Routledge Library Editions

ECONOMICS IN THE TWENTIETH CENTURY

ECONOMICS

Routledge Library Editions – Economics

HISTORY OF ECONOMIC THOUGHT
In 23 Volumes

I	A Select Bibliography of Modern Economic Theory	*Batson*
II	Early British Economics	*Beer*
III	Nassau Senior	*Bowley*
IV	The Theory of Marginal Value	*Birck*
V	Ricardo and the Theory of Value Distribution and Growth	*Caravale & Tosato*
VI	Productive Labour and Effective Demand	*Coontz*
VII	London Essays in Economics	*Gregory & Dalton*
VIII	Capitalism and the Historians	*Hayek*
IX	The Origins of Scientific Economics	*Letwin*
X	The Individual in Society	*Macfie*
XI	Essays on Hayek	*Machlup*
XII	The Economics of Physiocracy	*Meek*
XIII	Karl Marx	*Mehring*
XIV	Marx's Critique of Political Economy I	*Oakley*
XV	Marx's Critique of Political Economy II	*Oakley*
XVI	J R McCulloch	*O'Brien*
XVII	A Key to Ricardo	*St Clair*
XVIII	Roads to Freedom	*Streissler*
XIX	Economics in the Twentieth Century	*Suranyi-Unger*
XX	Elements of Pure Economics	*Walras*
XXI	The Common Sense of Political Economy I	*Wicksteed*
XXII	The Common Sense of Political Economy II	*Wicksteed*
XXIII	Social Economics	*von Wieser*

ECONOMICS IN THE TWENTIETH CENTURY

The History of its International Development

THEO SURANYI-UNGER

EDITED BY EDWIN R A SELIGMAN

Routledge
Taylor & Francis Group
LONDON AND NEW YORK

First published in 1932

Reprinted in 2003 by
Routledge
2 Park Square, Milton Park, Abingdon, Oxon OX14 4RN
or
270 Madison Avenue, New York, NY 10016

First issued in paperback 2010

Routledge is an imprint of the Taylor & Francis Group

British Library Cataloguing in Publication Data
A CIP catalogue record for this book
is available from the British Library

Economics in the Twentieth Century
ISBN 978-0-415-31339-1 (hbk)
ISBN 978-0-415-60730-8 (pbk)

Miniset: History of Economic Thought

Series: Routledge Library Editions – Economics

ECONOMICS

IN THE TWENTIETH CENTURY

THE HISTORY OF ITS INTERNATIONAL DEVELOPMENT

BY

Theo Suranyi-Unger

PROFESSOR AT SZEGED UNIVERSITY

EDITED BY

Edwin R. A. Seligman

MCVICKAR PROFESSOR OF POLITICAL ECONOMY, COLUMBIA UNIVERSITY

TRANSLATED FROM THE GERMAN BY

Noel D. Moulton

LONDON

GEORGE ALLEN & UNWIN LTD.

MUSEUM STREET

First Published in Great Britain in 1932

PRINTED IN U. S. A.

ERRATA

The letters F. B. are an abbreviation for "from bottom."

PAGE	LINE	
5	18	after "have" insert "not"
7	15	for "Romantics" read "Romans"
12	11	for "up" read "almost"
20	10	for "," read "as"
36	3	for "phenomental" read "phenomenal"
37	19	for "revolution" read "evolution"
46	24	for "static-" read "statistical-"
49	6	for "Black" read "Back"
49	20	for "Soda K. Chiro" read "Küchiro Soda"
51	11 & 19	for "Casualty" read "causality"
53	27	omit "science"
81	4	for "Volkswirthschaftslehre" read "Volkswohlstandslehre"
146	6 f. b.	for "Gold" read "money"
155	4	for "national" read "economic"
185	last	before "demand" insert "of"
197	8 f. b.	for "Ambrorovics" read "Ambrosovics"
213	3	for "French" read "English"
259	19	omit "eternal"
271	18	for "to" read "in"
285	11 f. b.	for "like" read "as"
285	10 f. b.	omit "of rent"
292	11	for "income" read "interest"
303	5	for "loan" read "wage"
320	5 f. b.	for "promience" read "prominence"
341	add Ztschr. f. d. ges. Staatswiss: Zeitschrift für die gesamten Staatswissenschaften	
350	line 23, for "Volkw" read "Sozwiss"	
371	Part Four, line 5, for "Jones D. Caradog" read "Caradog D. Jones"	

FOREWORD

WHEN the original version of the present work first came to my attention, I was forcibly struck by three facts.

The first was the remarkable erudition of the author. As is not unusual among his cultivated compatriots—Dr. Suranyi-Unger is a Hungarian—his familiarity with foreign languages is very great. He is equally at home in German, French, English and Italian, not to speak of the other languages with which he is acquainted. There is, to my knowledge, no other living economist who has such a complete mastery of the world literature. Furthermore, Dr. Suranyi-Unger has been educated in a good school and is meticulously accurate in all his references.

In the second place, Dr. Suranyi-Unger, probably owing to his study in the German universities, is especially interested in the philosophical aspects of economic science. This has been evidenced by his earlier works which have dealt more particularly with the philosophical foundations of economics. Although by no means aloof from the practical problems of the day, as is manifest from the numerous articles that he has published in the last few years, Dr. Suranyi-Unger shares with some of the leading founders of the science a predilection for the philosophical treatment of economic controversies. While this is not uncommon among German economists, it is something rather rare in the recent literature of other countries. This book will therefore be especially welcome to English and American readers because of the unusual starting point of his exposition.

In the third place, this is, I think, the first time that any elaborate discussion of economic literature has been undertaken by one who stands quite outside of the leading racial and linguistic boundaries. The consequence is that as between the German, the French, the Italian and the Anglo-Saxon writers, Dr. Suranyi-

Unger seems to be entirely without bias, so that the general survey of the contributions of the five outstanding countries to economic literature is presented not only with fidelity but with as much approach to impartiality as can reasonably be expected. The book will be especially interesting on this side of the ocean because of the relatively great attention paid to the recent American literature. It may also be remarked that owing to a sojourn of almost two years in the United States since the appearance of the German version, the sections devoted to American literature have been very much amplified and improved.

It was because of these considerations, as well as because of my personal regard for the author, that I was led to suggest its translation and was induced to act as editor. The book will, in my opinion, fill a decided gap in our economic literature and ought to be welcome not alone to the university student, but also to the wider public which is concerned with the international development of economic ideas.

EDWIN R. A. SELIGMAN

Columbia University
New York
June, 1931

THE AUTHOR'S PREFACE

Those who desire only a survey of the development of theoretical economics since the beginning of the century should omit the passages in finer print. These are intended only for those who are interested in the less important details or especially in the bibliography of the subject.

THERE are three ways of writing the history of theories. The first is the purely descriptive one, which deals with the doctrines of the past only in their temporal order. The second is the critical one, in which the author tries to offer a "critical" view of other men's opinions, and thus stresses the exclusive correctness of his own ideas, thereby giving the unsuspecting reader a consciously distorted and one-sided picture of scientific development. The third and best method is the genetic one, which tries to explain prevailing opinions out of their own development, and in their inmost connexion. The following work attempts to follow the principles of the genetic method.

Owing to the lack of the requisite historical perspective, however, comparatively few events in modern development can be studied in a purely genetical fashion. In the present attempt this lack is felt as a perpetual flaw, and hinders above all the choice of economic theories to be discussed. The critical means of the whole genetic method of representation is contained in this choice: the material for this historical survey of theories could be assembled only on the basis of a valuation of the various theories which come into consideration according to their intrinsic and fundamental importance. Anyone would be justified in objecting, from his own point of view, that I have mentioned much that is unimportant, and neglected other things of more weight. He need only remember the well known fact that Gossen was first brought to the notice of his "discoverer" Jevons by Kautz. Were not the great majority of leading economists in 1860, the year in which Kautz's history appeared, of the opinion that the mention of a writer like Gossen was quite superfluous? And yet it would have been a mistake if Kautz had paid no heed to Gossen's views. The same thing is even more liable to happen with us to-day, when everything in the development of economics is even more in a state of flux.

In order to avoid this as much as I could, I have tried to condense as many new ideas as possible in the three main divisions of the book, in which I set forth the most recent development of our science, according to the three main linguistic groups. I have tried to draw largely on the literature of the periodicals, which is generally overlooked, and for many scholars difficult to obtain. Quite unpretentious articles in periodicals often contain the most important new discoveries. I hardly need mention that I do not intend to make a complete survey in this work. At times the lack of an historical perspective has compelled me to give a consciously bibliographical tone to the description in the three main divisions. I have tried here to maintain the strictest objectivity, for I believe that I can be more useful to the reader by citing theoretical discussions and the reception of new doctrines by trained scientific criticism, rather than by offering him material in the shape of "dogmatic criticism" accompanied by my own remarks. In reading this, he will learn not one single point of view, i. e., my own, but rather the majority of modern opinions. This enforced objectivity is, I hope, balanced by the freer and more subjective tone of the first section, and especially of the summary. I consider it, however, my duty to warn the reader that the ideas in the summary on the present status and probable future development of economic theory contain only my own subjective opinions.

I have thought it necessary in the present volume to impose certain limitations upon myself in three different directions: with regard to subject-matter, time, and language. I have tried not to overstep certain boundaries in my literary material. First in respect to subject-matter, I limit myself to the development of so-called pure economic theory, and proceed in all the three main divisions according to a fixed plan. The division into linguistic groups seemed to be permissible only through this strict unity in the formal structure of the work. It is only through the arrangement of the material within this scheme that I could take account of the peculiarities of scientific development in the various linguistic groups. Certain minor repetitions were unavoidable in this outward structure, and occurred chiefly because of the separate handling of methodological development, which, however, could be appreciated in its importance only in this way. Nevertheless, in order to diminish as far as possible the number of repetitions, I have tried to discuss each theory in only one connection. When doctrines are mentioned in the main divisions without references, these are always to be found among the author's writings which have been mentioned previously. I have omitted the theories of money for two reasons. First, according to present conditions, the theory of money does not, in most cases, form a unified, organic part of economic theory. We need only compare the money theories of the best known economists with each other to see that they are often only loosely connected with the rest of their economic theory: economists of different general tendencies often hold the same theory of money, and different money theories can be found within the ranks of the same school. A discussion of these theories, therefore, would have disturbed the unity of the present work. On the other hand this somewhat special position of the theory of money in economics has led to some notable studies being devoted to its most recent development in the last few years. The excellence of these works was the second reason which influenced the omission of these theories. I was in a similar position in respect to questions of production and of the closely related theory of organization. In addition, it is my opinion that one cannot very well speak of these questions, and especially of the problems of credit and business cycles, without touching on the most important problems of economic policy. It seemed to me better to limit myself to a narrower field rather than to treat superficially all the complex problems of the science. I desire, however, to draw emphatically to the student's attention the fact that an important transformation has taken place in economic investigation since the war in the direction of questions of organization theory. The works on this subject will afford him abundant information.

As regards time, I have kept to those limits which are mentioned in the title of the book. In the revision of the German edition, which has been made for the English translation, I have tried to include the most recent development of the years 1926–1928. I have endeavored to show in various parts of the book that the choice of the turn of the century, as the other temporal limit of the work, was not entirely casual, and that at this period epoch making changes were taking place in economics. But I have had to renounce from the outset explaining theories or theoretical concepts which belong to the achievements of the previous century. Therefore the reader will need to have an acquaintance with earlier fundamental concepts such as marginal utility, the theory of imputation, the classical theory of distribution, etc., if he desires to follow me. I strongly advise the beginner to study one of the better known books on the history of economics, before attempting the present work. Perhaps the best suited for this purpose is the small book of the Hungarian Wolfgang Heller.[1] Other works which may be recommended are those of Othmar Spann,[2] Paul Mombert,[3] Gide and Rist,[4] Bousquet,[5] and Haney.[6] The more advanced student will find valuable help in the recent historical works of Joseph Schumpeter,[7] Edgar Salin,[8] Rudolf Stolzmann,[9] Sven Helander,[10] Hans Honegger,[11] O. Fred Boucke,[12] or Paul T. Homan.[13] My two-volume *Philosophie in der Volkswirtschaftslehre* (Jena, 1923–26), may also serve as a preparation. For any one who can secure that work, I recommend especially the following chapters: "Die Physiokraten" (I, p. 284), "Die klassische Schule der Nationalökonomie" (I, p. 372), "Die historische Schule und die Neoromantik (II, p. 141), "Der nationale Gedanke" (II, p. 203), "Die Careysche Volkswirtschaftslehre (II, p. 232), "Die exakt vergleichende und die mathematische Richtung (II, p. 281), "Die Mengerschen positiven Wirtschaftstheorien und die österreichische Schule" (II, p. 356), "Marxens volkswirtschaftliche Lehren" (II, p. 515), and "Die Stellung des Marxismus in der neueren Entwicklung der sozialistischen Lehren" (II, p. 524).

In the third place, finally, I have dealt only with works that are written in German, French, Italian and English. These contain the most important contributions to the modern development of our science. I might have dealt also with Spanish and a great deal of Slavonic literature, but I should have been as little justified in mentioning these as in treating works in my own tongue, Hungarian, considering that my linguistic knowledge did not enable me to deal with the more important Scandinavian and Dutch economic theories.[14] I have considered the theoretical works of these nations only when they have been translated into one of the four above-mentioned languages. Where there have been several translations I have mentioned them in connection with the language into which they were first translated.

I am conscious that this volume is but an incomplete attempt, and that I have been only to a small degree able to overcome the great difficulties that stand in the way of such an undertaking. I shall have reached my goal if the historian of the future is able to use this book as a useful reference for the first quarter of the twentieth century. Perhaps I have also succeeded in contributing toward bridging the gulfs which exist between the economic theories of the various linguistic groups. An international understanding in our science is best brought about by a division and co-ordination of labor. What I have to say about the marked contrasts between the German, the Romance and the Anglo-Saxon spirit in science is said freely and objectively, for I myself belong to a cultural environment which is different from all of these but owes perhaps an equal amount to each.

Finally, I acquit myself of a pleasant duty when I cordially thank all my colleagues, in both the old and the new world, who have helped me with their advice in preparing this work. Most critics of the German edition of my book will find that I have tried to take account of their objections in the corrections which have been made for the present translation. I am especially indebted to the courtesy of the various German and Austrian, Italian, French, English and American libraries in which I have worked for various periods on this book.

THE AUTHOR

Chicago, May, 1929.

CONTENTS

FOREWORD v

THE AUTHOR'S PREFACE vii

INTRODUCTION: THE DEVELOPMENT OF ECONOMIC THEORY IN THE VARIOUS LANGUAGES 3

PART ONE. PHILOSOPHICAL SOURCES OF THE MOST RECENT ECONOMIC TENDENCIES

1. THE BADEN SCHOOL OF PHILOSOPHY, THE QUESTION OF METHOD, AND THE PHILOSOPHY OF VALUES IN ECONOMICS 16
2. THE PHILOSOPHICAL BASES OF "VALUE-LESS" ECONOMICS 19
3. THE MARBURG SCHOOL OF PHILOSOPHY; CASSEL AND LIEFMANN 20
4. COMTE, SPENCER, AND THE THEORY OF ECONOMIC EQUILIBRIUM 22
5. UTILITARIAN ETHICS, THE CAMBRIDGE SCHOOL AND ECONOMIC LIBERALISM 26
6. STAMMLER AND THE SOCIO-LEGAL THEORY OF ECONOMICS 29
7. THE RENAISSANCE OF GERMAN IDEALISM, AND SPANN 30
8. THE INTERPSYCHOLOGICAL SYSTEM OF TARDE 33
9. PHILOSOPHICAL OPTIMISM IN AMERICA AND CLARK'S SCHOOL 34
10. THE NEW AMERICAN PSYCHOLOGY, AND ECONOMIC INSTITUTIONALISM 35

PART TWO. THE DEVELOPMENT IN THE GERMAN-SPEAKING COUNTRIES

Chapter I: METHODS AND SYSTEMS 45

1. THE ABATEMENT OF THE QUARREL OVER METHOD 45
2. LOGICAL CURRENTS 47

3. THE DISPUTE OVER THE VALUE JUDGMENTS 49
4. THE METHOD OF EXACT COMPARISON 55
5. ECONOMIC PHILOSOPHY 56
6. PRIVATE ECONOMICS, BUSINESS ECONOMICS AND WORLD ECONOMICS 59
7. ECONOMICS OF WAR 62

Chapter II: ATTEMPTS TO CREATE SYSTEMS 64
1. THE HISTORICAL SCHOOL 64
2. THE PURE THEORY OF MARGINAL UTILITY 65
3. SCHUMPETER'S STATIC AND DYNAMIC ECONOMICS 68
4. CASSEL AND HIS ADHERENTS 70
5. THE REALISTIC THEORIES OF LEXIS AND ADOLF WEBER ON THE ECONOMICS OF EXCHANGE 72
6. LIEFMANN'S PURELY PSYCHOLOGICAL SYSTEM 73
7. ORGANIC AND TELEOLOGICAL THOUGHT 75
8. THE SOCIO-LEGAL TENDENCY 79
9. THE SYSTEMS OF THE SOCIAL REFORMERS 81
10. OUTSIDERS 85
11. TEXT BOOKS 86

Chapter III: VALUE 88
1. CONFLICT IN THE THEORY OF VALUE AS BETWEEN BÖHM-BAWERK AND WIESER 88
2. SPANN'S THEORY OF EQUAL IMPORTANCE 92
3. RETURN TO THE OBJECTIVE THEORY OF VALUE 93
4. SPECIAL ATTEMPTS AT CLARIFICATION 95
5. THE "MORIBUND" THEORY OF VALUE 96

Chapter IV: PRICE 98
1. THE PRICE THEORY OF MARGINAL UTILITY 98
2. LIEFMANN'S "PURELY SUBJECTIVE" EXPLANATION OF PRICE 99
3. THE "PURELY OBJECTIVE" SOLUTION 100
4. ATTEMPTS AT SYNTHESIS 102
5. SPANN'S ORGANIC AND UNIVERSALISTIC THEORY OF PRICE 104

Chapter V: DISTRIBUTION 106
1. MARGINAL UTILITY AND THE THEORY OF DISTRIBUTION 106

2. SOLUTIONS OF THE PROBLEM OF DISTRIBUTION ON THE BASIS OF THE THEORY OF PRICE 108
3. SOCIAL THEORIES OF DISTRIBUTION 110
4. THE DERIVATION OF RENT FROM THE FORMATION OF PRICE 113
5. THE GENERALIZATION OF THE LAW OF DIMINISHING RETURNS 115
6. MUNICIPAL GROUND RENTS 116
7. THE DISCUSSION OF BÖHM'S AGIO THEORY 117
8. THE DYNAMIC EXPLANATION OF INTEREST 118
9. MONOPOLY, ABSTINENCE, AND PRODUCTIVITY THEORIES OF INTEREST 119
10. FURTHER DEVELOPMENT OF IDEAS OF WAGES THEORY 120
11. THE EXPLANATION OF WAGES ON THE THEORY OF MARGINAL UTILITY 121
12. THE SOCIALISTIC THEORY OF WAGES 122
13. THE DYNAMIC THEORY OF PROFIT 123

PART THREE. THE DEVELOPMENT IN THE ROMANCE COUNTRIES

Chapter I: METHOD 127

1. ABSENCE OF METHODOLOGICAL CONTROVERSY IN THE ROMANCE COUNTRIES 127
2. THE METHOD OF THE LAUSANNE SCHOOL 127
3. THE NON-MATHEMATICAL DEDUCTIVE METHOD 130
4. LOGICAL AND EPISTEMOLOGICAL ATTEMPTS 132
5. THE STATISTICAL AND THE HISTORICAL-INDUCTIVE VIEWPOINTS 134
6. THE INFLUENCE OF SOCIOLOGICAL TENDENCIES 136
7. GENERAL TENDENCIES IN THE DEVELOPMENT OF METHOD 138
8. NO INNOVATIONS IN THE SYSTEMATIZATION OF ECONOMICS 138

Chapter II: SYSTEMATIC IDEAS 140

1. SYSTEM OF THE LAUSANNE SCHOOL 140
2. ECLECTICALLY BUILT ABSTRACT-DEDUCTIVE THEORIES 146
3. THE CLASSICAL LIBERAL GROUP IN FRANCE 150
4. RATIONALISTIC SYSTEMS WITHOUT THEORIES OF VALUE 152
5. THE AFTER-EFFECTS OF HISTORICAL RELATIVISM 154
6. SOLIDARISTIC SOCIAL IDEAS 155

7. THE RELIGIOUS AND ETHICAL TENDENCY 159
8. SOCIALISTIC SYSTEMS 161
9. TEXT BOOKS 165

Chapter III: VALUE 168

1. THE LAUSANNE SCHOOL AND THE THEORY OF VALUE 168
2. SLIGHT SUCCESS OF THE PURE THEORY OF MARGINAL UTILITY IN THE ROMANCE COUNTRIES 171
3. ATTEMPTS AT A RECONCILIATION BETWEEN OBJECTIVE AND SUBJECTIVE TENDENCIES 173
4. THE CONFLICT OVER COST OF REPRODUCTION 175
5. MORE RECENT DEVELOPMENT OF THE THEORY OF COST-VALUE 176
6. TARDE'S THEORY OF VALUE BASED ON CULTURAL PHILOSOPHY 177
7. THE THEORY OF "ECONOMIC CONVENIENCE" 178

Chapter IV: PRICE 179

1. THE MATHEMATICAL THEORY OF PRICE 179
2. THE CONFLICT OVER THE CLASSICAL LAW OF SUPPLY AND DEMAND 184
3. THE EXPLANATION OF PRICE BY SOCIAL RATIOS OF POWER 186
4. THE "FAIR" PRICE 186

Chapter V: DISTRIBUTION 189

1. THE ITALIAN THEORY OF DISTRIBUTION BASED ON THE THEORY OF ECONOMIC EQUILIBRIUM 189
2. THE MODERN AND THE CLASSICAL THEORY OF DISTRIBUTION IN FRANCE 191
3. IDEAS OF POWER AND OF SOCIAL ETHICS IN THE THEORY OF DISTRIBUTION 192
4. THE UNIFICATION OF THE LAWS OF RETURNS 193
5. THE GENERALISATION OF THE THEORY OF RENT 195
6. CONSUMER'S RENT 197
7. THE ATTITUDE OF THE LAUSANNE SCHOOL TO THE PROBLEM OF INTEREST AND THEORIES OF SAVINGS 198
8. THE INFLUENCE OF BÖHM'S AGIO THEORY IN THE ROMANCE COUNTRIES 201

9. PARTIAL WEAKENING OF THE THEORY OF INTEREST 202
10. SOCIO-ETHICAL WAGE THEORIES IN ITALY 202
11. THE REALISTIC EXPLANATIONS OF WAGES BY LEVASSEUR, CORNÉLISSEN AND SIMIAND 204
12. THE MARGINAL PRINCIPLE AND SOCIO-ETHICAL VIEWPOINTS IN THE FRENCH THEORY OF WAGES 206
13. MONOPOLY THEORIES AND ECLECTIC EXPLANATIONS OF PROFITS 207
14. DIFFERENTIAL PROFITS 208

PART FOUR. THE DEVELOPMENT IN THE ANGLO-SAXON COUNTRIES

Chapter I: METHOD 213
1. THE MATHEMATICAL PROCEDURE 213
2. LOGICAL ATTEMPTS 215
3. THE QUARREL OVER PSYCHOLOGICAL PRINCIPLES 216
4. THE REALISTIC CURRENT IN AMERICA 218
5. METHODOLOGICAL DISCUSSIONS AMONG AMERICAN ECONOMISTS 219
6. "YOUNG AMERICA" 222
7. THE LEGAL, HISTORICAL AND SOCIO-ETHICAL ATTITUDES 225
8. THE PROBLEM OF VALUE JUDGMENTS 226
9. BUSINESS ECONOMICS, SCIENCE OF MANAGEMENT, AND THE ECONOMICS OF WAR 227

Chapter II: ATTEMPTS TO CREATE SYSTEMS 229
1. THE CAMBRIDGE SCHOOL, AND OTHER ABSTRACT THEORETICAL SYSTEMS IN ENGLAND 229
2. CLARK'S SCHOOL IN AMERICA 238
3. FISHER ON MONEY AND INTEREST 241
4. DAVENPORT AND THE POINT OF VIEW OF THE ENTREPRENEUR 242
5. FETTER'S DEVELOPMENT 243
6. CARVER AND OTHER THEORETICAL SYSTEMS IN POST-WAR AMERICA 245
7. REALISTIC AND ETHICALLY RELIGIOUS SYSTEMS, AND THOSE DEVOTED TO SOCIAL REFORM 247
8. TEXT BOOKS 250

Chapter III: VALUE 254

1. THE PREVALENT TENDENCY TOWARD COMPROMISE IN THE ANGLO-SAXON THEORY OF VALUE 254
2. DEVELOPMENTS OF THE THEORY OF DISUTILITY, ESPECIALLY IN A SOCIAL DIRECTION 255
3. EFFORTS TO SAVE THE LABOR THEORY OF VALUE 258
4. DAVENPORT'S PSEUDO-OBJECTIVE THEORY OF VALUE 258
5. FETTER, ANDERSON AND THE STRUGGLE AGAINST THE MARGINAL UTILITY THEORY OF VALUE 260
6. GRADUAL RETREAT OF THE WHOLE VALUE THEORY IN ANGLO-SAXON ECONOMICS 263

Chapter IV: PRICE 265

1. MARSHALL'S THEORY OF PRICE, AND ITS DEVELOPMENTS 265
2. THE EXPLANATION OF PRICE FROM THE POINT OF VIEW OF DEMAND. FETTER 267
3. CLARK'S THEORY OF PRICE, AND THE ANALYSIS OF PRICE BOUNDARIES 268
4. THE POINT OF VIEW OF COSTS 272
5. MONOPOLY PRICE 275
6. NORMAL PRICE AND PRICE FLUCTUATIONS 276

Chapter V: DISTRIBUTION 278

1. THE PROBLEM OF DISTRIBUTION IN MODERN ENGLISH THEORY 278
2. THE AMERICAN THEORY OF MARGINAL PRODUCTIVITY 279
3. DISTRIBUTION OF WEALTH AND THE SOCIAL CONFLICT OVER PRICES 281
4. DEVELOPMENT OF THE AUSTRIAN THEORY OF IMPUTATION 283
5. THE PASSING OF THE NARROWER CONCEPTION OF RENT AND THE PROBLEM OF RETURNS 285
6. NEWLY RECOGNIZED INCOMES RESEMBLING RENT 288
7. THE CLASSICAL DIFFERENTIAL RENT 290
8. NO NEW THEORIES OF INTEREST IN ENGLAND 291
9. THE IDEA OF PRODUCTIVITY AND THE THEORY OF INTEREST IN AMERICA 292
10. THE CONFLICT ON THE CONCEPT OF CAPITAL 293

11. THE RECEPTION OF BÖHM'S INTEREST THEORY IN AMERICA 294
12. ABSTINENCE, RISK AND THE RESIDUAL PRINCIPLE IN THE AMERICAN THEORY OF INTEREST 297
13. THE PROBLEM OF WAGES IN ENGLISH LITERATURE 298
14. THE MODERN AMERICAN PRODUCTIVITY THEORY OF WAGES 299
15. THE WAGE-FUND THEORY 301
16. MOORE'S INDUCTIVE EXPLANATION OF WAGES 303
17. THE PROBLEM OF THE WAGE LEVEL 304
18. THE AFTER-EFFECTS OF THE CLASSICAL IDEA OF PRODUCTIVITY IN THE THEORY OF PROFITS 305
19. RISK AND PROFIT 306
20. THE RESIDUAL PRINCIPLE AND THE DYNAMIC ELEMENT IN PROFITS 308
21. PROFITS AS A MONOPOLY INCOME 309

SUMMARY AND PROSPECTS 313

ABBREVIATIONS OF PERIODICALS 340

NOTES 343

INDEX OF NAMES 389

INTRODUCTION

THE DEVELOPMENT OF ECONOMIC THEORY IN THE VARIOUS LANGUAGES

INTRODUCTION

THE DEVELOPMENT OF ECONOMIC THEORY IN THE VARIOUS LANGUAGES

It is always presumptuous, in dealing with the development of the various sciences, to talk of an uninterrupted progress. Some advance is indeed indicated when only one short step has been taken toward a more systematic understanding of the truth. Yet even the nature of this truth which we are seeking appears to different eyes in different shades. Does the philosophy of the Enlightenment really represent an advance over mediæval thought? Or can anyone maintain, without fear of contradiction, that Karl Marx had a deeper insight into economic truth than Adam Smith? It is only the person who has surveyed the turmoil of intellectual currents from the position of his own school of thought, and appraised them according to his own personal bias, who can make a sharp distinction between progress and retrogression in science. The historian of thought, however, who, at the very least, should be above the disputes of parties and schools, sees nothing but a rolling sea of contradictory theories. One wave after another takes the lead, only to give way to those which in their turn advance with the pretentions of being the best qualified to discern the real core of Truth. And out of this raging tempest there emerges by degrees a small coral island, the only secure foundation for progressive science. Every controversy, to a greater or less degree, leads to an elucidation of opposing positions, whereby the positive and enduring treasure-store of our science is enriched by some sort of a contribution, however insignificant it may appear to be.

"Are my officers still grumbling?" the Austrian general Radetzky used to ask: "then all is well!" In the same way, we may brush aside all anxiety for the further growth of economic theory, so long as there are dissatisfied persons who regard the prevalent theories in a spirit of criticism, and strive to effect in our science more or less "revolutionary" reforms. It seems to be in the nature of controversy that we try to detect, in the position of our adversary, the fate of the proverbial cow, which we have all seen in the advertisements of a patent medicine, afflicted with every possible disease to which an animal is susceptible. In this state of affairs, however, only the most extreme pessimist can lose courage; for it is a fact that every system of economic theory, for all its errors and omissions, can be shown to have its merits. Every theorist strives to discern the same lone summit of the true relations between the various elements of economic life. Whether we view it from this side or that; whether we examine its general outlines from a distance or endeavor to climb up it and investigate the individual rocks at close range, the picture we get is always different. It is in intellectual controversies, in the great disputes between different schools of thought, that these pictures are compared with one another; so that seeming contradictions are seen to be unreal, and individual agreements are being increasingly recognized. Thus it is that we gradually approach an ever clearer apprehension of the one and central Truth.

The most invigorating factor of true progress in our science is an argumentative analysis of diverging theses; the more these take stock of each other, the more they can further the common cause. Wherever investigations of the same subject-matter are being carried on in complete isolation, without the opportunity of being challenged and fertilized, much energy that could profitably be employed for science as a whole is wasted. Although the losses which this isolation implies are severely felt on all sides, they seem in the present state of economics to be more pronounced than ever. Among the three chief linguistic groups which at the outset claim our attention—the Germanic, the Romance and the English—gaps exist which make it more impossible than ever to speak of a unified development of our science. A comparative study of the economic literature of these three groups forces us to conclude that each proceeds under lock and key, and without an appreciable regard for the achievements attained by the others. It is especially in personal intercourse that one sees how common it is for the leading economists of a nation to know astonishingly little about what their colleagues in other lands are accomplishing. It is often decades before the most important results of foreign research come to their notice, and by that time science has struck out in new directions.

The reasons for this deplorable separation are, now as before, only partially to be found in the purely external difficulties of linguistic differences. Of much more decisive import are the underlying cultural differences which have led nations and races to develop entirely different concepts of the nature of economics. We shall, therefore, be in a better position to understand the latest developments in economic theory, if we keep in mind the distinctive characteristics of German, Franco-Italian and Anglo-American culture.

Beginning with the national character of the Germans and their attitude toward science, we find that these have always been different from the prevalent culture of the west. Their peculiar status in the present culture of Europe dates from the intellectual revolution of the romanticists. It was then that the Germans attained a national consciousness and that German civilization, which had previously followed a course more or less parallel to that of western Europe, struck out its independent path. The romanticists turned their gaze upon life as a whole, tried to discover its deepest impulses and pressed their search even into the realm of mysticism. They saw in society a sentient whole, a living organism, composed of a mass of differing units. According to them there exist in each self-sufficing personality creative forces which express themselves in reciprocal social contacts and which ultimately react on the community. Foremost among their teachings was the æsthetic-religious ideal, to which they attributed not a continuous development, but a gradual advance, punctuated with conflicts due to differences in culture.

From romanticism emerged German idealism, with its strongly marked metaphysical character, which intensified the natural tendency of the Germans to metaphysical speculation and to interpret all experience, social as well as natural, in terms of the cosmos. It is perhaps in the music of Bach, Gluck, and Handel, that this spiritual trait of the Germans appears to the best advantage; just as the great strength of their plastic art, from mediæval Gothic up to the present, resides not in beauty of line or of form, but in expression and movement. The idea of a self-contained and organic social structure has given birth, on the one hand to the German conception of the State, with its emphasis on the subjection of the individual to a central power, and on the other hand to those feelings of duty, order and discipline, which are especially characteristic of the race. This is exemplified in their training, their education, and especially their scientific work, through a methodical and systematic procedure which foreigners are only too prone to call pedantic and doctrinaire. These accusations are all the more irrelevant when we consider the depth of feeling which, as everyone knows, not only characterizes family life, as in England, but also informs the whole German attitude toward life and society. In sociological studies, both Romanticism and Idealism led to a splendid development of the historical outlook, which became for the Germans the outstanding scientific method in linguistics, art, religion, politics and economics. In mentioning these leading traits of German culture, we do not wish to imply that there did not exist at the same time—notably under foreign influences—other intellectual currents. Especially in the seventies and eighties, a realistic movement came to the fore, of which the chief examples are the sober, nationalistic policy of Bismarck, the partly naturalistic doctrines of Nietzsche's later philosophy and last, but not least, the materialistic teachings of Marx. It is significant, however, that Bismarck, Nietzsche and Marx in their youth all came under the influence of Idealism. Nevertheless, because of its efficacy, Realism has won for itself a strong position in German culture and is today a worthy opponent of the pervading Idealism, although constantly influenced by it.

In contradistinction to this peculiarly German culture which started with the Romantic, we have Franco-Italian and Anglo-American cultures, which we can call West European thought. In view of the fact that Germans are generally said to be conservative and western Europeans progressive, our remark is only superficially paradoxical. The spirit of progress is the result of thousands of years of an unbroken development, which had already reached a certain maturity in the philosophy of the Stoics and in the underlying principles of Roman Law. First of all we find the notion of a divine providence, of the natural laws of the eternal wisdom of God, which had dominated the golden age but had been obscured later through folly, strife and cupidity. The aim, then, is to re-establish their supremacy, so that the god-like dignity of man, found in all of us, may again express itself in liberty, equality and fraternity.

Pantheism, which was at the bottom of this train of thought with the Romans was replaced in the Middle Ages by a deep-rooted Theism. But it accepted also the idea of a divine natural law, to which were added the doctrine of original sin and the supreme authority of a divinely instituted church; all of which profoundly influenced the art, the science and the life of the period. Even the system of estates and guilds, with all its social and economic inequalities, was unable to destroy the sense of equality achieved by this belief in a divine world order. Humanism and the Enlightenment, then, are the two great movements which have made western European culture what it now is, and through which the ideas of a divinely given law of nature, of an eternal and divinely appointed world order, and of the equality and common destiny of mankind have taken on their present form. In spite of the more recent positivistic tendency, this attitude has prevailed even to the present day, and the ideals of freedom and progress which have been built upon this foundation are even now in sharp contrast to the German notion of historical "unfolding of the Idea," and its embodiment in the fundamentally unequal structure of society.

Within this general frame of Western European culture, there are naturally important differences, between the "Latin" and the "Anglo-Saxon" minds. In France, the Revolution led to a decisive break with traditional institutions, and radical reforms were attempted everywhere. These took the form of a worship of popular rule, a strictly equalitarian democracy, and an inexorably materialistic and mechanistic rationalism, whose atomism sought only mathematical relations. This trait of the Latin mind is especially noticeable in contemporary Italian sociology. On the other hand the Anglo-Saxon holds fast to tradition, knows how to combine the ideal of personal freedom with a deep-rooted belief in a select class of leaders, and so achieves a peculiar Liberalism, quite distinct from similar intellectual currents on the Continent. The English middle class combine this dominant Liberalism with an ethico-Christian attitude to life, which is in sharp contrast to the unlimited feeling of power and mastery on the part of the upper classes; there is thus engendered the dualism which is so marked in every phase of Anglo-Saxon culture. In the United States, the deeply rooted democracy of the people unites them all in one great society for the promotion of interests and material welfare of the community. In philosophy, English empiricism is opposed to Latin rationalism; scepticism and materialism, likewise, as a rule give way to utilitarian and hedonistic ethics. In this we see the practical nature of the English and the American, which leads them to value everything according to its usefulness and which, with their remarkable optimism, may be considered the source of Anglo-Saxon supremacy.

It must be borne in mind that this rough sketch of the differences between the German, Latin and Anglo-Saxon cultures represents a more or less abstract picture which will, in practical experience, often be found inadequate. Nevertheless the dividing lines have always been sufficiently marked to cause a certain amount of isolation even in the separate sciences. Whoever tries to comprehend the scientific development of an alien culture will find himself, even after he has mastered the language, in an entirely different world of thought, often so difficult to understand that only a painstaking re-arrangement of his own ideas will enable him to grasp its meaning or to derive from it any useful stimulus. Even in economics there came, accordingly, certain national tendencies which were of course more or less adopted by other nations, but which could produce significant results only in their own cultural environment. Thus German economics has been able to achieve real results only in so far as it has been historical, universalistic, national and (corresponding to the German sense of organization) socio-political. Even Marxism is in essence historical and influenced by the idealistic philosophy. In the Latin cultures the only economic doctrines that proved themselves capable of a high development were materialistic and revolutionary socialism and a wholly rationalistic, atomistic, and mechanico-mathematical theory. Finally it followed that the Anglo-Saxons, who have always been greatly influenced by the optimistic ideas of natural law and divine providence, should have produced an essentially individualistic, liberal, hedonistic and utilitarian body of economic doctrine. On the other hand, a revolutionary socialism could not take root here. The outbreak of the war brought to the front in every way more acutely than ever the old contrasts between the German and the Western European minds. A strong effort was made by propagandists on both sides, but especially among the Allies, to turn this purely political struggle into a contest between two cultures.

The leaders of German art and science answered in September 1914 with their unhappily worded manifesto "*An die Kulturwelt*," signed by 93 leading thinkers. After characterizing as fantastic the accounts of atrocities supposed to have been committed by the German soldiers in Belgium and northern France, the manifesto proceeded in an exaggerated way to sing the praises of their own culture over that of the rest of Europe. This naturally excited the indignation of the opposition, and a whole literature now appeared, especially in France, consisting not only of newspaper articles and pamphlets but also of numerous volumes with scientific pretensions, which tried to prove, in various ways, the faults and the inferiority of German character and culture. To take but a few of these writings which refer especially to German science: Gabriel Petit and Maurice Leudet sent a questionnaire to the most prominent French scholars, and then collected all their answers in order to prove that leadership in every field of knowledge belonged to the Latins and Anglo-Saxons and that, therefore, a menace to German culture could not be fatal to civilization.[1] Joseph Lefort examined in turn all of the branches of knowledge in which the Germans had made so-called epoch-making discoveries, and tried to prove that they rested throughout upon the researches of earlier foreign scholars.[2] He considered the academic seminary an absurdity and found fault with the entire methods of German science which, according to him, wastes itself in gathering masses of undigested material.

Although his tone is free from the propaganda which was inspired by national hatred, the American C. E. Persons investigated the problem with especial reference to economics and demanded, in place of the German system which aims at training scholars and research-students, a return to the traditional English and American ideal of education as befitting a gentleman.[3] French economists were especially incensed at Lujo Brentano for signing the manifesto of 1914, and suspected that he, the descendant of a family of Venetian merchants who had always been intimately associated with foreign scholars, had been persuaded by some one else to do so. Thereupon a debate broke out in correspondence between Brentano on one side and Yves Guyot and Daniel Bellet on the other, published in the *Journal des Economistes*, and in which Brentano sought to defend the statements in the manifesto. It is all the more surprising, therefore, that after the war, he sent a letter to Charles Gide in which he confirmed Guyot's conjecture and blamed Schmoller, now deceased, for having persuaded him to sign the manifesto, the contents of which he did not even know until it was published.[4]

As a matter of fact, Brentano's recantation is not the only one. When the American journalist Charles Victor, of the New York *Evening Post*, went to Germany after the war, and seized the opportunity of interviewing most of the signers of the manifesto, they almost unanimously renounced its contents, and admitted that they had signed under the powerful pressure of public opinion.

This striking example of faint-heartedness can be paralleled in many realms of contemporary German culture. The propaganda developed by the Allies during the war must have had such a power of suggestion, that we hear today even of Germans who tend to attribute the great "débâcle" to a few especially prominent traits of German character and method, thus recognizing a victory of western European culture over their own. People forget, however, that in neither its origin nor its course was the war a struggle between two different cultures. This idea was invented and read into it afterwards. If the general who was in command on that fateful September night had not ordered the first retreat on the Marne, who knows what the result of the war might not have been? The faint-hearted, however, see in this and a hundred similar strategical and other occurrences fundamental mistakes and defects in the traditional German mind, and are consequently ready to welcome the influence of the foreign ideas, which have apparently stood the test of war.

This western spirit, ardently welcomed by many, boasts on the other hand of its recent material success and draws from this great period of trial new sources of further growth, which in its consciousness of victory it likes to consider as an uninterrupted continuation of pre-war tradition. Therefore, whereas both Latins and Anglo-Saxons are engaged in strengthening and developing these traits which we mentioned above as typical of their respective cultures, German intellectuals seem downcast and ready to relinquish the treasures of that culture which they have guarded for so long. Are we to see a repetition here of what happened after the Franco-Prussian war? To keep to economics: in those days, not only did the theories of the German historical school penetrate France, where Gide, Cauwès and other occupants of the foremost chairs of economics came under its influence, but the younger generation in Italy, England and especially America lent an attentive ear to the economic teaching of triumphant Germany. From the United States a stream of eager young economists came to the German universities to imbibe learning from the younger members of the historical school and later to create out of the ideas which they brought home the new American economics that ranks so high today. The fact, too, that German Marxism has spread like wild-fire over the whole globe is closely connected with the rise of German prestige after the victory over France.

Today it seems that in the Latin countries economics is developing more consistently than ever along the traditional lines which correspond to the general mental attitude. The same is true of England, and it is perhaps only in America, which was but slightly affected by the war, that we can notice a more active movement toward a partial reform of economic theory. In Germany, on the other hand, there has perhaps never been such confusion and such dismemberment in the various theories struggling for supremacy as we have seen since the war. Many seem to despair of their own fundamental scientific ideals, and it is perhaps only their practical isolation from foreign economics, so evident up to the present moment, which has prevented them from adopting those leading theories to a more appreciable extent. Nevertheless, it is a striking symptom of the attitude of German scientists to-day that the Swede Cassel has been able to make such an impression in Germany with his essentially Anglo-Saxon theories, whereas similar attempts made by Germans before the war were more or less doomed to failure.

To counteract these foreign influences, there has recently appeared in German economics a new movement which emphasizes the old traditions and consciously sets itself the task of continuing them. Nevertheless Latin and Anglo-Saxon scholars give it as little attention as they give to other economic currents in post-war Germany, and continue in complacent seclusion, almost untouched by foreign influences. Thus those comparisons between different economic theories, which are so fruitful and so important for science, are hindered to-day even more than before the war by these great cultural divisions. It is only at the end of the decade following the war that we again notice signs of international *rapprochement* in economic theory.

PART ONE

PHILOSOPHICAL SOURCES OF THE MOST RECENT ECONOMIC TENDENCIES

PART ONE

PHILOSOPHICAL SOURCES OF THE MOST RECENT ECONOMIC TENDENCIES

THE REAL and important cultural differences which we have noticed even in economics lead us to divide the development of our subject-matter in the last quarter century into three linguistic groups. First of all, however, we shall try to summarize the philosophical origins of these various tendencies.

At the end of the last century, where our study begins, there was considerably more intercourse between the economists of different nations than there is to-day. The historical school was still the official one: in Germany it dominated most of the universities, and it was respected in many European countries, as well as in America. The appearance of Schmoller's *Outline* was hailed by all as a great event. This, however, was to be the last great effort of the historical school, which was no longer able to halt the victorious advance of the newer theoretical tendencies that were reaching their greatest development about this time. Among the Anglo-Saxons the polished theories of Marshall's *Principles* were enjoying universal praise; Pareto in his *Cours* had given the Latins an excellent development of Walras's theories, and the Germans were still powerfully impressed by the works of Böhm-Bawerk. At the very end of the century there appeared in America the best work on the somewhat modified theory of marginal utility: Clark's *Distribution*. The criticisms of Veblen and others on the theory of marginal utility were scarcely noticed, and the Vienna school shone in the full glory of its far-reaching influence. Karl Diehl was still devoting himself to the problems of Socialism and Communism, Liefmann was busying himself exclusively with the Cartel, and few suspected that he would soon advance an abstract economic theory. The Swedish engineer Cassel had only just turned his attention toward economics, and a young student, Othmar Spann, now wrote his first work, soon to be published in Schäffle's *Tübinger Zeitschrift.*

The great changes which the last quarter century has seen in economic theory can be in large part traced back to philosophical sources. The war between general philosophical tendencies of recent years is at the bottom of the various economic view-points as well as of the great changes in economic theory and as one or the other prevails or else exerts a greater influence on our science, the economic picture also changes.

1. The Baden School of Philosophy, the Question of Method, and the Philosophy of Values in Economics

Before the birth of the theory of marginal utility, the condition of German economics was such that the historical method, which was already becoming stereotyped, threatened to put an end to all theoretical investigation. The only chance for improvement lay in a renewed attack upon the problem of method. The nature of economics, its tasks and its place in the world of science were all questions which demanded a thorough investigation. A close alliance was accordingly made with the Baden school of Neo-Kantian philosophy which was working upon the same subjects. Windelband had already dealt with the systematization of the sciences; his researches were continued by Rickert and developed with incisive logic. A two-fold division of the sciences was reached, on the basis of which one group seemed to be amenable to the deductive, the other to the inductive method. It was, therefore, the business of economists to decide to which group their science belonged. Thus it happened that German writers on methodology, especially of recent years, have as a rule made use of the philosophical weapons placed at their disposal by the Baden school.

There was, moreover, a second point of contact between the new economics and the Baden school. Windelband already investigates the problem of knowledge with reference to its value as truth, rather than to its psychological origin, and connects epistemology with normative ethics and æsthetics. The idea of value is becoming prominent and idealism again takes precedence over thought. Rickert developed this tendency by his two methods of epistemology: transcendental psychology and transcendental logic. By the first we distinguish truth from error; there is, therefore, a judgment: affirmation or denial, acceptance or refusal. Behind this behavior is a transcendental idealism, which is recognized by the second method as a transcendental value, and appears to the consciousness of the knower an entirely different and independent principle. Consequently the whole dualistic structure of the Baden philosophers rests upon the epistemological theory of value.

The division which the Baden school made between natural and cultural, social and historical sciences has given weight to the theory of transcendental values. For if the aim of the natural sciences is to discover general laws, the cultural sciences can approach their subject, individual phenomena, only on the basis of an acknowledged system of cultural values. This is furnished by the principle of selection, which involves the choice of criteria in determining the particularity or uniqueness of phenomena. It is the eternal values, therefore, which have made possible for us an ordered and systematic knowledge of all external phenomena that are subject to change. They constitute the *a priori* basis upon which the transcendental idealism of the Baden school rests. Thus every systematic interpretation of the meaning of life starts out from a system of established values which attaches to all goods, or otherwise, in the present or the future, and with regard to which the scientific appraiser takes his own stand. We see here how the whole theory of knowledge resolves itself into a theory of value, and that historians of philosophy are right when they call this Neo-Kantian tendency a critique of values.

We can largely attribute to the success of value concepts in philosophy the fact that economists adhere so persistently to a theory of value as the foundation of all economic theory. Proponents of the theory of marginal utility invest it with a kind of tabu, so that no one dares question it, and they assign to it considerably more importance than do the exponents of newer economic tendencies, as far as these are still influenced by values.

We meet of late increasingly frequent attempts to connect abstract-deductive theories, especially the philosophy of marginal utility, with the idealistic and pragmatic positivism of Hans Vaihinger. The assumption is made that the theory of marginal utility works with the same fictions that Vaihinger emphasized in his *Philosophie des Als-Ob* (Berlin 1911), in developing the connection between science and being. This, however, seems to be a serious error. Perhaps Vaihinger himself is partly responsible when he quotes the authority of Adam Smith and the latter's apparent fiction of pure egoism. According to Vaihinger, all modern economics owes its origin to this fiction. Historical research, however, has proved more than once that the matter is not so simple with Adam Smith. Vaihinger is no economist and we ought not to blame him too severely. Even the younger economists seek at most to posit new hypotheses which correspond to reality, and which may be verified by it. Nevertheless, it is not their intention to play around with fictions, which are obviously not a picture of reality and do not even intend to be. A popular attack on the theory of marginal utility is to accuse it of unreality; but the argument does not seem to rest on firm ground. On the other hand, if some young writers purposely select Vaihinger's philosophy as a basis for their economic theories, it is easy to predict certain failure for the attempt. A conscious "Fictionism" will never discover a satisfactory path to reality, especially in our field. Thus the first and most important demand which we make of every economic theory remains unfulfilled.

Hugo Münsterberg, who had been influenced by other philosophical tendencies as well, brought the value criticism of the Baden school to America, and developed it to bold conclusions in his comprehensive *Philosophie der Werte* (Leipsic, 1909).

Reality, for him, consists of perception which in turn consists in pointing out values of existence and of relationship. Values exhibit, however, not a mere imperative, but at the same time a superindividual will, which is independent of pleasure or pain and is founded, in final analysis, on the "self-assertion of the world." In this way Münsterberg's epistemology, as well as his ethics and æsthetics, is merged in a theory of values; and, in addition, logic and metaphysics share the same fate. There are two main fields in his system of values: life-values, which are given directly, and cultural values, which are created. Each of these main categories includes the four subsidiary groups of logical, æsthetic, ethical and metaphysical values, which appear respectively as values of existence and relation, values of joy and beauty, values of development and performance, values of God and belief. Over and above this hierarchy of values is the original striving of the spirit, a super-individual fact of which all particular values are to be regarded as the formal expressions.

These ideas of Münsterberg succeeded in directing attention in America to the general problem of values. In this way this attitude, which had already been stressed by Clark and Seligman among others, penetrated even further into American economic theory. The same result was attained by the theories of the more recent American sociology, which is both biologically evolutionary and psychologically voluntaristic (Lester F. Ward, F. H. Giddings, C. H. Cooley), and which directly influenced certain young economists who are attempting to bring about an extension of the concept of economic values, and to put it in its proper place in the hierarchy of the other, more general, values. It is partly on this basis that B. M. Anderson Jr. attempted to reform current economic theories of value. Later on we shall see how other students, for example Dibblee, Perry and Usher, have been stimulated by him to similar researches.

2. *The Philosophical Bases of "Value-less" Economics*

The difference between what is and what should be, based on the concept of value, and especially the preparatory work of Rickert formed the starting-point of the important debate concerning the possibility of scientific value judgments in economics, which began at the turn of the century with Max Weber, and remained as one of the chief topics of German discussion until the war. It seems to be definitely established that Max Weber was closely connected to the Baden school. This we shall explain more fully later.

Starting from entirely different premises, French students reached methodological conclusions which were closely related to those of Weber. In contrast to the epistemological psychology which we have just noticed among the followers of the Baden school and which, as it is well known, has been adopted by numerous Latin scholars, Émile Durkheim offers a strongly objective conception of sociology.

He notices an essential difference between social and psychic phenomena, and vigorously denies the possibility of the psychic functions discovering the laws of social life independently, through purely rational and deductive thinking. Durkheim wishes to separate sociology as sharply as possible from philosophy, hoping thereby to expel all those elements of deduction which give to sociology, when it forms part of a general philosophical pattern, at once a certain direction and some kind of a special character, whether it be spiritualistic, positivistic, evolutionary or what not. By logically developing this postulate, he desires to exclude from sociology all practical norms which contain, however vaguely or indirectly, a flavor of idealism. Sociology should be neither individualistic nor collectivistic, neither conservative nor progressive, but should endeavor, with as few premises as possible, to attain an objective knowledge of social phenomena as they appear in their causal relationships. Contrary to Max Weber, who works out the principle of causality, the only possible viewpoint in social studies from the angle of a rationalist, Durkheim sees in it an empirical postulate. This attitude leads him to choose a purely inductive method, through whose development or transformation he seeks the perfection of social research.

Durkheim's adherents, the enthusiastic circle of the *Année Sociologique,* which he edited, tried to apply the leader's views to the separate social sciences and to make these views conform to the peculiarities of each discipline. François Simiand was especially successful in carrying out this work. Not only did he develop his economic researches, which were inductive, sociological and methodologically free from value judgments, but he indicated it in practice by his thorough investigation of highly important economic problems. It is certainly owing only to the rationalistic and mathematical dispositions of the French mind that Simiand's valuable thoughts have found, at least up to the present time, but scant response.

We can mention only briefly here the Italian idealistic philosopher, Benedetto Croce who, by postulating Hegelian dialectics purged of the misuses of later followers and by settling his score with the historical materialism of Marx—thus in an entirely different way from that of Weber and Simiand—reached the demand that in economics a sharp distinction must be drawn between the purely economic and the moral effects.

3. The Marburg School of Philosophy; Cassel and Liefmann

In its rejection of epistemological psychology, Durkheim's sociology resembles that of the Marburg school; after the Baden school the most important development of Neo-Kantianism in Germany. It was founded by Hermann Cohen, after whose death it was continued by Paul Natorp and Ernest Cassirer.

Like the Baden thinkers, this school starts by rejecting Kant's "thing in itself." On the other hand, it teaches that it is not the business of philosophy to investigate the growth of the perceptions of each individual, but rather to explain the immanent and logical conditions of scientific experience. Therefore they are concerned not so much with systematically developing an independent theory of knowledge, as with scientifically analysing the logic of the functional relations which govern scientific thought. In their choice of a scientific ideal they follow Kant: the only sciences which can give us true knowledge are the natural sciences which can be treated mathematically; consequently they disclose a strong leaning toward the methods of mathematics. They thereby formulate general laws which are not transcendent, but transcendental. These they do not deduce from *a priori* major premises, but always remain within the domain of thought, of which they conceive the relationship of subject and object as a subsidiary corollary. Thus the Marburg philosophers attain a monistic and logical idealism and set themselves the task of discovering the principles of uniformity as well as their various manifestations in the realm of the logical sciences. Evidently this point of view can be of use only in sciences which are already more or less fixed in their method, and it is only when they build upon such foundations that the methods of the Marburg school can produce results.

This is the maturity which economics has reached in the eyes of those students who ignore methodological disputes and concentrate on the logical and mathematical developments of the science. Cassel shows the influence of the Marburg school when he criticizes the theory of marginal utility as barren and empty and throws overboard as well the whole theory of value which had led to so much quibbling. His explanation of all economic phenomena is the unitary principle of scarcity upon which he tries to build, with the help of his objective attitude, a purely logical structure of economics. Cassel was also influenced by positivistic and pragmatic theory as well as by the realism of Alois Riehl and Oswald Külpe, and endeavored to reject from economic theory all the traditional elements which, in his opinion, did not further the knowledge of the logical and partly mathematical relations of real economic phenomena.

Liefmann tries to found his purely psychical economics on the results of the Baden school and expressly quotes Windelband, Rickert, Münsterberg and Max Weber as his authority. In reality he owes much to the Marburg school. Even here we notice a certain eclectic trait for which his economic system has often been blamed. He rejects the theory of value for very much the same reasons as Cassel and endeavors also to build his system upon a principle of unity: his law of psychic returns. By theory he understands a systematic explanation of the object of experience under discussion on the basis of its correct principle of identity e. g.—in dealing with economics—on the basis of a comparison between profits and costs. He does not miss an opportunity of blaming other economists who quarrel over questions of method instead of dealing with the real problem of their science—but he is often guilty of the same fault. Apart from these rather formal influences of the Marburg school, the purely psychic structure of his system can be traced back to the influence of the Baden philosophers. Even the pragmatic-realistic trait which we noticed in Cassel can be found in Liefmann. He purposely and consistently retains the "money-veil," and considers the real subject-matter of economics to consist in the phenomena of money economy.

4. Comte, Spencer, and the Theory of Economic Equilibrium

We shall deal later with the further influences which the Marburg school has exerted on the most recent developments of German economics. For the present we shall follow the strongly marked realism and pragmatism of both Cassel and Liefmann, which lead us to recent Latin and Anglo-Saxon economics. The positivism of Auguste Comte, which had influenced the formal methodology of the German historical school as well as of the few followers of Durkheim and Simiand, left a deep impression on the following generation in respect to the contents and aims of economic theory. Comte wished to rid sociology of metaphysics and to make of it an exact and positive science, based on sense experiences and concerned with a limited number of social relationships. In the same way subsequent Latin and Anglo-Saxon economists concerned themselves with the study of a few relationships which could be exactly ascertained and which, when free from disturbing and extraneous considerations, might form the kernel of an exact and positive theory of economics. At the center of their thought is the doctrine of economic equilibrium, from which their various theories develop, as do the branches from the trunk of a tree. It is unlikely that this idea would have attained its present wide popularity without the support of Herbert Spencer's evolutionism.

After formulating his well-known general law of development, Spencer tried to modify it from various angles, so that it should fit in with the concrete phenomena of evolution. Accordingly he first asserts that evolution is a transition from a simple to a more complex state, and tries to prove this in the evolution of the solar system, the earth, plants, animals and human society. With these and other examples he also shows that in most cases evolution is also a transition from a greater to a lesser similarity or from homogeneity to heterogeneity. An organism, therefore, evolves from a simple, homogeneous seed to a complicated structure of organs just as a language, which was originally common, divides into several dialects. At the same time that this differentiation takes place, the being is also becoming more definite; i. e., it evolves from an indefinite to a definite state. All natural and social organisms are made more precise and defined by the growing complexity and development of their parts. This is the way in which Spencer developed his famous evolutionism, according to which evolution is an integration of matter, accompanied by distintegration of motion, while at the same time matter moves from undefined, simple homogeneity to defined, complex heterogeneity, and motion goes through similar changes.

Whither does this process of progressive differentiation and integration lead? Surely the dissipation of motion and the concentration of matter must end somewhere! But then, says Spencer, a state of absolute equilibrium is reached, where all forces and counterforces have cancelled each other, motion is abandoned and dispersed, and therefore everything is at a standstill. Meanwhile, individual substances have reached a state of moving equilibrium, where only their separate parts continue to move, while the whole has reached a state of rest. In such an unstable equilibrium is, for instance, our solar system, which is in its most general relationships fixed and stable, but within which the individual planets continue to move. This moving equilibrium becomes gradually, in every development, a stable and absolute one, in which even the parts cease to move, perfect differentiation and order are reached, and the being can react to continuous exterior forces only by a process which is opposed to development, by its gradual disintegration. In its course, all the phenomena of evolution repeat themselves in reversed order, until finally matter is again dispersed and disintegrated by the attainment of complete motion, and returns to a condition of imperceptibility. Since, however, matter must continue to exist, it remains there until the course of a new development begins. Thus, in organic and in social life and in the cosmos, development and disintegration repeat themselves in an eternal rhythm, the course of which provides us with the key to the understanding of the universe.

However much this impressive outline of Spencer's outwardly resembles materialism, we think that we should emphasize the fact that it is essentially very different. For Spencer the expressions matter, motion, and force are symbols, behind which is the much more complex absolute. He is never tired, however, of emphasizing that the absolute is unknowable, and that both materialism and spiritualism lose themselves in verbal quibbling, when they think it knowable.

Spencer first applied his evolutionism to biology and psychology, and then made it the leading doctrine of his sociology and ethics. He conceives social life as an organic development, and as a part of the general unified cosmos. Comparing it with the evolution of individual organisms, he seems to distinguish a similar integration and disintegration of matter, the social relationships, and a similar transition to a more coherent and definite state. Social organisms—according to Spencer—differ from individual ones in that they have no definite external form: their units form no continuous substance, in which their positions may be relatively determined, but are scattered, and move freely from place to place. Finally they are all endowed with feeling, whereas in the case of individual organisms the seat of sensation is a special tissue. From all of this there emerges the main distinction; namely, that with social organisms the whole must serve the parts, whereas with individual organisms it is the other way. Nevertheless the evolution of social organisms, like that of all others, aims at a state of equilibrium, so that here too we find the great cosmic rhythm of development and dissolution, rise and fall, which guides the fate of the universe.

These imposing thoughts of Spencer's synthetic philosophy spread swiftly over the whole civilized world, and it is not surprising that the science of economics should have felt its influence. When we consider that Spencer's *First Principles,* which contained the main features of his evolutionism, appeared about ten years before Walras's *Éléments d'économie politique pure,* we can see more plainly than ever what a close connection exists between Spencer and the theory of economic equilibrium. The interplay of supply and demand, the manifold actions and re-actions by which the Lausanne school explains the formation of prices and the distribution of incomes and tries to solve many problems of economic organization are all dealt with in the manner of Spencer's evolutionism. According to the Lausanne school, economic relationships also are trying to attain an ideal state of perfect equilibrium. This, however, is never reached in practice; for in the moment that it is reached, economic life would come to a standstill and gradually disintegrate. All the more important, then, in practice is a state of unstable equilibrium. The followers of the Lausanne school, as we shall see later, investigate the bearings of this on the most various economic problems, and with great enthusiasm. Nevertheless, even if they are generally unconscious of it, Spencerian philosophy is the source of their inspiration as well as the link by which the theory of economic equilibrium has been connected with the most important problems of society, of natural science and of the universe in general.

Most of the followers of the Lausanne school adopted the main thoughts of Spencer, with modifications of a more or less materialistic or mechanistic kind. Pareto alone left them in their pure and original form. In his youth he was one of the most enthusiastic admirers of the great English philosopher and studied him zealously as long as he lived in Italy. Later on, in Switzerland, he gradually turned away from Spencer's thought but always remained very much under its influence. For instance, the theory of social equilibrium is at the center of his whole sociology and the problem of economic equilibrium receives a treatment from him which reminds us forcibly of the general views of Spencer. In Pareto's later development, however, the influence of Spencer gave way to the increasing influence of Comte. In the *Manuel* and in the *Trattato*, this influence is again and again visible. Pareto's positivistic ideal of science is exactly the same as Comte's: the human race has progressed through theology and metaphysics to positive science, from which all elements of the former ruling ideas must be abolished. Accordingly he takes as the object of scientific observation only what is given in time and space and believes that we can know only movements, though not the forces which cause them. We could continue to enumerate at length the resemblances between Comte and Pareto, especially in phenomenology, and gnosiology. We may also trace to the influence of Comte who, as is well known, was a believer in government interference, Pareto's gradual abandonment of the liberal ideal which he had maintained so strongly in his youth. Beside Comte and Spencer, we can trace in Pareto, among other philosophical influences, that of Darwin's evolutionism, and Alexander Bain's logic, based on the psychology of association.

5. *Utilitarian Ethics, the Cambridge School and Economic Liberalism*

The doctrine of economic equilibrium was also adopted by Marshall and his followers, of the Cambridge school of political economy, who made of it a cardinal principle of their teaching. In this respect they come into contact with Spencerian thought, by which they have also been much influenced in the domain of ethics. For this reason we shall say a few words about Spencer's ethics.

The great English philosopher considered his "Ethics" the crowning achievement of his whole philosophical system. He was, first and foremost, a hedonist, who saw in pleasure the final ethical goal. But since, as he taught, everything which is conducive to pleasure is also conducive to life and since life itself is the goal of the whole evolutionary process, one can make of life itself the direct ethical aim. According to this, all actions which subserve life are good, whereas all those which tend to diminish life, or to deny it, are to be considered bad. Morality should, however, as far as possible, further not only self-preservation but also the life of one's own and of future generations. Here we see plainly the utilitarianism of Spencerian ethics. While he makes the most of his evolutionism in this respect, he manages to steer a sound middle course between the radical ethical empiricism of the earlier utilitarians, for whom morality originated in our experience of the good and bad results of our actions, and the philosophy of intuition, which perceives the origin of all morality in the will of a supernatural being, in something therefore which is innate and *a priori* to us.

In the beginning, Spencer says, our judgments of good and evil undoubtedly arose out of our everyday experiences and out of the consequences which usually accompanied our various actions. This capacity to judge, then, originally purely empirical, is carried on by countless generations of mankind and gradually hardens itself into an ethical intuitive faculty which is *a priori* and innate to us; a potent feeling which has nothing to do with the individual will and which we call conscience. With respect, therefore, to the individual, morality is innate; with respect to the whole of mankind, in process of evolution, morality is rooted in practical experience. Closely connected to this *a priori* evolutionism is the fact that Spencer separates himself further from the barren empiricism of traditional utilitarianism in relating ethical experiences to the most universal conditions of human existence, from which he attempts to derive them, thereby laying a foundation for deductive research in the field of ethics.

Owing to the spread of these ideas, which have been taken from his general evolutionary teaching, Spencer succeeded in breathing new life into utilitarianism, and in again making it popular in wide circles. It is largely owing to him that the hedonistic-utilitarian doctrine has been considered by many as one of the most important starting points in economics right up to the present day. The doctrine can be clearly traced, not only in Pareto, but in the whole Lausanne school. Its importance, however, was greatest in Anglo-Saxon economic theory, where it predominates even today in the works of most American economists, especially in those who carry on the traditions of the Cambridge school. In the system of Pigou, the basic thoughts of utilitarianism have the deciding word. At this point, however, we note the appearance of another, more modern trend of utilitarianism. Henry Sidgwick is the scholar who, at the end of the nineteenth century, sent forth its doctrines on their triumphant journey.

Sidgwick boldly attempts to divorce utilitarianism from its empirical basis, and to give it an entirely new philosophical foundation. The importance of this step will be perceived only when we consider how deep were the roots of empiricism in England where, since Hume, the indestructible foundation of all morality was placed in feeling. Sidgwick, however, rejects the practice of Mill and Bentham in subordinating the ideal to the real, and makes the ethical aims be determined once again by reason and moral consciousness. In this way he especially rejects psychological hedonism, which managed in a particularly agreeable way to unite utilitarianism with egoism and then, with great insight, he brings out the contradictions between these two tendencies. As a matter of fact Sidgwick perceives a truth in Spencer's evolutionary ethics and willingly concedes that the evolutionary period is of great importance in the genesis of moral judgments. He decides, however, that the origin of our morality is not to be found in empiricism, but in intuition. According to Sidgwick, our perception of a moral constitution of the world, in which all men have the same moral duties under the same conditions, cannot be founded on experience. It is due rather to an intuition, under the influence of the instinct, implanted by nature into all of us, of benevolence toward our neighbor. Sidgwick, then, goes back to the teachings of the early Scotch philosophers, especially to Butler, unites them with the point of view of the Kantian categorical imperative and gives thereby a new content to utilitarian ethics; although the outward frame of Bentham and Mill is preserved intact. He is strongly influenced by Kant in his theory of knowledge. In metaphysics he is a sceptic and his recommendation of a belief in God and in morality is due merely to its social utility.

It is well known that Sidgwick applied his ethical views himself to political economy. When his system of political economy appeared in the eighties, it was noticed only in his own country where its success was but moderate. His rational-utilitarianism, however, has been recently brought into prominence by Pigou whose system is now one of the most prized possessions of world economic science.

Nearer to Spencerian ethics is the still flourishing economic liberalism of the classicists, which is especially strong in France. Although it derived its hedonistic-utilitarian views from the later classical school, it is in sympathy with the innovations of Spencer. Spencer himself was one of the most indefatigable champions of the ideal of economic freedom. This was in keeping with his fundamental individualism, and proved to be a means of contact between him and the French liberals. Gustave de Molinari even took over Spencer's general evolutionism and built his whole economic theory upon this foundation.

6. *Stammler and the Socio-legal Theory of Economics*

We shall now go back to the philosophical bases of the most recent German economic doctrines. We have already shown how from two directions, Cassel and Liefmann, the Marburg school of philosophy gave rise to serious objections to the theory of marginal utility. To these we may add a third direction, springing from the same source. It can be referred directly to Rudolf Stammler, legal philosopher, a follower of the Marburg school, who undertook to build a structure of social philosophy with the help of the critical-epistemological points of view of the Marburg Neo-Kantians. He treats social evolution monistically and tries to explain motion and change in the social world by antecedent social phenomena and to perceive them in the unconditional unity of social experience. He does not admit, however, an independent causal series for social currents. Stammler sees the essential characteristic of social life, that which distinguishes it from a mere collocation of units, at the time of external regulation: that is to say, in the existence of a legal order created by man. He means, therefore, by social life a community of men whose conduct is regulated by exterior norms. It is only through this exterior regulation that society becomes an object of study, and consequently every social investigation must direct its attention to it, to its composition and nature. Therefore, according to Stammler, the form of society is the law, whereas its material substance is economics. Every consideration of economics should be based on a knowledge of the legal form, or frame, which contains the only conditions that are possible for economic life.

Karl Diehl based his socio-legal system of economics on Stammler's social philosophy. In this he retained the theory of value, although in an entirely subordinate position, but criticized with telling force the abstract procedure of the theory of marginal utility. One of those who agree with Diehl on this point is Rudolf Stolzmann, whose philosophy is closely related to that of Stammler, and who took from him a teleological attitude toward social phenomena which, according to Stammler, are but elements in the general teleological structure of society. Alfred Amonn, a member of the Austrian school, likewise tends toward a socio-legal point of view, but he also relies largely upon the logic of the Baden philosophy. In his earliest writings he played the part of a kind-hearted peace-maker in the great dispute on method. It is all the sadder for the theory of marginal utility, that he should recently have given himself up to entirely different aspects of economics. Marginal utility fared no better at the hands of Othmar Spann, who had been one of its most prominent younger champions. He too shows many points of contact with the teleological attitude of Stammler in sociology; the real roots of his philosophy, however, reach down into entirely different realms.

7. *The Renaissance of German Idealism, and Spann*

With the renaissance of German philosophy which took place toward the end of the last century, an idealistic attitude becomes more and more prominent. The Baden school of Neo-Kantianism is deeply influenced by the idealism of Fichte, such as we see in Windelband, more clearly in Rickert and, above all, in Münsterberg. These thinkers are, however, especially occupied with criticism of knowledge, which is the direction in which Fichte influences them. But a real renaissance of traditional German idealism could be achieved only by a philosophy which interested itself once more in metaphysics, as Rudolf Eucken advocated. He was opposed to naturalism, and taught the existence and the ruling of a super objective spiritual world, without which we must view even human society as a senseless farrago of selfish individuals who obey only their hedonistic impulses. This idea of a higher spiritual world was the center of Eucken's philosophy, and became the foundation of the new idealistic movement in German thought. Even Richard Falckenberg, who is more under the influence of Lotze, tries to breathe new life into the idealism of Fichte, and Hermann Schwarz, Fritz Medicus, and Johann Maria Verweyen, from among the younger philosophers, take this same direction. Hegel, too, is studied with increasing fervor and an attempt is made to achieve, with his aid, a revival of speculative thought. This was the direction chosen by Adolf Lasson and Otto Pfleiderer; the two leading schools of Neo-Kantian criticism both absorb the thoughts of Hegel.

It is in this environment that Spann attempts to utilize the buried treasures of German idealism for a reform of economics. Like some other representatives of modern science and poetry, Spann has recourse especially to Romanticism, the culmination of idealism, and opposes its universalism to individualism in economics. In the new psychology Spann examines Dilthey, Franz Brentano, Ehrenfels, Meinong and Külpe, in the philosophy of history Lotze, Windelband and Rickert, and perceives in the achievements of these men a more and more marked transition from mechanism and causality to an attitude which is both organic and teleological. He quotes with especial insistence the biological metaphysics, of which Hans Driesch is the most important representative.

Driesch had originally devoted himself to zoology. He soon felt called upon in his studies to challenge Darwinian evolution. After much successful inquiry he came to the conclusion that the innermost secrets of zoology can be probed only by adopting a teleological attitude and that its first principle was dynamic vitalism—a theory which J. v. Hanstein, G. v. Bunke, and J. Reinke had proclaimed shortly before, after making similar investigations. In this way he became interested in philosophical, more especially in metaphysical, problems, to which he has recently been giving all his attention. The starting point of his philosophy is the original state of knowledge which he understands somewhat in the sense of the Cartesian "*cogito ergo sum.*" He develops the rule which is implied in this primary conception of knowledge in his "theory of classification." In this work he supplements the categories of Kant by adding to them the category of "the whole and its parts" in which the outline of vitalism is implied. Driesch sees in every organic structure, in every whole the seat of a plurality which cannot increase fundamentally in degree of its own accord in the course of its becoming.

He goes on in his metaphysics to inquire more closely into this growth, or organic development, and tries to explain it by means of the principle of Vitalism alone, rejecting mechanistic notions. Driesch also teaches that the life of an organism is moved and ruled by a superindividual entelechy, besides the natural psychic and chemical factors. This presents no special form of energy but is subject nevertheless to the general principle of energy, the activity of which consists in productions of order, that is to say in the development of their inherent and intense plurality, and which can best be compared, as to its nature, with the platonic idea of species. It is by the action of the entelechies that the various organisms articulate themselves and their system is already implied in that of the entelechies. The highest and most unattainable goal of this theory is to conceive the world as an unique organism of which individuals are the parts, graduated according to their importance for the whole.—Jacob von Uexküll developed a similar theory of a systematic structure of the organic world, and Karl Jellinek undertook to explain society and economics from this aspect.

The principles of this biological metaphysics as developed by Hans Driesch and his followers were still unknown to Spann when he started to construct his own system. It was only later that he came upon them unawares. Spann himself would admit the agreement of his general attitude with that of Driesch even though Driesch retains some elements of causality in his philosophy, whereas Spann tries to keep one consistent attitude. Moreover both reached similar conclusions by different routes: i. e., biological researches and social investigations. Their agreement, therefore, seems to be all the more remarkable and important.

Spann constructed his system by interweaving his organic and teleological thoughts with the main tendencies of German romanticism, especially that part which consists of his doctrine of categories in which his universalistic philosophy is especially noticeable. According to this, the statement of individualists that the part comes before the whole is untrue. The prevalence of this attitude is even an "unspeakable misfortune" and the knowledge which it produces is barbaric, teaching a negation of life, truth, spirit and God. The fallacies to which this philosophy leads are atomism, mechanism, individualism, capitalism, socialism of the future and sensualism. To this Spann opposes his first and most important category of being, that of the whole, in which he sees the only correct attitude for metaphysicians and sociologists. The whole, according to Spann, has in itself no existence; it is, however, superior to its members: it comes into being with the members, but does not perish with them. Spann derives his other categories from that of the whole: the mode of agreement, development, birth, fate, etc. Right in the center, however, is the indestructible, and invisible spark, which can be called the first source of Driesch's entelechies. Spann got the idea of this spark from Meister Eckehart, the greatest of German mystics, and tries to show its presence in Aristotle, Plotinus and St. Thomas. Freedom and dependence in Spann's system are no longer, ethically speaking, opposites, since both concepts meet in a relation of membership in the "re-association of the member in the whole." Spann derives all morality and all ethical values from this relationship of members, this ordered articulation of the whole and then, going over to economics, derives also the concept of equal importance or equivalence with which he tries in his latest phase to supplant what he now considers the untenable theory of marginal utility.

8. The Interpsychological System of Tarde

The nearest approach in modern Latin literature to the inclusive systems of philosophy and economics, like that of Spann, is probably the philosophy of Gabriel Tarde, who belonged really to an earlier generation but who published authoritative works in economics at the beginning of this century. As a matter of fact, there is only one essential point of contact between the two, namely, that Spann's outline of a universalistic structure of society, with which we shall deal more fully later, shows a certain resemblance to Tarde's interpsychological view of society.

The general features of Tarde's philosophy are essentially optimistic. There is a great harmony in the universe, within which all particular phenomena adapt themselves under certain inherent relationships. The first of these general relationships is that of adaptation, which appears in the inorganic world as chemical union, in the organic world as fertilization, and in human society as the creative activity of invention. Undulations in inorganic nature, procreation in the organic world, and imitation in social life are the various aspects of another universal relationship, that of repetition. The third and last is opposition which appears in the three separate phases of existence as violence, murder and war.

The process of social, organic and cosmic evolution is a result of the interactions of these three main relationships. It is governed by a universal harmony in which it finds its goal. But within this process a law of *irreversibility* operates, according to which the strict series of evolutionary phenomena ordained by nature can never be upset. The second fundamental law of development is that of *progressive extension* which is the same as Spencer's law of the multiplication of effects, which we have discussed above.

Later on we shall show more fully how Tarde tried to connect the whole structure of economics with this philosophical system, often with cleverness but often, also, with artifice and effort. Indeed, his system differs fundamentally from that of Spann in its general outline; but some parts show much similarity. Thus the idea of a *just price* plays an important role with Tarde; the same idea which Spann "theoretically reconquered" in his latest phase, although in an entirely different way.

9. Philosophical Optimism in America and Clark's School

The main current of recent economic theory in America, which is best represented by the elder Clark, consists of the principles of marginal utility and of modified aspects of the classical tradition. Its philosophical origins, therefore, are similar to those of these two economic trends. It is especially characterized by hedonism and utilitarianism, which form the basis of the attacks most often made against it. Besides this, Clark's school is marked by an optimistic tendency, which is one of the most important ingredients of American culture.

Jonathan Edwards, the first American philosopher of importance, and perhaps the greatest, looks upon nature and society as a magnificent harmony, created by God, which is holy and devoted only to the happiness of man. This attitude became, through Benjamin Franklin, the typical attitude of American philosophy. He succeeded, through his maxims of "poor Richard," in planting his conviction that the happiness of every being lies in its end into the consciousness of all classes of Americans. Even social units exist only for the well-being of the individual. Franklin tries to base these ethical concepts upon aspects of natural philosophy which bring him into close spiritual affinity with the French physiocrats. In economics, this optimistic philosophy reaches its fullest expression with Henry Charles Carey. He founds his entire system of political economy upon the divine harmony in which, according to him, the organic and inorganic, the spiritual and social worlds are ruled by fundamental laws.

The tradition of optimism is more or less adhered to in the doctrines of Clark. He uses it especially in his theory of distribution and above all, through the ethical adoption of the principle of marginal utility.

According to Clark, the share which the various factors in production get out of the social dividend because of their marginal yield, is their just share, which cannot in the long run be curtailed even by the influence of social forces. Seligman draws a liberal conclusion from the theory of marginal utility, which he utilizes to explain business life in general. Patten develops this optimism still further, makes it the corner stone of his theory of price and value, and sees in the distribution of goods the hope of harmony, even with a retention of the present wages system.

10. The New American Psychology, and Economic Institutionalism

In the present century, Clark's school has been severely criticized in America. The leaders of this attack are an active group of young economists, who rely especially upon the findings of the so-called new psychology and attack the fundamental principles of hedonism and utilitarianism in modern economics. The new psychology, which arose in America partly in the eighties, but especially in the nineties of the last century, developed its theories out of the teachings of two important European schools. The first of these is the old English psychology of association, especially in its Spencerian modifications; the second is modern German experimental psychology.

The psychology of association is a branch of that empirical, explanatory psychology which, in contrast with empirical descriptive psychology, not merely enquires into the purely phenomental manifestations of spiritual life but also tries to discover the psychic dispositions which are at the back of them. Its origins are to be found in Greek philosophy. Apart from a few passages in Parmenides of Elea and Diogenes of Apollonia concerning the phenomenon of forgetting, Plato was the first to attempt an abstract analysis of memory. Aristotle advanced some interesting laws concerning association and imitation, which show keen observation. The Romans, who were interested in mnemotechnic inquiries, and the mediæval scholastics, who made the soul the agent of memory, did not go beyond him in this respect.

It is the seventeenth century philosophers, especially Hobbes and Locke, who developed the subject, while Hume made the idea of association the corner stone of his psychology. He looks upon association as the mode of transition from one idea to another, and explains thereby the perpetual change and continuation of simple and complex ideas. Upon this doctrine Hume bases his whole empirical theory of knowledge, since he refers our consciousness of existence to associative relationships. Hartley on the other hand rehashes some of the theories of older French thinkers, Descartes and Malebranche, and tries to explain the psychic fact of association by bodily functions of the brain, and by drawing upon a psycho-physical theory of vibration. The French enlightenment was exceptionally favorable to this materialistic conception of association, and German scientists gladly accepted and developed the theory that association was due to the stimulating of closely related fibers. On the continent, Kant and the romantic movement put the psychology of association into the background, but the English continued it and James Mill gave it a fresh impetus. John Stuart Mill was the first who gave the psychology of association as well as classical political economy logical and precise expression. He considers thoughts, emotions, volitions and sensations the chief kinds of states of consciousness, formulates general rules for their regular associations, and makes them the object of scientific psychology. Alexander Bain follows the way of abstract unification, makes all simple associations depend on similarity and contact, but recognizes also complex and constructive associations which are brought about by fancy.

The psychology of association reached its greatest development in the evolutionary thought of Spencer. He divides psychology into objective and subjective. The former deals with an inner observation of the phenomena of consciousness, whereas the latter tries to discover psychic phenomena only in the actions of men and beasts. This is the objective status of psychology: the doctrine of a certain group of general vital manifestations, closely related to biology and presupposing an accurate knowledge of the functions of the nervous system. Spencer imagines the subjective basis of these objective nervous functions to be a combination of the fundamental psychological atoms or units of consciousness and derives from this all the different phenomena of consciousness. The motive power and concrete expression of these combinations are the associations, as they were understood by earlier English psychologists. Spencer goes on to say that the real essence of these physic manifestations of life can be understood only in terms of evolution. In their course the inner, psychic relationships adapt themselves in a continually better manner to the outer world, whereby a scale of constant development takes place among organisms, so that their reactions to the environment become more and more diversified. The psychic activities become, in the course of their development, more and more regular, in contradistinction to physiological manifestations. The relations of the spirit to the environment take on, thereby, a more and more differentiated character, not only through individual experience but also through heredity.

Besides this emphasis on revolution, Spencer falls back largely upon the psychophysical theory of Hartley; but he expressly refers to the later researches of the German scholar Helmholtz. He was the first who, in developing the theories of Johannes Müller, treated the close relations between physiological and psychological processes upon a mathematical basis. Moreover, his physiology of the senses provided a groundwork for experimental psychology, the theory which was so flourishing in Germany in the latter half of the last century.

The first important results in this field were due to Ernst Heinrich Weber, who tried to measure with precision the innate instruments of feeling and made use in this connection of the experimental method. The connecting link between the researches of Weber and the older psychological theories, especially the metaphysical ideas of Schelling, was provided by Gustav Theodor Fechner. He considers body and soul to be different expressions of the same fundamental thing and states the proportions and mathematical equations of the interactions of their functions. Out of this he builds an entirely new science of psychophysics: something between psychology and physics. In the meantime quite different investigations, especially those in the much-discussed problem of mistakes in astronomical registration, led to conclusions which were somewhat similar to those of experimental psychology. Wilhelm Wundt deserves the praise of having gathered together the results of these various investigations into an unified system in which the theory of senseperception, the psychology of the senses and, as a culmination of them all, experimental psychology, are represented as the three main currents of modern psychology.

In Germany, experimental psychology was developed especially by the Würzburg school. In America, its union with aspects of earlier associationism, especially with the psychological teachings of Spencer, gave birth to the new American psychology, which was destined to play such an important rôle in the development of modern economics on the other side of the Atlantic. Of the numerous Americans who helped to found or to continue this science, we shall only mention the names of William James, J. Mark Baldwin, J. B. Watson, E. L. Thorndike, W. B. Cannon, E. B. Titchener, R. S. Woodworth, K. Dunlap, R. M. Yerkes, and J. R. Angell. Its anthropological and biological aspects are represented especially by F. Boas, R. H. Lowie, T. H. Morgan and the Englishman, W. Bateson; while its socio-psychological relationships are developed by such men as C. A. Cooley, W. McDougall, W. F. Ogburn, and the Englishman, Graham Wallas and later, with especial emphasis on the economic aspect, by Thorstein B. Veblen and some of his followers. Since we must abandon the attempt, in the space at our disposal, to discuss these men individually, we shall try to give a short summary of their chief views, in so far as these tend to renovate economics.

According to them, human nature is not the simple phenomenon directed by pure reason, which it was formerly supposed to be. On the contrary, an infinitely complicated psychophysical mechanism is at work which always reacts in a different way according to the nature of its environment. In these reactions, or in human behavior, the role of reason is not to determine, but merely to choose, since it is able only to crush certain undesirable forms of reactions and to select the useful actions which should be accomplished. If these actions tend to satisfy the needs of individual and social life, they are due originally to psychophysical particularities of our nature, and not to reasoned calculation which accomplishes the secondary function of a choice of actions striving for accomplishment and psychically already implied. This is not contradicted by the fact that the influence of reason upon behavior increases with the growth of civilization and that in the mental advance of mankind culture more and more assumes the form of activity directed by reason. For in reality we are dealing only with an ever increasing differentiation of psychophysical reactions which always give a suitable response to the changing influences of the environment and, by their speedy adaptability, differentiate man from the rest of living creatures.

It is impossible to say, therefore, that economic behavior is determined by a general law of reason as, for example, by the principle of hedonism. For even in its most fundamental principles the economic behavior of mankind is always adapted to the contemporary evolutionary development of economic institutions and of the social environment. Moreover, the development of human nature and that of economic institutions move parallel to each other, as in Spencer's doctrine: even the smallest action of mankind produces changes in the economic environment which react in turn upon human nature in a thousand different ways and produce counter-reactions. This process continues uninterruptedly and keeps a perpetual parallel development and change going on on both sides. It is useful, of course, to inquire into the relationships between the economic behavior of man and his economic environment, apart from its evolution, for a given time; e. g., for the present. But this method will give us only a static picture. It is also a mistake to start from an abstract *a priori* assumption of a certain type of economic behavior, which is changeless and logically observed in all its details. For all needs and desires, ends and means, the place and direction of individual behavior are merely functions of an institutional development, always changing, and infinitely complex.

The real essence of economics can be understood only by a thorough study of economic institutions, their nature, their origin, their growth and the changes they undergo in the course of their development and of their relationships to the parallel changes of psychophysics or of practical economic behavior.

This is, in outline, the principle of the most modern current in American economics, known as *Institutionalism*, or *Behaviorism*, which is based on the new American psychology and has become more and more prominent in recent years. It repeats, in logical sequence, the points of view of German experimental psychology and Spencerian evolutionism, with a background of the traditional English psychology of association. We should, however, not overlook the fact that the idea of relativity, which is at the center of this new economic theory, is partly connected with the fundamental principles of the German historical school and, within this school, especially with the attitude of Bruno Hildebrand.

One can scarcely talk of a special school of institutionalism in America or even of a clearly defined current which goes its own way, unrelated to other economic tendencies. The outlines are blurred, and many students appreciate it in a greater or less degree, without thereby being known as institutionalists. Nevertheless, next to Veblen, we may call W. C. Mitchell, J. R. Commons, W. H. Hamilton, L. D. Edie, and R. S. Tugwell, the leaders of this movement, which A. B. Wolfe, J. M. Clark, F. C. Mills, O. F. Boucke, D. Friday, among others, approach to some extent from different directions.

H. J. Davenport pretends to have nothing to do with the institutionalists; nevertheless he has some contacts with them since he severely criticizes the theory of marginal utility on the basis of a psychology which is quite distinct from utilitarianism. He calls himself a psychological *voluntarist,* emphasizing the importance of the element of will in both spiritual matters and practical behavior. This theory, so readily adaptable to the American idea of progress, had already been formulated by the American philosophers of the eighteenth century: Jonathan Edwards, Samuel Johnson and Benjamin Franklin. F. A. Fetter has derived some valuable ideas on economics from this voluntaristic psychology, but this scholar cannot be classified, for he tries to retain the most important results of the theory of marginal utility and even attacks institutionalism.

It is thus obvious, that the Americans have not arrived at a consistent economic program on the basis of their new psychology. Up to the present time, the adherents of institutionalism have not succeeded in forming a unified group. They all differ according as their attitude is more historical, statistical, purely quantitative, merely realistic or psychological. The adherents of the new psychology agree only on one point: they all attack orthodox political economy, as it is represented by the elder Clark and his followers. This attitude has recently been defended by Zenas Clark Dickinson, who tries to prove, with much ability, that economics should keep to its traditional hedonistic principles, regardless of the results of the new psychology. Nevertheless, public opinion in America seems to be more and more sympathetic to the arguments of the new tendency.

We may conclude, from this general survey, in which we have touched lightly upon the philosophical origins of the chief economic tendencies in the first quarter of the twentieth century, that the development of our science, now as much as formerly, has been more influenced by various philosophical movements than is generally believed. This influence becomes all the clearer when we advance from a consideration of pure theory to that of socio-economic policy. For it is in the nature of the case that the important differences and contradictions between the various philosophical convictions are more clearly discernible here than in the formulation of economic theories from which they are generally extricated only with difficulty. Consider, however, what closely defined relations exist between the cultural ideas of Nietzsche or Oswald Spengler, the ethico-social thoughts of Tolstoi or Dostoevski, and some of the most recent systems of economic policy. Consider, in the Romance countries, what an overwhelming influence Henri Bergson exerts on the prevailing tendencies in social and economic policy; an influence from which few French theorists escape. Thus Charles Rist, whom one certainly cannot accuse of a co-operative or syndicalistic attitude, quotes the authority of Bergson, as his champion, in purely methodological questions.[1] However important the various relations may be between philosophy and practical economic and social tendencies, we cannot deal with them in a book which is devoted only to the latest theoretical developments.

We have referred to various international points of contact in the philosophical origins of the most recent theories. Cultural differences do not make themselves felt so much in the higher regions of thought as in the development and very structure of economics itself. National and political distinctions do not play a very important part in pure philosophy; consequently the influence of literature is all the more active. While we have been able, therefore, to present a coherent sketch of the philosophical origins, it seems better for us, in dealing with the most recent economic theories themselves, to portray their development according to the three chief linguistic groups.

PART TWO

THE DEVELOPMENT IN THE GERMAN-SPEAKING COUNTRIES

CHAPTER I

METHODS AND SYSTEMS

1. The Abatement of the Quarrel over Method

THE GREAT quarrel over method between the adherents of the historical and the supporters of the abstract-theoretical doctrines of political economy had been subsiding for more than a generation. The new theorists were gaining more and more recognition until they were able toward the end of the nineteenth century to devote the energy which had been previously consumed in a methodological demonstration of their own right to live and work toward some constructive ends. The historical school was at first jealous of their success; soon they too began to make concessions and were the first to attempt a rapprochement. It was gradually perceived that one could deal adequately with the complexity of economic problems only by a "distribution" of the scientific research involved, so that even the deductive method should have an important role to play. In the present century only a few individual attempts have been made to revive the historical attitude in its old rigidity.

Among them is the work of Stanislaus Grabski,[1] which is distinguished by its logical foundation; also the rectoral address of Rudolf Eberstadt,[2] which has a similar content, and in which he tries to preserve in general the historical attitude toward the political sciences. Ludwig Stephinger [3] defends the historical school by cleverly drawing on Rickert's logical theory of perception, and even in his most recent works exhibits his preference for the historico-organic attitude.[4] Notwithstanding his recognition of theoretical investigation Waldemar Mitscherlich favors the realistic attitude; [5] and amongst the latest experimenters of this kind, we may also mention Louise Sommer.[6]

Wilhelm Hasbach, a strong supporter of Schmoller's views, tried to bring about a mediation in the methodological dispute by opposing to the method of inductive research an equally justifiable method of abstract-deductive presentation and by himself admitting the claims of deduction in the research field.[7]

The treatises of Gustav Bunzel,[8] and W. Ed. Biermann,[9] which appeared about the same time, are written in similar vein. Two years later,[10] Hasbach approached the Austrian school even in material questions of economic theory and endeavored to prove that it would be wiser and more practical to put the theory of demand and consumption before that of production: a clear concession to the idea of starting out from the theory of wants in the pure theory of modern abstract tendency.

In the meantime, the leader of the historical school, Gustav Schmoller, wrote more and more conciliatory articles on the work of the opposite side and in his famous contribution called "Volkswirtschaft, Volkswirtschaftslehre und Methode," in the third edition of the *Handwörterbuch für Staatswissenschaften* (1911), the old differences seem to have been completely wiped out. Whereas Schmoller emphasizes only the general claims of deduction as well as of induction in economic research, Andreas Voigt endeavors, in the corresponding essay in the fourth edition of the *Handwörterbuch* (1928) to point out the special problems in the attempted solutions of which either of these methods should be preferred.

This conciliation, however, was most practically effected by Werner Sombart in his monumental *Modern Capitalism.* The third volume (1927) especially shows a successful union of static historical investigation with the theoretical attitude. The present writer has elsewhere tried to show this in detail.[11]

From the very beginning of the quarrel, the representatives of the abstract-deductive tendency have fallen more and more upon the defensive, so that even in the present century their attacks have become less and less important. Among these are the writings of F. Lifschitz.[12] The leaders of the school, however, try to conciliate the enemy in every way and maintain that they posited the abstract economic man in the last decades merely in order to bring economics back to the right track. But they recognize more and more the importance of social factors that are abstractly unaccountable in the real formation of economic life.

Thus Friedrich Wieser,[13] and a few years later Böhm-Bawerk,[14] emphasize the important social factor of "Power," and oppose it to the economic laws which are so rarely valid in practical life. In his last work,[15] Wieser applied the same thought to sociology. The younger generation which grew up in the spirit of the modern doctrine follow their masters in this path. The most important among them is Alfred Amonn, who works out the necessary conditions of the social and legal order as the indispensable foundation of economic theory.[16] Joseph Schumpeter is also able to appreciate the great services which the historical school has rendered to economics.[17]

A few years before Amonn, the Hungarian Akusius Navratil made a sharp distinction between "elementary" and "secondary" economic phenomena, according as they were independent of the legal order or originated from it.[18] More recently some German writers, who do not belong to the Austrian school, have written some distinguished works which exhibit similar tendencies. Karl Wasserab [19] and Rudolf Kaulla [20] especially have done fine work in their investigation of the social and legal limitation of all economic phenomena, while Otto V. Zwiedineck-Südenhorst [21] and Hans Honegger [22] continue the researches of Böhm and Wieser on the relations between the idea of power and economic laws. While this relation is loose with Zwiedineck, Honegger deals with it all the more fully and vividly. Karl Landauer finally explains the essence and the behavior of economic power.[23]

It is well known that one of the essential points of the historical school was to emphasize the importance of social factors in economics. As soon as some of the adherents of the theoretical tendency began to devote their attention to this aspect of the subject, the old enemies were bound to meet in the same endeavors.

2. *Logical Currents*

Hand in hand with this reconciliation, the chief interest in the dispute over method was gradually transferred to its purely logical aspect. Here the effort was not so much to lay one's opponent low as to give a clear and complete account of one's own attitude. The leading aspects of the respective investigations are so varied as to defy all systematization.

At the very beginning of the twentieth century the chief representatives of the logical attitude were Friedrich Gottl and Othmar Spann. The former visualizes an inclusive system of economics which is independent of concrete forms of organization and at the same time inveighs against the "verbal slavery" of economic theory: the temptation to rely upon definitions instead of penetrating into the very essence of the problem under consideration.[24] Spann approaches the methodological questions of political economy from the sociological point of view and even in his earliest works inquires into the mutual relations of the whole and its parts in economic theory. He analyses finally the "idea of function," and investigates the relations or the achievements of the part as related to the whole.[25] The idea of function was adopted by the representatives of other economic tendencies, such as Schumpeter and Cassel and the tendency to substitute it for the somewhat rigid idea of causality is growing today.

Karl Muhs has had success in this direction. He discloses with much penetration the difficulties in the way of basing economic theory upon a purely subjective and psychic, or a purely objective and materialistic attitude. Such attempts can only lead to one-sidedness and to irreconcilable differences such as we have seen between the general conceptions of Schumpeter and Liefmann or between the value theories of Marx and Böhm-Bawerk. Nevertheless, Muhs hopes to have discovered an adjustment of these differences by means of his "principle of identity." In place of the factual attitude in economics, one should substitute a functional concept, by which socio-economic viewpoints are seen in their true essence, as relations between subject and object.[26] J. Marschak also makes a contribution to the functional theory of economics,[27] but takes a more objective and mathematical position. Arno Lamprecht tries to replace the idealistic attitude of present-day pure theory by a geneticological attitude, of functional tendency.[28]

Richard Strigl [29] attempts to develop the formal elements of economics as its first premises, and distinguishes thereby "meta-economic" elements, which are shown only by a special organization of economic life, from "pure economic ones." Herbert Schack endeavors to reconcile the different concepts of the fundamental problems of the economic science by a logical analysis of the concept of the economic man.[30] In this way, somewhat like Strigl,[31] Schack has recently formulated a "theory of data," in which he tries to grasp the various intellectual adjustments that men have made to the means at their disposal—the gifts of nature—and to build up in this way a formal theory of economics, with some of the elements of idealism.[32]

Other writers direct their interest in methodology especially toward mathematical procedure. Joseph Schumpeter,[33] Walter G. Waffenschmidt,[34] Otto Kühne [35] and just before his death, Knut Wicksell,[36] analyse the essence of this method and strive to achieve thereby far-reaching clarity. Kühne goes far beyond these questions in his latest researches,[37] and proposes, on the basis of a discussion with Spann, Driesch, Cassirer and other scholars, to found a phenomenological philosophy of economics. Joseph Black [38] makes a similar attempt, relying strongly on the phenomenological doctrines of Husserl. Rudolf Streller, starting out from the viewpoints of Sigwart, tries to give a methodological solution to the fundamental economic problem of statics and dynamics, by making use of the idea of time, somewhat after the fashion of the Böhm-Bawerk theories.[39] In a critical discussion with Streller, Emmanuel Hugo Vogel emphasizes the fact that an understanding of economic problems can come only from dynamics, as an empirical concept of the imagination.[40]

The old question of the logical status of economic laws remains unchanged in the foreground of methodological research. In the wider realm of general social laws, Franz Eulenburg,[41] Gustav Ratzenhofer [42] and, after a profound study of Hegel, Walter Köhler,[43] have made valuable studies in the questions and have lifted them above the traditional dispute over method; while the Japanese Soda K. Chiro [44] and Albert Haas [45] look upon the problem partially from the sole standpoint of the historical school. This attitude is the contrary of that of the Hungarian Karl Schlesinger, who tries to render the historical method more fruitful by engrafting upon it some of the elements of deductive-mathematical thought.[46] Josef Dorbretsberger [47] has some illuminating remarks on the nature of economic law, due to a normative interpretation derived from the philosophy of law.

3. The Dispute over the Value Judgments

In all these investigations, which are closely connected with the great quarrel over method, we notice some kind of attempt to elucidate more fully and to develop more securely an existing compromise. In this set of problems, as soon as a mutual understanding developed, little more could be done for the real methodological dispute. Consequently, at the beginning of the century, a new matter began to claim the attention of students. After the quarrel over method in theoretical economics had subsided, a new one started on a fundamental scientific question of economic policy. The question was the "possibility of a scientific judgment of value," that is to say, whether the science of economics ought merely to explain the possible means of controlling practical life, to analyze them logically and empirically in their material relationships, and therefore to treat its subject in an explanatory fashion, or whether it is also its duty to proceed in a normative fashion: to determine the ends at which we should aim in directing economic life.

We can distinguish with precision two periods in this dispute. In the first, which lasted until 1904, only scattered and desultory remarks were made on the problem, which did not develop into a genuine discussion. The fundamental dogma of the historical school was the doctrine that validity of social ideals and sociological discoveries was limited by time and place. Armed with this relativistic attitude, they fought the "eternal laws of nature" of classical political economy and, later, the doctrines of the abstract-theoretical tendency. For the same reason, they abandoned, from the very first, the attempt to prescribe general ends as inherent guides to economic procedure within the science and questioned the scientific character of all judgments of value which arose in this way. We find the same ideas in Wilhelm Roscher; and especially clearly in the nineties, in Gustav Schmoller and Lujo Brentano.[48] These attribute the lack of cohesion in our science especially to the fact that we are always too much inclined to say what we "*should* do," instead of contenting ourselves with the discovery of what "really *is*." Werner Sombart, toward the end of the last century, is even more decided and explicit in adopting this attitude. He attacks all the "ethical, religious and political ideals" which have been transferred to the subject of economics. He substitutes for these foreign elements an autonomous ideal, derived from the very nature of economics, that of "the greatest productivity," which he tries to make the fundamental principle of our science.[49] The radical expression of Sombart's attitude aroused at the time strong antagonism, and Gustav Cohn[50] especially admonished him that a complete elimination of ethical postulates in our subject would lead to serious abuses.

But the problem became one of first-rate interest only in the second period of the development, when it came to be conducted upon epistomological lines, and became the object of heated dispute. The signal was given by the appearance of Max Weber's famous treatise (*On the Objectivity of Sociological and Socio-political Knowledge*) in 1904.[51] In this, Weber starts out from general criteriological considerations. His problem is one that goes back to the philosophers of antiquity: the problem of knowledge which science is able to prove on an empirical basis.

Originally, unsophisticated mankind based its judgment of phenomena and events not on the idea of causality but on that of ends. Therefore natural and social facts were appraised only according to the use or effect which they produced: the idea of casuality was only in the background of this inclusive concept of ends. Our whole philosophy is still founded on this, as were the leading philosophical systems of antiquity and of the Middle Ages, and it was only the appearance of the law of causality during the period of enlightenment which revolutionized our attitude, so that we viewed the phenomena and nature of the soul in their connections of cause and effect instead of from a teleological point of view. Kant stands about in the middle of these two tendencies since, although he first posited the principle of casuality to explain the phenomena of the outer world, yet because of the limitations of the human capacity for knowledge, he retains the teleological principle to supplement it. In later German philosophy, especially in the works of Windelband, Simmel and Rickert, the division between the subjectivity of teleological assumption and ideals and the objectivity of causal connections becomes more and more apparent until the latter become the only objects capable of scientific demonstration.

Here is the contact with the studies of Max Weber. He teaches that the social sciences, to be real sciences, should deal only with such facts and truths as can be demonstrated by means of an unbroken chain of cause and effect based upon intuition or direct perception or universal axioms. "But ethical and social ideals must be absolutely ignored," since they exist only in the consciousness of particular individuals—however numerous these may be—and therefore exist only subjectively. Or, as the historical school had put it: the social sciences should deal only with what "is," and not with what "should be." Therefore, social postulates as well as economic ideals should be excluded from science, nor should any social value judgment be passed, since their first principles lie beyond the limits of scientific knowledge. Weber does not regard empirical phenomena as existing in the form in which we directly perceive them; he invents, rather, after the pattern of the "real types" of Karl Menger and Oskar Jäger, "ideal types," which have arisen, in the course of the historical development of our concepts, through synthesis out of the individual traits of our practical observation. According to Weber, only these should form the contents of our objective knowledge. True, we have no assurance that these ideal types do actually cover reality; they are, however, the ripest fruits of objective knowledge and at least come nearest to absolute reality.[52]

It should be especially emphasized that it was far from Weber's thoughts to exclude value judgments from every aspect of social science, in the application of epistemological conclusions. In fact, he appropriates from the idealism of Simmel the concept of "super-individual ends" which in strict logic have no objective validity but are so widespread and obvious that they can be considered as objects of science. He counts among these in social politics, for example, the concrete objects of social hygiene and care of the poor, the individual postulates of factory supervision, industrial legislation, labor arbitration or labor protection. This judicious tolerance of Weber's should be all the more noted, since the violence of the quarrel which later broke out over value judgments was due chiefly to the fact that most of Weber's followers exaggerated his doctrine and angrily rejected all ethical postulates. This generally goes with a misconception of the profound epistemological basis of Weber's doctrine which produces, instead of Weber's "critical objectivity," a "naïve" objectivity, that has brought more harm than good to the new tendency.

In 1908, Sombart rejected his principle of productivity, which he had so long defended,[53] and became converted to Weber's standpoint,[54] which he developed as radically as possible at the famous meeting in Vienna of the Union for Social Politics in the autumn of 1909. He said that it is as impossible to discuss value judgments in economics as it is impossible for science to decide which are the prettier—blondes or brunettes.[55] In general, Weber's followers have made relatively few fruitful suggestions, whether in the two Vienna discussions (1909 and 1913) or in their own polemical treatise.

Pohle [56] tries to bring his attack on value judgments, together with a violent broadside against professorial socialism, to the notice of the general public. Julius Wolf [57] is another who has very little new to say. Andreas Voigt, who had formerly taken an active part in this dispute in defense of Weber's position,[58] has recently made a sharp distinction between technical and pragmatic value judgments according to which he conceded universal validity to the former but, like M. Weber, considers the latter subjective and therefore unscientific.[59] Hasbach is more concerned with the historical and practical aspects of the problem.[60] The researches of Adolf Weber [61] and Richard Ehrenberg [62] on this point are epistemological in character. While we are disconcerted to find the former putting his methodological inquiries at the service of his proposed solution of the problem of property in land and houses, we are somewhat mystified at finding the latter, even in his attitude towards value judgments, occupied only in making propaganda for his idea of so-called exact-comparative economic theory, which later will be developed more thoroughly.

The attacks of Max Weber and his followers on value judgments were bound to produce a reaction. Weber's own profound epistemological ideas were at first considered rather startling and were opposed only with timidity. Gustav Cohn was the first to do so. Although he stresses the fact that Weber's teachings are the product of entirely new talents in a powerful personality, he takes the position that there are in our science discipline certain value judgments which, in spite of their subjective origins, may be considered "scientific" and objective; for they have their roots in the general culture of the age and correspond to certain ethical views which are held by all educated people and are generally recognized as authoritative.[63] This attitude is similar to that of Gustav Schmoller, who abandoned his former dislike of value judgments and tried to meet Weber's school with philosophical arguments, drawn especially from Wundt. Schmoller considers that every act which is useful not only to society but also, as far as possible, to the agent himself, is the absolute socio-ethical ideal, which has always to some degree predominated in the course of civilization.[64] He therefore considers all value judgments which are made in accordance with this ideal objective and thus admissible in economic science. Schmoller does not tell us in what departments of economics such value judgments may come into consideration; and his attitude to the whole problem remained somewhat vague and vacillating.

Similar in content, but more decided in expression, are the views of Eugen v. Philippovich, published after the Vienna discussions. He entrusts to political economy, as a science, the duty of adopting "an attitude, in the quarrel between the different economic factions," and to bring the direction of economic development into harmony with the ends of general cultural progress.[65] Heinrich Herkner, who occupies a similar position, sees the economic ideal which is to be realized in the general "welfare of the people." [66] As a matter of fact, it is the difference of opinion concerning the "welfare of the people" which is at the bottom of the difference in value judgments.

Another group of Weber's antagonists devote their attention chiefly to the broader, more "philosophical" problem, as to whether scientific value judgments are even possible and treat economic value judgments as a side issue.

Eduard Spranger starts with a general systematization of the sciences and with the necessary and constant prevalence of value judgments in human consciousness; [67] Walther Köhler attacks the problems of normative science from a metaphysical and logical point of view; [68] while Oskar Englander attempts a systematic development of the ethical ideal of economics.[69] Albert Hesse arrives at a certain systematization of scientific economic value judgments by relying on Kantian criticism, and the teleological opinion of Rudolf Stammler's sociology.[70] He kept this position for more than a decade [71] and has only recently returned to a more relativistic attitude, like that of Max Weber.[72] There is a treatise of Herbert Schack,[73] which is somewhat similar to the earlier treatment by Hesse, which returns to a consideration of the more general problem of social judgments of value but shows no advance over the investigation of Hesse. Notable studies have been made by Karl Eugen Nickel, who, on a psycho-physiological basis, attacks with much erudition the doctrines of Weber with the help of the theories of the well-known Danish psychologist Lehmann.[74] Nickel gives, among other things, a good historical survey of the quarrel over value judgments. Walter Weddigen has recently disclosed teleological and normative tendencies.[75] The present writer sees a solution in a sharp differentiation between what he calls heteronomic and autonomic economic ends.[76]

Robert Wilbrandt has made valuable contributions toward a solution of the whole dispute on value judgments since the war. He was at first a follower of Max Weber, from whose influence he has never quite freed himself. He believes, however—as we shall see later—that he has found a comprehensive and inherent purpose for economics in the concept of industry as an activity to avert distress. On this basis he desires to review the connection between economic theory and economic policy. As a consequence, disregarding all political and cultural considerations, as well as all norms and dictates relating to natural law, the economist should be able to frame the rules suitable to each particular case.[77]

4. *The Method of Exact Comparison*

In the first two decades of the present century another dispute arose over method, which was of considerably less importance. It hinged on the doctrine of Richard Ehrenberg, professor at Rostock. Starting with a criticism of the two dominant methods of economic research, Ehrenberg tried by uniting their best traits to make propaganda for a new method, that of "exact comparison." This consisted in offering certain fixed points of departure for economic investigation, which according to Ehrenberg could be attained only through exact observation. There is no difficulty in the natural sciences, since their objects are measurable and amenable to the experimental method. Although the social sciences do not as a rule possess these two advantages, we should do our best to attain them, even in a round about way. As regards the measurableness of its objects, economics is favorably placed since it can refer all that relates to its field of research, through the cardinal idea of value, to money prices. The valuation, however, of economic factors, by which they can alone be measured, can be attained not by the historical method nor by statistical collections of data, but only by exact calculation. But since every social economy is in the last analysis composed of individual economies,

Ehrenberg turns his attention to these and makes a thorough study of their accounting methods in the hope of attaining measurable units of comparison. Through the arbitrary grouping of these, the necessary conditions of our observations may be changed according to the ultimate purpose of economic investigations, so that finally certain typical causal connections may be perceived. In this way economic students can secure for themselves the advantage of the experimental method which had formerly been inaccessible.

Ehrenberg turns next to more particular studies and makes a thorough and comparative study of the accounting needed for the understanding of the wider relations and rules of economic life. This part of his program was destined, unfortunately, to be the decisive factor in the debate which arose over his method. His enemies did not direct their attention primarily to the methodological content of his doctrine but accused him of "partiality toward the interests of the entrepreneur." [78]

It was Ehrenberg's fate to bear the cross of the misunderstood champion of scientific ideals. The embitterment with which he was compelled to defend himself against attacks until the hour of his death [79] is perhaps the reason why no school worthy of mention grew up around his methodological ideas—with the possible exception of Harms' group, with which we shall deal later.

5. *Economic Philosophy*

The problem of method (in the wider sense of the term) touches upon a question which has been much discussed in German literature both past and present: the question whether an independent philosophy of economics is possible and what its nature may be. Few problems of our science have remained so obscure, notwithstanding the relatively active interest which it has aroused. The term (*Wirtschaftsphilosophie*) had often been used by the Physiocrats, and since then by all manner of writers in the most varied connections, so that no one has been able to form even an approximately coherent idea of what the concept means.

At first the phrase seemed to mean economics in its more profound theoretical connection. This was a legacy from the time when people dealt with economic problems as a part of social philosophy. Scarcely had economics become emancipated from philosophy, scarcely had some sort of boundary been drawn than a reaction set in: no sooner does the independence of economics seem assured than a longing is felt to reunite it with the science of sciences—philosophy. In its new meaning, the phrase *Wirtschaftsphilosophie* refers to the realm of knowledge which lies between economics and philosophy. Its purpose, therefore, is essentially to connect and to relate. This connection can take place in two fundamental ways. If we keep in mind the purpose of philosophy, which is to place at the disposal of all sciences the implements of thought, the most important contrivances for building a foundation, we find that the philosophy of economics too is meant to discover the first formal points of departure, the logical, epistemological and conceptual content of economics. But philosophy has also the task of uniting the conclusions of the various sciences: in this way *Wirtschaftsphilosophie* would mean the study of economic theories from the general standpoint of the various philosophies.

Many attempts were made in both directions in the nineteenth century. They have been continued in the last twenty-five years, without, however, reaching even a fairly coherent attitude toward the main question of a system of economic philosophy. Fritz Berolzheimer, in his monumental work in five volumes [80] considers economic philosophy from the standpoint of a "juristic-economic monism," relating economic life closely to law and the state (Stammler!), and treating it together with ethics and social organization as one of the constituent forces of general cultural development. In the second volume of his work he tries to consolidate his doctrines from the point of view of the history of literature by means of a historico-cultural and socio-psychological method; and in the fourth, a positive philosophy of economics is explained as a philosophy of wealth and business. Berolzheimer rejects contemporary theories, and builds his own upon the concept of wealth, which leads him to deal with questions that could be answered very much better by theoretical economics or even jurisprudence than by an independent philosophy of economics. In 1907 the *Archiv für Rechts-und Wirtschaftsphilosophie* was founded, for a similar purpose and in its introductory article,[81] Ferdinand Tönnies expressly stated that the purpose of economic philosophy was to deal with the fundamental relationships of economic life and law, economic life and politics, and to check up on the universally accepted truths and doctrines of economics from the point of view of general philosophy.

Rudolf Stolzmann adopts in his latest writings a somewhat similar attitude toward economics.[82] He too examines economic theories and endeavors to unite the fundamental differences of opinion in economics by means of philosophy. This attitude is really that of social unity which averts all contradiction between individualism and socialism or between subjectivism and objectivism. This tendency leads in final analysis to a program of practical social politics. Nevertheless, Stolzmann, relying upon Stammler's theories, has valuable suggestions to make through his teleological theory of knowledge.

We find the two possible attitudes toward a philosophy of economics in the works of Robert Wilbrandt.[83] In his philosophical investigation of economic problems he too gives expression only to his own social views. These are considerably more radical than those of Stolzmann: his social ideal being a socialistic and communistic commonwealth (a kind of communistic socialism) developing finally into a sacrifice economy on altruistic lines, strongly anarchistic in tone. Wilbrandt, however, starts from a thorough epistemological analysis of the fundamentals of economics and sees in the Ideal of *Wirtschaftlichkeit* (economy) a norm which is derived from the very nature of the subject and which helps to build our whole conception of the science.

Nickel, too, in his methodological work, which has already been mentioned, tries to compose a scientific philosophy of economics out of the norms dealing with the natural necessity of economic behavior. Sergei Bulgakoff, adopting an entirely different attitude, understands by economic philosophy "a natural philosophical analysis of economic phenomena." [84] According to him, it is a philosophy of objective behavior which, beginning with labor, also includes the exchange of the products of labor.

Besides these systematic attempts to lay the foundations of a philosophy of economics, we may mention the works of Georg Simmel,[85] Richard Krzymorski,[86] Eleutheoropulos,[87] Hans Freyer,[88] Wladislaw Zalesky,[89] and the present writer.[90] These have made contributions to the new branch of learning, either by their philosophical treatment of certain details of economics or through a theoretical investigation into the history of the problems of economic philosophy.

6. Private Economics, Business Economics and World Economics

Questions of economic philosophy used to be, and still are to a certain extent, discussed as a branch of general economics. In the course of development, however, these questions have been grouped under one heading and have formed a more or less separate branch of learning, somewhere between philosophy and economics. This general tendency to differentiate within a science has recently been especially noticeable in Germany. Violent discussions have arisen over the systematization of the economic sciences which, like the great methodological dispute, have at times attracted the attention of wide circles.

Ehrenberg starts with a comprehensive investigation of individual enterprises and their relations to economics. He demands, at the turn of the century, a theory of business economics, which should be a systematic study of the life of private industry, an independent branch to be sharply distinguished from political economy of which it is to serve as the foundation.[91] He soon abandoned this attitude, however and expressly stated later that he desired through the observation of private industry to find a correspondingly exact foundation for political economy.[92] As a matter of fact, Ehrenberg's earlier demand for a special theory of business economics was nothing new in German science. It was at the bottom of the whole Cameralistic movement of the eighteenth century and, since then, some of the leaders of the German

Classical school, especially Rau, have demanded the retention of private economic researches as a special branch of economic science. In our day Georg V. Mayr has adopted a similar attitude. He attempts to introduce a special economics of enterprise (*Haushaltslehre*), which is to study individual industries as the active constituents of economic society.[93]

Two younger authors, Moritz-Weyermann and Hans Schönitz, proceed from a different angle. They too wish to found a theory of business economics,[94] but endeavor to remain within the boundaries of political economy and to develop the new science as one of its fields. In this sense they understand by business economics that department of economics which deals with the activities of private industries considered by themselves as enterprises for profit and which in opposition to social economics in the narrower sense approaches these activities from the point of view of private interests and deals with them separately according to their individual types.

In contrast to these attempts, we have the insistence of some authors on industrial technique and their efforts to build through its systematic development a theory of private economics. Thus Eugen Schmalenbach and Heinrich Nicklisch,[95] each of whom achieved a considerable reputation, are only two of those who attempted to develop a theory of business, closely related to economics. J. F. Schär, on the contrary, deals with business problems only within the bounds of general economics.[96] Rudolph Dietrich takes a much broader view of the subject. He criticizes all systems of private or business economics for remaining apart from the main structure of economic science and endeavors to found an industrial science, independent of economics, which should devote itself to a study of the structure and inner workings of the various industries.[97]

Bernhard Harms, a pupil of Ehrenberg, is also of the opinion that there should be a theory of private or business economics in between political economy and social economics. His system, however, is especially remarkable because, on the top of political economy, he erects a fourth division—that of world economics.[98]

The idea is old. Fulda had spoken of international economics; Rau had stressed the importance of world wide economic relations, and Heinrich Dietzel [99] had called attention to this problem at the end of the century. Harms draws a sharp distinction between political economy and world economics. By the term political economy he understands the conditions and interrelations of the economic life of a state, made possible through freedom and technical perfection of transportation, regulated by law and encouraged by political measures. By world economics he understands "the conditions and interrelations of the economic life of the world regulated and encouraged by perfected transportation and by national and international agreements." Since economists are becoming more and more interested in the affairs of a particular state, world economics should become a correspondingly more important branch of the science. Its first part is "general," and deals geographically with the problems of the international division of labor and exchange of goods, other international relationships, balance of trade, and finally with the economic status of colonies. Next come the legal and political regulation and encouragement of world trade. The special part deals with the details of business and world trade, as well as with world production, circulation and consumption. At the end comes a study of world-wide economic expansion. All through the system we notice the idea of comparative economics which Harms took from Ehrenberg.

Herman Levy's attempt to give a short systematic review of world economics is not very successful.[100] After a modest preliminary study,[101] Sartorius von Waltershausen has succeeded in his recent works [102] in giving a good account of the moral and material foundations of world economics, as well as in sharply distinguishing its problems from those of political economy.

There has been much discussion on the status of business economics and of world economics in scientific systems. Some were for making each of the special disciplines an independent science, whereas others thought that they could find a place in the traditional structure. In the former group were W. Prion,[103] Rudolph Kobatsch,[104] Kurt Albert Gerlach,[105] while their opponents numbered such men as Karl Diehl,[106] Karl Bücher,[107] Götz Briefs, [108] Moritz Julius Bonn,[109] Herbert v. Beckerath, [110] Louis Kraft,[111] etc. Their attacks, however, were unable to stem the tide of the new science, which continues to develop today.

7. *Economics of War*

Although business economics and apparently world economics have triumphed over their opponents and are becoming independent sciences, a third movement, that of war economics, has been less successful. A few years before the war, when the political atmosphere of Europe was already charged with electricity, problems of war began to engross the attention of economists, and led to many stimulating theories.

We may mention here the prophetic book of H. Völcker,[112] and the comprehensive war theory of Reinhold Wagner.[113] Arthur Blaustein has written a detailed bibliography of the subject, arranged according to the economic problems involved.[114] Naturally enough, the literature on the subject increased a hundredfold during and after the war. Johann Plenge,[115] Emil Lederer,[116] Bernhard Harms,[117] Sartorius v. Waltershausen [118] and W. Ed. Biermann,[119] are the authors who have dealt most searchingly and scientifically with the relations between war and economic life. We draw especial attention to the volumes of the *Archiv für Sozialwissenschaft und Sozialpolitik* [120] which are entirely devoted to the problems of war economics.

While these investigations were going on, a demand in methodology was voiced to build a separate economics of war. Otto Neurath proposed this even before the war and demanded an independent science which should systematically discuss the economic advantages and disadvantages of war.[121] In the final year of the war he became more concise and demanded that the new science should make a comparative study of the influence of wartime economics on wealth—that is to say, on real income, wages of labor, etc., in the widest sense, and their assurance through war expenditures. Nevertheless, he always insists that the economics of war be treated as an independent science, so long as the present systems of economics remain as they are.[122] In the second year of the war, Ferdinand Schmid undertook to publish a systematic survey of the economics of war.[123] He agrees with the proposals of Neurath but believes that the new science should try to explain the economic causes of war as well as study its consequences. On the whole, however, he too fails to give a comprehensive system of war economics and, like Neurath, has thought out only a few of its aspects coherently. Georg v. Mayr, on the other hand, tries to give a thoroughly systematic outline of the new science.[124] According to him the economics of war should form the third independent part of the general science of economics, while war finance, assigned by Schmid to the new science, should be an entirely separate discipline. Mayr assigns to war economics the study of the changes undergone by the principal phenomena of economics (wants, production, transportation, consumption, etc.) as a consequence of war.

Franz Eulenberg was the first to oppose these attempts to found an independent science. He tries to prove, in a thorough study,[125] that war economics is but a modification of the general science of economics, which suffers some changes during wartime but remains fundamentally unaffected. Therefore, we should view its phenomena as mere deviations from the normal trend of economic life, whose laws alone should guide us. Wolfgang Heller too rejects the idea of an economics of war, and tries to show that traditional political economy is able to cover the field.[126] According to him, the specific phenomena of war economics occur especially in commercial life and could be adequately dealt with, if one got rid of the money illusion and made better use of national economics and of the dynamic development of business. Recently, Adolf Weber has identified himself with the position of Heller, and uses the argument that the phenomena of war economics belong especially to economic policy, and not to theory, as even Georg v. Mayr had to admit. This means that there is no real theoretical foundation for an independent economics of war.[127] The same opinion is voiced by Götz Briefs who considers the phenomena of war economics as pathological modifications of normal economic phenomena and therefore thinks it as absurd to found a special economics of war as to make a special science out of business crises.[128] The result of this controversy seems to be that the idea of an independent science of the economics of war has been finally stifled.

CHAPTER II

ATTEMPTS TO CREATE SYSTEMS

1. *The Historical School*

WHEN we devote our attention to the development of economic theory in the German-speaking countries in the first quarter of the twentieth century and especially to the comprehensive systems which were then produced, we are at once struck by the treatise of Gustav Schmoller which stands as a symbol of the new age. The publication of this work,[1] the fruit of long experience, was epoch-making. Not that it showed the way to anything new; it represented rather the high-water mark which the historical school had reached. When Schmoller started upon his work, the authority of his school was almost unquestioned in Germany, and it still remained strong at the time of its publication. The author's fame and the inadequacy of previous works on the same subject were sufficient to arouse the greatest curiosity. The founder of the older historical school, Roscher, could never free himself completely from classicism, whether in his treatise or in his later text books. Neither Hildebrand nor Knies wrote a comprehensive treatise. Kautz and Cohn were more complete; but while the former modestly suppressed his personality and any original contributions the latter allowed his philosophical and ethical ideas to prevail over strictly economic considerations. Thus, when the historical school was in power it possessed no general survey of its doctrines. At last this was accomplished by Schmoller.

It is impossible to describe the contents of this book without reciting all the leading ideas of the younger historical school. It is a rich store house of historical and sociological material in which economics is so often illumined by social viewpoints that one may with justice call it a comprehensive theory of society, looked at from the standpoint of the economist.[2] The province which Schmoller allows for the working of economic law is a very small one, and his treatment of pure economic theory is decidedly meagre. Not even his adherents have followed him all the way in this direction. Inama-Sternegg, for example, reproaches him for not giving a real theory of production.[3]

After the appearance of Schmoller's treatise, the historical school produced no new systematization of its doctrines. Friedrich Kleinwachter wrote a carefully prepared text book[4] in which he criticized past and contemporary theories from an historical standpoint, but offered nothing new. Gustav Ruhland[5] gives an account rather of his practical preferences than of economic theories. His views are concerned chiefly with the attainment of a healthy condition of property in land, and a corresponding organization of production. Although the influence of the historical school began to decline at the commencement of the century, the new editions, published even during the war, of the chief works of Roscher[6] and Hildebrand[7] testify to the continued interest in the systems of this school.

Heinrich Sieveking has recently published a system[7a] which he intended to base entirely on the principles of the younger historical school. He accordingly emphasizes the social and historical side of economics and deals with the phenomena of circulation only insofar as they relate directly to the real object of economic theory, that is, to the economic considerations of human beings. Consequently, like Schmoller, he gives too little attention to the important problems of exchange.

2. *The Pure Theory of Marginal Utility*

The opponents of the historical school, the Austrian school, produced in the new century only one comprehensive treatise in which their method and their theory of marginal utility are expounded in their purest form. The work of Friedrich Wieser[8] is as important in its way as the treatise of Schmoller. He too was one of the outstanding leaders of his school, aroused the greatest interest, gave the most complete and valuable account of the whole field of economics and, if indications do not deceive, his book too was destined to mark the highest achievement of his school, after which it disintegrated. It is now possible to say these things in all calm.

The central and creative idea of Wieser's book is the theory of marginal utility, to which he subordinates everything in economics, including the theory of money. He even goes so far as to found a science of economic policy upon this theory. He derives the necessity of private property from the theory of utility [9] and bases his economic idea, which is an harmonious interplay of unrestricted competition and government interference, on the legal institutions of private property. It would appear that we have here the missing link between abstract theory and economic policy. The question is, how strong is this link? Nevertheless, one of the main advantages of Wieser's system is the steady progress it shows from the abstract ideas of economic theory to the more realistic considerations of everyday life. First of all he analyses the phenomena of simple economic life, and formulates its elementary laws; secondly, he studies political economy, in which social power plays an important part; thirdly, he presents his theory of national economics which describes the influence of the State; and lastly comes his theory of world economics. The system is of enduring worth, even though parts of it have become antiquated. Wieser published before his death (1926) the results of his investigations on the law of power, which contain the sociological basis for his doctrine. It was not vouchsafed to him to forge the link between his sociology and his economics.

One of his former pupils, Alfred Amonn, has recently pointed out the logical shortcomings in Wieser's system.[10] He tries especially to show that marginal utility is a phenomenon of individual psychology which explains many phases of individual economics but which cannot be made the basis of a sound system of political economy. Since there are just as many margins of utility as there are individuals, Wieser's doctrine is condemned from the outset as fruitless.

Besides Wieser's, there are in German literature two systems built upon the theory of marginal utility which deserve attention. One is a translation from the Swedish; the other from the Dutch. Knut Wicksell [11] as a matter of fact belongs to the mathematical school, even partially to the Lausanne school. His algebraical deductions, however, are such that their elimination does not hinder a comprehension of his thought. His system is unusual in that he introduces the quantitative aspect of consumption by a theory of population, which is more statistical than theoretical. After this, he presents in order his theories of value and exchange, production and distribution, capital, money and credit. Verrijn Stuart,[12] too, bases his theory upon marginal utility, although he seems to aim at a synthesis of the doctrines of the historical school with the abstract deductive theories. Besides the abstract concept of business, which is at the bottom of his theory, he advanced other first principles, such as nature, mankind, society, etc., which he calls social categories. His scientific ideal is one of causality, devoid of the principle of value and he recognizes only one standard in economics: the general welfare. In sociological matters he is always liberal and individualistic and consequently opposed to all organized force.

It is with some hesitation that we mention here the work of the Hungarian scholar, Wolfgang Heller.[13] Although he resembles Wieser in his insistence on the theory of marginal utility and in the formal structure of his doctrine, he is also anxious to do justice to the tenets of other schools. He resembles Spann in his emphasis on organic thought at the expense of atomism. Like Diehl, Amonn and Oppenheimer, he stresses the social, legal and authoritative elements of economics. Following Cassel, he bases his theory of distribution on his theory of price; and he resembles some of the American writers in his conception of capital. By reconciling such different tendencies and by some of his own researches Heller manages to produce a well-rounded system.

Emil Lederer [14] has written a concise survey of economics. Although the theory of marginal utility predominates, he does justice to the cost of production theory which explains how the exchange of products takes place and how the social dividend is distributed among the different classes of society. Apart from value, the other problems are only sketched by Lederer. His attitude is, on the whole, mathematical and mechanistic as well as functional. Moreover, he seems to come under the influence of Schumpeter when he deals with the dynamic phenomena of economics. Alfred Amonn considers the Austrian interpretation of marginal utility one of the weak points of Lederer's system.[15]

Besides the second edition of Menger's *Grundsätze* (1923) and the new editions of Phillippovich's text book, Schullern zu Schrattenhofen has written a notable survey of economics, viewed from the standpoint of marginal utility.[16] Its purpose is purely didactic, and it does not pretend to offer anything new.

3. *Schumpeter's Static and Dynamic Economics*

The theory of marginal utility is also the foundation of Joseph Schumpeter's system; but he is original enough to go beyond its traditional limits and to create his own mechanistic and mathematical system of economics. His main characteristic is a sharp distinction between static and dynamic economics which produces two entirely different attitudes towards economic phenomena. In his first important work [17] Schumpeter adopts the static point of view. He rejects all political, philosophical and ethical considerations, and adopts as a foundation of his pure economic theory the hypothesis that economics is in a static condition, in which there are no new combinations of production and consumption and no modifications or changes in the whole of its course. Once this is taken for granted, there exists a state of equilibrium between the quantities of goods in the possession of various individuals, and the aim of Schumpeter is to ascertain how the other quantities within a given field of observation will re-act as soon as one of them is affected. The more subtle causes which motivate these changes are not analysed here. He is interested only in their outward, formal relationships which appear to him functional between the movements of individual quantities of goods. According to Schumpeter, the relation in which the functions themselves appear is, for economics, that of exchange, which has its origin in the principle of value as determined by marginal utility. Every movement of these commodities becomes objectified in the making of price in which the laws of the distribution of income hold sway. In static economics there are only three kinds of income, which correspond to the three possible kinds of production goods: labor, land and the results of previous production. Schumpeter explains the laws of these fluctuations in his mathematical variation method, in which he assumes that other elements in the equilibrium of static economics are constantly being modified, and tries to discover what effects these changes exert on the elements which he considers invariable.

Schumpeter realizes perfectly well that these results can be applied to the actual phenomena of economic life only for a certain point in time or at best for a short period of time, and that this is the only way in which the static viewpoint can be applied. For longer periods, and especially for the modern capitalistic organization, only the dynamic attitude comes into consideration. The changing, developing nature of economics is, for Schumpeter, essentially dynamic and at the center of all the new combinations and progress stands the entrepreneur who governs the course of all production. His activity gives rise to capital which creates a demand for credit. The dynamic aspect of economic life is the subject of Schumpeter's second large work [18] in which he especially analyses the categories of income which consist of profits and interest.

We can gauge the sensation which this work caused by the amount of criticism directed against it. Karl Diehl [19] criticizes Schumpeter especially for having built his theory upon so many hypotheses that it is valueless as an explanation of the real phenomena of economics. Othmar Spann [20] directs his criticism against the mathematical method in general. He doubts the existence of direct, purely causal, and mechanistic relationships between commodities, since these become economic phenomena only through the primary phenomenon of the economic activity of the individual. Friedrich Wieser [21] defends the psychological method of the Austrian school against the attacks of Schumpeter, whereas Hans Mayer [22] criticizes him from the point of view of the pure theory of marginal utility itself. He opposes in especial Schumpeter's main thesis that the change in any one given commodity will cause changes in all of the others. He also attacks Schumpeter's concept of value and criticizes the application of differential calculus to economic theory. Ludwig Pohle [23] accuses Schumpeter primarily of being remote from actual life, attacks each separate doctrine, and tries to refute the theory of wages, alleged to be based on a caste-like division of the social groups. Wilhelm Lexis [24] tries to prove that Schumpeter's theory of economic development should not have been made dependent upon the theory of marginal utility and that it often contradicts the facts of actual life. Akusius Navratil [25] sees nothing new in the glorification of the entrepreneur's function. More modern critics are Leo Schönfeld [26] and Otto Conrad.[27] The former, from a rather novel interpretation of the subject with which we shall deal later, points out several alleged errors in Schumpeter's solution of the problem of imputation, whereas the latter bases his attacks on the elements in his work which touch upon marginal utility. Nearly all these critics, however, recognize the highly scientific character of Schumpeter's work. Only Pohle takes an opposite view.

The Hungarian Karl Schlesinger who was deeply influenced by Schumpeter tried to develop on the one hand a theory of price and value, on the other hand a theory of the practical problems of banking, both based on modern monetary theory and with the help of the mathematical method.[28] He too attempts to view prices as functions of quantities and discloses an entirely objective attitude to economic phenomena. Consequently he does not touch upon their psychological background although the concept of marginal utility plays an important part in his work.

4. Cassel and his Adherents

The Swede Gustav Cassel published in Germany a system of economic theory which is as important as that of Schumpeter, with which it has many points of contact. [29] He makes frequent use of the mathematical method and makes the doctrine of price the central part of economic theory. Nevertheless, there are important differences between the two theories: for Cassel completely rejects the theory of marginal utility and, instead of the mechanistic relations of quantities of goods, emphasizes economic activities themselves. The core of his system is a thorough analysis of the concept of economy itself, upon which he builds his theory of scarcity. For economics, as for every activity whose end is the satisfaction of human wants, there come into consideration only those means whose amount is limited in comparison with the wants. Combining this principle with the concept of exchange, Cassel takes it out of the theory of simple economic life into that of political economy and makes of it the foundation of the problem of price. He has thus passed over the whole problem of value which he considers an unnecessary part of our science.

Cassel's system has generally been considered as destitute of the idea of value. This characteristic has been attacked by Franz Euhlenburg,[30] and defended by H. Mannstädt.[31] In a similar way Hans Neisser[32] seeks to explain Cassel's teaching, while Alfred Amonn,[33] Hero Möller,[34] Edgar Salin,[35] Eduard Lukas,[36] in a comparison between Cassel and Ricardo, and finally Karl Diehl[37] have all pointed out that Cassel has rejected only the nomenclature, but not the concept, of value.

The principle of scarcity is already found in Karl Menger at the bottom of the subjective theory of value, in the concept of "economic relations of quantity." Moreover, Cassel's concept of valuation is fundamentally a representative of economic value. Cassel tries, however, to be independent of the formal theory of value and endeavors to replace it by a broad price theory. From this he derives his doctrines of distribution and money as well as a notable theory of crises. These always maintain the closest connection with his theory of price.

Cassel was not spared the reproach of having composed a "monograph on prices," rather than an entire system of economics with all its organic functions (Eulenburg).

Diehl's principal objection to Cassel is that his neglect of social and authoritative factors leads to absolutism in his solution of economic problems. Schumpeter[38] and Wilhelm Kromphardt[39] try to show how Cassel contradicts some of his own main theories by retaining some of the elements of the imputation theory in his doctrine of distribution. Otto Conrad[40] attacks him on the same score, as well as for his conception of cost. Ewald Schams[41] claims to notice an important mistake in Cassel's theory of price, in an insufficient distinction between positive judgments of necessity and general judgments of choice. A very severe foreign critic of Cassel is the American Fabian Franklin, who finds Cassel not only deficient in originality but also guilty of a complete misapprehension of Ricardo, as a result of which he seeks to explain Cassel's utter lack of influence on American economic thought.

Cassel's influence is also seen in the survey of Hans Oswalt,[42] especially in his theory of price and in his effort to ascertain the natural categories of economics: those which are independent of fortuitous conditions. He differs from Cassel in his attempt to retain the theory of value which he supports by means of the theory of marginal utility. He has some notable introductory remarks on the concept of economics and on the satisfaction of wants. The distinguishing feature of his system is the clarity which comes from the pen of an excellent technician. Siegfried Budge[43] builds his system on the theory of scarcity but has a more static attitude towards economic phenomena than Cassel. Like Oswalt, he retains the theory of value which he also supports by means of the theory of marginal utility. The central part of his theory, however, is not price, but production. Some of his ideas are borrowed from the socialists; e. g., he explains profits on the surplus value theory. Nevertheless, Budge is no social reformer. Like Cassel, his attitude is liberalistic. The short introduction of Hans Gestrich [44] is the last we shall mention as coming under the influence of Cassel. He combines in an original way the most important attitudes on the great economic problems of the day with the corresponding theories of other authors, and his own opinion. But his system is neither clear nor unified.

5. *The Realistic Theories of Lexis and Adolf Weber on The Economics of Exchange*

If historical perspective allows us to divide the economic systems of the first quarter of our century into distinctly separate schools, the theories of Wilhelm Lexis [45] should come somewhere between the systems of Schumpeter and Cassel, although he also has much in common with the historical school. Like Schumpeter, he restricts his investigations to a relatively small and definite field and many of the material solutions which he offers remind us of Cassel, while his general attitude recalls to us rather more of the historical school. Above all, he distinguishes between "abstract" and "realistic" theories, rejects the former, is sceptical of all economic laws based on natural science, considers the result of the historical school the most valuable thus far and concedes that his realistic theory holds good only for a definite stage in the development of economics. The object of his inquiry is the question how the production of goods takes place as a social activity in a given social system and how the various persons engaged in their divers activities obtain their share of the goods out of this social process. Consequently, production, consumption and the distribution of income comprise the entire field of Lexis's study. He is as impatient as Cassel of the theory of marginal utility and shows a certain Marxist trait when he explains profits as a deduction from wages. As a rule, Lexis is no slave to the traditional classification of the various elements in the theory of economic circulation, but arranges them in an entirely free sequence as they occur to him. This has a refreshing effect. The value of his contribution is enhanced by the truly realistic way in which he maintains close contact with actuality and tries to do adequate justice to the most complicated phenomena of practical economic life.

Adolf Weber too, is above all a realist in economics. Nevertheless, he shows some striking analogies to Cassel in his recently published system.[46] He too starts with the idea of scarcity, makes the theory of price the center of his system and derives from it his doctrine of distribution. He retains, however, the theory of value and, unlike Lexis, explains it by means of the theory of marginal utility, although in another connection he considers this vastly overrated. The formal arrangement of his system is entirely his own. His book is illustrated with a wealth of historical data and social background; and he surpasses Cassel in questions of social power and in the general methodological foundation of his system.

6. *Liefmann's Purely Psychological System*

In striking contrast to the above systems, Robert Liefmann [47] tries to build a whole system of economics on a purely psychological basis. The Austrian school had already made much of the psychological element. Liefmann goes far beyond them and rejects all materialism and quantitative aspects in order to interpret economics in the light of psychological phenomena. For him the end of economic theory is to refer everything to subjective judgments of value, the desires of the consumers. Like the adherents of marginal utility he quotes Gossen in order to find a basis for his theory. But the former's subjective theory of value consisted only of the varying utilities of the goods themselves. Liefmann is struck by the fact that Gossen opposed the idea of cost to that of pleasure, which he did not value for its own sake. Therefore Liefmann works out a concept of psychological returns which consists of the difference between utility and cost, and recognizes economic activity only where returns can be ascertained: that is to say, where utility and cost (not quantities of things or value, but psychological units of pleasure and pain) may be compared.

The idea is not entirely new; but Liefmann deserves praise for his clear and logical development of the subject and for the absence of technical jargon.

Another discovery of Liefmann's is the fact that the smallest returns, which occur in the satisfaction of our various wants, tend to balance each other at a certain minimum height. A man will always take care to arrange the costs for the satisfaction of his wants in such an order that the smallest item of cost will bring in a return which, according to his own sense of value, could not be surpassed by another expenditure. The necessity that all the final returns obtained in the satisfaction of various wants will be of approximately equal height, Liefmann calls the law of the equalization of marginal returns. Upon this he builds his theory of price, which is followed by a theory of distribution and money erected along similar lines.

Liefmann's haughty attitude toward other economists, and the arrogant way in which he extols his own theories led to many disagreeable debates, often of a personal nature. Both Amonn [48] and Joseph Bergfried Esslen [49] tried to prove that he was not original. Amonn endeavored to show, point by point, that the essence of Liefmann's law of the equalization of marginal returns is contained in the theory of marginal utility, which Liefmann did not adequately grasp. Esslen stated that Liefmann's idea of utility is only another name for value, and that his idea of cost should be taken in the sense of loss of utility. Therefore, there is nothing new in the foundation of Liefmann's system, and whatever original contribution he makes is in contradiction with it. Similar criticisms are made by Franz Oppenheimer.[50] Liefmann answered these attacks with accusations of falsehood and dishonesty. Milder, but no less decisive, were the criticisms of J. Steinberg,[51] Zwiedineck-Südenhorst,[52] and Rudolf Stolzmann.[53] Steinberg goes to the heart of the matter when he says that political economy cannot be isolated and treated from a purely psychological point of view, and that the law of the equalization of marginal returns means nothing. Zwiedineck criticizes the unhistorical and unsocial attitude of Liefmann and calls his psychological foundation of economics a purely individualistic one. He bases his scepticism on the fact that there must be a certain materialistic and quantitative aspect to the concept of returns. Stolzmann accuses Liefmann of wasting time in describing the causal and individualistic side of his theory of returns since in reality it is merely teleological and social.

Diehl [54] and Lederer [55] reject Liefmann's law of the equalization of marginal returns. Karl Engliš severely criticizes the theory of marginal returns in consumption and reaches the conclusion that a law of the equalization of the relatively smallest utilities of the price unit should take the place of the law of the equalization of marginal returns.[56] Eduard Kellenberger recognizes this law for consumers, but not for producers.[57]

Weyermann [58] draws attention to the sharp separation of economic problems from technical, social, ethical and political problems, and the building of an economic system on nothing but a psychological foundation in Liefmann's work. Jaffe [59] considers it an improvement on Sombart's *Modern Capitalism*. Otto Mayer's [60] praise of Liefmann has a hollow sound. Arnold Kupper's [61] attempt to push Liefmann's pure subjectivism to its logical conclusion and to build thereby a new theory of value has not been attended with much success.

7. *Organic and Teleological Thought*

The three chief economic systems published in Germany in the first quarter of the century and mentioned hitherto, those of Schumpeter, Cassel and Liefmann, are built upon a purely individualistic social philosophy, a characteristic of which is most noticeable in Liefmann. In their conceptions of the essence and the functions of society they first study the individual and derive the whole from the consideration of the individual parts. Othmar Spann starts with the whole of society, which has its own existence and should logically be considered before its parts. These parts, the various individuals, are not independent things, but merely ancillary units which derive their existence from the whole. In considering how society functions Spann stresses the reciprocity which exists within the multiplicity of individuals.

In this, he reverts to the social and political philosophy of the romantics, especially to Adam Müller and tries to bring their spirit back into modern science and to revolutionize economics with their universalistic outlook. In his chief work [62] he considers economics a notional structure in which only the idea of an end predominates. He wants to bring our science back to its "natural" state and to reject the causal and individualistic innovations of Smith and Ricardo. Therefore economic theory should not begin with a causal and mechanistic concept of value but with the concept of service, which alone corresponds to the facts and which he considers the organ of the whole, the purposeful functioning of the entire organism. Starting from this idea, Spann makes of economics a theory of service in four parts: factual services, spatial relation of services, temporal relation of services, and finally, magnitude of service. The first part deals with simple services, such as goods, capital, etc., and services of a higher order, as exchange, credit, commerce, etc. The next two parts which deal with the spatial and temporal relations of services discuss monogenetic and polygenetic relations and those of a higher order, such as the inner movement of various economic phenomena and transition. The last part is devoted to theories of value and price. This part, however, is in need of a thorough revision in view of Spann's subsequent desertion of the theory of marginal utility with which we shall deal later.

Spann realizes the difficulties involved in this new conception, which he considers the only possible one for his teleological attitude. To make it harmonize with the older concepts, he starts by analysing the concept of economics itself in which he contrasts, from a purely teleological point of view, the close connection of the ends with that of the means. One part of his system is concerned with the nature of the formation of economic concepts, the theory of method. With his far-reaching transformation of all economic theory, Spann tries to compress all the parts of economics, and therefore all its phenomena including their formal elements, into one co-ordinated and coherent system. Under our traditional concepts this had thus far been possible only with the economics of exchange (*cf.* Schumpeter, Lexis).

The theories of Othmar Spann created a great sensation in Germany and they are even to-day the subjects of much discussion. It would take too long to mention all the reactions toward his work.[63] We shall restrict ourselves to the more important ones.[64]

Rudolf Stolzmann is the most distinguished of the many economists who regarded Spann's contributions as a step in advance. Being somewhat similarly disposed, he can appreciate the value of Spann's universalistic outlook. He rejects, however, Spann's solutions of the problems of value and price, thinks that his concept of service retains some causal elements and claims priority in the foundations of teleological organic economics.[65] The following pupils of Spann have defended him enthusiastically: Wilhelm Andreae,[66] Jakob Baxa,[67] Walter Heinrich,[68] and Gustav Seidler-Schmid.[69] The following are sympathetically disposed toward the idea of universalism: Waldemar Mitcherlich[70] (with his own theory of plurality), Emanuel Hugo Vogel[71] (for the fluctuations of economic life), Ludwig Stephinger,[72] Walter Weddigen,[73] and Horst Wagenführ.[74] It is also a remarkable fact that many leading German historians consider Spann's results a worthy contribution to the social sciences. Georg v. Below deems him the most distinguished successor of the historical school of economics.[75] Theodor Mayer also considered a knowledge of Spann's work of importance for an historian.[76]

Some economists, while they appreciate the teachings of Spann, try to bridge the gulf between his theories and traditional individualistic economics. Wolfgang Heller stressed the fact that the individual does not become submerged in the economic whole, but retains all the definite elements which are independent of the whole.[77] Richard Kerschagl, too, tries to reconcile Spann's universalism with individualism.[78] Others who have attempted this thankless task are Albert Hesse, in the methodological studies which we have mentioned above, and Alfred Amonn in his system which we shall discuss later. Hans Honegger recognizes the concept of credit as a category of exchange, from a "neo-romantic" point of view; but he considers the expression "universalism" unhappily chosen, and thinks that Spann's ideas, although correct, are not sufficiently "objectified."[79]

The numerous adherents of individualism are naturally anxious to answer Spann's attacks. The most thorough and energetic of these has been, thus far, Fritz Sander.[80] Liefmann's criticism contains nothing new, but surpasses the others in bitterness.[81]

It does not seem probable that any of these criticisms and attacks will be able to crush Spann. On the contrary his prestige appears to be increasing, especially among the younger generation.

Friedrich Lenz's recently published system has many points of contact with Spann.[82] He too conceives of economics as an organic and social entity which is in direct opposition to traditional individualism. As Spann was influenced by Adam Müller, Lenz is influenced by Friedrich List and makes economics the handmaid of nationalism. He tries to avoid the opposition between the theoretical and the historical attitudes by his emphasis on the historical and cultural, legal and political aspects of state economy as the central concept of his system. Instead of a mechanistic theory of value and price, he gives us List's organic theory of production and explains all economic relations by the principle of the political whole. The determining goal of economics is the satisfaction of a nation's entire wants; therefore prices and distribution are organically related to each other. His aim, then, is to do away entirely with the analytical and atomistic attitude toward economics.

In his earlier works, Rudolf Stolzmann [83] had, like Spann, a conception of economics as a means toward a social end. Both Spann and Stolzmann were influenced in this by the teleologically inclined social philosophy of Rudolf Stammler. Spann gave the most weight to his social universalism, which was his starting-point for the analysis of economic concepts and phenomena. Stolzmann is influenced by an idea of social ethics, which somewhat resembles doctrinaire socialism and which he uses to solve problems of theory as well as of practice. He also tries to illumine his theory by means of the "natural categories," which he relates closely from the very beginning to the socio-ethical category. He rejects without exception all that is built upon an unsocial, and untrue utopian hypothesis, since the results obtained in this way cannot be brought into any relation with the actual social facts. His attitude toward economics is from the outset practical and directed toward a realistic and ethical end. It is this which gives Stolzmann's system its peculiar aspect of eclectic compromise. He is always trying to find a compromise between the "natural" theories, which are abstract and causal and the socio-ethical attitude which is directed toward an end. He tries to do this especially for the theory of marginal utility and that of distribution. Stolzmann is particularly strong in the criticism of prevailing theories; but in his own doctrines we notice a certain restlessness and lack of finish. We have mentioned above how this restlessness caused him to plan a philosophy of economics.[84]

Stolzmann's teleological attitude has been, on the whole, fairly well received in German literature.

Among his critics, Emil Lederer,[85] considers the causal attitude better suited to economics. Joseph Schumpeter [86] can see nothing essentially new in Stolzmann's work and Karl Diehl,[87] although fundamentally in sympathy with Stolzmann's social outlook, attacks some of his doctrines and chides his eclecticism and hesitancy. The value of Stolzmann's contribution is, however, fairly generally recognized.

The only resemblance between the system of Karl Engliš,[88] which has been translated from Czech into German, and the works of Spann and Stolzmann is its teleological character. He is, however, rather individualistic. The great principle which runs right through his book is the postulate of the minimum of displeasure. He starts, therefore, on a course of psychological analysis which brings him very close to Liefmann, especially in his criticism of the theory of marginal utility. His price theory represents a compromise between the psychological explanation of utility and the equilibrium idea of the Lausanne school, while in his theory of distribution he emphasizes the principle of social power. His system, therefore, is eclectic, in the best sense of that word. An interesting discussion took place on methodological points of view between Engliš and Streller.[89]

Like Stolzmann, Berthold Josephy [90] keeps out of his system all the fictions of pure theory and makes of the social aspect the main independent category of economics. The philosophical basis of his system, however, does not lie in the direction of Stammler and the Marburg school, but consists rather of his own interpretation of Bergsonian metaphysics. He resembles Stolzmann in contrasting the "natural" with the social category, and advances as the origin of the former the dependence of mankind and human society on nature. He considers this "natural" category the more elementary and important of the two. In the course of his work, however, Josephy stresses more and more the sociological aspect and especially the legal premises of economic phenomena. In this again he resembles Stolzmann, as well as Diehl, whom we shall mention later. It should be noted that there is an historical aspect to Josephy's work, and also apparently some traces of natural law.

8. The Socio-legal Tendency

Karl Diehl has all the more reason to approve of Stolzmann, since he is himself an adherent of Stammler's social philosophy. During the war he started to publish, after a long preparation, a comprehensive survey of economic theory, built upon this foundation. Three of the four volumes have appeared so far.[91] Diehl himself calls his tendency "socio-legal," and considers Rodbertus, Marx, Stammler, Stolzmann and Amonn his predecessors in this field. It is a characteristic of this attitude to consider each particular economy as a subordinate part of the whole organization of economics, from which it derives the "manner, extent and pace" of its activity. Consequently every effort to found economic theory on a study of particular economies, the economic activities of the individual, his wants, etc., is immediately dismissed, and only a concrete legal system is considered a sound basis for the comprehension of economic life. The only way to obtain a theoretical knowledge that is consistent with the actual facts of economics is to consider the most elementary phenomena in close relation to the legal structure which underlies them.

The volumes of Diehl which have appeared up to the present contain first of all a somewhat polemical discussion of the nature and aims of economics. This treats of political economy as a part of sociology, discusses the relation between law and economics and between technology and economics; and finally studies the question of the systematization of the economic sciences. There follow an historical account of the development of economic doctrines and a criticism of the leading ancient and modern theories. The second volume deals with production, discusses its natural and technical foundations as well as its social aspects and finally examines the capitalist method of production. The third volume treats of the theory of the circulation of wealth and the problems of value, price, money and credit. The fourth volume will contain a theory of the distribution of income. The difference of Diehl's system from that of other economists is noticeable even in the arrangement of his material: as in treating price and value under the head of circulation of wealth, instead of under the more general and basic problems of economics.

Alfred Amonn comes fairly close to the socio-legal attitude in his fundamental ideas of method. This is very noticeable in his early work which we have mentioned above.[92] He distinguishes between individual and political economy, and tries to prove that it is a mistake to base the latter upon the economic principle which holds good only for particular phenomena. In political economy everything depends upon social and legal necessity. Its central point is not the phenomena of value (whether understood subjectively or objectively), but the social problem of price. Therefore, the subject matter of economics, according to Amonn, consists of the phenomena of exchange as determined by private economics and the quantitative relations between prices, wages, interest and rent. But as soon as we go into matters which belong to the aim of all economics—the general welfare—we are entering another field which can best be called *Volkswirtschaftslehre* or, to use an expression coined by Adam Smith—"the pure theory of economic welfare." Applied economics or, to use Amonn's favorite term, applied economic welfare, deals with the methods of furthering well-being.

The second of these three spheres, the "pure theory of economic welfare," is explained by Amonn in his latest work.[93] Here he studies, from a social point of view, the various divisions of economics, such as production, exchange and the distribution of income. To these "static" relationships he opposes "dynamic" phenomena which he examines in connection with his theory of business cycles and crises, and the general development of economic institutions.

Much attention has been paid by economists to Amonn's methodological ideas. In the second edition of his *Objekt und Grundbegriffe* (1927) he tried to answer the earlier objections. Karl Diehl has recently blamed him for neglecting the legal postulates of economics in favor of the social ones, and disagrees with Amonn's partial retention of the theory of imputation as well as with some other aspects of his theory of distribution.[94] Franz Oppenheimer takes exception to Amonn's epistemology and claims that he has confused the aim with the concept of the science.[95] Robert Liefmann accuses him of eclecticism[96] and Hans Honegger considers that he has not sufficiently noticed the structure of our present-day capitalism.[97] The present writer considers Amonn's threefold division unnecessary and objects to his omission of the economic concept.[98]

Helmut Stammler's slight system[99] is chiefly methodological. He tries to prove that the socio-legal concept of economic phenomena founded by Rudolf Stammler and continued by Stolzmann and Diehl is the only correct one.

9. The Systems of the Social Reformers

The socio-legal idea leads us to a further group of economic systems which, while also founded on the social idea, tend in the direction of reform.

At the beginning of the century, Julius Platter [100] published a system based upon the theories and ideals of Marx, which found little favor with scientists. He ignores the recent discoveries of our science, and tries to support his socialistic theses with arguments which have been abandoned long ago. The slight survey of Robert Wilbrandt [101] is also socialistic; smaller in extent but more valuable in essence than Platter's. His book deals chiefly with the causes of the great increase of prosperity in our times, which leads him to discuss the most important problems of population and of the general organization of our science. The second part of his book contains his theory of price and of distribution, in which the influence of Marx, and the theory of marginal utility are discernible. The same ideas are contained in a small and recent work,[102] in which Wilbrandt tries to develop and simplify Marxism by uniting it with the main results of the theory of marginal utility.

The important work of Franz Oppenheimer [103] also belongs to the group of social reform. His social ideal, however, is not that of Marx, but that of land reformers. He is even opposed to Marxism and uses much historical evidence to show that the sole cause of social evils is private property in land. His entire system of economic theory is subservient to this idea and he uses every argument in favor of the abolition of large landholding. His tendency is apparent at the outset in the general tenor of his whole concept of economics. He contends that the motive to satisfy wants or the economic urge makes use not only of the economic means of labor and exchange, but also of political means. These political means are robbery and the state, both of which appropriate alien labor without compensation. Similarly, the other elements of his theory are arranged in such a way as to lead straight to his theory of land reform. The greatest importance, in Oppenheimer's system, is assigned to distribution and crises. We may note the numerous analogies to the natural sciences, especially biology, which are characteristic of all of Oppenheimer's work. This gives his teachings almost the same kind of objective coloring which we have noticed in Schumpeter.

In the most recent revision of his system Oppenheimer tries especially to develop further its epistemological and methodological aspects. Even thus, however, Amonn [104] attacked it severely, and rekindled an old dispute. First and foremost, he is opposed to Oppenheimer's treatment of the concept of economy. He attacks next the purely objective explanation of the social theory of power upon which Oppenheimer builds his theories of monopoly and of the distribution of income. The rest of the discussion over Oppenheimer's system does not interest us much, as it deals chiefly with its socialistic aspect. Insofar, however, as it touches upon certain theories of Oppenheimer, we shall mention it later. A most futile dispute was started by Fritz Sander's intellectual attack against the naturalistic sociology of Oppenheimer,[105] in which Julius Kraft also took part against Sander.[106]

In spite of all these attempts to offer systematic surveys of political economy, the need has been felt in Germany both before and after the war to enrich the economic literature of social reform with translations. Omitting the works published first in English or in the Romance languages, with which we shall deal later, mention should be made here of the works of two Russian Marxists. The system of Peter Massloff [107] is suffused with historical materialism, and Marxian tendencies are evident in the treatment of individual economic problems. The whole system is based on a study of economic forces of production, and the laws of their distribution and development are the chief considerations which throw light on the other problems in the general field. Massloff devotes equal attention to industry and agriculture, and always supports his statements with a wealth of statistical material, drawn chiefly from conditions in Russia. The much more important work of W. Gelesnoff [108] has met with greater approval in German scientific circles. In his fundamental social views Gelesnoff is also a Marxist; but he belongs to the left wing of the revisionists who criticize nearly all of Marx's fundamental doctrines, and he also assigns a place in his system to other doctrines such as those of the classical school and of the theory of marginal utility. His is a carefully worked and eclectic system of economic theory. One of its advantages is an ingenious arrangement of the material, whereby it becomes possible to treat in the framework of theoretical economics certain problems which would otherwise come under the head of economic policy. The form chosen is that of lecture, which considerably helps the directness of the exposition. Especially useful are the practical examples, taken from statistical material of the most different countries.

The short work on land policy by Alexander Tschajanov [109] contains suggestions for basing the whole of economic theory on a cleverly conceived concept of family economics.

The last-mentioned writers have offered a system of economics based upon socialistic ideas, but the weighty system of Heinrich Pesch, of nearly 4000 pages, which was the result of twenty years of intensive study, contains the social idea in its orthodox catholic form.[110] His starting point is twofold. Above all is the religious conception of heaven and earth, between which God's moral law is the connecting link. This is the supreme law and should always be observed in the conduct of economic life. Man should not be considered an object of social life, but an independent subject ruling in sovereignty above the material world, whose one aim in life is to follow the path prescribed by God's moral law. Besides this fundamental idea, we find in Pesch an anthropological and teleological conception of the reasonable and unchangeable nature of man. By merging these two main viewpoints, he ends by rejecting both individualism and socialism and opposes to them his solidaristic social ideal, the social labor system in which the "natural" end of economics, public welfare, can be achieved by an accord between individual and social interests, between individual freedom and state regulation.

In his first volume, Pesch presents the foundation of economic theory somewhat in the above sense. In the second volume he criticizes the various modern systems in a thoroughgoing manner and discusses conditions of territory and of landed property, questions of population, race and classes, as the foundation of the public welfare to be reached by solidarity. The third volume is taken up with the various forms and factors of economic life, with especial attention to representation of interest. In the theory of production, price, and distribution of income in the last two volumes, Pesch's ethical zeal is especially well exemplified. Although he often makes an eclectic use of some of the prevailing ideas of economic theory, he especially stresses the solidaristic social idea and the demand for the moral behavior of the individual: his results are a theory of fair price and just distribution based thereon. In spite of its constant Christian social character, Pesch's system is marked by a broad and tolerant consideration of the opinions of others and a willingness to point out their strong as well as their weak points. Thanks to this, his system has been on the whole well received by scientific criticism, and its good qualities have been universally acknowledged. Pesch also unfolded his social ethical ideas in a smaller work.[111]

10. Outsiders

Without any political tendency, but also entirely from the aspect of the prevailing social movement, Max Schmidt offers a system [112] in which he claims to found a new "ethnological" economic theory. He thinks that up to the present ethnological aspects have been too much neglected, and he accordingly tries to analyse the social elements of trade, reducing them to ethnological considerations. Nearly all of his ethnological material is taken from the life of primitive American peoples. Useful contributions from the point of view of ethnology, anthropology and the history of culture are contained in the work of Emmerich Schubert,[113] although it cannot be called a complete economic system. The repeated attempt of J. Offner [114] to bring about a closer connection between economics and our general modern scientific knowledge has not proved successful. Rudolf Goldscheid's work,[115] which is also based on natural science, is more logically constructed. In building the framework of a new system of chiefly normative economics, he places in the center not the interest in the process of goods, not the economics of purchasing power, but the further development of the human race as an end to be attained with the help of all economic means.

We may notice also the attempt of the Norwegian Wilhelm Keilhau,[116] to transpose all that happens in the realm of economics through a well-founded methodology of clear and definite concepts into the realm of thought, and to build an original system out of the doctrine of economic determination, economic behavior and economic valuation. While clarity and logical unity are especially characteristic of Keilhau's work, the absence of these qualities is felt in the somewhat similar scheme of Edmund Herzfelder.[117] He uses Hans Vaihinger's philosophy of the "As if" (Als ob) as his basis, and tries to discover new truths in our science by the use of the fictitious method. He perceives the foundation of the law of exchange value not in the actually accomplished transactions, but—obviously under the influence of Oskar Engländer's price theory, to be mentioned later—in the offers on the supply side, as they develop objectively on the market out of their originally purely subjective shape. From these offers on the supply side and the psychological reactions which they occasion on the demand side Herzfelder derives the variation of values and then tries to build a whole system of economics on the theory of value changes. He endeavors to give it a strictly mathematical stamp and develops it through a theory of money value right up to the boundaries of ethics. Although his work contains some valuable thoughts, especially in his examination of the theory of marginal utility, it needs to be considerably improved before it will find a wider recognition.

General ideas at systematization are contained in other works, which their authors have neglected to develop in detail. Rudolf Meerwarth, for instance, published an interesting book,[118] in which he tried to base economic theory on the principles of statistics, but succeeded only in offering a business statistics more or less connected with economic ideas. Both Stephinger and Haenel have planned original systems, but have produced what may be considered broader studies of value and of money. We shall deal with them, therefore, later. Johann Plenge [119] and Otto Neurath,[120] without attempting a thorough treatment, sketch the broad outlines of new systems, the former with reference to trade, the latter with reference to the whole field of economic life. Plenge shows traces of the influence of the younger historical school, especially of Schmoller, Bücher and Sombart, and tries to found a "natural" system of exchange economics based upon the interacting functions of economic structures. Neurath is interested in an entirely original system based on an eudaemonistic theory of chance, as free as possible from any consideration of exchange. In this way he attempts to bring all the possible forms of economics, e. g., exchange, enterprise, money and land economics, under one theoretical treatment.

11. Text books

After mentioning the more or less independent new systems of economic theory which have appeared in the German-speaking countries in the first quarter of the present century, we may draw attention here to a few works which, although they really make no new contributions to our science, offer useful summaries for pedagogical purposes. Besides the various editions of the first part of Conrad's *Grundriss*, which has recently been revised by Albert Hesse, as well as the *Elements* of Wilhelm Neurath, which have maintained their popularity, we have also the works of Adolf von Wenckstern, Julius Wolf, Josef Gruntzel, Eugen Schwiedland, Wilhelm Wygodzinski and Georg Jahn.

Wenckstern's introduction to economic theory [121] has had little success. It purports to reproduce not the acknowledged principles of economics, but only the author's personal views which are opposed to socialism and the modern co-operative movement and which favor a bourgeois policy. This tendency does not appear consistently throughout the book. On the whole it has an unpleasant authoritarian aspect and the peculiar arrangement is not very lucid. Julius Wolf claims to offer a system of economics as an exact science [122] but has no really new theories. He considers those sciences exact which, because of their logical nature, attain conclusions whose truthfulness cannot be questioned by new theoretical investigations and new facts. He tries to reach conclusions for economics in order to prove experimentally that it too is an exact science. He piles up a great deal of theoretical material, which he illustrates with a great many examples, especially from technology, but manages to offer only a few stimulating ideas. His larger work, which appeared four years after this unsuccessful attempt, is written along the same lines.[123]

With less pretentions, but with more valuable results, Josef Gruntzel published after his earlier popular survey [124] a system of economic theory [125] in which, basing himself on the organic conception of society, he offers a methodologically well founded outline. Gruntzel claims that his attitude toward economic phenomena is that of a realist and wars against all abstractions which tend to isolation. He recognizes no absolutely valid economic laws but only certain rules of experience. His chief strength is as a critic and he offers little that is positive and creative. The most valuable part of his system is its sociological foundation. Another Viennese professor Eugen Schwiedland published before the war a small text book, well founded historically and socially,[126] which he followed with a more comprehensive work.[127] After a cursory survey of general theoretical problems, this deals chiefly with the ethnographical and cultural aspects of the subject. The thorough discussions of questions of organization as well as of problems of social ethics are other advantages of the work. Both Wygodzinski [128] and Jahn [129] offer short and clear introductions to economic theory in which they try to pay equal regard to all the main problems of theory. We may also note the excellence of Wygodzinski's numerous technical examples.

CHAPTER III

VALUE

Although the development of economic theory in German-speaking countries during the last decade seems to have taken a direction in which the earlier importance attached to the problem of value appears to be forgotten, at the beginning of the century this problem was indisputably the chief one. At the bottom of all attempts to solve it was the theory of marginal utility which reached its culmination at this time.

1. Conflict in the Theory of Value as between Böhm-Bawerk and Wieser

To the outer world the Austrian value theory showed a united front, but within it suffered from a controversy which had made its appearance in the closing years of the nineteenth century. The difference of opinion was on the valuation of stocks of goods, as found on one side in Friedrich Wieser and on the other in Böhm-Bawerk. Wieser takes the stand that all the units of a divisible stock should be valued according to their marginal utility, and that therefore the entire value of a stock of goods results from multiplying the number of units by the marginal utility. Böhm-Bawerk, on the other hand, holds that, in consequence of the law of diminishing marginal utility (i. e., in consequence of the fact that the marginal utility is always dependent on the last unit which is used for the satisfaction of wants, and the other units of the supply show an ever increasing utility), the entire value of a stock is the sum of the unequal fractional values of the individual units. These contradictory attitudes had appeared in the early works of these two leaders of the Austrian school, and were developed in their later works,[1] sometimes in a polemical spirit, to a point which admits still less of reconciliation. Both have had their zealous adherents, and the attempts to unite them form the chief subject-matter of the development of the value theory of pure marginal utility in the first quarter of the twentieth century. With regard to the adherents of Wieser's attitude, the first one was Robert Zuckerkandl,[2] who contributed, however, no new ideas to the debate. Ernst Broda[3] introduced the concept of the "marginal fraction," that portion of a stock of which the loss in a concrete case is questionable, as well as the concept of the "marginal quotient" which shows how many times the marginal fraction is contained in the whole amount. On this basis he formulates Wieser's law of value so that the entire value results from multiplying the marginal value by the marginal quotient. In this he does not keep strictly to the concept of a "given stock" so much emphasized by Wieser. Kläre Stier-Somlo[4] has recently tried to show that Broda's theory is untenable from the point of view of the general principle of substitution in economics. Hans Mayer,[5] Wieser's successor in the chair at Vienna, goes further in defending his predecessor's attitude. He admits the logical construction of Böhm-Bawerk's value formula, but maintains that it is contrary to the valuation of goods in a given stock as it is regularly found in actual life. Through a subtle analysis, reminiscent of Spann, of the concept of economy as an opposition of systems of ends and means, he reaches the conclusion that the time element is a real factor in determining economic dispositions in addition to scales of wants and quantities of goods in their technical and causal aspects. Böhm-Bawerk would be right only if we wanted to use the entire amount of goods in stock for the satisfaction of our wants, which arise in a certain order at a given point of time. As a matter of fact, we consider also future wants of the highest intensity, so that the actual satisfaction of our wants takes place in certain shifts spread out in time. In view of this fact, Wieser's value formula is nearer to experimental reality.

Most of the writers who joined in this controversy sided with Böhm-Bawerk. They try to prove that Wieser was misled by an "equivocation" when he thought that he could deduce from the discovery that the value of each unit is equal to the marginal utility the fact that the entire value of the stock corresponds also to the sum of these equal and individual marginal utilities. This equality of the marginal utility can be conceived only "disjunctively," and not "conjunctively," and the entire value of the stock results from the sum of the different unequal fractional values. This is the gist of Oskar Kraus's [6] argument against Wieser and also of the other objections to his law of value, especially those of Schumpeter.[7]

In this author, the difference of opinion born of this conflict in the solution of the problem of imputation by Wieser and Böhm-Bawerk is largely clarified. If Wieser wanted to remain consistent with his conception with regard to the valuation of goods in a stock, he should have adopted the standpoint, in determining the value of complementary factors in production by the value of the product, that the sum of the imputed fractions of the yield should in no case be greater or less than the value of the product itself. In opposition to this idea of "apportionment," Böhm-Bawerk stresses the fact that the whole advantage of the complementary co-operation depends on the disposal over each single element of production, and that therefore the value of each element of production must necessarily be greater than the fraction of the production value which it receives from Wieser's apportionment. The conclusion which follows, that the total value of a complementary group or the product value is smaller than the sum of the values of the individual means of production, is as little a logical contradiction as the fact that the total value of the stock is greater than the values which it contains, considered separately, for in these summated values we are dealing with only imaginary quantities, which have no real meaning. Schumpeter [8] then tries to offer a solution, strongly reminiscent of Böhm-Bawerk's attitude, by means of his ingeniously constructed concept of the value function and by his value curve. Unfortunately, we cannot here further discuss these ideas or the other views of Schumpeter that are important in this controversy. To settle the dispute he maintains, as the results of Böhm-Bawerk showed, that a satisfactory solution of the problem can be attained only on the basis of Wieser's investigations.

Although Friedrich A. von Hayek leans rather toward Wieser's attitude, he too reaches a similar conciliatory conclusion. His aim is to clarify the problems of the theory of imputation chiefly by means of a *rapprochement* with the American theory of marginal productivity.[9] Lilly Katser tries to establish the connecting links between the theory of imputation and Spann's universalism.[10]

Leo Schönfeld has recently subjected Schumpeter's stand to a sharp criticism (*cf.* above, p. 70), in which he tries to prove it untenable and contrasts it in another work [11] with an original conception of the whole problem of marginal utility. Fundamentally he endeavors merely to continue the results that have been thus far obtained; but since he also wishes to uncover certain aspects which have been hitherto neglected, he starts with a thorough change in our present-day stock of concepts. First he enlarges Gossen's law into a "law of partial utility orders." Then he rejects the concept of a given system of wants of the individual independent of economic arrangements and derives the individual utility of goods from a "general economic utility," by taking into equal consideration in their evaluation the judgment delivered both on their dedication and on their renunciation. Each time we apply goods to satisfy certain needs, in each dedication, there is necessarily a sacrifice of other goods or a renunciation to satisfy other needs, which should also be considered in valuation (*cf.* Liefmann's principle of returns!). Proceeding from the said source Carl Landauer is inspired in another direction. His starting point is also the conflict of meaning in the theory of imputation [12] but he tries to decide it in favor of Böhm-Bawerk. In his positive attempts to solve the problem of imputation [13] he undertakes to build a systematic foundation for the functionally conceived relationships between product value and production factors. In this he accepts value, price, rent, wages and interest as premises, and does not trouble himself with investigating them. Landauer devotes special attention to a study of the workings of extra-economic force on the distribution of the functional produce, that is, on the main phenomenon of theory of imputation.

Besides these more important attempts to continue the value theory of marginal utility other contributions have been made which stand somewhat apart from the main current. The Dane Will. Scharling [14] continues his former attacks against Böhm-Bawerk's deviations from the Menger-Wieser principles of marginal utility. The Russian A. Bilimowitsch [15] tries to view the chief phenomena of exchange value and of imputation more clearly from general aspects of the theory of marginal utility, while Arthur Salz [16] studies, on the basis of modern American literature, the importance of disutility in the formation of value as well as the elasticity of value and price building factors. Käthe Bauer-Mengelberg has recently made the nature of disutility the object of study of the theory of value and distribution.[17] Ludwig Mises [18] tries to point out a few objective elements which have been retained in the subjective system of marginal utility; Otto Weinberger offers an historical survey of the development of this theory.[19] Mention should also be made here of the studies of Franz Čuhel [20] and Joachim Tiburtius,[21] in analysing economic wants, as well as of the attempt of Emil Sax [22] to develop further the application which he made about forty years ago of the marginal utility theory to taxation.

2. *Spann's Theory of Equal Importance*

Othmar Spann's struggle with the problem of value deserves a chapter by itself. Originally he was an adherent of the theory of marginal utility, and retained this aspect of the theory of value in the third edition of his *Fundament*, published in 1923. Thus, although he necessarily had to recognize the subjective origin of value, he tried to treat it rather from the objective point of view by paying more attention to the objective phenomenon of the goal that is reached than to the psychic content of utility as a satisfaction of wants. This is the objective concept of value that Spann tries to introduce into his system. One of his followers, Richard Kerschagl, undertakes even to prescribe the attitude of Spann's conception of values to the other theories of value and tries to secure a more exact mathematical comprehension of the new concept of value.[23] The year 1925 witnessed a notable change in Spann's ideas. In examining more carefully Gossen's law, he finds that utility does not always decrease with increasing means but in certain cases even noticeably increases. He therefore considers the whole theory of marginal utility to be wrong, rejects it, and tries to put in its place an entirely original system of concepts as the starting point of economics.[24] According to this, it is not the amount of service of the various members that is relevant for theory, but only the state of service reached by an organization as a whole; i. e., that approximation toward the goal which is given by the services of the members of an organization. Within this limit of services there follows the partial apportionment of the share of the individual services according to the principle of equal importance, the equal indispensability of each member. This does not mean that each member of the whole is equal in importance to each other member; it means rather the equality of the members within the organization according to their ramifications. Descending upon the whole, we have first only the branches of services that are equal in importance, then only the sub-units and finally the last members. This whole theory of equal importance is entirely organic in structure and is best understood in connection with Spann's general universalistic theory of society and economics. We refer the reader to the earlier passages where we have dealt with them.[25]

Spann's sharpest critic was Julius Wyler who tried to prove that essential elements of the idea of equal importance are already contained in the doctrine of marginal utility. He claims that Spann's efforts to be objective led him to misunderstand the sense of this doctrine and that he neglected especially the difference between primary intrinsic value and secondary value, or utility, which is derived from it.[26] Before Wyler, Rudolf Stolzmann had found the weakness of the idea of equal importance especially in the fact that it provides no measurement for the individual members. i. e., for individual goods; consequently this concept means little or nothing for the value and the price of the goods themselves.[27]

3. Return to the Objective Theory of Value

A group of critics of the theory of marginal utility try to soothe their consciences by not directly rejecting the main principle of the Austrians, the derivation of value from utility, but by trying to bring it somehow or other into harmony with the ideas of the classical school on the subject. We shall see later that they follow a path which has been especially popular in the modern economics of the English-speaking countries. As early as 1902 Richard Schor [28] had maintained in an unpretentious article that we should make use of the subjective as well as of the objective concept of value in order to understand this phenomenon correctly. In his studies of the subject, which are derived from the criticisms of Liefmann,[29] Otto Conrad makes use of the idea of cost as well as of utility in explaining economic value [30] but treats it rather from the subjective point of view. Both Ludwig Stephinger [31] and H. G. Haenel [32] attempt to bring about a synthesis of the subjective and objective theories of value in their works, which are directed toward finding new foundations for all economic theory. The former declares war on all nominalism, all "isms" in economic theory and, with reference to the problem of value, wants to recognize the "stuff of reality" through a parallel consideration of subject and object; while Haenel, relying partly on the criticisms of Karl Diehl, tries to overcome the contradictions between the objective and the subjective theories of value by deriving the organic origin of value, influenced by social factors, from individual valuations.

H. C. Boden has recently offered a somewhat similar, but smaller, study of the subjective origin and the social economic workings of value; and he too rejects the pure marginal theory of value.[33]

Besides these efforts to effect a compromise between the old and the new, reactionary attempts to bring back the old supremacy of the objective theory of value have not been lacking in the first quarter of our century. Undoubtedly the most important of these was made by Franz Oppenheimer.[34] He distinguishes principally acquisition, and attributes an active function to the former only in evaluating a stock of goods which is ready for the disposal of the economic subject. In practical economic life, in modern trade, this role is somewhat subordinate, for the main question here is the supply of goods destined for the satisfaction of wants on the market. For this kind of valuation, the use value is inadequate, and its place must be taken by the objective acquisition-value, the source of which is the objective costs of acquisition. Oppenheimer understands by costs all expenditures of energy which are not devoted to relaxation (amusement, recreation, etc.). Evaluation according to these costs can be transposed also to those goods which can be obtained only by relinquishing goods that cost something.

The reaction in the scientific world toward Oppenheimer's bold attempt took the shape of much adverse criticism. Alfred Renner [35] and Alfred Amonn [36] went furthest in defending the subjective attitude. An extremely interesting discussion [37] ensued between Amonn and Oppenheimer, which seems to lead toward a clarification of the different points of view. Oppenheimer has thoroughly revised his original ideas, and Amonn seems to be willing to meet his objective attitude half way. The whole debate then resolves itself into an analysis of purely conceptual premises, especially of the concept of "statics." Wilhelm Vleugels makes of his criticism of Oppenheimer's theory a strong defense of the theory of marginal utility.[38]

Besides Masslov and Gelesnoff, who keep more or less to the Marxian theory of labor value in their works which we have already mentioned, Edward Heimann has written an excellent treatise [39] in the same vein. For Josef Gruntzel [40] there exists, besides a value in use and a value in exchange, a cost value by which he means the importance of goods for the satisfaction of human wants, measured by the expenditure of labor and capital in production. Bernard Rost [41] tries to set up a theory of lasting "intrinsic" objective value of goods on the basis of a more comprehensive criticism of the familiar theories of value. The criticisms leveled at the theory of marginal utility by Werner Sombart, in the third volume of his *Moderner Kapitalismus*, then by Friedrich Kleinwächter [42] and by other adherents of the historical school are mostly concerned with objective representations of the nature of value. A similar attempt of Warthold Mohrmann [43] may be considered a failure because of its insufficient theoretical background.

4. *Special Attempts at Clarification*

The three main tendencies in which the theory of value has developed in the first quarter of the present century are the subjective and objective attitudes, and the attempt to combine the two. On the other hand we encounter during the same period, experiments to treat the problem from another, quite original, side, in order to bring about a satisfactory solution. We shall mention only a few of these attempts, which were all doomed to failure. Perhaps the most successful is the large work of Alfred Schwoner,[44] who had pointed out at the beginning of the century a useful aspect for the solution of the problem, the temporal movements of value.[45] He has tried recently to continue the value theory of the Austrian school, gave an original classification of values, but then lost himself in a tangle of partly clever but entirely incoherent ideas on value. The Pole Anton von Kostanecki undertook in 1900 an audacious attempt [46] to synthesize dogmatic and historical studies of value, but met with little success, partly perhaps because of his unfortunate analogies between mediæval tallies and modern value theories. Both Johannes Leonhard [47] and Gerd von Ketelhodt [48] try to maintain an independent attitude in their studies of the nature of value, but both make the mistake of not distinguishing with sufficient clarity, or even noticing the difference between economic value and teleological value judgments.

5. *The "Moribund" Theory of Value*

Although we notice on the one hand the most varied attempts to develop further the theory of value, we must point out on the other hand that the position of this theory in the economics of German-speaking countries during the last decade has suffered many serious assaults. Heinrich Dietzel and Gustav Cassel started their attacks at the turn of the century and tried to prove the superfluity of the whole theory of value with even more caustic arguments in their later writings.[49] Liefmann joins them in his earlier works and his *Grundsätze der Volkswirtschaftslehre* which we have already discussed. These scholars, with their adherents and other writers desire to substitute for the theory of value a correspondingly enlarged theory of price.

Gottl-Ottilienfeld, in his fight against the "supremacy of the word," attacks not only value but all the other abstract dogmas of economics and has recently tried to replace the concepts of value and price by a general "economic dimension" comprising number as the valid magnitude.[50] Only in this shape does he expect to make of them organic members of his realistic and empirical "general theory of economics." He works out the theoretical foundation for this systematically.[51]

Many have felt themselves bound to defend the threatened position of the theory of value against these attacks. At the turn of the century and again recently, Knut Wicksell opposed sharp arguments[52] to Cassel. Otto Neurath tries in an excellent essay to determine the systematic place of the theory of value in the structure of economics,[53] and since the war Hero Möller has proved himself one of the successful defenders of value.[54] Karl Diehl is similarly disposed and counters the attacks anew with his theory of value, composed of subjective and objective elements.[55] On the basis of an epistemological and philosophical foundation of value Andreas Voigt favors the retention of the value theory in its modern subjective form.[56] Alfred Amonn subjects Gottl's new theory to a harsh criticism to the advantage of the traditional theory of value,[57] while Karl Muhs tries to show, more mildly, that the idea of value is contained in the final analysis in Gottl's concept of economic dimension.[58] Josef Back gives us the whole epistemological problem of this conflict in his methodological work[59] and reaches the conclusion that Gottl himself has fallen a victim to the "tyranny of words" of which he had so bitterly complained and was exaggeratedly one-sided in his criticisms.

Among the numerous dogmatic histories of the theory of value written at this time in German, the work of Rudolf Kaulla[60] is the best. He tries to base his positive ideas on value on his socio-legal aspect of economics, upon which we have already touched.[61]

CHAPTER IV

PRICE

A NOTICEABLE change has taken place in the German economic literature of the first quarter of the twentieth century between the positions of the theories of value and price. At first value was almost indisputably supreme and all economic investigations were constrained to use it as a starting point. But the importance of the problem of price gradually loomed larger and at the same time some of the leaders of our science came to consider the whole theory of value superfluous. At the present moment the issue has not yet been decided, but everything seems to point to the fact that the theory of value will not in the long run be able to withstand the attacks of its adversaries.

1. The Price Theory of Marginal Utility

We might think that the Austrian school would be the first to maintain the traditional equilibrium in science by continuing to develop both theories. Unfortunately its accomplishments with respect to the theory of price leave much to be desired. Even the remarkable performances of Schumpeter and Wieser, upon which we have often dwelt, are apparently no longer able to consolidate the position of marginal utility in this respect. Schumpeter takes as the premise for his theory of price a state of perfectly free competition, through which, by the undisturbed exchanges between consumption and production goods, there will be reached in economics a state of equilibrium which can be considered the maximum. He then tries to show that the reciprocal value of the condition of marginal utility of the goods exchanged would be the prevailing price. He tries further to show with much subtlety that all prices and the quantities of all goods to be exchanged can thereby be determined without ambiguity, since there are unambiguous reciprocal actions between their prices and their quantities. In opposition to this objective and mechanistic attitude of Schumpeter, Wieser tries to restore the position of the psychological, and especially of the social, element in the price theory of marginal utility, by working out the influence of social forces on the formation of prices. In analogy with the classification of income and property, he assumes a graded marginal utility and builds thereupon his theory of graded prices. According to the goods which are available for the widest or only the well-to-do classes, he distinguishes between mass values, intermediate values and luxury values. In his detailed study of the formation of prices Wieser moves gradually from competitive price to monopoly price, and distinguishes a market regulated by free competition, law and morality, from one which is without regulations, under the influence of panic, anxiety and extortion. In this way he manages to treat with much ingenuity the formation of prices in all its social and psychological factors.

The theories of Schumpeter and Wieser, which have been continued chiefly by Robert Zuckerkandl [1] and in part by Hans Mayer [2] are the chief contributions of the theory of marginal utility in the last twenty-five years to the problem of price. We may also mention the recent attempt of Friedrich A. von Hayek, to bring the element of time into the theory of price, on the basis of modern American studies, especially the results of Fetter.[3] We have no room to deal with outside contribution, such as the sketch of Eduard Kellenberger,[4] which limits itself chiefly to a criticism of Schumpeter's doctrine.

2. *Liefmann's "Purely Subjective" Explanation of Price*

It is only at first sight that Liefmann's theory of price seems very different from that of the Austrian school. He makes use of some other concepts but finally comes quite close to the marginal price theory. We have already discussed the meaning of Liefmann's law of the equalization of marginal returns. Upon this law he bases his price theory and develops it first from the point of view of supply and then from that of demand. The costs by which the seller can reach the equalized minimum of marginal returns, i. e., the costs which are necessary for manufacturing the last good sold Liefmann calls the "marginal costs." These marginal costs, increased by the marginal returns of exchange, determine under free competition the "normal price" of goods, below which level they could not be sold in the long run in actual life. This price level determined by marginal costs and marginal returns represents only the lower margin of the competitive price and is contrasted with the higher margin of demand. Even with the consumer comparisons of utilities and costs, made with regard to the good to be purchased, are decisive and there too the principle of returns, the principle of consumer's returns, is always maintained. For every good that is offered on the market there is at every price level, theoretically speaking, a consumer, the marginal consumer, who can just buy it with retention of the principle of consumer's returns, and for whom this good represents a marginal enjoyment: he would have to do without it if a consumer were found with a greater purchasing power. In the case of demand, then, the price level is determined by the marginal returns of the marginal consumer. Under free competition, according to Liefmann, both price margins meet, the lower one determined by supply and the higher one determined by demand. Thus we see how Liefmann's ideas lead on the whole to the same conclusion as that reached by the school of marginal utility through its analysis of demand. Closely related to Liefmann's theory of price is that of Otto Conrad, although he does not start from the idea of returns, but bases his doctrine on a concept of value considered as a synthesis between the principles of utility and costs.[5] Recently Herbert Schack has tried, relying on Liefmann's results, to oppose an empirically concrete, changing price level to the theory of absolute price.[6]

3. The "Purely Objective" Solution

Franz Oppenheimer's "purely objective" explanation of price, which he offers in his works which we have already mentioned, is somewhat similar to Liefmann's "purely subjective" theory, although its formal structure is entirely different. In order to study the phenomenon of price exactly and free from all disturbing influences, Oppenheimer assumes a series of bold abstractions. He dismisses all social inequality and takes for granted that the personal capacities of all men are equal. If all producers worked equally long, all incomes would have to be equally high. Consequently a static condition of market economy is presupposed in which, in spite of free movement, there are no changes in the data, in the given state of equilibrium. Under such conditions, according to Oppenheimer, the price of every good and of every performance will have to aggregate so much as to assure each producer of the same net income after deduction of his prime costs; for price consists of prime costs plus the "load," or profit of the producer. From the equal "normal income" the price of goods valued on the market can be obtained in such a way that it is divided equally among their numbers with the prime costs added. This abstract law of price is also the basis for the price which prevails in actual economic life, by again taking into consideration all the factors that correspond to concrete reality which we have omitted in the course of our abstraction and by examining what influence they have on the formation of price. Oppenheimer's studies have been especially fruitful in the various forms of monopoly price, which confront us as soon as we let fall the equal material or personal qualifications of the producer. The relation of this to Liefmann's price theory is seen chiefly in the fact that while Liefmann's law of the equalization of marginal returns, the foundation of the "subjective" theory of price, contains under careful scrutiny some objective elements, certain subjective elements are also apparent in Oppenheimer's "objective" theory, based on the equalization of incomes.

The solution which Werner Sombart offers in the third volume of his *Moderner Kapitalismus* (1927), is based entirely on the traditional objective viewpoint, but his realistic analysis of supply and demand contains some notable ideas. Thus he distinguishes between external (exogenous) and internal (endogenous) demand

(p. 479), according as the purchasers stand within or outside of the narrower capitalistic circle. In supply he stresses the artificial influences which it undergoes from cartels, combines and other associations of manufacturers. Sombart finds the effects of the social forces of big business on the whole in a rationalization, mechanization, systematization and leveling of prices.

4. *Attempts at Synthesis*

Gustav Cassel tries to solve the problem of price in an entirely different way.[7] He takes as his premise exchange values, and thus refuses to discuss once and for all the nature and psychological assumptions of these values. These exchange values are economically founded on the principle of scarcity, which we have already discussed, and the prices depending thereon have, according to Cassel, the economic function of maintaining the balance between the unlimited wants of individuals and the limited means of satisfying them. But although these prices depend on exchange values, the latter also depend upon prices. This reciprocal dependence is best expressed by mathematical equations. This first system of equations of Cassel, the mathematical aspect of which we may here omit, determines price, under a given amount and quality of goods as well as a given range of demand, at the level where supply and demand meet. Further on he rejects the assumption that supply is known by the amount and quality of the goods, puts in its place only a knowledge of the means of production devoted to the manufacture of the goods offered and proceeds under these changed assumptions to the determination of price. This leads him to the realization that a single definite function exists between the supply of finished goods and the prices of the means of production and that finally a similar relationship exists between the prices of final products and the range of the means of production. In the further development of his theory, Cassel tries to prove that the various incomes of the members of an exchange economy depend also upon the formation of prices so that this finally determines all economic distribution.

In this universal price theory, Cassel consciously unites objective and subjective elements. Among the former are the quantity of the given means of production and its technical conditions; while the demand for finished goods which sets the whole process of price formation in motion is a subjective element.

We find numerous points of contact with Cassel in the price theory of Otto von Zwiedineck-Südenhorst, which has thus far not received the attention that it merits.[8] He too tries to show that the phenomenon of price is of a multiform character and that consequently it is equally false to treat it on a purely objective or a purely subjective basis. He defends this principle against Liefmann's theory of price with cogent arguments [9] and developed it recently to greater clarity in a critical discussion with Cassel and Spann.[10] He draws attention also to the relations to be considered as functional between valuations and prices and to the direct connection of the social problem of distribution with the formation of price. His profound methodological studies of the price problem have been recently continued by Amonn,[11] who had offered interesting views on the subject in his early methodological work which we have often mentioned.

Oskar Engländer's [12] attempt to solve the problem resembles Cassel's theory in another direction. He too starts with the objective phenomena of the market and investigates valuations only in their effect on the behavior of the parties in the formation of prices. He criticizes, moreover, the marginal utility theory of price partly in the same way as Cassel.[13] Engländer tries to explain price by the "highest offers" made on the market for the good in question according to the individual budgets of the buyers. In the formation of price, the highest limit is represented by the highest offer of the marginal buyer, and the lowest limit by the highest offers of the marginal buyer and of other buyers for further units of the same good. Engländer then tries to develop these relationships between highest offers and the formation of price, by bringing in the element of cost and the connections between the income and the highest offer of the marginal buyer, to a concise theory of price, embracing many problems of detail.

Hugo Müller has tried to demonstrate the epistemological value of Engländer's theory of price for other economic problems.[14] We have already touched upon Herzfelder's theory [15] which is closely akin to that of Engländer.

The synthetic theory of price expounded by Karl Diehl in the third volume of his text-book (1927) is characterized by its realism. He tries to supplement the abstract laws of price by the establishment of general tendencies of market-price formation according as we deal with consumer's or producer's goods, wholesale or retail prices, agricultural or manufactured goods. In a special theory of price, he also works out the tendencies of price formation for certain specific markets.

Of other independent explanations of price in the first quarter of our century, we may call attention to the theory of the Czech Karl Engliš, who inclines rather to the subjective attitude. He starts not from exchange valuations, but from use valuations, which he considers exactly measurable on the basis of the utility units with which they are connected.[16] Riedenauer makes a good contribution to the mathematical conception of the problem of price,[17] and Gruntzel, in his work which we have mentioned above, studies by means of his "realistic" method, individual cases of price formation as they occur in practical life, somewhat in the same manner as Diehl has done more recently.

5. *Spann's Organic and Universalistic Theory of Price*

In his most recent work, mentioned above [18] Othmar Spann sketches a theory of price which completely rejects the concept of valuation, and has, therefore, a purely objective foundation. We remind the reader of what we said in dealing with Spann's latest theory with reference to the equal importance of the members within the same degree of articulated structure. He considers price the embodiment of equal importance on the basis of the proportions in size of the services of the members, whereby these proportions of size, through an equal treatment of the branch-services and services, result as members of the entire activity. If, according to Spann, regroupings of members are to be expected in the economic structure, the basis of the formation of price is not the actual, but the expected condition of the members whereby, according to the expected increases or losses in service, the concepts of greater and less importance appear besides that of equal importance. According to this point of view, each price can be explained only by the systematic and temporal universal relationship of all prices. From the special character of all members and structures in the organic concept of economics there is another result, price can be balanced only by a corresponding organization: no equal prices for goods can be attained by free competition. If the price is the right expression of a right arrangement of the whole economic organism, Spann calls it a right price, and believes that he thus has recaptured in a purely theoretical way a concept which was possessed by the universalistic, organic, and teleological science of the ancients and the mediævals as well as by the moral consciousness of all other times, but which was ridiculed by "individualistic science with its mechanistic formulas of causality." It is obvious from this that his bold theory of price will stand or fall with Spann's general principles of sociology and economics. This will be decided by the outcome of the active discussion now taking place on the subject. The criticisms which have been made thus far, and which we have already noticed in connection with the theory of equal importance, apply also to Spann's theory of price.

CHAPTER V

DISTRIBUTION

1. Marginal Utility and the Theory of Distribution

As ALWAYS, the development of the theory of distribution in recent economics is intimately connected with the progress made in the theory of value and of price. As long as the theory of marginal utility still dominated German economics, its doctrine of distribution, the theory of imputation, was zealously prosecuted. The more fundamental, however, the criticisms directed against the theory of marginal utility, the more prominent did other theories of distribution, besides that of imputation, become. The problem of distribution and the theory of value are so closely connected in the doctrine of marginal utility that we felt impelled to discuss them jointly in the earlier part of the book. The development of the theory of imputation is also characterized in the first quarter of our century by the conflict between the two active leaders of the Austrian school, Böhm-Bawerk and Wieser and their adherents, and so it seemed appropriate to discuss this conflict in one group of subjects. In the meantime many members of the Austrian school have devoted themselves to studies of the theory of production, and have tried to regain in this direction a counterweight to the theory of imputation.

We shall return later to the investigations of Richard Schüller and Josef Schumpeter, in the problem of returns. The Hungarian Paul Fleischl keeps closely to Böhm-Bawerk's general ideas, and succeeds in erecting on their basis a theory of production based entirely on the principle of marginal utility.[1] Omitting all problems of social organization, Hans Mayer has recently outlined a theory of production on purely natural and technical foundations, of which the sole theoretical assumption is to be the law of economic utility.[2] The last work of Robert Zuckerkandl was also to be on production theory. In the first excerpt that has been published[3] of what was to be a general theory of the subject he makes a scholarly attempt to unite the ideas of the Austrian school with the new American viewpoints, especially those of the elder Clark and his followers.

Among those which are outside of the theory of marginal utility we can mention only briefly the production theory of Spann which is based on an analysis of the productive functions of exchange in the organic structure of economics.[4] Jakob Baxa tries to develop Spann's ideas in a history of the theory of productivity.[5] Perhaps we should also mention for Germany the work of A. Nordenholz, which appeared at the beginning of the century, but which remains on the whole within the frame of the classical theory of production.[6] An ambitious attempt was made by Karl Diehl, who devoted the entire second volume of his *Theoretische Nationalökonomie* to a development of his socio-legal theory of production. We may also refer to this work in reference to the whole recent development of production theories, which we have not room to discuss here. Frieda Wunderlich reaches important conclusions on the question of productivity in a normative-teleological way.[7] Werner Sombart tries to solve the same problem in his realistic manner.[8]

The fact that the young Austrian school is increasingly devoting its attention to questions of production theory is undoubtedly one of the reasons why they seem somewhat to neglect the development and defence of the theory of imputation, which has been attacked from so many sides. There have been some isolated attempts—as we have noted—to unite the theory of imputation with the closely related American theory of marginal productivity, and thus to prepare the way for the union of the Austrian school with the tendency of the elder Clark; but so far these have had no success worthy of record. Perhaps J. W. Schiele has been most successful in the German-speaking countries in continuing the American theory of distribution based on the principle of marginal productivity, and in applying original ideas.[9] His originality lies in a clever union of marginal utility with labor-value. Consequently he views labor as the only source of value and transfers the concept of surplus value which he thus obtains to the theory of distribution. He succeeds in this difficult theoretical feat without giving his ideas the slightest trace of a social reformistic tendency.

2. *Solutions of the Problem of Distribution on the Basis of the Theory of Price*

Robert Liefmann criticizes most severely both the theories of distribution which prevailed at the beginning of the century, that of marginal productivity as well as that of imputation.[10]

He tries especially to show that Karl Landauer's studies are untenable, and entangles himself in an unprofitable discussion with the latter.[11] It is always regrettable when the political attitude of an opponent is drawn into a debate on purely theoretical questions, as Landauer's socialism was in this case.

According to Liefmann, the greatest mistake of economic theory is to refer wages, interest and pure rent to the factors of production: labor, capital and land. For these factors bring forth products only in a purely technical sense, and it depends on the subjective valuation of man whether the products can be considered as economic goods showing profits and returns. Therefore we can talk of income only on the basis of considerations of profit between utility and costs, such as we have discussed more fully above, and it is accordingly quite false to impute directly a share of value to the factors of production. The actual problem of distribution is a purely practical question of the concrete formation of price, and what alone matters is how much of the real returns accrue to those who contribute to production. In distribution, Liefmann considers as decisive the method of origin of supply and demand, and their interactions on the market, which he tries to explain on the theory of price discussed above.

The idea of explaining distribution directly from the process of price formation, has become markedly prominent in German science during the last decade. Although Böhm-Bawerk keeps largely to the basis of the theory of imputation, he too contributes clearly to this attitude in his theory of interest, to be discussed below. For instance, he places the element of time in the center of the problem of production and investigates first of all how the entrepreneur acquires use of the soil, tools and labor, i. e., future goods, in exchange for the present goods which he possesses,

i. e., for the means of subsistence which he offers to the persons engaged in production. In this way Böhm comes to analyse the market of productive goods, and draws attention to the two important facts, that the formation of income really takes place here, and that social elements, e. g., especially the conflict between the owners of present goods and those of future goods, play an important role.

It is in Cassel that we first find a clear and accurate theoretical development of the close relation between price formation and the distribution of incomes. We have already seen in discussing his price theory how directly and spontaneously he moves from the price of final products to the price of means of production, and thence to the chief aspects of distribution. The idea of a valuation of consumption and production goods does not appear, and the price formation of productive goods, which Cassel considers here the same as factors of production, contains the entire distribution of incomes. He is somewhat influenced in this by the concept of Walras, according to which the entrepreneur stands in the center of economic life and, in conformity with the same laws of price formation, buys with one hand factors of production and sells with the other consumption goods. He pays for land, capital and labor, forced by their "scarcity," a price which is just as much subject to the general laws of price formation as is the price level of final products. Cassel has thus constructed a unitary theory of price and of distribution.

Similarly, both Wolfang Heller and Adolf Weber, in their new systems, derive the distribution of incomes directly and entirely from the formation of prices. These scholars also stress the social limitation of the problem. The realistic trait is even more pronounced in the theoretical ideas of Sombart on distribution, based on the theory of price (*Moderner Kapitalismus*, vol. 3, 1927).

Oppenheimer's theory of distribution is also derived from his theory of price. We have already shown how, in the course of uniting his abstract price theory with the actual conditions of social life, he came to a thorough analysis of monopoly price. Among the various kinds of monopolies which he distinguishes, he devotes especial attention to class and exchange monopolies. By class monopolies in opposition to personal monopolies, he means those positions of power based on constitution and law which constitute a relationship of monopoly between an upper and a lower social class. These have appeared in history in three different forms: slavery, serfdom and finally land monopoly, which is the foundation of the contemporary capitalistic system. Landowners also possess an exchange monopoly, since workmen can sell their labor only to them or to other capitalists who in the last analysis also rest upon a land monopoly. Since every exchange monopoly causes a rise of price above the level of competitive prices, the income of the monopolist class is increased by the monopoly profit; this increase is reflected on the other side in a diminution of earned income. This theory of distribution is indeed curiously built, and has an unusually marked character of social reform; nevertheless, it is clearly and directly connected with a theory of price, which constitutes its foundation.

Among many other writers who deal with Oppenheimer's attempted solution of the problem of distribution we may mention especially Schumpeter. He criticizes Oppenheimer for having too broad a concept of monopoly, which is consequently false, and maintains that modern private ownership of land is fundamentally not a monopoly, so that Oppenheimer's whole theory of distribution built upon this concept falls to the ground. The latter defended his standpoint and a most interesting debate [12] ensued, which for its friendly and courteous tone—and this unfortunately needs especially to be stressed nowadays—may well serve as a model for such discussions.

Besides these writers, Ernst Schuster also envisages a solution of the problem of distribution based wholly on a theory of price and has recently made the bold attempt to omit the concept of income entirely from economics, on the basis of Kant's critique of knowledge.[13]

3. *Social Theories of Distribution*

The second point of view which Böhm-Bawerk stresses in his theory of distribution, the great importance of social relations of power in the formation of income, had often been considered by earlier writers. Many members of the historical school, and especially those who were also leaders of professorial socialism, have held distribution to be a problem of social power. We can see this in the earliest writings of Brentano, and Schmoller takes a similar view of distribution in his *Grundriss*. In this circle it has been recently Wilhelm Lexis above all who, in his *Allgemeine Volkswirtschaftslehre*, holds the social factor of power as alone decisive for the actual level of the various branches of income. On the whole, however, he still follows the principles adopted by the classical school in solving the problem of distribution, and accordingly he too starts from the value of production goods. Lexis deserves much praise for connecting closely the theory of distribution with a profound theory of production, in which he again stresses against other points of view the fact that the end of all the media of production is the production of consumption goods, wherefore their future marketability alone determines the producing capacity of all investments. Lexis distinguishes a primary, a secondary and a derived income, according as income is obtained from actual production, for personal services or from another source (e. g., rent). We have already touched upon the socialistic elements in his theory of distribution.

In 1913, three years after Lexis, the Russian socialist Michael Tugan-Baranovsky, active in Germany, published a theory of distribution [14] in which the supremacy of the social element is pushed to its furthest limit. The critical basis of Tugan's theory is the principle that the problem of distribution is in the first place not a problem of value. Thus his attitude is essentially different from that of Lexis. He energetically attacks not only the distribution theory of Marxism and of the school of marginal utility, which depends on a theory of value, but also all other theories which try to explain distribution by the formation of price. Tugan considers that the problem of distribution has absolutely nothing to do with that of production or of exchange. Distribution should be viewed merely as the process in which the various social classes meet, in which are expressed the relations of dependence between the income of the social classes joined together by the necessities of capitalistic production and of exchange. Tugan sees the real business of the theory of distribution in a systematic study of these conditions of dependence. Here again we notice a far-reaching divergence from Lexis's view of the problem: while the latter endeavored to join the theory of distribution with that of production, Tugan makes a sharp distinction between production, as a purely economic process and distribution, as an historical, social and political category.

Tugan's theory aroused much interest in economic circles. Wilhelm Wirz,[15] in spite of his regard for it, rejects Tugan's theory chiefly because it considers the process of distribution as a conflict between entire and homogeneous classes. Wirz maintains that the class as a whole disposes of no power over its means of production and that the conflict therefore takes place principally between individuals, or at the most between groups of limited size. Gerhard Albrecht[16] studies the relation between Tugan's distribution and that of other modern writers and points out that Eugen Dühring had several decades ago attempted a solution of the problem similar to that of Tugan. Rudolf Stolzmann went far in this direction in his earlier and later works, which we have mentioned above. Nevertheless, he submits Tugan's work to a comprehensive and detailed critical examination[17] and comes to the conclusion that he is wrong in trying to solve the problem of distribution independently of the concept of value. According to Stolzmann phenomena of distribution are phenomena of value, like all other economic phenomena, and should be derived not from each other, but both together from a third superior entity: from the immanent socio-organic functions of purpose. Under the influence of Stammler's social philosophy, which also affected Stolzmann, Paul Schröder endeavors to oppose the idea of institutional distribution, limited by law and society, to the prevailing abstract theory of personal distribution, which refers only to the various personal activities.[18] The social element is also strongly emphasized in the theory of distribution of Bernhard Josephy in the small systematic work mentioned above.

The Hungarian Karl Von Balás comes rather close to the German socio-legal attitude.[19] He is not satisfied with considering legal institutions as a mere framework of economics, but tries to explain the conditions of distribution by means of the collection of legal concepts which have developed through the ages. He considers income in its modern shape of purchasing power and then develops the process of distribution entirely from its aspect of social power. It should be noted that these ideas of Balás were published in Hungarian in 1913 at the same time as the partly analogous theory of Tugan-Baranowsky.

Spann also considers the process of distribution as socio-organic function of purpose but goes even beyond the modern point of view on the subject in his universalistic study of this entire complex of problems. He sees the basis of distribution, not in subjective valuations and in the formation of price but in the economic whole and its articulated arrangement. In the general economic organization it is already determined what goods will be produced and in what order; what goods therefrom fall to income and to what branches of income. Therefore distribution is already contained in the process of production, and it is the sign of an individualistic and materialistic mind to want to interpose here a special theory of wages, interest, and income based on the theory of price. The truth lies rather in the fact that distribution is only facilitated by the process of price formation, since in distribution the principle of equal importance based on the principle of the relativity of the members is decisive. The individual branches of income share equally according to the requirements for restoration and the surpluses: what is decisive here is only the relativity of all members and means. Where there are only a few workmen, for instance, each may receive a relatively larger share from the surplus which is allotted to the productive branch of "labor," and also within this branch the individual labor functions receive a corresponding share according to their equal importance in the articulated organization, i. e., in the given organization of labor.—Was not, *mutatis mutandis,* a similar idea contained in the wage-fund of classical economics?

4. The Derivation of Rent from the Formation of Price

The first quarter of the twentieth century has witnessed no new theory of rent of land in the German-speaking countries. We can, at most, see an original solution in a negative tendency: namely, that the scholars abandon the attempt to explain rent of land in a special way. In our discussions of the development of the theory of distribution, we have seen that the tendency is to find if possible a single explanatory principle for all branches of income; consequently all special theories of rent of land automatically disappear. This tendency is especially noticeable in those systems which derive the whole process of distribution directly from the formation of price. With Cassel the problem of the rent of land is treated principally according to the aspects of the general formation of price, where the supply and demand of the productive factor land play the chief roles. Cassel, however, clings to the concept of the classical differential rent, applying his principle of scarcity, and tries to develop it further and more exactly. He achieves this by considering in his theory of rent the possibilities for substitution of land on one side and of capital and labor on the other.[20] Liefmann generalises Ricardo's law of rent, and lets it prevail everywhere where products manufactured at various costs are brought to the market by numerous sellers. On the whole he endeavors to derive rent, like interest on capital, entirely from the concept of interest on lent goods. Otto Conrad accepts fundamentally the classical theory of rent,[21] but also gives it an entirely general meaning. Because of the scarcity of good land, its owners possess a monopoly, which enables them to attain a greater or a smaller margin between price and costs. Wherever the restriction of free competition leads to such a margin in the traffic of goods, a rent arises, and the rent of land is only one of its special cases. This monopoly theory of rent—as we have already seen—is logically developed by Oppenheimer, and applied to the other branches of income. Tugan-Baranowsky, and all economists who derive distribution only from the social relationship of power are even more clear in giving an explanation of the rent of land which is essentially like that of the other branches of income.

5. *The Generalization of the Law of Diminishing Returns*

Schumpeter urges emphatically the unification of the whole theory of distribution. He tries to suppress the special position which rent of land has always held by showing that the law of diminishing returns is not peculiar to agriculture: when industrial methods, organization, technique and capital power remain the same, i. e., in static economics, it applies even more to industry, and in dynamic economics it is valid neither for agriculture nor for industry. Consequently Schumpeter holds that it is meaningless to speak further of a special law of diminishing returns on land.[22] While Schumpeter is influenced by modern American theorists in these respects, Richard Schüller seems to have proceeded independently on his parallel investigations, which he began a few years previously. In his detailed study of problems of tariff policy, he recognizes first that the special natural and other advantages which enable certain industries to produce more cheaply are available only up to a certain limit of production. If production is extended beyond this limit, this is possible only with comparatively higher costs.[23] In this way Schüller develops a general law of diminishing returns applicable also to industry. Walter Weddigen reaches similar conclusions, although he starts from essentially different premises.[24] On the basis of a thorough methodological study, he formulates from the subjective psychological point of view the "exact law," which is to the effect that an increasing amount of consumption goods produces at first a comparatively increasing utility but, after a certain level, a comparatively decreasing utility. He also makes use here of the marginal analysis. Weddigen's exact laws of productivity and yield then, which are intended to solve the objective material problem of the formation of profits, correspond in their total organic conception to the generalised theory of diminishing returns. This solution is distinctly based on Spann. Individualistic (Schumpeter, Schüller) and universalistic (Weddigen) attitudes meet here.

The studies of Schumpeter and Schüller provided occasion in the German-speaking countries for a more thorough examination of the law of diminishing returns on land, which led to an interesting discussion. Otto Auhagen[25] and Zwiedineck-Südenhorst[26] adopt attitudes which resemble that of Schumpeter, while Friedrich Aereboe, Knut Wicksell, Joseph Esslen, Hans Neisser, Theodor Vogelstein, Karl Diehl, Rudolf Stucken, Franz Xaver Weiss, etc., stand for the traditional form of the law.

Aereboe[27] and Esslen[28] devote their attention especially to the purely technical and agrochemical aspects of the problem, and try to prove that the law of diminishing returns on land is based on the imperfection of our scientific knowledge or on the impossibility of a complete utilization of natural forces. Wicksell[29] and Neisser[30] approach the question rather from the point of view of political economy. The former proposes to start from a given amount of labor and capital instead of from a given area of land while Neisser, through his studies of price and money, also reaches the conclusion that a special law of returns on land should at all costs be retained. Vogelstein[31] is of the opinion that diminishing returns in industrial production can take place only in cases where this is somehow inwardly dependent on limitations of soil. Karl Diehl considers all efforts to formulate a single law of returns for agriculture and industry a retrogression, since returns in each branch of production should be examined according to the special conditions and peculiarities of the case.[32] Working from the same premises, Rudolf Stucker shows some of the typical differences between the agricultural and the industrial problems of return.[33] Franz Xaver Weiss believes in a special category of land rent since land is one of the original factors of economics to which the theories of value and price must always be directly applied.[34]

All these important objections to extending the law of diminishing returns on land to industry have contributed, at least for the present, toward the prestige of the special theories of land rent in the German-speaking countries. It is likely, however, that the influence of Anglo-Saxon and Romance science on a unification of the theory of distribution will before long overcome the present German tendency.

6. *Municipal Ground Rents*

The last century witnessed the beginning of the discussion of the views of Rudolf Eberstadt concerning municipal housing policy and municipal ground rents. Adolf Weber [35] and Andreas Voigt [36] take part in this with their detailed investigations published in 1904 and 1905 respectively. Both reach in the main the conclusion which Philippovich expounded in 1901 in his report to the League for Social Politics, namely, that both municipal land prices and municipal ground rents are to be explained by the general theory of rent. Relying partly on a pamphlet of Friedrich Wieser,[37] Friederich Kleinwächter Jr. later made a similar attempt to give a satisfactory solution of urban ground rents from the most general aspects of the theory of marginal utility.[38]

7. *The Discussion of Böhm's Agio Theory*

While the problem of land rent is one of the questions which have been most neglected in German-speaking countries during the first quarter of our century, the problem of interest has been constantly in the foreground and has aroused great interest in all quarters. Böhm-Bawerk's famous agio theory of interest was published at the end of the last century, but the discussion which developed around it held our interest until the World War, and even beyond. We can mention here only the most important aspects of the voluminous discussion which took place, and the names of only those authors who took a leading part in it. As is well known, Böhm-Bawerk founded the difference in value between present and future goods, to which he referred interest, not only on the difference of provision in the present and the future and on the systematic undervaluation of future needs, but also on the greater productivity of roundabout production. Here we see the element of time as the foundation of a superiority in value. Böhm's critics have correctly recognized in this principle of the greater yield of roundabout production the weakest part of his theory, and concentrate their attacks on this point.

Otto Conrad [39] holds that, in comparing the two methods of production, we can take as a standard either the requisite time or the quantity of goods produced, but not both. Since Böhm makes this logical mistake, his formula is devoid of meaning. Diehl [40] also attacks this point of Böhm's doctrine and consider that on general methodological grounds it is impossible to solve the problem of interest, which he deems part of a historical and legal category, in an abstract-deductive way as Böhm has attempted. We find similar views in the comprehensive criticism of Emil Sax [41] which greatly influenced the supporters of the doctrine. Sax is one of the strongest adherents of marginal utility; nevertheless he tries to contradict the arguments of his Viennese colleague point by point and endeavors to show that a distinction of value between present and future goods has been rendered possible only through an erroneous private economic interpretation of the whole problem of interest. In real economics the source of interest is represented by the unequal distribution of property with its unequal reactions of social power. These critical and positive views of Sax are followed in the main by Michael Hainisch.[42] Perhaps the most typical of the remaining German critics of Böhm is Bortkiewicz [43] who rejects categorically the principle of the greater yield of roundabout production and considers Böhm's other arguments for the explanation of interest irrelevant. Consequently he denies the value superiority of present over future goods and tries to prove that Böhm's theory of interest belongs essentially to the well-known productivity theories. Among foreigners, J. B. Clark [44]—to whose famous discussion with the Austrian scholar we shall return later—attacks Böhm's doctrine from the point of view of a productivity theory of interest, while others such as N. Schaposchnikoff,[45] Z. Zankoff,[46] and more recently important figures such as Knut Wicksell [47] and L. V. Birck,[48] devote themselves entirely to criticizing the principle of the greater yield of roundabout production. Böhm himself answered the objections raised up to the summer of 1911,[49] and recently one of his most zealous disciples, Franz Xaver Weiss, has undertaken to defend the master's teachings,[50] and also to perfect them further independently. F. A. von Hayek tries to accomplish this by bringing the element of time into the static theory of interest.[51] Erik von Sivers gives a clear, if somewhat incomplete, survey of the German critics of Böhm's theory.[52]

8. The Dynamic Explanation of Interest

The only original theory of interest in the German literature of the first quarter of the twentieth century is to be found in Schumpeter. Relying upon recent American theorists, he is unable to see the sole source of interest in the time element stressed by Böhm-Bawerk. According to him, there must be a further factor which guarantees more surely a value premium of the capital spent, and at the same time effectively opposes the tendency of competition to level values as well as to engender the equalizing revaluation of production goods. Schumpeter believes that he has found this factor in economic development which can continuously guarantee the creation of surplus values through the perpetual transformation of the processes of production. There is no interest on capital in static economics, since interest can arise only in the dynamic form of economic life.

Schumpeter develops his theory with unusual logic and is able to defend it even in a dispute with Böhm-Bawerk.[53] Rudolf Stolzmann rejects Schumpeter's theory of interest on general methodological considerations and tries to derive capitalism solely from the interplay of social relationships of power.[54] Georg Halm, in connection with Böhm-Bawerk's objections, tries to show that Schumpeter's economic system would collapse as a result of the tremendous inflation caused by the constant product of value surpluses.[55] Oskar Engländer's chief argument against Schumpeter is the fact that loans, for which interest is paid, are quite generally accepted,[56] even from capitalistic producers, who are not dynamically efficient entrepreneurs in the sense of Schumpeter. G. Heinze has recently tried to prove that interest exists in static, as well as in dynamic economics.[57]

Karl Muhs [58] offers a theory of interest which is related in part to that of Schumpeter and recognizes the possibility of interest neither in manual trade nor in small landownership, but only in the branches of production of big business. For here the greater yield of material means achieved in production appears as a function of the monopolistic accumulating process of capital. Emanuel Hugo Vogel's [59] studies are on similar lines and deal with the relations between interest and the business cycle.

9. *Monopoly, Abstinence, and Productivity Theories of Interest*

The interest theories of the new century which are based on social reform are not different from the older ones. Otto Conrad [60] bases interest on the monopoly of capital belonging to the propertied class and allows certain considerations of technical exchange such as that of friction only tentatively as a secondary source of interest. A very systematic monopoly theory of interest is offered by Oppenheimer, and a similar tendency is expressed in numerous less important attempts, such as that of the Marxist Wilhelm Hohoff.[61] Oppenheimer's theory is subjected to a thoroughgoing criticism by Siegfried Budge,[62] who contrasts it with his own theory of interest composed of elements of the classical labor theory and Senior's abstinence theory. With reference to the rate of interest, he takes into consideration Schumpeter's distinction between static and dynamic economics.

The element of abstinence, the capitalist's "waiting," also plays an important role in Cassel's interest theory, but he makes the concrete rate of interest depend only on the process of price formation. This is also true of Liefmann; but, following his subjective attitude, he refers the origin of interest to the consumer points of view. Richard Strigl [63] tries his luck with a residual theory of interest modeled somewhat after modern American writers and brings the old productivity theory back into honor. Besides Böhm-Bawerk, Max Gebauer [64] stressed the importance of the element of productivity much earlier and Oskar Engländer [65] rejects Böhm's agio theory in favor of this attitude. Götz Briefs criticizes very severely the classical theory of interest in his historical work,[66] whereupon Knut Wicksell succeeds in defending the real essence of the productivity theory of interest with well-considered arguments and much polemical skill.[67]

10. Further Development of Ideas of Wages Theory

Among theories of individual branches of income in German-speaking countries in the first quarter of our century, the most unified development has taken place in the theory of wages. In the opening years we find many expositions of which the roots are to be sought in the wages-fund theory of the descendants of classicism: e. g., especially in Böhm-Bawerk, Arthur Spiethoff, and later in Karl V. Balás. This theory, on the whole, comes to an end with the extremely thorough criticism of Arthur Salz.[68] He has recently contrasted it emphatically with the modern price-theoretical analysis of the formation of wages.[69] Heinrich Sieveking also advances some telling arguments against the wages-fund theory in his recently published text book.

Thünen's productivity theory of wages has recently been strongly emphasized by Paul Arndt [70] and, among others, by Adolf Weber in his text book. More fruitful, however, has proved to be another tendency which most successfully unites the leading points of view of this doctrine with the Ricardian theory of wages. In his work which appeared at the turn of the century, Zwiedineck-Südenhorst [71] emphasizes demand on the part of the employer and supply on the part of the laborer as of equal importance for determining wages. He does not forget the important role played by the traditional scheme in the formation of wages. Ernest Klien [72] develops clearly the principle that the process of price formation, which produces wages, is determined by two factors: an historical one, tradition, and a contemporary one, the interplay of supply and demand. Schmoller stresses similar views, especially in the second edition of his survey, and attributes great importance to the historical factors.

In addition to other, less important, attempts like that of Franz Saspach [73] to interpret the problem of wages within the framework of the general process of price formation, but more from the abstract theoretical side, we may mention the work of Cassel, who offers an excellent analysis of supply and demand in the formation of wages.

11. The Explanation of Wages on the Theory of Marginal Utility

From the standpoint of analysis, two adherents of the marginal utility theory, Richard Schüller and Verrijn Stuart, are especially prominent. Schüller [74] studies in detail what value labor possesses for the entrepreneur and how demand will in consequence shape itself on the labor market. In this way he reaches the conclusion that, for the shaping of demand in the formation of wages, not only the marginal value—the value which the employed laborer has for the entrepreneur—is decisive, but also the whole inner structure, the interior arrangement of demand itself. After studying the unequal intensity of demand, he formulates the principle that increasing the wages causes no noticeable decrease, and reducing the wages causes no noticeable increase, in the demand for labor. Schüller then analyses supply on the labor market and studies the psychological and social conditions on which the laborer's demands depend, and which lead to a classification of these demands. Decisive, for the level of wages, according to Schüller, is the supply of that class of laborers employed by the entrepreneur which upholds the highest demands. Under a given demand, a class with higher demands is the standard for supply according as the classes claiming more favorable conditions are wider and more profitable for the employer in proportion to those who make more modest claims. This is all the more the case, the more excellent workmen predominate, the more performance is increased by higher wages or by better labor conditions, and the more complete and the better the organization of labor is.

Hilde Oppenheimer [75] investigates in a successful dissertation the importance of the last-named factors, the organization of labor, in the formation of wages. Richard Strigl is convinced that the marginal analytic theory of wages is also able to explain the effects of the factor of power in the wage struggle. Consequently he tries to emphasize the ideas of social policy in the results of the Vienna school on the theory of wages.[76]

Verrijn Stuart reaches a similar conclusion [77] as Schüller. First he posits the main question, whether the origin of wages is to be sought in the needs of the laborers or in the value of the work performed. After rejecting all the arguments in favor of the first solution, he recognizes only the value of the performance as a foundation for wages, relying partly on the investigations of Wieser. The marginal productivity of labor is the standard of the entrepreneur's valuation; and the supply of the laborer depends also on the valuation of his own performance. The needs and the traditional standard of life of the laborer enter only as an element in this valuation. The actual level which wages will reach between these two marginal values depends, according to Stuart, on the psychological, technical and social factors which Schüller had already pointed out.

12. The Socialistic Theory of Wages

The socialistic theories of wages of the new century, such as those of Otto Conrad, Oppenheimer,[78] Tugan-Baranovsky, David Lewin,[79] etc.—like the similar theories of interest—offer no essentially new ideas. We always have in the foreground, with more or less modifications, the concept that the social relations of power, which are unfavorable for the labor class, depress wages to the level of minimum subsistence. In the last analysis, the needs of the laborer are decisive for determining the wage level—an idea which, as we have just seen, Verrijn Stuart and other adherents of the theory of marginal utility do their best to combat.

Rudolf Stucken offers a good survey of the recent development of socialistic wage theories.[80] He deals also with the doctrines of the professorial socialists, but is unable to share their optimism with respect to the increase in wages to be expected from changes in social power. Joachim Staberow has recently stressed the elements of power in the formation of wages in opposition to the theory of productivity.[81]

13. The Dynamic Theory of Profit

The only progress in the theory of profit in the German literature of our period is to be found in Schumpeter. Other studies of this subject have led to no results worth mentioning. Schumpeter derives profit like interest solely from the economic development, of which the leaders are according to his opinion—as we have already pointed out—the entrepreneurs. In static economics there is no profit; it is only in the transition from one economic form to another, i. e., in a dynamic state of economics, that a surplus results from the price of production beyond the prices of the means of production, from which alone profit arises. Since the entrepreneur's activity consists essentially in the dynamic further development of economic life, the source is formed of a special permanent income. We have already mentioned that this theory is largely based on the recent American literature of the subject.

A considerable part of modern German literature on the theory of profit centers around Schumpeter's doctrine. Eduard Kellenberger[82] and the more profound Adolf Lampe[83] are of the opinion that profit can arise also in static economics, for it comes under the same aspect as rent, since both kinds of income can be referred to special, monopolistic, personal (or material) characteristics which are above the average. Oskar Engländer tries to prove the presence of profit in static economics on the basis of considerations of price and wages theories,[84] while Rudolf Streller, who is generally successful in analysing the income of the entrepreneur in dynamic economics, tries to interpret profit in static economics as a residual income.[85] A residual explanation is also given in Werner Sombart's *Moderner Kapitalismus* (vol. 3, 1927). The recent attempt of Bruno Moll[86] to refer profit again for the most part to an exploitation of the laborer, is based on the traditional socialistic attitude. Ludwig Pohle offers a good short historical survey of the dynamic role of the entrepreneur in modern capitalistic development; [87] Kurt Wiedenfeld published a comparative study on the nature and importance of entrepreneurship in its typical differences between individual nations on the one side, and between individual branches of industry on the other,[88] while E. H. Vogel studies the connections between the level of profit and the variations of the business cycle [89] in much the same way as he has done concerning the problems of interest.

PART THREE

THE DEVELOPMENT IN THE ROMANCE COUNTRIES

CHAPTER I

METHOD

1. Absence of Methodological Controversy in the Romance Countries

In Romance economics, there has never been a controversy between inductive and deductive methods such as was known in Germany toward the end of the last century. This can only in part be explained by the fact that scientific interests are different and that, as far as pure theory is concerned, discussions are conducted in a more quiet and friendly tone. The real reason is that the influence of the historical school, which is of German origin, was unable to displace the classical tradition in France or in Italy. The small number of adherents of the historical attitude were aware of their weakness and wisely refrained from attacking the dominant classical method too openly. Consequently they also remained aloof when at the end of last century the abstract-deductive method underwent a renovation, which partly transformed it into a mathematical one.

2. The Method of the Lausanne School

It was not long before the Latins adopted the mathematical method with such enthusiasm that in the first quarter of our century it became in Italy and later in France the chief instrument of scientific development. In his long scientific career, terminated by his death in 1924, Maffeo Pantaleoni published numerous essays,[1] all of them the products of a distinguished mind, in which he discussed problems of economic method from every angle and gave special consideration to the mathematical method. We may ascribe to him the growth of this method in modern times, at least on the Continent, for it was he who induced Vilfredo Pareto, the acknowledged leader and champion of the movement, to study economic problems.

Although Pareto started as a mathematician and an engineer and was thus naturally inclined toward a mathematical attitude, he was not blindly prejudiced. His whole career exhibits a striving toward the most perfect attainment of truth, so that he does not hesitate, where necessary, to sacrifice former principles and attitudes for the sake of newer and more accurate knowledge. He repeatedly tests the foundations of his mathematical method and is always ready to reconsider as well as to defend it with new arguments.

The basis of his economic attitude may best be illustrated by the following anecdote: Once, during a speech which he was making at a statistical congress in Berne, Pareto spoke of "natural economic laws," whereupon Schmoller, who was present, said that there was no such thing. Pareto said nothing, but smiled and bowed. Afterward he asked Schmoller, through one of his neighbors, whether he was well acquainted with Berne. When Schmoller said yes, Pareto asked him again whether he knew of an inn where one could eat for nothing. The elegant Schmoller is supposed to have looked half pityingly and half disdainfully at the modestly dressed Pareto—although he was known to be well off—and to have answered that there were plenty of cheap restaurants, but that one had to pay something everywhere. At which Pareto said: "Les lois naturelles de l'économie politique, les voilà."

A general economic law may be easily derived from the fact that food is nowadays prepared only for a consideration. We could, if so desired, interpret this as a law of nature. Every economic investigation involves the recognition of certain economic laws. For—according to Pareto—we bring certain phenomena A, B, and C . . . into relation with certain other phenomena A′, B′, C′. Why especially with these, and not with A″, B″, C″? The reason is that we consider the relationship *a priori* as determined by law. Any further investigation makes an unconscious and spontaneous use of mathematical deduction. In addition to the systematic works, which we shall mention later, Pareto has developed and defended his ideas in a number of small and large treatises [2] which were later collected in one volume.[3]

The influence which the methodological views of Pantaleoni and Pareto exerted even in France is not generally appreciated. In the latest edition of his history of economics in collaboration with Charles Rist and in his contribution [4] to the publication in honor of Brentano, Charles Gide complains that Cournot and Walras have been especially ignored in their own country.[5] We shall now mention the works of some of the younger French economists who have been ardent promoters of the mathematical method.

At the beginning of the century, we find the essay of Émile Bouvier [6] who, while admitting then that he did not possess the necessary mathematical qualifications himself, was all the more persuasive in bringing others over to his way of thinking. In a notable essay,[7] Charles Rist demands a sharp separation between the various sections of economic theory. For him the chief mistake up to the present has been the tendency to attack all problems according to some one or other of the various methods, with the result that certain elements have had to be distorted in order to fit into the particular Procrustean bed which had been chosen. To avoid this, Rist desires a sharp separation to be made between questions of social ethics and of social law, between theories of social organization and matters of political economy on the one hand, and all those problems of pure theory which are grouped under the head of the mechanism of exchange on the other. For the first class, he accepts the historical and inductive method, but for the second he recommends the mathematical method as it is applied by the Lausanne school.—The dissertation of Pierre Bovens [8] has the same content as the work of Bouvier, but is also mathematically well founded. The Pole, W. L. Zawadawski,[9] tries to justify, in a comprehensive work, the mathematical method chiefly by dogmatic and historical expositions. All these attempts, however, have been surpassed in precision and clarity by the works of the engineer, Jacques Moret,[10] written before the war, in which the author undertakes to defend the mathematical method by every possible means and to dispose systematically of all the objections which have been raised against it. The practician, A. Leroux, demands, in a short pamphlet, a more intensive application of this method through graphical illustrations in university teaching.[11]

These works go to prove that the French were more interested in the mathematical method before the war, than is commonly supposed.

A few isolated mistakes; e. g., that of Professor Sp. C. Haret,[12] who instead of the mathematical explanation uses the laws of pure mechanics, which he tries to apply to sociology and economics, do not change the general situation.

Not even in Italy, where it has been so widely used, has the mathematical method been so extensively discussed, and defended. Luigi Amoroso is about the only follower of Pareto who seizes every opportunity to justify his method.[13]

It was he who so spiritedly refuted the assertion of Pasquale Jannaccone [14] that modern Italian economics was largely degenerating into a servile imitation, even a plagiarism, of Pareto.[15] Like most other followers of the mathematical method, Amoroso knows perfectly well that we can use it to explain only a relatively small amount of economic phenomena, and even then only by observing the utmost abstraction. Vito Volterra sketched rather accurately the boundaries involved in this attitude, at the beginning of the century,[16] and tried to define in his rectorial address what could be expected of the mathematical procedure and what lay outside of its scope.

Most economists will be interested in the efforts of Erminio Juvalta to introduce the mathematical aspect of pure economic theory into ethics,[17] by studying the behavior of a "homo justus" as our theorists had studied the "homo economicus." Domenico Berardi contributes to the spread of the mathematical procedure by studying the purely causal aspect of economic relations.[18] Augusto Graziani, one of the leaders of modern theory who stands outside of the Lausanne school, had stressed the fact, a few years before, that there are economic problems which are not subject to strict causality.[19] Consequently, as we shall see later, he does not expect unusual advantages to result for our science from the mathematical method.

3. *The Non-mathematical Deductive Method*

In Italy the adherents of the mathematical method have been on the whole successful in their struggle for supremacy. Not so in France. Although, as we have seen, the new method had several champions, it still remains in the minority: even today, the leadership belongs to a different kind of abstract-deductive method—the one which had been used by the Physiocrats and the classical school, and which makes use only of verbal expressions, not of mathematical symbols. The reasons for its survival are the same today as they were in the past, as may be seen from the historical and dogmatic literature on the subject. It survives because it corresponds more than any other to the whole structure of French economic life: the Académie des Sciences Morales et Politiques is still the decisive factor in the development of the science; and the other scientific institutions, which cherish and guard orthodoxy with the greatest care, are still flourishing. The foremost leader of this method in the present century was until his death in 1928, Yves Guyot, an old jouster, a redoubtable fighter and to the end a courageous champion of his scientific creed.

His belief in the supremacy of natural economic law recurs like a refrain in all his voluminous writings. The liberalism founded upon it he maintains methodologically against all other tendencies like protectionism, but especially socialism. He maintained his views during the war with iron determination: even in these critical days, he thinks of nothing but the eternal, natural, economic laws, and warns against their being overlooked.[20]

The most important adherent of classical traditions after Guyot is Gustave Schelle, who has also passed away recently. He dealt with questions of method from the liberal point of view, and finally decided against the mathematical method,[21] objecting that it demanded, as a rule, too much abstraction and that certain important economic laws could not possibly be represented by mathematical formulas. In a discussion by the Société d'Economie Politique, which took place in January, 1907, on the modern method of teaching economics, the traditional liberal school again seized the opportunity of formulating their principles with the utmost precision; we might almost say with unbending dogmatism. The reporter, Auguste Béchaux, led the way, and received all possible support from Guyot, who desired to anticipate any objections that might be made by the opponents of the classical school.[22] Less important contributions toward a defence of this view have been made by M. Rouxel,[23] Edmond Villey [24] and Louis Baudin,[25] who attempted to justify it either in connection with distribution, or within the more general framework of liberalistic discussion. In this connection, special mention should be made of the works of Albert Schatz,[26] and of the Italian, Oliviero Zuccarini,[27] who stresses the "eternal" laws of economics. More recently the Russian emigrant Peter Struve [28] has made a thorough historical study of these laws, which he cleverly interprets in the sense of Marxist economic determinism.

Besides the two leading schools of the mathematical and the non-mathematical deductive methods, there are other economists in the Romance countries who, though they show leanings toward one or the other method, maintain their own individuality. Perhaps the most important of these is Graziani, whose psychological attitude is most closely akin to the Austrian school of marginal utility. There is also a small group of Italian theorists who lie somewhere between the modern mathematical attitude and conservative classicism.

Camillo Supino recognizes the existence of economic laws, but is emphatic in stating that they are not of mathematical precision.[29] According to him, there are differences of time and place in economic life, which should be taken into account by theorists. Vincenzo Tangorra attacks the problem of subjective or objective economics. Although he defends the subjectivism of the Austrian school, he recognizes also the value of some of the views of the more objective classical and mathematical economics.[30] The sociologist, Roberto Michels, has recently tried to determine the bounds of psychological investigation in economics by comparing it with the objective attitude.[31] We may finally mention Ghino Valenti with his attitude of independent criticism midway between the mathematical and the classical methods.[32]

4. Logical and Epistemological Attempts

Another group of writers bury themselves in studies of logic and epistemology which tend more or less toward a criticism of the classical as well as of the mathematical school. The most penetrating of these is François Simiand, who tries to lay the foundations of a modern "positive" method of economic investigation.[33] According to him, the chief methods of our science are all in some way normative and finalistic. They are interested merely in the relationship of the means to the end. The classical school, for example, concerns itself with the way to the greatest wealth, by the best method of distribution, etc.; and even the mathematical school has in mind, in the theory of equilibrium, a postulate which it tries to realize. Simiand, on the other hand, endeavors to comprehend economic life only from the point of view of cause and effect and gives a purely causal explanation of economic phenomena. It is easy to recognize in this "positive" method, an echo of Max Weber's postulate of freedom from value judgments. We shall see later how Simiand's idea of causality is entirely different from that which we have noticed above in connection with the mathematical method, as for instance with Berardi.

The same tendency, leading to somewhat different results, is found in the studies of the Italian, Emanuele Sella, which were published at about the same time as the investigations of Weber.[34] Under the influence of Pantaleoni, he dismisses from the field of pure theory all value judgments, but allows them some space in applied economics so long as they do not go beyond the measure of purely economic, i. e. not also moral, postulates. His attitude toward economic laws is that they have only a relative or logical importance but no absolute validity. Sella has also made other important methodological studies in which there is expressed his organic conception of economics.[35]

The critical studies of Guido de Ruggiero [36] are based upon an inadequate acquaintance with modern economics and a dissatisfaction with its results, which is not sufficiently well grounded. He does not go beyond a somewhat nebulous demand for a better logical foundation of our science. In a similar vein but, owing to post-war conditions, with somewhat more justification, Charles Bodin thinks that the loftiest aim of economics consists in ascertaining the means whereby the sufferings of mankind may be diminished and their productivity increased.[37]

Léopold Leseine has accomplished a useful work in trying to establish the logical limits within which the different economic theories supplement each other and contribute toward an integral whole.[38] He omits in his historical survey the critical parts of each doctrine and tries to bring their positive contributions into harmony with each other. His ideas were well received, and even induced Guyot to write an especial study of method, in which he merely develops the principles which we have already mentioned.[39] In an essay written with the collaboration of Louis Suret,[40] Leseine gave a short description of the mathematical requirements that are necessary for a comprehension of the theories of the mathematical school.

5. *The Statistical and the Historical-Inductive Viewpoints*

In the present century the statistical method has come to be held in increasing regard in France and in Italy by economists of all complexions. It is a kind of neutral zone where the most different minds may meet and work in peace. The most important students of this method are Rodolfo Benini [41] and Lucien March.[42]

The former tries to make use of the results of the statistical method for economics even from a mathematical point of view, whereas the latter is especially interested in pointing out the limits up to which this method can be at all relevant, i. e., useful. Jacques Rueff has recently called economics a statistical science in which theoretical laws can be applied only to a majority of isolated individuals living next to each other; whereas the economic life of an organic whole can be studied only by means of the statistical method.[43]

We come now to those students in the Romance countries, who are well disposed toward the historical-inductive method and whose methodological views lie somewhere between it and the deductive method.

Examples of these are Maurice Defourny,[44] and Roberto Murray.[45] The former is of a compromising disposition, and seeks—although somewhat obscurely—to bring about an understanding between the leading methods in our science. The latter, although an ardent adherent of the Lausanne school, narrows the scope of the mathematical method and assigns to the historical-inductive method the leading place in economics.

Even G. H. Bousquet gives the historical attitude its due, although his views are largely molded by those of Pareto.[46] Emilo Cossa,[47] who has evidently more than his name in common with the great Italian economist of the 19th century, is an extreme critic of the abstract deductive methods in his varied writings.

Another critic of the abstract method is Achille Loria, one of the most distinguished figures in the recent development of our science. His numerous works represent the historical attitude, although he holds no brief for an unrestrained relativism, such as Schmoller, in the criticism of economic phenomena. In his methodology, Loria is influenced by sociological rather than by epistemological considerations and he makes an unusual synthesis of historical materialism [48] and an idealistic conception of the ends of all sciences.[49] This is the explanation of his attitude toward method; the insistence on differences of time and place in all socio-economic phenomena, while recognizing certain historical laws of society.[50] His attitude in this question is perhaps most closely related to that of the older historical school in Germany, especially to the methodological doctrines of Roscher and Hildebrand.

In France too we find a few more uncompromising adherents of the historical and inductive method. For instance, the historian, Charles Seignobos, in his lectures at the Collège Libre des Sciences Sociales at the turn of the century, attacks every abstract method, whether it be mathematical, biological or psychological and admits only the historical method.[51] Even here he rejects all tendencies to explain everything by a single historical principle, such as race, religion, matter, etc., and demands an historical method which takes cognizance of every phase of cultural development. One of the leading adherents of the historical method in France, which is disappearing, is Henri Hauser, who has tried to defend it in numerous writings.[52] His methodological thoughts, however, are only too prone to merge into considerations of practical politics, whereby he attacks the classical school not only in its scientific method, but also in its liberalism, and opposes to it his doctrines of state protectionism. On the whole, however, he stands for a rejection, based upon epistemology, of the laws of nature, and a correspondingly relativistic attitude toward the phenomena of economic life. The Belgian Guillaume de Greef [53] has attacked the abstract method just as vigorously with his "myth of the economic man" and his "Robinsonades." Relying upon certain ideas of Comte, he tries to consider economic life only from an historical and sociological point of view, partly placing it in the historical stream of development and partly bringing it into close connection with its juristic, political and general social environment until in this shape it has again become a proper subject for investigation. In his remarks on the theory of distribution, he has developed his pious methodological intentions in a somewhat unsatisfactory manner.

Arturo Labriola exhibits certain similarities with the method of Loria. While in the latter, the sociological aspect, historical materialism, is only of secondary importance, it is the chief thing with Labriola, and his disquisitions on method are placed entirely at the service of his general socialistic doctrines. To the abstract, rationalistic attitude, which has developed steadily from Quesnay to Pareto, he wishes to oppose a realistic, historical and social attitude. He transfers the center of gravity from here into the criticism of the individualistic and liberal attitude, which is generally associated with the deductive method and he hastens at once to attack it from the point of view of his socialism.[54]

6. *The Influence of Sociological Tendencies*

The methodological tendencies of the last-named writers lead us to a further group of economists who work entirely with sociology and who wish to apply the principles of method which they have acquired in that broader field to the more special one of political economy. To begin with, we must again refer to the work of Simiand, in which the sociological ideas of Émile Durkheim (published at the end of the last century) find their most mature expression for economic method. The purely causal concept of economics, which has been discussed above, is only one half of the demands which Simiand makes upon what he considers the only "positive" method. According to the second half of his postulate, it is just as important that it be from the start social; i. e., it must examine economic phenomena only in their social connections, in order to get a correct picture. Consequently Simiand rejects every kind of abstract procedure in so far as it is connected with an hypothetical isolation. In his comparison of concomitant variations, taken from Durkheim, i. e., in his comparative study of the relations between economic phenomena and their various accompanying phenomena, certain points of similarity appear with the method of Richard Ehrenberg. We may add that Ehrenberg found an enthusiastic adherent in France in the person of Maurice Bellom.

Of the followers of Durkheim, after Simiand, we may mention René Maunier, who tried in a promising opening work[55] to state systematically the relations between economic phenomena and all other fields of human endeavor, which he considers the proper field of sociology. He too comes to the conclusion that these various fields of endeavor should not be separated from each other in scientific research and consequently that the only correct method in economics is one which is socially directed. Arthur Bochard attempts to reconcile the teachings of Durkheim with those of Gabriel Tarde in the field of economic method, by adapting to the system of Durkheim certain elements of Tarde's interpsychological sociology—the socially important factors of invention and imitation, adaptation and repetition—and by utilizing his results for the method he advocates in economics.[56] The sociologist, René Worms, too, stresses the importance which a sociological attitude can have for the development of our science: it broadens our horizon, and places all the well-known facts in a new and truer light.[57] For the time being, Worms is decidedly against the deductive method. According to him we should content ourselves with the inductive method, within which he enjoins the statistical and monographic procedure for the immediate environment—the ethnographical for the countries which are not yet quite civilized, and the historical for distant epochs. Émile Worms, an older writer probably related not only in thought to René Worms, suggests a closer union of economics with sociology, even in university teaching.[58]

In Italian literature we may mention the interesting attempts of Benedetto Croce, at the beginning of the century, to arrive at a satisfactory solution of the problem of economic method from the point of view of sociology. He starts with a criticism of Marxian historical materialism,[59] which he considers but a partial explanation of social development, and then makes a sharp distinction between the moral and the purely economic theory, having established a few years before the principle of *de gustibus non est disputandum* for economics,[60] by stressing which Sombart later created such a sensation at the Vienna meeting of the Verein für Sozialpolitik. Croce discovers the first principle of pure economics in constantly following an egoism which is independent of all moral considerations, whereby he necessarily reaches a subjective attitude toward economic phenomena. This leads him into a heated discussion against the objective attitude of Pareto and consequently against the mathematical method in general, his objection being that it can offer at best only a more or less imperfect representation but never at the same time also an explanation of socio-economic relationships.

7. *General Tendencies in the Development of Method*

The various procedures which we have mentioned above,—the mathematical, the unmathematically deductive, the "positive," the statistical, the historically inductive and the sociological,—have been the chief tendencies in the development of French and Italian economics in the first quarter of the twentieth century. It is a program which is rich in material and which is not so easily to be summarized. Its manifold variety is increased by the fact that the types, as we have had ample opportunity to notice, are represented in their purest state by only a few writers. Most economists stand somewhere in the middle between two or even more of these main tendencies and, owing to their eclecticism, show marked differences from one another. This very eclecticism, however, brings about by degrees a reconciliation of the various methods, and the scholars gradually agree as to what may be expected from this or that method for the furtherance of our science. In this way a division of labor is attained, whereby the different methods become parts of a larger entity, developing systematically, in which they meet, no longer in a spirit of enmity but in more or less friendly and peaceful integration. If one wishes to discover the position of the opposing forces, it would appear that the chief tendency, in France as well as in Italy, is the steadily increasing predominance of the mathematical method, whereas the purely historical method is slowly losing ground. Between these opposite poles, the positive, the statistical and the social methods hold their own with tenacity.

8. *No Innovations in the Systematization of Economics*

No worth-while discussions about the systematization of the economic sciences have taken place in France or in Italy since the beginning of the century, nor has a new branch of our science appeared. The development continues in more or less fixed grooves, and the science is not in such a perpetual state of ferment as we have noticed in the German-speaking countries. We shall touch later upon the various attempts at reform with reference to the systematic arrangement of the individual groups of problems within economic theory. The weak skirmish which takes place in Italy over the closer union of the "Ragioneria" (corresponding approximately to what is called in America business economics) with economic theory, has not been able to claim the attention of broader scientific circles.[61] Gino Aria published during the war a thorough and theoretically well-grounded system of business economics, which appeared as an independent *Economia commerciale*,[62] a separate science which corresponds to the newer and similar book of the Frenchman, P. Clerget.[63] The validity of this was as little discussed from the point of view of system as the similar, though much more modest, attempt of V. Tosi to build a system of Industrial Economics,[64] a theory of industry based on private economics. Exhaustive researches have also been made in problems of world economics, and the World War has given birth in the Romance countries to some excellent studies of its economic aspects; but no one dreams of maintaining the validity of an independent world or war economics. Neither the French nor the Italian mind has any disposition for discussions which deal only with the method and systematization of the sciences.

CHAPTER II

SYSTEMATIC IDEAS

In the first quarter of our century both France and Italy have been fairly productive of new theoretical systems. The very variety of the leading methodological tendencies was bound to bring forth a large body of doctrines which attempt to embrace systematically the whole of economics from the point of view of one particular method. It is largely through the power of logical persuasion and the scientific success of these systems that the method which underlies them finds its relative position in the struggle with others.

1. System of the Lausanne School

Undoubtedly the most important recent economic development in the Latin countries has been the mathematical school. It had received a rich inheritance from the writings of Walras and, later, of Pantaleoni in the closing decades of the nineteenth century and henceforth it was merely a question of managing and increasing this inheritance worthily. The man who appeared for this task, Vilfredo Pareto, accomplished a highly important work. The course of his development went first from mathematical studies to theoretical economics, which he began by treating quite dogmatically. Besides the strictly abstract and mathematical character of his pure economic doctrine, liberalism appeared to him in his *Cours d'économie politique* (1896) as an incontrovertible dogma which no one must touch. Later on, he devoted himself more than ever to the analysis of economic phenomena, thus separating himself still further from the great facts of real social life. His intellect, however, was too honest not to perceive this soon, so that the second half of his development is taken up in recovering the way to a knowledge of actual social-economic phenomena. He devotes his attention more and more to other fields of social life outside the realm of pure economics and tries to find out, with an increasing range, how his economic man behaves in other social relationships—how for instance the other half of his being, *homo ethicus*, influences his actions. This course can be clearly seen in the last two decades of Pareto's activity until finally, during the World War, he published the crowning achievement of his studies, his great sociology.[1] Indeed, a great deal remained for Pareto to do. His economic theory, which appeared before his sociology but logically follows it, should have been brought into closer relationship and in full harmony with it. To other fields also, namely, to the theory of finance, Pareto intended to apply the results of his sociological investigations for their further development. But fate did not grant him this, for in 1922 he died.

Notwithstanding the looseness of Pareto's whole system, and its consequent lack of temporal sequence, we shall, even in a short survey of his economic doctrines, deal first with the principles of his general sociology. This is all the more necessary since its chief ideas are clearly to be found, although in an undeveloped form, in his earlier works. The first thing is to distinguish in human actions the unlogical ones—those which cannot be referred to reason, and in which beliefs and feeling predominate—from the logical ones, in which the means tend in an orderly way toward a goal. Pareto then analyses clearly the inner workings of these various activities and their influence on human culture and attains in this way, by synthesizing the results of his study, a theory of social equilibrium. By this he understands the equalization of all forces which operate in social life and of the obstacles which hinder them; an equilibrium that not only is static, but also appears, in the process of social evolution, as dynamic. Throughout this whole process of thought one can detect a flirtation with historical materialism.

That which corresponds to this conception of general social life in Pareto's economic theory is the central doctrine of economic equilibrium, which is supposed to explain immediately all those phenomena about which economic theory has up to the present been totally in the dark or else turning helplessly in a circle. Here too economic forces such as wants are opposed by obstacles, such as the wants of others just as in commercial life production and consumption, in the distribution of goods the prices on the labor market and those on the produce market, have a tendency to remain in constant equilibrium. Walras had already used this idea of a tendency toward equilibrium to explain the most important social-economic relationships and Pareto's merit is to have comprehended it more exactly, to have enlarged its horizon by applying it to the interplay of mere desires and obstacles and to have used it in certain fields of economic life which Walras had not analysed mathematically to a sufficient extent. According to the last point of view the most important facts to be considered are the theories of production, of international trade and of foreign exchange, all of which Pareto endeavored to develop with reference to the principle of economic equilibrium.

In his chief economic work, the *Manuale*,[2] Pareto offers us a complete theoretical system based upon these principles, which differs from the above-mentioned *Cours* (published ten years before) not only in arrangement, but also in a few leading ideas. Pareto refers to his own previous work in the introduction and readily admits that he is not in a position to prove empirically the sole validity of liberalism of which he had formerly been such an ardent advocate. Fundamentally, even in this work his theories are based upon the idea of marginal utility but, in order to avoid a disturbing ambiguity of expression, he coins the word "ophelimity" for subjective utility. Whereas in the *Cours* he still looks upon the ophelimity which has reference to a particular good and to a particular moment as a certain magnitude, in the *Manuale* he merely retains the assumption that the individual can judge at any time which of two or more goods gives him the greatest ophelimity. In order to throw more light on wants, Pareto also makes use of the curves of indifference which he found in Edgeworth and then develops, principally with their help, his individual theories. In his exposition he makes use to a high degree—as we have already said—of mathematical signs; although in his restless efforts to attain the truth in economic life, he occasionally employs other methods as well. It would do Pareto an injustice to accuse him of methodological bias or narrowness.

Although Pareto's system made a great impression on scientific circles in Italy and France, it was followed by no such discussion as we have noticed after the publication of important systems in German science. His adherents, as for instance, Luigi Amoroso,[3] burst into torrents of praise of the master's work and try to comment and enlarge upon his individual theses, whereas more distant economists, as for instance Vito Volterra,[4] at most merely point out a few holes in his theory. The Frenchman G. H. Bousquet is the one who deals most thoroughly with the doctrines of Pareto. Although he brings out all the merits of the master, he cannot suppress some qualms with reference to his excessive use of the mathematical procedure.[5] The recent criticism of U. Spirito is directed especially against Pareto's social-philosophical views.[6] Besides these writers, even the adherents of partly opposed tendencies are somewhat reserved in their objections against Pareto, as we have already mentioned when speaking of Benedetto Croce. This can be traced back to the extraordinary importance of Pareto's work, before which even his enemies had to bow.

Pareto's influence is felt in the compact, but for that reason all the more substantive, system of Enrico Barone.[7] In the arrangement of his material, as well as in his mathematical exposition he follows his master, though he is able at the same time to advance some original ideas in his concise synthesis.

If purely theoretical discussions play a considerably more important role in Pareto's system than the presentation of actual facts, this is still more the case with Barone. He emphasizes the fact, however, that his work although meant as a text-book can only be considered by such readers to whom the necessary factual material is already known. As with Pareto, his central doctrine is the theory of economic equilibrium and it is from this aspect that he undertakes to determine the rules to be observed in the various divisions of economic life. The best parts of his book are the fifth and the sixth where he offers an explanation of the formation of prices under producers' monopolies, as is the case in an age of modern trusts and combinations, and where he analyses economic crises. Here he starts with a searching criticism of the doctrines of Rodbertus and Marx and tries to explain the periodically recurring crises through the cyclical movement which results from the temporarily uneven possibility of a corresponding investment of savings. Unfortunately the formal structure of Barone's work is far below its intellectual level in excellence. This is the only reason why it has not attained the popularity which it really deserves for its scientific merits.

In a similar frame, with the same intentions and, we can add, with a success not far below that of Barone, A. Roberto Murray published a small systematic survey of the main problems of economic theory.[8] We have mentioned above how Murray, in the course of his methodological studies, clearly recognized how narrow was the field in which mathematics could be applied. In this narrow field, however, he moves all the more surely. Relying on Pareto's theory of equilibrium he deals not only with the questions treated by Barone but throws light especially on the problem of credit and a few difficult points of international trade in which he attempts a solution from the unitary point of view of the economic equilibrium. After the war Murray published his system in French in a considerably augmented form.[9] Luigi Amoroso, in his university lectures, made a successful attempt to create a compact theoretical system out of the principles of the Lausanne school.[10] He too is one of those adherents of the mathematical school who never forget what is to be expected from their method and where those economic problems begin in the study and solution of which other methods must be employed. He makes independent contributions to the theory of economic equilibrium especially through a careful and delicate working in of the time-element with respect to problems of equilibrium. To this is joined his analysis of interest based on the same principles. No less interesting is his analysis of value as well as his theory of consumer's equilibrium and producer's equilibrium, the scientific importance of which has been recognized by authorities such as Edgeworth.[11] Amoroso has recently had an interesting discussion with Ugo Broggi, which turned around fundamental aspects of the mathematical theory of the Lausanne school.[12]

The outline of E. Caesari,[13] which keeps fairly close to Walras, is remarkable for its clear and concise formulation of ideas. Next to a faithful reproduction of the theories of the Lausanne school he lays the most stress on those problems of economics which have not been exhaustively treated by this school. For instance, by means of his mathematical procedure he advances a theory of international exchange rates which is more far-reaching than Pareto's. The one disturbing element in his work is the fact that through discussing separate goods, utility, wants, etc., both in general and again in the specific manifestations of these categories there is necessarily much repetition and unevenness. A short mention should also be made of the *Lectures* of Gustavo del Vecchio.[14] In these lectures too we find a complete mathematical system of economics in the manner of the Lausanne school, in which the attempt is made to solve every economic problem by means of the one cardinal principle: that of economic equilibrium. The fact that because of this attempt the problems of static and dynamic economics, so different in themselves, are intertwined and offered as a unit, strikes the reader occasionally as somewhat artificial and doctrinaire. The chief strength of Vecchio lies in the union of Walras's and Pareto's ideas with the results of modern American theoretical investigation as well as in his consistent regard for the facts of economic life. Thus he is able to harmonize with his system the problems of applied economics. Politically del Vecchio leans to government interference in economic life.

Contemporary French literature does not lack concise summaries of the teachings of the Lausanne school. First in point of view of time is the pamphlet containing the lectures that Hermann Laurent delivered at the technical high school in Paris. In this booklet, published at the beginning of the century, he claims to keep in mind not so much the usual literary point of view but above all a scientific one.[15] In sixty pages Laurent undertakes to offer not only a solution of the problems of pure economics, but in addition his views on a series of questions of organization, even on evolution, civilization, population, public education, socialism, etc. He is naturally compelled to express his views quite apodictically and generally without the slightest proof of their validity, a fault that impairs the scientific quality which he intended. We really do not know what to make out of the statement in which he laconically declares that he is theoretically a socialist, a collectivist, an opponent of nationalism, but practically a liberal, and a good patriot. Nevertheless, the attempt to keep as close as possible to Walras and to Pareto, which appears in the subtitle, is very evident here. The Lausanne professor, Boninsegni, blames Laurent especially for behaving as a mathematician rather than as an economist and for having sorely neglected the specific economic points of view through a kind of "chrematistic" bias.[16] A few years later Boninsegni himself issued a concise Handbook,[17] in which he deals more thoroughly and scientifically but with considerably less clarity and acuteness than did Laurent with the theories based on economic equilibrium and on the principle of ophelimity.[18] The system of E. Antonelli, is less independent, but more useful.[19] He goes back to the teachings of Walras and sets himself the task of giving a clear exposition of the main tenets of that scholar, defending them in their original form against newer interpretations. He retains Walras's assumption of an independent standard of subjective utility, a somewhat shaky hypothesis, which has meanwhile been successfully criticized by American theorists and, as we have already mentioned, also by Pareto. Contrary to most of the mathematicians whom we have already named Antonelli limits himself to problems of pure economics in the narrower sense: exchange, production, distribution, credit and circulation of wealth. For this he presupposes individual responsibility and perfectly free competition. More recently Antonelli showed himself especially anxious to lay a proper philosophical and theoretical foundation for a more elaborate development of his system.[20] His attempts at a realistic, historical social exposition are quite successful. The Lausanne idea of economic equilibrium lies also as the heart of the system [21] in which F. Divisia tries to develop the traditional economic theory by adding to it a further equation between the quantity of money and the exchange of goods, somewhat like the well-known formula of Irving Fisher. Although he makes ample use of the mathematical method, Divisia also points out the limits beyond which more is to be expected from other methods.

2. *Eclectically built Abstract-deductive Theories*

We cannot sufficiently praise the small book in which Bernard Lavergne boldly sketches a system of economic theory.[22] Of the Lausanne school he retains only a few more formal viewpoints. On the whole, he relies upon the pure theory of marginal utility, and tries to work out its principles in every problem of economic theory. Besides a few original ideas, to which we shall return later, the clever structure of Lavergne's system is especially noteworthy, since through it he gives us an entirely individualistic continuation of the main tenets of the Lausanne school. He tries to deal with the phenomena of economic life according to different markets, such as the market for consumption goods, the gold and credit markets, the producers' market (raw materials, labor, circulating capital, etc.), or the market of "capitaux producteurs," by which he means fixed capital: land, buildings, machinery, etc. This last market is governed by the principle of differential utility or of absorption of excess profits, according to which all savings which are made possible by production are absorbed in the rent. If Ricardo's theory of rent is noticeable here, Lavergne tries to bring the rest of his work into close contact with the most modern results of psychological economics as well as into harmony with the position of the Lausanne school.

Entirely different from these slight systematic surveys is the imposing system published by Léon Clément Colson, professor at the École des Ponts et Chaussées.[23] First of all we can see, if only from its outward appearance, that it is by far the most comprehensive economic system published in France in the present century. Colson's position is essentially different from that of the other adherents of the mathematical method which we have mentioned. He descends from the liberal school of French economics and remains on the whole, however much he may make use of mathematical exposition, an adherent of classical economics. He considers the mathematical method useful for exposition only and not, as the Lausanne school does, as a method of investigation. He tries to reach his theoretical conclusions through simple deductive processes of thought and then translates these conclusions into geometrical form, in order to make them more intelligible. Substantively, too, his theories are nearer to classical views than to modern tendencies: his theory of value is based on Adam Smith. He is closest to Marshall of modern economists, especially in his theory of price, although he claims not to have known the Englishman's theories when he wrote his book. Undoubtedly the influence of Leroy-Beaulieu is evident, as well in the treatment of individual questions of theory as in a great part of Colson's views on economic policy.

Only the first volume of his work deals with pure economic theory. The other five volumes take up questions of practical economics, including public finance. They contain a wealth of factual data, part of which is of interest only for technical teaching. This is especially true of the last volume where questions of transportation are treated with great thoroughness and knowledge of the facts. The leading aspect of Colson's work is its liberalism, the principles of which he developed also in a separate work,[24] although he did not cast it in a stiff dogmatic form.

He shows much acuteness as well as party spirit in his attacks on government interference, but in certain questions such as protection of workers he realizes the necessity of moderate state legislation.

After the *Manuale* of Pareto, the most important system in modern Italian economic theory is the well-known comprehensive text book of Augusto Graziani.[25] It stands below Pareto's work from the points of view of profundity and originality. His intention to write a text book has occasionally prevented him from going to the root of certain problems and a certain eclecticism, although in the best sense of that word, is very evident in his work. He is not even so partial to the mathematical method as Colson, for although he recognizes its validity he has a poor opinion of the services which it has already rendered to economics or which one may expect from it for the future. He believes that even the most abstract theories can be expressed in ordinary speech just as well as in mathematical formulas and more simply. Graziani is today one of the most distinguished representatives of the theory of marginal utility as expounded by Menger and Böhm-Bawerk. In certain problems, however, he willingly resorts to the classical school, in which cases it would be hard not to recognize the influence of Marshall. Thus in his theory of value he is impressed by the idea of a kind of natural or normal value which is to be referred to the greatest costs of production, i.e., to the costs of marginal producer. Although we find in Graziani's work a few other similar attempts to synthesize old and new theories, he is as a rule interested in the most modern problems of economic theory in which he exhibits unusual knowledge and skill. Especially noteworthy is the way in which he applies the idea of marginal utility to his theories of production and distribution, thus making a valuable contribution to our science. Graziani follows the classical system in the arrangement of his system, starting, after a preliminary exposition of the function of economics, with the theory of production, going through the circulation of wealth to the theory of distribution, and ending with a study of the technical side of commercial life. He claims to be an adherent of liberalism though at times he seems to join to it certain tendencies toward socio-political ideas.

The works of Colson and Graziani lead us to consider those new systems which stand between modern theory and the doctrines of the classical school. Viewing on the one hand his mathematical method of exposition and on the other the general tendencies of his teachings, Colson really belongs to this group and even Graziani discloses certain endeavors to unite these two tendencies. Perhaps the most fruitful inherent union of classical theory and the modern school of marginal utility is to be found in the systematic outline of Camillo Supino.[26]

Supino exhibits a conscious eclecticism by trying to give a systematic survey of the latest results in all the different schools of economic investigation. In his views on economic policy he is inclined to be a professorial socialist; for the solution of some of the problems belonging to practical economics he uses the results of the historical school; whereas in theoretical questions, with which most of his books deals, his position midway between the classical and the modern psychological schools is most evident. In his theory of value, for instance, he is an adherent of the latter, whereas in his theory of wages he is influenced, with certain limitations, by the classical wage-fund theory. Noteworthy is his attempt to derive the validity of the *lex minimi* for economics from the feeling of pain associated with work and effort.

This idea, somewhat differently presented is one of the first principles of the system which Ghino Valenti [27] published two years later. With him the principle of hedonism becomes the law of *tornaconto* which he makes the basis of his theory of production: the producer endeavors to secure the greatest possible return or, in other words, to attain the greatest possible producer's surplus. Valenti deals with this theory and with others, such as that of wants, of economic goods, etc., in the first part of his work, which is devoted to problems of "individual economics." This treats of questions of isolated individual economics, as well as of those which arise from the special relationships between society and the individual. In the second part, value, price, circulation of goods, distribution, etc., are studied as phenomena of social economics. Whereas Supino tends more toward the Austrian school Valenti, in so far as he takes stock of modern theory, is closer to Pantaleoni and the Lausanne school. For instance, he uses certain elements of the theory of economic equilibrium, which he applies especially to his explanation of price.

While the modern parts predominate in the system of Supino, in the case of Valenti they are overshadowed by the classical school. As an example, he explains value quite according to the classical pattern by the cost of production, and in distribution he is unable to accept the modern theory of imputation. Consequently he attacks the mathematical school on many points. This provoked numerous answers; e. g., that of Umberto Ricci [28] who blames Valenti for decrying the mathematical method although he recognizes his contribution to science.

More recently G. H. Bousquet has outlined a system [29] which exhibits an attempt to form a logical union of the Lausanne tenets with the results of the Austrian school of marginal utility; even the many years which he devoted to fathoming Pareto's viewpoints could not induce him to become an adherent of the pure mathematical attitude. In addition, Bousquet is inclined to diminish the importance of pure theory in relation to the other parts of economic science. He thinks, for instance, that the theory of applied economics should be taught before pure theory.

C. Bodevelle has had little success with his attempt to mediate between the old and the new theories. In an original, but quite inadequate, systematic frame he places the theory of division of labor in the foreground, develops a subjective theory of value and, in questions of economic policy, claims to be an interventionist.

3. *The Classical Liberal Group in France*

In Italy, the doctrines of the classical school have been able to hold their own only by remaining in close connection with modern theories. The case is different in France where, besides defences of the unmathematical method, the new century has seen some remarkable systems of economics which are almost entirely based on classical theory.

First of all we must mention the new editions of the works of Paul Leroy-Beaulieu,[30] and of Yves Guyot,[31] which were first published in the last century. In these the natural laws of classical economic theory appear in their perfect, original form. The more uncompromising is Guyot who mercilessly attacks all forms of socialism and government interference, whereas Leroy-Beaulieu has some respect for the historical method and in certain questions makes concessions to government interference. He does not wish to be associated with any school and recognizes only Adam Smith as his master. At the beginning of the century Gustave de Molinari published as a defence of the fundamental principles of liberal and individualistic economics a few works which did not embrace the whole field of the science, and in his last book [32] he again expounds his principles, defended during two generations, and this time applied to modern questions: "Presque arrivé aux limites de la vie humaine—je suis maintenant dans ma 92e année—je vais publier mon dernier ouvrage. Il concerne tout ce qui a rempli ma vie: la liberté des échanges et la paix . . ." Another enthusiastic defender of economic liberalism is the Italian, Luigi Einaudi, in some of his rather unsystematic works.[33] Einaudi's chief contributions lie, however, in the field of public finance.

Among the more important new systems, also classical and liberal, which have appeared in France in the last twenty-five years, we must mention first in point of time the work of Octave Noël,[34] a professor at the École des Hautes Études Commerciales. He is a faithful adherent, in his whole intellectual complexion, of the school of Bastiat. He refers all economic evils to an ignorance and neglect of the eternal economic laws which the classical school recognized and which he tries to present in a new light. Nevertheless he relies upon thorough historical investigations and he has gathered together a goodly store of factual data. He is also able to make his demands for the protection of labor harmonize in theory with his consistent liberalism.

Two other professors, a Parisian, Henri Truchy,[35] and one from Brussels, Maurice Ansiaux,[36] published after the war systems which belong to the classical liberal school. Both retain certain elements of the theory of marginal utility, especially to explain economic value. This is, however, only a forced concession to modern theoretical tendencies and both writers hurry back to protect themselves behind the walls of classical thought.

Truchy compresses the theoretical part of his work to a minimum: the most important problems are disposed of in one or two pages; a few words suffice for an explanation of supply and demand as well as for the formation of prices; whereas he plunges into hundreds of pages over problems of practical economics. The whole value of the book lies in the amount of data which he has amassed. Truchy has also worked out with remarkable care the role of capital in production and he has successfully emphasized the relation of distribution of income to the formation of prices. His liberalism is by no means dogmatic: at times he allows other attitudes full scope, and he is especially partial to the ideas of Gide of whose system, to be mentioned later, Truchy's work often reminds us, even in its outward form. Ansiaux goes considerably deeper into the study of theoretical problems, and the thorough methodological foundation of his system is especially successful. He tries to build his theoretical structure on a secure foundation from the psychological, technical and legal points of view as well as from a profitable study of a few questions of economic organization. The fine distinctions which he draws in discussing the interplay between supply and demand and the elasticity of these two factors is of lasting scientific value. In general, his theoretical system is characterized by a constant realistic trait: he is always trying to illustrate his theories from the social point of view and to make them harmonize with the experience of practical economic life.

4. *Rationalistic Systems without Theories of Value*

Before we go on to those economic systems which exhibit even more realistic traits, so that the deductive method is almost displaced, we shall deal briefly with a few attempts which are indeed far removed from classical theory in essence but which, owing to their rationalistic strain, possess some close points of contact with it. The concise system which Alberto Zorli published at the beginning of the century [37] remained almost unnoticed, in spite of the high reputation which the author enjoys among Italian scientists. The original and noteworthy ideas of the work have suffered from the unusual form in which they were couched. Zorli comes from the study of public finance and, true to his general theories, tries to form out of this field a principle for the explanation of all economic activity. He considers state finance a great cooperative undertaking characterized by compulsion, in the management of which the balancing of assets and liabilities appears as in any private enterprise. The undertaking, or the business, is the final irreducible social unit for economics as well as for theoretical research. Economic theory, therefore, has to deal not with aggregates of goods but always with aggregates of persons and goods and it should study the interactions of these: the manner in which an asset or a liability arises for private undertakings and for the sum of these constitutes political economy. In this framework, there is no place for the traditional theory of value, which is replaced by a theory of "economic convenience."

The founder of the theory of economic convenience, which

Zorli uses in place of value and which we shall discuss more fully later, is Ulisse Gobbi. Whereas Zorli endeavored at the beginning of the century to work this theory into a system which covered all of economic theory, Gobbi did not publish till after the World War a system based upon this doctrine.[38]

In his comprehensive work, Gobbi expounds his own independent system, which is quite different from the one usually followed by the French and Italians and which closely resembles that of German textbooks. He emphasizes especially, and has a preference for, questions of private economics and law and neglects the historical aspect in his entire exposition. In the first part, which deals with pure abstract theory and makes use of the mathematical method, he develops above all his fundamental principle of economic convenience and supplies an introduction which is thoroughly methodological, analysing the fundamental concepts of economics. Next come the theories of price and distribution, in which the various kinds of income are referred to the mechanism of demand and supply. Not till the second part of his work does he bring in the social environment and the aspects of practical economics and in this he starts with a discussion of questions of organization and of problems of political economics. This arrangement engenders a certain amount of repetition: the same problem is sometimes treated theoretically in the first part of the work and practically in the second. Socially Gobbi claims to be a mutualist.

Like Zorli and Gobbi, the Frenchman, Charles Bodin,[39] has dismissed the theory of value from his system. He still holds to the concept of value but assigns to it a very subordinate place. He declares war on the theory of marginal utility as well as on the classical theory, reproaching the former for confusing the concepts of utility and desirability and the latter for not distinguishing sufficiently between the pure psychological concept of value and objective economic relationships of exchange. His system is based on a theory of exchange of which the starting point is the assumption of an equilibrium between the mutual advantages of the exchanging parties.

As we have already remarked, he considers economics the science of the working of human endeavors and in this light he tries to arrange the concepts of economics with the help of a new and difficult terminology and arrangement. Although he goes about it in the most abstract way, he is of the opinion that our science is in the last analysis teleological and practical in character. We shall have to wait for the publication of the second volume of Bodin's work in order to judge the value of his views. Those which have appeared so far are principally morphological and methodological. We shall then be able to see how far he succeeds in using the extremely difficult ideas of this "économie simple," to explain the complicated phenomena of real economic life: with these he intends to deal under the title of "économie complexe."

5. *The After-Effects of Historical Relativism*

Among the systems which stand between classical deduction and historical relativism, we may mention those of Camille Perreau [40] and Bertrand Nogaro.[41]

Perreau is still very much influenced by classical theory. He recognizes the validity of most of its laws but uses these in his system only insofar as they seem to throw light on the phenomena of practical economic life. As regards the remainder his attitude is thoroughly realistic and consequently he always studies the problem of economics from their historical and practical social side. On the whole Perreau claims to be a liberal. In certain cases, however, he makes use of induction, and points out the natural and social factors which justify, for instance, agrarian or industrial protection. He does not pretend to offer new and original theories and looks upon his work merely as a text-book. Nogaro stands even closer to realism. He gives his system a broad social basis and resorts to abstract theorems only in case of need and even then, as in his curves of supply and demand, only very cursorily. With reference to the problem of value, in accordance with his realistic social attitude he is interested only in the question of exchange value which he is inclined to solve in a rather objective sense. At the core of his whole system is his well-known "chartalistic" quantitative theory of money, with which he tries to associate the remaining problems of political economy. He takes an especial interest in questions of organization which leads him to a noteworthy theory of crises. This is built upon the idea of a constantly necessary equilibrium in production.

The modern French literature possesses a system devoid of all abstract theories in the comprehensive outline of Professor Charles Brouilhet [42] of Lyon. Even before this, he published a work in which he claimed to offer a purely objective account of the prevailing economic controversy; but between the lines he attacked all abstract-theoretical doctrines and all hypotheses.[43] Brouilhet's attitude is fundamentally the same as that of Stammler and Diehl in Germany. His chief idea also is the constant stressing of the social and especially the legal conditions of all national phenomena. But whereas in Germany an attempt is made to unite this attitude with the leading contemporary theories, Brouilhet abandons himself to a complete relativism, under the influence of which he is inclined to recognize a provisional validity, depending on time and place, in the laws of value and price as well as in all other economic theories.

He considers an analysis of the phenomenon of value quite unnecessary for an understanding of economic factors. He refers the origin of prices and of distribution to social forces: to the contest between buyers and sellers on one side and those interested in production on the other. Brouilhet also rejects the general arrangement of economic theory which he replaces by a new attempt to treat the main fields of economic life in independent divisions. He expects to find the solution of social questions in a kind of unrevolutionary syndicalism; a union of employers and employees in a great, integral league of interests, without believing in the possibility of a perfect concentration of production or consumption which would quite suppress the mediating activity of commerce.

6. *Solidaristic Social Ideas*

Gabriel Tarde approaches economics with the aim of studying social life in its broadest aspects. The economic system which he has outlined is characterized by a remarkable unevenness.[44] On the one hand we perceive Tarde's extraordinary broad horizon, which embraces parts of nearly every science besides possessing a brilliant philosophical equipment, and on the other hand we note his inadequate knowledge of the real meaning of economic life as well as of the latest results of economic theory. This inner discord gave birth to a hybrid, "economic psychology," which contains certain brilliant, detached ideas and an artificial systematic framework which is contrary to truth, and unadapted to the specific quality of economic phenomena. Tarde's system is above all metaphysical, well suited to all the phenomena of being, and sufficient as a framework for his "interpsychological" sociology: all the more reason why his attempt to force a system of economics on the same Procrustean bed should be doomed to failure.

The three categories of adaptation, repetition and opposition prevail, according to Tarde, in the whole organic and inorganic world, and the phenomena of social and spiritual life are also ruled by these three same categories. The manner in which he founds his sociology upon this basis reminds one in part of the corresponding views of Othmar Spann. Tarde too stresses the spiritual bond which exists between separate individuals; but he calls this bond "interpsychological," whereas Spann calls it "universalistic." Within this bond, there is, according to Tarde, a universal tendency for the behavior of an individual to be imitated by the rest. If the evolution of the environment compels man to adopt a new and different behavior; i. e., to adapt himself, and if the way to this appears in the shape of an invention, this is imitated by the others; i. e., repeated. Therefore the categories of adaptation and repetition appear in social life as discovery and imitation. If different harmonious entities, composed of invention and imitation, come together in social life, either they can supplement each other or else a sundering is possible only through a conflict which is the sole way in which they can attain a still higher harmony. Wherever such a conflict takes place in social life, we have the third universal category—that of opposition.

Tarde tries to make economics, like all the other sciences, fit into the scheme of these three fundamental categories. First of all he is bold enough to try and prove that all traditional economics has worked with erroneously formed concepts, and that therefore its whole structure is wrong. He attempts to show especially that the concept of value is not specifically an economic one, but a much more general one, which can be met in various forms in all the social sciences. In the same way, he blames traditional economics for treating production and consumption, the circulation of wealth, distribution, etc., from totally wrong angles. In order to erect a satisfactory new structure in place of what he has demolished, Tarde separates all economic phenomena according to the three categories and tries to build his system upon this foundation. Under the category of imitation he places wants, since one is always stimulated by them to continuous production, as well as labor, money and capital, all of which increase in importance with production. Under the category of opposition belong phenomena which arise from economic conflict: the formation of prices, competition, crises and the various other phenomena of business cycles, rhythms. Under economic adaptation he treats finally of invention, property, exchange, and unions. In discussing these, he also exhibits his views on economic policy, which tend toward a realization of the real idea of solidarity in the shape of a thorough co-operation of all activities in economic life.

We can see, even from this slight sketch of Tarde's system, that it contains some fruitful ideas, which open out onto broad horizons, but which are mixed with factual errors and an artificial scholasticism. This distinguished sociologist has been praised for his economic endeavors by certain authors; e. g., Ernest Mahaim,[45] August Dupont [46] and Maurice Roche-Agussol; [47] but some of the most important writers in the field of political economy have accused him—not without reason—of dilettantism.

Tarde's economic doctrine culminates, as we have seen, in the praise of the idea of solidarity. Following his work, we come to the scientific leader of solidarity and the co-operative movement in contemporary France. The economic system of Charles Gide was published, it is true, in the preceding century,[48] and has appeared since then in numerous editions and translations. Before the war, however, Gide published, besides repeated editions of his earlier survey, a new one, twice as large, in which he expounds his system more thoroughly.[49] This book gives us the opportunity to discuss Gide's economic views within the framework of our present considerations.

Gide comes from the historical school of economics, although his teachers were Auguste Comte and other French sociologists. Of the two German historical schools, Gide is closer to the older one. He studied for some time with Roscher but could not accept him unreservedly. Although he naturally considers the problems of economics first of all according to their historical and social aspects, he recognizes the validity of economic laws, although not in their naked, apodictic form, and can give excellent reasons for their defence. He tries to realize this conciliation, which he has effected between the historical and the theoretical attitudes, also in his own theoretical views between classical and modern doctrines. The way in which he does this is somewhat similar to that of Marshall. This is especially the case in his theory of value where Gide tries to draw upon and harmonize both the subjective and the objective principles of explanation. Gide's larger work owes its popular success also to this impartial regard for all the main currents of economic investigation, the clarity of its exposition and the perfection of its style. Whenever he comes upon problems which touch upon his own solidaristic attitude toward economic policy, he always criticizes himself, so that his discourse never appears to be inspired by prejudice or propaganda. This is not the case, indeed, with his numerous other writings, in which he defends the idea of solidarity with singularly perfect dialectic, and awaits the abolition of the wage system and of all other institutions which he considers as not entirely ethical and under which society is now suffering, from the future development of the co-operative movement.

The slight survey of all economic theory that Georges Valois [50] published after the World War expresses the idea of a social reform based upon mutual help, not in a co-operative form but in one of unrevolutionary syndicalism. This booklet cannot be mentioned in the same breath with the work of Gide. The latter offers us the ripe fruits of long and studious experience whereas Valois, insufficiently acquainted with economic literature and intoxicated with the sense of victory engendered by post-war days, offers us the outline of a bold system which contains interesting points but which also exhibits obvious imperfections and contradictions.

He is especially opposed to Marxian socialism, and tries to replace the main principle of this tendency, historical materialism, by an entirely idealistic conception of cultural evolution. He objects as strongly to liberalism, the origin of which, as well as of most of the chief social errors of the 19th century, he traces to the basic evil of the subjective theories of value. A similar evil is the explanation of the formation of prices as due to supply and demand; for, according to him, these theories obscure the idea of one right normal price which can only depend upon the degree of costs of production. In the economic structure which he built upon these foundations and which deals partly with practical problems of contemporary politics, many heterogeneous elements are united under the same heading; the most difficult questions are simply omitted; and the whole process of thought resolves itself into what is at times but a verbose prophecy of nationalism and syndicalism. Valois's position as leader of the French Fascists has enabled him to make a great deal of propaganda for his work. This is also the purpose of his periodical, *L'Economie Nouvelle.*

Not only did scholars, such as René Gonnard,[51] object to the unscientific character of his work, but writers of Christian-socialist tendencies accused him of a hypocritical idealism, and of falling into a materialism similar to the one which he attacked through his separation of the scientific aspect of economics from general philosophical questions. An enthusiastic adherent of Valois, Nel Ariès, has tried to defend him from the last accusations in a special work.[52]

The system of Gaetano Napolitano [53] has many close analogies with that of Valois, for which reason we think it best to mention it here. He too has an almost sovereign contempt for many of the most important results of recent economic investigation, and objects strongly to the law of supply and demand, the idea of free competition, and the other principles of liberal economics. On the other hand, he also attacks socialism, and considers the theory of class conflict an absurdity. The foundation of his new system is not the idea of syndicalism, as with Valois, but that of Fascism, especially as expressed in the thirty articles of the new Italian labor law: the co-operation of employers and employees, regulated by the state. Instead of explaining the economic phenomena of Fascism as far as possible in the light of the recent developments of our science, Napolitano follows the opposite course and tries to do away with all economic theory on the ground of the economic demands of Fascism. The futility of his attempts is hardly altered by the fact that he is bound to retain, in his positive structure, many elements of traditional, and especially of classical, theory.

7. *The Religious and Ethical Tendency*

Among those economic systems influenced by religion which appeared in the Latin countries in the first quarter of our century, the work of the Belgian Victor Brants[54] stands foremost. To him, the most important principle of economic theory is the recognition of the divine laws of social life. All economic life is subject to religious and moral law and it is the business of science to investigate how the most perfect harmony may reign under this rule.

Brants is more inclined to the inductive method, but he rejects the exaggerations of historical relativism and recognizes also the right of the deductive method in economics. In his theory of distribution, he criticizes the proposals of the socialists but willingly justifies, on the other hand, the increment value tax. He considers free competition harmful, since it leads to rank materialism and is one of the causes of the periodic economic crises. In other questions, too, he is against liberalism and stresses the importance of state intervention to protect the interests of the socially and economically weaker classes. He looks for the solution of social questions to a general return toward the ideals of the inner, religious life. This should be accompanied by the abolition of luxury, the amelioration of the condition of labor, and other reforms, the main lines of which Brants derives from Thomas Aquinas.—The small book of the Belgian, F. Denoel,[55] written in the form of questions and answers, tries to solve the most important problems of economics according to the papal encyclical *Rerum novarum*, and has no scientific pretensions. Even less scientific is the system of the Frenchman, F. Jollivet-Castelot,[56] which contains a program of Christian and spiritualistic communism. He attacks not only materialistic and atheistic socialism, but also the social and economic teachings of the Catholic church.

In Italy Guiseppe Toniolo planned to publish an ambitious system of economics, based on Christian social ideas, but did not carry it out beyond two volumes.[57] His ideas have a broad philosophical and sociological foundation, and start with a definition of economics in which the supernatural aims of man, his subjection to the higher laws of God, are the main factors.

He thereby consciously sacrifices the whole independence of economic science for which we have struggled so arduously for five generations. In details Toniolo tries to adapt himself to the discoveries of modern theory; e. g., in his theory of value which he founds upon the principle of marginal utility, or in his theory of price which he derives from a twofold equilibrium between supply and demand, between the costs of production of the seller and the marginal utility of the buyer. In the second volume Toniolo expounds his theory of production.

In structure, and in its philosophical and ethical-social framework, if not in its Christian foundation, the broad systematic outline of Giulio Alessio, of which the first parts appeared in the form of a student's note-book,[58] is most closely related to the unfinished work of Toniolo.

Alessio attracted the attention of scientific circles forty years ago with a work which was in essence dogmatically historical,[59] in the positive part of which he tried to reconcile subjective and objective theories of value in an eclectic theory of social use-value, founded largely upon ideas of Turgot, Rau, Hermann, Bernhardi, Neumann, Schäffle and Knies. In that part of his system which has been thus far published Alessio's chief aim is to consider the essence of national wealth from general social points of view. He therefore studies the ethical, social and cultural conditions of the economic mechanism, as expressed in the formation of prices, in distribution, in the circulation of wealth and in international trade. An adequate criticism of Alessio's system will, of course, be possible only when it is completed. Another incomplete system is that of M. Houques-Fourcade,[60] which is also based on social ethics. He blames classical as well as modern economic theory, the objective as well as the subjective theory of value, for not concerning themselves with justice or morality. He confronts them with his principle of a just price, the standard of which is the continuance of the present social order. We find here the same conscious negation of scientific "objectivity," which appeared at the beginning of the century with Brants. On the same foundation Houques-Fourcade builds his system, of which the chief characteristics are a realistic stressing of the social aspects, and a far-reaching consideration of problems of economic policy. The two volumes which have been published thus far contain no theory of distribution.

8. Socialistic Systems

Among the comprehensive surveys of political economy written in Latin countries in which the idea of social reform becomes more prominent the most important is the work of Achille Loria.[61] This contains an exposition of his well-known views of land reform: his conviction that social questions can be solved only by the freedom of the soil and the abolition of private property. His historical materialism, which we have mentioned above, is also permeated by this idea: he refers all human cultural development, not to economic factors in general, but especially to the institution of private property. His ideas are based above all on a morphology of economic phenomena, and in his theory of production he deals at great length with the technical aspects of the case. His historical attitude and his modern social illustrations of economic problems give his work a realistic aspect. Noteworthy also is his wealth of factual data.

The actual text was put together from Loria's lectures by one of his disciples, Giulio Fenoglio. The new editions contain, after the earlier chapters on production, distribution, circulation of wealth, population and the state as an economic factor, three more sections, which deal with rent, income and insurance. Loria's system is remarkable, on the whole, for its proportion and for its attention to the latest results of economic theory which, in spite of his historical and reformatory attitude, he does not neglect.

In France, the nearest approach to the work of Loria is the system of Adolphe Landry.[62] Landry is a pupil of Charles Andler, who did much in France for the dissemination of state socialism, and an enthusiastic adherent of the German socialist, Otto Effertz, whose doctrines have found greater favor in Latin countries than in his own.

Effertz tries to treat the question of social reform in a scientific and unprejudiced spirit. He discusses with subtlety the possibilities of development of a hypothetical society with absolutely equal economic rights and duties among its individual members.[63] By distinguishing between means of existence and the media of civilization he reaches the conclusion that in a socialistic society the decline of civilization can be prevented only when its members maintain the necessary means of existence by dint of a quantity of labor which will at the same time suffice to produce the necessary media of civilization. But even this forced union of the two main groups of productive activity does not do away with certain difficulties caused by the problem of population. The "ponophysiocratic" system of economics that Effertz finally proposed is something intermediate between industrial and agrarian socialism.

Landry undertook, at the beginning of the century, to give a clearer and more concise exposition of Effertz's doctrines in a book which was primarily a criticism of private property in productive goods,[64] and even in his principal work, which interests us here, he is perpetually referring to the ideas of the German socialist whom he admired so much.[65] After an introduction which discusses the psychological and sociological foundations in general, he makes some interesting dogmatically historical remarks, in which he recognizes the former supremacy of German science, at least in so far as it consists of the investigation of facts and individual matters, but prophesies a marked change of intellectual leadership in the immediate future and especially an advance in French economic theory. He tries to show that the mathematical method, which he considers a branch of the general deductive method, cannot be used for research; but he himself employs it to explain matters which are already known. He has an especial predilection for the study of statistics and offers in his work a wealth of relevant material. Landry has a wide regard for modern theories, quotes everywhere the latest foreign works on his subject, and discusses their ideas, as for instance, the doctrine of marginal utility. We shall revert later to some of his own more important theories. On the whole we notice in his work the effort to harmonize the points of view of the abstract-theoretical method and the experimental facts of practical economic life. Of lasting value, for instance, is the part in which he opposes to the economic man of pure theory the real individual as he appears in practice.

The Italian, Enrico Leone, although one of the most ardent adherents of syndicalism, tries in his popular outline [66] to suppress as far as possible his socialistic views and to offer an objective and purely scientific treatise. As a matter of fact, his attempt is not always successful and there are parts especially in the second half of his book which are clearly socialistic.

The first part of his work contains a purely scientific theory of economics, largely in the manner of the Lausanne school. He is careful, however, to make eclectic use of certain elements of classical doctrine and of Austrian theory for the solution of the more complicated problems. Nothing better proves the purely theoretical attitude of Leone, undisturbed by practical and political considerations, than the fact that he fully estimates the value of economic individualism. He even tries to prove, with the help of his mathematical demonstration, that free competition causes the greatest benefit to all producers. This, indeed, is true only of pure economic theory, in dealing with which all ethical considerations must be neglected. These, as well as the political and legal aspects of the subject, he also omits from the second part of his work which deals with production, circulation of wealth and distribution; and he tries to treat the questions which arise from these as purely quantitative problems of equilibrium. We have already hinted that he is less successful here than in the first part of his book. The dynamic problems of economic theory, which received only a summary treatment in the first edition of Leone's work, are studied more thoroughly in the second. In dealing with crises and economic evolution in general, he not only analyses the principal theories on the subject but also is able to grasp theoretically some of the practical problems of the most recent social-economic development.

Entirely different is the system, which was published after the war, of Arturo Labriola,[67] a no less ardent Italian socialist. Whereas Leone is anxious to remain as objective as possible, Labriola emphasizes as much as possible his Marxian views. He accuses the whole of modern economic theory of falling, because of its subjective theory of value, into psychological prejudices, and of neglecting its specifically social character. As the master, Marx, taught, value can be referred back only to human labor as the sole means of satisfying our material wants. Labriola, nevertheless, does not continue to follow the theoretical path pursued by Marx. He follows rather a relative and "realistic" lead, and takes for the object of our science, "the study of the economic aspects of contemporary social life," which may be quite different from the past or the future and consequently limits himself to a study of modern capitalism with its industrial, agricultural, commercial and financial implications. He admits that social life has certain laws, but he thinks that they do not affect economics to any extent, and considers it sufficient to dispose of them in thirty pages of his work, under the collective title of "Economic Logic." At the end of his system, Labriola tries to explain again the relative validity of the traditional theories of economics, by illustrating them through the relations between the state and the individual. For instance, in the present age of state-capitalism, where the state has frequently a great deal of influence on the formation of prices, where paper money is flourishing, and where wages are generally decided on ethical and political grounds, the traditional theories of price, money and wages, which rested upon the acceptance of free competition, intrinsic value of money and free understanding between employers and employes are, according to him, quite antiquated. It is the same with the other theories of the prevailing economics.—Perhaps Labriola's system is best characterized by this exaggerated relativism.

9. Text books

After these systems, which purport to be the results of more or less independent scientific studies, we may mention, as we did for German literature, a few works which also offer a survey of the whole field of economics, but can be considered only as text books with a pedagogical value. These books contain neither new theories nor an original arrangement of material. As a rule they do not pretend to have any independent scientific value.

To begin with the works of mathematical tendency, we may mention the book of Giuliani Balbi,[68] in which he attempts merely to give a clear exposition of the results of mathematical investigation. On the whole, he limits himself to reproducing the doctrines of Cournot and Pareto and almost ignores the other chief representatives of this tendency such as Walras and Jevons. A very useful work is the larger text book, of almost a thousand pages, which Alfonso di Pietri-Tonelli published after the war.[69] In this he outlines a well-built structure of economic theory which is based entirely on the views of Pareto. He illustrates these with elaborate examples, and tries even to develop them by making an extended use of statistics. The outline of Lamberto Paoletti,[70] which is built upon the standpoints of the Lausanne school, has the advantage that it undertakes to conceive the questions of production as problems of equilibrium and thereby extends the theory of economic equilibrium.

The popular university lectures which H. L. Follin, a zealous adherent of individualistic and liberal views, published in the shape of a booklet,[71] are founded upon the ideas of Bastiat and claim to follow Yves Guyot. Exchange, distribution of labor, law of supply and demand are the main headings according to which this system is divided. In his strongly liberalistic emphasis on the importance of the economic factor for the other departments of human culture, Follin approaches even a materialistic interpretation, such as one is accustomed to find—in quite different surroundings—with the Marxists. Paul Ghio, in the short essays which he entitles an outline of economic theory,[72] tries to defend the philosophical foundations, based on natural law, of moral, political and, above all, economic liberalism. He finds in the principle of liberty the quintessence of all economic theory, which has nothing to do with the discussion of practical questions. Unfortunately Ghio opposes liberalism to the social doctrines of the church, thereby falling into fruitless hair-splitting arguments.

The great text book of Professor Georges Blanchard,[73] of Cairo, is quite eclectic. Theoretically he is influenced principally by the older systems of Gide and Cauwès, and by the more modern Colson. Above all, he interprets theoretical problems in the light of dogmatic history, studies all the solutions that have been proposed in international literature and then concisely gives his own opinion. This opinion generally consists of his adhering to one or another of the parties without even attempting to solve the problem according to his own lights. Thus, with respect to value, after explaining at length all the relevant theories he throws in his lot with the objective attitude. His work is noteworthy, nevertheless, for its wealth of historical and statistical material. This is its chief importance. In his arrangement Blanchard keeps to the traditional divisions according to production, consumption, distribution and circulation of wealth.—The eclectic work of P. Reboud [74] has chiefly a didactic value. In his explanation of the elementary phenomena of economics he retains certain aspects of the theory of marginal utility but on the whole he remains faithful to the traditions of classical political economy. The best parts of his work are those which deal with the problems of applied economics; we find intelligent solutions here for some of the most recent questions.—Agatino Amantia [75] devotes more attention to theoretical questions. The influence of Marshall and of Gide, which does not harm his sociological basis and his general social attitude, is very evident in his book.

The expert Maurice Journé addresses the general public in his comprehensive work,[76] which attempts to popularize economics. He touches upon questions of the most varied social sciences but keeps close to contemporary economic events and considers as antiquated all theories which fail to deal with the burning questions of the post-war period. In this way he lets the actual theory of economic science crumble and offers only a series of more or less connected opinions on questions of economic policy.

Leaving aside the other text-books which have appeared fairly frequently in the first quarter of our century, occasionally intended even for high schools, we may mention the lucid and well-arranged popular university lectures of Alberto Carlo Giovannini,[77] which as a matter of fact do not touch upon all the questions of economic theory. Giovannini is an enthusiastic disciple of Mazzini but counts neither his master nor himself as a socialist. He is friendly to municipal socialism and recognizes the ethical functions of the state in the regulation of economic life—fundamentally, however, he claims to be a liberal.

CHAPTER III

VALUE

1. The Lausanne School and the Theory of Value

SINCE WE have just shown that the most important contribution of the Latin countries to economics in the first quarter of the century was the application of mathematics, we shall now come to the development of the theory of value in these countries and examine the attitude of the Lausanne school toward this subject during the last two decades.—Since Walras, the efforts of mathematical economists have been directed toward minimizing the concept of value, in order to become independent of it and to avoid as far as possible all the theoretical discussions which gather around it. The Lausanne school tries to explain all economic processes in the light of exchange and to place production, consumption and distribution of wealth in a series of acts of exchange in which one merely gives goods for goods. Therefore the question is one of objective relationships of exchange between the various goods and groups of goods, and value as a subjective phenomenon may readily be omitted. We have already pointed out, in discussing the similarly objective theory of Cassel, that this attitude can easily avoid using the expression "value" and a separate theory of value when its meaning is already contained in the concepts "evaluation," "relations of exchange," etc., employed by them.

Likewise the question of utility, which is the basis of conditions of exchange between various groups—or in other words: the fundamental problem of the modern subjective theory of value—caused Pareto much difficulty. In his *Cours* he still tried to flirt with the idea of "elementary ophelimity," by which he means the enjoyment which arises in the course of using goods and which he considers a "function of all complementary goods which come into consideration." He realizes quite clearly that the range of this "complement" is extremely large and that it can, taken literally, embrace all goods. For the pleasure—Pareto teaches—which we get from a cup of coffee depends not only upon the mixture of coffee and sugar, the heat of the drink, etc., but also upon the fact whether the cup itself from which one drinks, the room in which one sits, its temperature, the people who surround one, the servants, etc., are to a greater or to a less degree pleasant to us. That the range can be extended still further is a fact of everybody's experience. As a function of the already used, or still to be used, crowd of relevant goods, we have ophelimity as a basis for the conditions of exchange. There has been much argument about the validity of the expression "ophelimity." Many think that "ophelimy" would have been grammatically more correct; others wish to retain the traditional names such as "subjective utility" or "enjoyment." On the whole, Pareto does not seem to have had much success with it for, with the exception of a few enthusiastic students, his innovation has not been followed.

We have already mentioned, in dealing with the general foundations of his system, how Pareto was dissatisfied with these thoughts in his *Manuale*, and how he went on to build an opposition of mere wants and obstacles until he comes to his curves of indifference. Especially subtle is the way in which he analyses wants on the one hand and obstacles on the other. In dealing with wants, it is all the same to him whether the enjoyments to which they tend are measurable or mathematically comparable among each other. He finds it enough to know what series the individual chooses for the satisfaction of his wants in all the possible combinations of consumption-goods, or—since each of these combinations has an index—what is the series of these indices. Once this is known, the individual can go away: even if we were to subtract from his own person, we should be able to compute his economic activities, his acts of exchange and his whole economic behavior, and derive them with mathematical exactness. Among the obstacles Pareto distinguishes those of the first and those of the second order. The obstacles of the first order embrace the wants of the person with whom we come economically in contact, the quantitative limitations, the spatial and temporal condition of the goods at our disposal, or to be sacrificed in the course of production, as well as the limitations which are rooted in the structure of social life. Obstacles of the second order are those circumstances which cause changes in price immediately before or during the exchange. A further study of this analysis will lead one to the conclusion that, with the exception of his wants, everything else is an obstacle for the individual.

Unfortunately we cannot here go into a more complete exposition of these interesting ideas by which Pareto unfolds the whole mechanism of the interplay between wants and obstacles. Our brief remarks will at least show that, in spite of Pareto's attempts to treat his theory objectively, his main ideas are essentially similar to those of modern subjective theorists of value. Pareto's analysis also contains useful contributions to the theory of value which rests upon the concept of marginal utility.

In this connection some of Pareto's followers have accomplished some notable work. We may mention above all Umberto Ricci who has often successfully continued the master's thought.

He constructs out of a few stray remarks of Pareto and Marshall a law of increasing utility, of growing ophelimity, which he opposes to that of decreasing utility and which means that in certain exceptional cases the enjoyment which corresponds to the ever larger quantities of goods applied to the satisfaction of wants does not perish, but on the contrary constantly increases.[1] He tries to prove that enjoyment can theoretically be measured with precision and that the *minimum sensibile* can be taken as a theoretical standard. In practice, however, he admits that only the comparison worked out by Pareto, between two or more satisfactions is to be considered since evidently one cannot construct a "hedonimeter" as one can a thermometer.[2] Antonio Osorio, on the other hand, goes back to Walras, and tries to prove his principle of the presence of a general standard of utility.[3] Arrigo Bordin is of the opinion that Pareto's index of ophelimity is not able to deal with the satisfaction of wants quantitatively. He tries to replace Pareto's *homo oeconomicus* by the less abstract assumption of a subject who acts according to certain pre-ordained tendencies (preferences), and on this assumption he tries to build the theory of equilibrium of exchange.[4] V. Furlan again attempts to transfer the idea of ophelimity from pure theory to the theory of social economics as well,[5] whereas Corrado Gini tries to treat the same concept objectively.[6] Roberto Murray considers Gini's ideas erroneous, and tries to prove that such efforts can never lead to satisfactory results.[7]

2. *Slight Success of the Pure Theory of Marginal Utility in the Romance Countries*

It is a curious fact that the results attained by French and Italian economists in the first quarter of our century with reference to the subjective theory of value remain far behind those with which the mathematical economists of the same nations enriched this doctrine—as we have just seen, unwittingly. The reason for this contradiction is to be found in the fact that whereas the modern mathematical theory, through the half French and half Italian school of Lausanne, is a national one, predestined to a wide expansion, the purely psychological modern subjective theory of value had to be imported from foreign literature and was able to obtain a position only gradually, after much heated conflict. Even today, it has not been able to maintain itself independently of foreign influences.

As regards the purely psychological and not mechanistically mathematical theory of wants , we have at the beginning of the century the researches of Camillo Trivero who tries to prove that the theory of wants is the solid foundation, not only of economics, but of all other social sciences.[8] By working out logical, ethical and æsthetic needs he manages to avoid the attitude of historical materialism. He considers the sequence in the satisfaction of our wants a "normal" one, given by nature. Charles Bodin wrote a lucid sketch of the relations between the intensity of our wants, the available or requisite quantities of goods and the enjoyments attained,[9] but he had little to say that was new. Upon this foundation he comes, in his recent systematic work, to a conception of value which is closely related to the American theory of disutility, especially as expounded by Davenport.

Of considerable importance are the researches on the satisfaction of wants and on the magnitude of the pleasure which results therefrom by Antonio Graziadei, who published them at the beginning of the century in a booklet of scarcely fifty pages.[10] He tries to show, with admirable arguments, that the conception of the modern hedonistic theory as resulting from a decreasing curve of satisfaction is only one side of the picture. For in reality, with the increasing satisfaction of wants, the intensity of enjoyment shows at first a rising curve, which does not start to fall until it has reached a certain high point. Only the first half of the curve, in which enjoyment constantly rises, is of importance for practical economic life, for one does not usually push the satisfaction of wants beyond the point where the proportional enjoyment reaches its maximum. But if the law of decreasing enjoyment is useless for practical life, then the whole hedonistic theory is built on sand and the doctrine of marginal utility falls to the ground.

Besides this, Graziadei tries to show that the doctrine of marginal utility cannot possibly remain valid even if the law of diminishing utility really had the importance which is attributed to it, since this law is connected with the idea of marginal utility only through a logical fallacy.—Graziadei's criticism caused a sensation among the adherents of marginal utility and many different attempts were made to dispose of his arguments. Among these, we shall mention the most important: that of Augusto Graziani, who, in his *Istituzioni*, which we have already mentioned, gives much attention to the endeavor to overcome Graziadei's objections, although even he regards the principle of marginal utility inadequate as a single explanation of value.

The Böhm-Bawerk theory of value found an enthusiastic adherent in Riccardo dalla Volta. Like most followers of the Austrian school in the Latin countries, he limits himself to a repetition of their views, without making any noteworthy contributions himself.[11] Maurice Roche-Agussol undertakes the difficult task of finding the essential kernel of the modern subjective theory of value, as represented by the English, the Americans and the Austrians, and of interweaving in his synthesis the ideas on value of Tarde, Durkheim and other philosophers.[12] In self-interest on the one hand and subjective desire on the other he sees the opposite poles of thought to which all differences between objective and subjective theories of value should be referred.

While the Italian adherents of marginal utility have a preference for the most subtle abstractions, the French try, as far as possible, to simplify this theory. Albert Aftalion tries to enrich it especially with aspects of the American theory of marginal productivity, and to work out its meaning for the explanation of price-formation and money-value.[13] We find an attempt to simplify the doctrine of marginal utility and to continue the eclectic contributions of the old French theory of value, joined to some unfavorable criticism, in the comprehensive works of Charles and Charles-Henry Turgeon.[14] Both father and son try to make the theory of value the cardinal point of all economic theory, analyse thoroughly the old and the new doctrines, and expound in this way the whole problem of value.

They recognize that the general idea of the value theory of marginal utility is correct. They point out, however, that the two chief factors of this explanation of value, utility and scarcity, have always been acknowledged by French economists, and that therefore one should not attribute too much importance to the discovery of the Austrians. The Austrian far-reaching abstractions and their deductions, however subtle and flawlessly logical, which may be looked upon as progressive, would lead them, according to the Turgeons, because of their frequent artificiality, to contradict the complicated phenomena of real economic life. Therefore the Turgeons try to explain the phenomenon of value on a subjective basis, while avoiding as far as possible the difficulties of marginal utility. They thereby make some use of the objective factors of value and attempt to construct in this way a realistic foundation for the explanation of all economic facts.—Gaëtan Pirou [15] is of the opinion that they have exaggerated the subjective contributions of the French theory of value and have thus, in spite of their eclectic attitude, neglected the objective side of the problem.

3. *Attempts at a Reconciliation between Objective and Subjective Tendencies*

Christian Cornélissen criticized the theory of marginal value at the beginning of the century [16] still more thoroughly than the Turgeons and leads us to those French theorists who consciously strive after a reconciliation and union between the subjective and objective theories of value.

Cornélissen blames the theory of marginal utility especially for its exaggerated and artificial abstractions and also thinks that it contains some logical fallacies. Especially noteworthy is his objection that the substitution utility, with which the representatives of marginal utility used to work is, in reality, a valuation according to the price. Therefore in explaining value as the basis of price formation, the knowledge of the price is already presumed. If Cornélissen also in this way rejects the theory of marginal value, he starts to build a theory of use value, which should be determined by the advantage that goods have for the individual on the ground of their quantity, quality and other characteristics. To this subjective use value, he opposes an objective production value which, in the present economic organization, is composed of the socially necessary costs of production and circulation of goods as well as of the average profit. In order to give a complete explanation of value, Cornélissen draws upon both use value and production value, since the former arises from the relation between goods and consumers and the latter from that between goods and producers; so that both should be equally recognized.

Next to this somewhat difficult and halting theory of Cornélissen we may mention here Charles Gide's theory of value, in which the union between the subjective and the objective attitudes is accomplished with unequaled elegance. Originally Gide was an adherent of the theory of labor value, and was only gradually influenced by the Viennese and the Lausanne schools. In his *Cours* he reaches an attitude which—as we have already mentioned—is closely akin to that of Marshall. He considers it a mistake to determine value from one point of view only: either that of the enjoyment which a good can give us, or that of the sacrifice which is necessary for procuring it; i. e., from the point of view of costs. Just as the most intense of all loves, mother-love, consists of both elements, so also does the valuation of economic goods as well as of the enjoyment that their possession procures and of the sacrifice that must be made to obtain them. Value flits between these two poles, like a ball hit by two racquets.

In Italian literature, the theory of value of Graziani corresponds to that of Gide. While Gide accepts the subjective and the objective explanations of value as something entirely parallel, Graziani selects only certain elements from both theories and combines these, in the way that we have already mentioned, to form a single theory. What Graziani offers us is a kind of theory of cost value built upon the principle of marginal utility.[17]

Fabrizio Natoli proposes a further kind of compromise.[18] According to him, the source of value is entirely subjective, for it is to be found in the utility that goods have for us. The amount of value, on the contrary, is determined only by cost of production. Although Natoli tries to relate this to exertion as the only immediate sacrifice that man makes in production, he is bound to admit that not the amount of labor is the standard, but the manner in which it is related with capital and land to production. Recently Filippo Carli has made a sharp distinction on the basis of value on the one hand and the measurement of its height on the other, while attempting at the same time—like some modern American scholars—to treat the whole problem of value from a social angle.[19] In solving the first problem, he opposes the concept of social utility to that of individual utility, whereas in answering the second question with the social element of cost he stresses the importance of cost of reproduction.—In opposition to all these attempts at reconciliation, Domenico Berardi pointed out the other side of the picture at the beginning of the century, and tried to show the contrasts which separate the subjective from the objective theory of value.[20] These contrasts exist not only—as is generally assumed—in the question of the degree or the quantitative determination of value, but also in the questions of the knowledge and the origins of the phenomenon of value. In all three points we must reach essentially different conclusions, according as we view the problem of value subjectively or objectively. Although Berardi offers no positive theory of value in this book, he discloses more or less sympathy for the theories of cost value, but rejects the theory of marginal utility even in an earlier critical work.

4. The Conflict over Cost of Reproduction

Berardi also took part in the heated discussion which occurred in Italian science at the beginning of the century about the theory of reproduction costs, as represented by Francesco Ferrara. A slight passage of arms first took place between Vincenzo Tangorra and Ottilio Cabiati. The former remarked, in an exhaustive critical study,[21] that Ferrara had assigned too much importance to his theory of reproduction costs, and he emphasized the epistemological value of the modern subjective theory of value. Cabiati then tried to defend the theory of Ferrara in all its dignity.[22] Barone too recognizes its importance, even though he feels obliged to say that it throws light on only one of the numerous problems of economic equilibrium.[23] The discussion did not become acute until Loria published an essay,[24] in which he severely criticized the theory of reproduction costs, considering its inner structure illogical, and regarding it as useless for the explanation of value, since we are in no way influenced, in a transaction, by the hypothetical costs of production. The harsh tone of this criticism challenged Ferrara's adherents, who saw in it a depreciation of the scientific contribution of their master and who now made a passionate defence. Tullio Martello's attack on Loria [25] is marked by personal animosity and Berardi too undertakes to defend Ferrara by trying to represent the theory of reproduction costs in its true light.[26]

5. *More Recent Development of the Theory of Cost-Value*

We are now in the midst of the attempts to explain value objectively, in spite of all the efforts of modern theorists to the contrary. Neither the French nor the Italian literature on the subject offers any new views: both merely revive older theories, which they try to harmonize with the results of modern theoretical investigation.

Among the most recent comprehensive investigations we might call especial attention to Salvatore Majorana's [27] study which also takes a position as to this theory. In the main he seeks to emphasize that while marginal utility explains only the demand side and while cost of production explains only the supply side in the promotion of value, the cost of reproduction is of equal importance for both sides.

Perhaps the best study is that of Umberto Ricci, who develops the sound kernel of Senior's abstinence theory and illumines it by means of his mathematical attitude.[28] Labriola, on the other hand, in his above-mentioned text-book, represents himself as an adherent of the theory of labor value as propounded by Marx and is not inclined to make the slightest concession to modern views. Antonio Graziadei has recently achieved some success in continuing the revisionistic criticism of this theory of value.[29] The careful analysis which caused so much trouble to the school of marginal utility is again presented here, and he points out the logical reasons for which, in the third volume of *Kapital,* Marx himself was forced to dilute his theory of surplus value. According to this, surplus value is regarded only as a class phenomenon, which is related not directly to the individual worker, but merely to the difference between the value of the entire production of society and the entire amount of wages. Graziadei regrets that even this social conception of surplus value cannot possibly be measured with precision. Thus we find the traditional objection to the theory of marginal utility also turned against the Marxian theory of value.

In connection with the objective theories of value, there are some interesting studies by Jannacone,[30] in which he investigates the costs of production as an independent economic category according to their social nature and measurability, and tries to posit as their basis the modern organization of enterprise. He sees in the concentration, the increase and the acceleration of production, the true explanation of diminishing costs.

The cost theory of value has naturally found a strong support in the French followers of the classical liberal school. Nevertheless, even these economists have recently become less prejudiced, and at times make important concessions to the subjective theory of value. Thus, a few years before his death, their leader, Yves Guyot, defined value as the relation between the utility which is in possession of one person and the wants as well as the purchasing power of another person. For the objective basis of value he accepts the costs of production unchanged.[31]

The reduction of value to the costs of production, which Valois opposes in his *Économie Nouvelle* to the subjective theory of value, one of the reputed sources of all the ills of our day and in which he finds a new theoretical discovery, can only be ascribed to his ignorance of the literature of economics. It is consequently of no scientific value.

6. Tarde's Theory of Value Based on Cultural Philosophy

Tarde's theory of value, expounded in his *Psychologie économique*, has, like the theory of Valois, made little use of previous discoveries. Nevertheless it is of considerable interest, because of its cultural and philosophical basis. Tarde distinguishes first between a cost value dependent on the evaluation of the sacrifice to be made and a use value dependent on utility. He believes that goods constantly increase in utility; i. e., in use value, through discoveries and cultural progress, but that their cost value diminishes because of the technical improvements of production. Since, however, cost value, because of the sacrifice or spiritual conflict which pertains to it, belongs to the category of opposition, whereas use value belongs to that of adaptation, the change in the importance of both forms of value advances parallel with the development of culture toward the universal harmony which is the key-stone of Tarde's sociology.

More recently, S. Théodotou has offered a theory of value, in which he regards value as a relation between the good and bad characteristics, the advantages and the disadvantages of the object which is to be valued.[32] It is not likely that this theory will arouse much interest.

7. *The Theory of "Economic Convenience"*

To complete our exposition of the French and Italian theories of value in the first quarter of the twentieth century, we may say a few words about the theory of "economic convenience" of Ulisse Gobbi.[33] Although it is meant to supplant the theory of value, yet its main idea is closely related to that which is at the bottom of every theory of value and is contained in the very concept of evaluation. In its original form, Gobbi's theory starts with the fact that the individual must always in his economic activity utilize certain things and personal energies which are in his own possession. In undertaking a given action, the individual will let himself be determined by a judgment of convenience which arises from a comparison between the importance of the good which is to be obtained and the energies which are to be sacrificed. This basic comparison, in its turn, always appears as a function of certain physical quantities. Gobbi believes that this idea of economic convenience provides a more real and stable foundation for the theories of price and distribution than is possible with the more or less abstract theories of value.

Although his innovation was generally well received; e. g., by Benedetto Croce [34] and Montemartini,[35] Boninsegni [36] reproached him that the concepts which build up his theory, such as those of personal energies, importance and physical quantities, are not defined with the mathematical precision which one should always observe in a science like economics. Gobbi tried to defend his ideas vigorously against the attacks of Boninsegni in an interesting discussion,[37] but the form which he gave his theory in the text-book published after the war shows that he has taken stock of his opponent's objections.

CHAPTER IV

PRICE

1. The Mathematical Theory of Price

THE PROBLEM of price is the axis around which the whole modern mathematical theory of economics turns. Neglecting the phenomenon of value, its adherents devote all their attention to the analysis of price in which they perceive the element which can be apprehended quantitatively, with the help of which the whole mechanism of economic life becomes accessible to mathematical formulas. In price they find incorporated all the conditions of exchange which comprise production, distribution and consumption, and by means of which all the questions of economic theory can be regarded as problems of equilibrium. It is self-evident that as a result of this central position of price in mathematical economics the Latin countries should have become more and more interested in it in the present century. The greatest interest was shown in Italy where the renaissance of the Lausanne school, instigated by Pareto, made some notable contributions toward the development of this theory.

With regard to the master himself, Pareto took advantage of the broadening of his horizon which he had attained in the *Manuale* for enriching the theory of price. Perhaps Pareto's contribution can be summarized as follows: Walras assumed that the exchanging members must always approach a certain point in which the stable economic equilibrium establishes itself. Marshall and, under his influence, Pantaleoni studied the problems of stable as well as of unstable equilibrium but always limited themselves to the treatment of single problems of equilibrium. Pareto, on the contrary, through his far-reaching abstractions arrives at a system of thought in which he embraces the problems of stable and unstable equilibrium in a single theory; or, in other words, he constructs a theory to which the phenomena of both equilibria are equally subjected. For his predecessors, the phenomenon of exchange was a problem by itself; but Pareto builds upon it a theory of "general economic equilibrium," in which only wants and obstacles stand opposed to each other and into which the problem of exchange can easily be fitted even though the prices change during the exchange. The general laws of equilibrium unite especially for Pareto the two fields of economic theory: the theory of exchange and that of production, two systems of equations each of which leaves indeterminate another group of unknown factors.

The special problems which Pareto studies within the theory of exchange on the basis of his mathematical equations are the conditions of exchange under free competition with fixed and variable prices, as well as the conditions of exchange with fixed prices in case of monopoly. Within this second group of phenomena of exchange, he distinguishes various individual cases, according as there are one or more monopolists or one or more monopolized goods respectively. Pareto sees the "maximum of social ophelimity" only in exchange, which takes place under free competition. This attitude is expressed somewhat apodictically in the *Cours* but with great care and considerable limitations in the *Manuale*.

This last-mentioned change in the attitude of Pareto may partly be due to the sagacious criticism which Gaetano Scorza directed to parts of the *Cours* in which, although recognizing all the merits of the Lausanne school, he tries to show that their attempt to connect the mathematical theory of exchange with the postulate of free competition is based upon false logic.[1] Among the immediate adherents of Pareto, with reference to the further development of his theory of price, we must mention first Ricci who works out carefully the differences between the corresponding doctrines in Marshall and the Lausanne school, as well as the results of his theory of increasing ophelimity for the formation of the demand curve. He has also started some interesting researches on the elasticity of the two factors of price formation: supply and demand.[2] Boninsegni has made a clear and concise formulation of the law of price, as it follows from the basis of Pareto's theory of equilibrium.[3]

The powerful work which Graziadei, the sagacious critic of the theory of marginal utility, published after the war, moves on the same lines.[4] He manages to maintain a certain independence of the Lausanne school, from which he borrows only the principle of economic equilibrium. In erecting his theory of price, Graziadei goes back to the analysis of the problem of utility, and then comes to the study of supply and demand, which he examines especially with reference to its elasticity and to its varying aspects under free competition or under monopolies. In the course of his abstract mathematical procedure, he is especially anxious to maintain the connections with the phenomena of practical economic life. This is the reason why he tries to demonstrate his results in a branch of practical industry.

Among the other contributions of Italian mathematical economists to the theory of price in the first quarter of our century, the most interesting is the work of Pantaleoni on the nature and the socio-economical effects of "political prices." By political prices he means all prices, as distinct from economic prices, which change for the same object according to the political, social, ethical, religious, national, psychological, etc., condition of the buyer or seller, such as the more favorable prices which are made to employees or poor people, special prices which serve for boycotting, etc.[5]

Amoroso tries to give a mathematical and graphical exposition of the laws of monopoly prices by developing the doctrines of Cournot on the subject.[6] Marco Fanno has made valuable studies in which, founding himself upon various premises, he investigates the condition of supply under joint costs of those goods of which the production is necessarily interconnected.[7] He has recently considered the problem from the other side and offered a theory of "substitute goods": goods which replace each other in the satisfaction of the same or of different wants.[8] The works of Corrado Gini[9] and Costantino Bresciani-Turroni[10] are essentially statistical. In these they examine the manner in which the consumption of various goods re-acts upon the changes in their prices or the differences which usually arise between the height which had been previously calculated and the future condition of the prices in fact. Gini has also more recently published a similar searching analysis of the relations between cost of production on the one hand and the formation of prices and size of income on the other.[11] Del Vecchio interests himself [12] in the movement of prices; namely, in the problem whether a slow and gradual decline of prices is possible. Pietro Scraffa has devoted a more comprehensive work to the reciprocal relations between the cost of production, the price-level, and the extension of production.[13] In this he has principally continued the results of Marshall, Edgeworth and Pareto. Del Vecchio directed some well chosen arguments against Scraffa, objecting, among other things, that he had not sufficiently distinguished the static conditions from the dynamic developments.[14] In this dynamic connection, G. M. Papi has enlarged our knowledge by trying to consider realistically the concept of money costs by applying the tools of the modern investigation of business cycles in the process of price fluctuations.[15] Attilio da Empoli has published a survey, for the time being only abstract, which offers a noteworthy development of the theory of production costs.[16] In this he tries to explode the traditional theory that normal exchange value is determined by the marginal costs of production in agreement with marginal utility. He believes that there arise from the nature of the technique of production additional factors of price formation: the "ultramarginal costs," and "ultramarginal utility," the reciprocal relations of which can, under certain conditions, cause a special producer's or consumer's surplus. Antonio Osorio offers a systematic exposition of the teachings of the Lausanne school, centered around the theory of exchange and price. He goes back to the theory of Walras; and defends some of its propositions against Pareto, but has no original views.[17] Marcel Lenoir, on the other hand, is influenced more by the Cambridge school. He makes use of Edgeworth's famous curves of indifference, sets himself many abstract problems of price and tries to solve them with the help of mathematical formulas.[18] A successful study is that of J. Moret on the mechanism of supply, demand and price, the mutual interplay of which he works out with great clarity.[19] Although the work is intended to be primarily a practical explanation of the mathematical method, it contains also some useful points of view. In theory it tends toward a confession of the liberal faith. Gaston Leduc has recently published a scholarly work on the theory of monopoly in which he considers, during the formation of price, the effects of absolute as well as of relative monopoly and throws much light on his problems from both the static and the dynamic sides.[20]

The modern literature of France is rather poor in mathematical investigations of the theory of price. Interesting studies like that of J. Delevsky, in which he tries to justify the once celebrated law of Gregory King on the relationship between the harvest yield and the price of wheat,[21] are very few and far between. All the more remarkable, then, is the clear exposition of a purely psychological theory of price, based on the principle of marginal utility, which Lavergne includes in the text-book which we have already mentioned. The subtle psychological points which he develops in his theory of marginal demand, his intelligent treatment of consumer's surplus and his analysis of supply, for which he gives the size of production cost as a secure quantitative basis, are a delight for anyone who has a taste for economic theory. The central position which he assigns to the idea of exchange, by means of which he divides his whole system according to different markets, is derived from the Lausanne school. We have already noticed the importance of Aftalion's researches into the theory of exchange. He tries by means of psychological analysis, which is connected with the marginal idea, to probe those elements in the formation of prices and in the dynamic development of price, which are not amenable to the statistical method. He calls them qualitative elements, and contrasts them with the quantitative elements, which can be treated by statistics. Both Lavergne and Aftalion remain more or less on the basis of the traditional theory of marginal utility. Mentor Bounatian, however, makes the psychological assumption of the formation of prices the object of an investigation which is supposed to lead to revolutionary results.[22] He starts with the distinction, coined by Gide in the last century, between "utilité" and "désirabilité," and believes that, in the case of numerous goods, the latter decreases in geometrical proportion when the amount of goods increases in arithmetical proportion. In order to reach a generalisation of these relations, he finally concludes that a geometrical change often corresponds to an arithmetical one between price, supply and demand; e. g., it often happens that prices increase geometrically if the demand decreases only arithmetically. King's law and the quantitative theory of money, as well as most of the results of mathematical economics, would be supplanted by this discovery,—if it could have been made more persuasive by factual material than Bounatian made it.

2. *The Conflict over the Classical Law of Supply and Demand*

As in his theory of value, Cornélissen tries also in his theory of price to connect elements which he has taken on the one hand from the subjectivistic tendencies and on the other from the older objectivistic attitude. According to him the exchange value which determines price is a result of the co-operation between use value and production value. We have explained above the meaning which Cornélissen ascribes to these two kinds of value. This co-operation takes place in many different ways: the value of exchange approaches sometimes the value of production, sometimes that of use. On the whole, with goods that can be reproduced at will the determining factor is production value, whereas with goods that are not reproducible the exchange value will be very close to the use value, or else coincide with it. In the first case the element of personal sacrifice, of labor, with which the production of goods is connected, is more evident, whereas in the second case our attention is directed to the end of goods, or their use, which is consumption. Cornélissen considers the law of supply and demand meaningless but uses its fundamental principles in part in order to explain price.

Although Colson's theory of price also belongs to those which try to unite classical and modern tendencies, it is essentially different from that of Cornélissen. Colson believes thoroughly in the law of supply and demand and it is only on this solid foundation that he tries to utilize some of the ideas of the modern theory of price.

This is especially true of his analysis of supply and demand in which the results of modern science are given a certain amount of consideration. In this way he arrives at the construction of his theory of consumer's surplus, one of the most valuable parts of his learned treatise. The importance of Colson's theory of price is largely limited by the fact that it is closely related—if only by chance—to Marshall's theory which was published much earlier. The solutions of the problem of price which we find in most of the French surveys; e. g., in those of Antonelli, Reboud, etc., run along somewhat similar lines. In this connection we may mention the ideas on price of the Russian Peter Struve, which were published in French in the form of an extract. He claims to stand on the same ground as Turgot, Simmel, Pareto and a Hungarian writer, Olivér Gömöry.[23] He considers price an entirely independent category of economics, and tries to contrast it, as the expression of a "real" relation between exchangeables, with value which is a norm and the expression of a merely ideal connection between exchangeable goods. He clings, nevertheless, to the law of supply and demand.

In Italian literature, Graziani's theory of price is the most important attempt at a synthesis between classical and modern science. Although he makes use of the idea of marginal utility in his analysis of price, he is of the opinion that the basis of a theory of price must always be sought in the classical law of supply and demand, and that all the new viewpoints can only serve to perfect this fundamental doctrine.

On the whole, even the French liberal school exhibits an effort gradually to take more account of some of the aspects of the modern theory of price. Colson, as we have just seen, was the first to give the good example, which was followed by Ansiaux in his text book. Especially noteworthy is the way in which the latter analyses the elasticity of supply and demand. With regard to demand, he recognizes that in respect of many, and especially the most important, articles it does not diminish much in spite of important increases in price, whereas the elasticity of supply is generally much greater. As a matter of fact, there are certain absolute limits beyond which the elasticity of supply, for instance, cannot be stretched. In his lecture of 1924, quoted above, Yves Guyot did not shut the door on modern ideas of price so tightly as he had formerly done. The law of supply and demand, however, still holds its own as much as before. Jean Lescure tries to show the practical importance of this law in an historical study of economics.[24] Herman Schoolmeesters [25] has recently made a useful contribution to the law of supply and demand. He starts with a study of the internal relations between production costs and returns, inquires into the consequences that necessarily follow for the shaping of supply, and finally works out the relations of price formation to the changes demand.

3. *The Explanation of Price by Social Ratios of Power*

The law of supply and demand naturally plays an important part in the price theories of the socialistically inclined economists, with whom ideas of social ethics or of social reform are fundamental. Landry studies, with his mathematical procedure, all the particularities of supply and analyses with equal thoroughness the nature of demand. He does this, following the ideology of Effertz, by taking first the case of "monoonium," or of buyer's monopoly, and next that of seller's monopoly and then calculating all the consequences that follow therefrom for the formation of price. Not till the end does he take up free competition on both sides. The price equilibrium is for Landry the level upon which supply and demand are equal. If the latter is crushed, the equilibrium is disturbed and all economic life suffers: general economic crises ensue in this case, with all their devastating social and economic consequences.—Emanuele Sella tries to explain price entirely as a result of the social conflicts between various groups of interests.[26] Nevertheless, he recognizes the correctness of the fundamental principles of the classical theory of price and even tries to show how their validity is apparent at the back of the social conflicts. Labriola is much more radical; engrossed in his relativism he rejects the theoretical law of supply and demand and endeavors to explain the phenomenon of price only by the given social and economic ratios of power of the modern capitalistic system. Raymond Sachot has recently stressed monopoly in the theory of price, and attempts to solve it by means of the subjective and mathematical doctrines of older French economists, such as Cournot and Dupuit.[27]

4. *The "Fair" Price*

The theory of price which Gabriel Tarde sketched in his "economic psychology" has its origins in a purely sociological trend of thought. According to him, price belongs to the category of economic contrasts, since its source is the internal and exterior conflicts which take place partly in the individual's mind and partly between buyers and sellers. In the final conflict the seller is nearly always the stronger and all economic development tends toward a constantly increasing monopoly of sellers. Consequently we may say that the seller alone determines the amount of the price. In his opinion, the determining factor is not only, as the school of marginal utility supposed, the intensity of the wants that are least felt as they reach their satisfaction in the presence of a given supply of commodities, but also the purchasing power possessed by the subjects of these marginal wants, as well as the greater or less range of the wants in question. Besides this purely chrematistic, quantitative moment, Tarde recognizes a further, essentially ethical factor, which is of great importance for the actual determination of price. This is the idea of a "fair price," an interpsychological phenomenon, which has its foundation in our deep-rooted and inextinguishable moral conviction that the advantages arising from a transaction must somehow be divided equally among the contracting parties. The seller, therefore, cannot avoid considering this idea in some way or other in determining the price. Even if he suppresses it entirely, he still has the consciousness of having acted unjustly.

With these ideas as a foundation, Alfred de Tarde, probably a near relation of Gabriel Tarde, attempts in his comprehensive Paris dissertation,[28] to include nearly all the problems of economics in a single theory of a fair price. This is for him not a mere ethical postulate, but rather a practical fact, which should be considered on one hand as an important element of economic judgment of value and on the other as a noteworthy factor in the price of special individual goods. Therefore he undertakes in the first part of his work the bold attempt to prove the presence of the idea of a fair price in all theories of value, from the mediæval canonists to the most modern doctrines, a task which he can achieve at times only with the help of hair-splitting sophistry. He is led by the notion that the valuation of a good arises in the individual consciousness only in virtue of this idea; through imitation, social or general value arises from this individual value, which in turn becomes the foundation of the actual prices. In the second part of his book, de Tarde investigates what practical influence the idea of fair price exerts on the level of wages, interest, etc. He thus reaches the concepts of "fair wage," "fair interest," etc., to which he attributes an importance which seems scarcely to correspond to the facts of actual economic life.

In the years following the war, in which the exaggerated profits of a few speculators contrasted with the general rise of prices and the necessary restriction of the wants of entire classes of the population, the idea of a fair price became increasingly prominent, and numerous demands were heard, especially in France, that its ethical requisites should likewise receive a foundation in economic theory.

Of these demands, we may here mention again the *Économie nouvelle* of Valois, in which the law of supply and demand is called the "worst nonsense" (*la plus creuse sottise*) that economic theory has ever invented. Apart from the fact that it contains an untruth, it tries scientifically to justify cheating, deception and the exploitation of one social class by another. The "fair price," on the contrary, can be founded only on the costs of production, the sum of which augmented by a small amount, the usual profit of the producer or of the merchant, must at the same time represent the actual price. The theory of a fair price of Houques-Fourcade, upon which we have already touched, is founded entirely on socio-ethical considerations. The price of every product should be settled so that the material foundation of a suitable livelihood can be offered to all.—These and similar views have been recently opposed by Charles Turgeon.[29] He states with convincing arguments that the blame for the social ills of our day should be laid not on the traditional doctrines of economics, which are in themselves correct, but on the general decay of the moral sense. He appeals to the voice of conscience, to which more attention should again be paid in economic life and he proposes, in case it is not listened to, the intervention of the state by means of strong legal sanctions. In another study,[30] Turgeon takes up the defence of the law of supply and demand and tries to show that it is not a rigorous and mechanical law of nature, but only a social rule which must therefore be subject to higher moral considerations, and—if necessary—give way to them.

CHAPTER V

DISTRIBUTION

1. The Italian Theory of Distribution based on the Theory of Economic Equilibrium

ALTHOUGH WE have stated, in dealing with theories of value and price, that the adherents of the Lausanne school made important and fruitful contributions in the present century, the matter is quite different with respect to distribution. Although the whole theory of economic equilibrium culminates in this, the founder of the school, Walras himself, wrote his finest work on this subject, which he apparently definitely exhausted. Even today, one still keeps to the essence of Walras's distribution and it is hardly likely that the immediate future will see any important changes made. The doctrine of the two markets of products and of productive factors, to which is annexed the third market of the formation of capital, is still the back bone of the Lausanne theory. In the market of productive services, land, labor and capital receive from the hands of the entrepreneur their shares of the output, the level of which is determined by the general laws of price formation and the sum of which must be in equilibrium with the entire price of the products sold by the entrepreneur. The entrepreneur's profits are explained by the friction and unevennesses which result from the oscillations of this equilibrium.

The relatively slight contributions which Pareto made to this trend of thought, are contained in essence in his *Cours,* which was published in the last century. Since the *Manuale* contains on this line nothing new that is of importance, we shall deal with it very briefly here. Pareto works the principle of marginal productivity into Walras's theory of distribution with much clarity and points out in this connection the fact that the coefficients of production are partly constant and partly variable in different ways. Many depend on the amount of the products whereas others are interconnected in various relations. For instance, if a change takes place in the amount of capital used in production, one will also necessarily take place in the quantity of labor required. On the whole, however, there is a tendency for the amounts of all factors in production to balance on the level of equal marginal utility. There corresponds to this equal marginal utility the equal marginal productivity of the factors of production on the basis of which the distribution of goods takes place. Barone perfects these ideas of Pareto in an extensive synopsis and develops it in all its details by means of mathematical analysis and graphic representation. In certain parts of his text-book he comes very close to the doctrines of Marshall.

Among Italian economists of mathematical tendencies, Pareto's income curve is the object of general admiration. Nevertheless, a few writers point out certain respects in which it could be improved.

Bresciani, for instance, relies upon English and German, as well as Italian, statistical material to show that the master's curve of income is too rigid and does not take into sufficient consideration the social and economic conditions of the formation of income which differ according to time and place.[1] Both Alberto Beneduce[2] and Furlan[3] advance similar objections. Giorgio Mortara aligns himself with Pareto in a polemic directed against Gini, in which he presents some interesting views with regard to the whole external picture of the distribution of incomes of various levels: their average, concentration, density, etc.[4] The most valuable contributions are here again made by Ricci who, besides studying the nature of income and its various forms in "static" and "dynamic" (or, as he calls it, "progressive") society,[5] examines the correctness of Pareto's curve of income.[6] On the basis of well-founded mathematical considerations, he too reaches the conclusion that Pareto has not devoted enough attention to the multiplicity of the phenomena of actual economic life. For the distribution of income not only has a different character in different countries, but changes also in the same country according as differences occur in the number and the social order of the population, in the Finance acts, or in the general level of prices.

2. *The Modern and the Classical Theory of Distribution in France*

Although a few French writers, such as Rist,[7] accepted the main doctrines of the Lausanne school on distribution, none of them has made any original developments of the idea in the last twenty-five years.

All the more remarkable, however, is the attempt of Albert Aftalion to perfect the Austrian theory of distribution, that of imputation.[8] He first distinguishes between three kinds of productivity: general productivity and the special physical and economic productivities. By general productivity (*productivité globale*) he means the relation between the entire production achieved in a given period of time and the sum of all the factors of production in which each factor is evaluated by its own particular unit. The special physical productivity of a factor of production is the share in the material production achieved within a given period of time which can be imputed to the unit of this factor. Economic productivity, finally, is the share which falls from the value of a product to the cooperation of the factor of production in question. Since this share is dependent on the marginal yield, the economic productivity of a factor of production becomes the same as the net yield which is achieved in a given period of time by utilizing the final unit of the factor in question. Aftalion derives the individual branches of income from this third kind of productivity, making use of the principles of the doctrine of imputation as expounded by Wieser and Böhm-Bawerk. He refers all the discord and disorder that prevail in the leading theories of distribution to the fact that we always confuse these three kinds of productivity. Therefore he tries in the third part of his book to ascertain where they correspond and where they differ in space and time. We cannot overestimate the value of his well-knitted studies for the theory of imputation. In a recent essay Aftalion tries to show that Wieser's theory of imputation is in need of revision in view of our modern experience with regard to the nature of money.[9]

Lavergne, whose system we have often mentioned, offers an original interpretation of marginal productivity in his doctrine of distribution. In his criticism of Liefmann's theory of distribution, Maurice Bellom broaches the question of a theory of remuneration which is meant to replace the theory of distribution and which will also make use of the principle of residue.[10]

The attention of the vast majority of French economists, however, is directed, even today, to the distribution theory of the classical school. At the beginning of the century, the theory was represented, as for instance by M. Rouxel,[11] in its original shape. More recently, and especially since the war, attempts have been made, even by the liberal group, to take modern theoretical ideas into consideration and to use them in their own theories of distribution.

The influence of subjectivistic and mathematical literature is very noticeable in the text-book of Truchy who tries to explain the entire process of distribution by the formation of price, much more directly than the classical school did. The principle of productivity upon which Ansiaux bases his theory of distribution contains many modern views, besides classical ones.—As a matter of fact modern French literature is not lacking in refutations of the classical theory. Paul Cahen [12] tries to refute the optimistic ideas of Bastiat's theory of distribution: that the proportion between interest and wages gradually changes in the course of economic development to the advantage of the latter. Charles Rist too is of the opinion that neither this theory nor the pessimistic view of Ricardo, developed by the socialists, can be positively proved by the facts of actual economic life.[13]

3. Ideas of Power and of Social Ethics in the Theory of Distribution

Among the modern writers in the Latin countries who make the idea of social power the first principle of their theory of distribution, the most important is Loria. In his famous work, which has since been translated into many languages and in which he gathers the results of years of social and economic research,[14] he tries to explain distribution in the light of historical materialism as well as of his famous proposals of land reform, upon which we have already touched. Accordingly the entire yield of production falls into two different parts. The first is the yield that "isolated labor" could achieve and the second is the result of the organization of labor. In our present economic system this second part is only partly due to labor; most of it being divided among interest, rent and monopoly profit. Loria then tries to show the important part that this monopoly profit has always played in the distribution of wealth, in the framework of his historical and sociological studies. The source of monopoly profit is only the socio-economic power which is always in the hands of the monopolist and which remains the fundamental principle of distribution so long as private property in land is not abolished.

Gino Arias correctly points out the fact that it is this idea which renders insecure the foundations of Loria's system, so excellent in its details.[15] Labriola inclines toward a theory of social power and seems to depart from his earlier attitude that distribution takes place only in proportion to the relative importance of the services rendered in production.[16] Natoli tries to explain the distribution of income principally by the social conflict between capitalists and workers. He was not able, however, to reach a perfectly clear conception of these problems.[17]

Landry worked out the socio-ethical aspects of the distribution of wealth in his book: *L'utilité sociale*, which appeared at the turn of the century and which we have already mentioned. There are also some stimulating ideas on the subject in the text-book of Tarde, in which the distribution of goods is subordinated to the phenomena of adaptation. Unfortunately, the theory is not developed in a consistent way.

4. *The Unification of the Laws of Returns*

In dealing with the theories of the individual kinds of incomes, and especially with the development of the theory of rent, we may state at once that in the Italian economic theory of the last twenty-five years it was the criticism of the classical law of diminishing returns on land which led to new and fruitful ideas in the theory of rent. In France, too, attention was directed to the laws of returns, but as a rule no new consequences were drawn for the theory of rent.

Antonelli, for instance, is content to show the boundaries which separate the purely technical, agronomic aspects of the law of diminishing returns on land from its economic consequences.[18] Relying upon the researches of foreign scientists, Pierre Aubry recognizes that the law of diminishing returns applies not only to agriculture but also to a certain extent to industry. He uses this knowledge only to combat socialism and to defend his own liberalistic ideal.[19] The Italians go much more deeply into the problem. In his work on the theory of production, Jannacone arrived a few years before Richard Schüller and Alfred Weber at an analysis of the causes in the technique of production of the law of returns. As we have already mentioned, he works out with care the relations between, and the mutual effects of, concentration, increase and acceleration, the three means through which a decrease can be brought about in the costs of production and mentions the discord of these mutual effects as the real reason for the proportional decrease of return in all branches of production. The work of P. Avenati [20] on private economics which appeared immediately after the war contains some valuable ideas with similar tendencies. It was the remarkable studies of Ghino Valenti which directed general interest in Italian literature to the law of returns. As early as the nineties, he interested himself, with the help of Liebig's studies, in the agronomic problems of agricultural production,[21] and later, in his text-book, utilized his results for economic theory. At first he states the law of definite proportions (*legge delle proporzioni definite*), according to which the factors of production must always stand to each other in a definite quantitative and qualitative proportion, in order to achieve a given favorable yield. The only difference in this connection between agriculture and industry is that, whereas in the latter even a slight deviation from the given proportions may lead to a marked decrease in production, in agriculture there is often more room for changes in these proportions. If we only had an exact knowledge of its technical laws, production could be extended with constantly increasing returns in both agriculture and industry. There is of course everywhere a certain limit of absolute satiety, beyond which a further extension of production is possible only with diminishing returns. This absolute limit, however, is still fairly distant in agriculture, in view of the progress which we may expect in our technical knowledge. Consequently the law of diminishing returns on land need not worry us for the time being. Valenti would prefer that attention be concentrated on the law of definite proportions, on a closer acquaintance with which we could after all speak only of increasing productivity in general. Graziani opposes in his text-book this theory of Valenti, as well as the analogous views of Cabiati and Virgilii and tries to show that the limit of absolute satiety admitted by Valenti is much nearer in practical agriculture than these writers admit.

5. *The Generalisation of the Theory of Rent*

On the whole, the studies in the theory of production which have been mentioned, succeeded in proving that there is some kind of a uniform law of returns for industry and agriculture. This provided the basis for a generalisation of the rent concept. The foundation for this had already been laid in the preceding century by the mathematical school, and even Pareto was able at most to give a more concise exposition of the theory of rent in his *Cours*, without adding any essentially new points. According to this, rent is exclusively a phenomenon of dynamic economics, of the transition from one state of static equilibrium to another. For, according to Pareto, in static economic equilibrium, the costs of production exhaust the entire price, so that any further constituent of price can appear only in the course of development. The existing savings can be brought into the required shape of capital only with more or less difficulty, wherefore the capital which is always ready at hand enjoys so to say a transitory monopoly. This is all the more noticeable in land, because of the relatively great difficulty of changing the savings into this form of capital. Because of its situation as a monopoly, capital can attain a price for its co-operation with production, which is greater than the strict costs of production: a difference which is the origin of rent in general.

Guido Sensini confines himself on the whole to a more complete development of this rent theory of Pareto,[22] but also ruthlessly criticizes the earlier theories of Ricardo and Carey and even the theory of Loria,[23] which is based on the idea of private land-monopoly. By extending the old concept of rent to that of a general producer's return, in which every surplus attained by the producer above the level of costs of production is considered a rent,[24] Sensini himself has recently drawn very near to the monopoly theories of rent. He also deems it necessary in a special study to point out the differences between rent and monopoly earnings, which he considers slight.[25] The smaller book of another follower of the Lausanne school, the Russian, Basile Samsonoff, which appeared earlier than Sensini's, is somewhat similar.[26] He too starts out with the dogmatic historical development of the rent concept, but deals more thoroughly with German theorists, such as Hermann, Mangoldt, Schäffle, Oppenheimer, etc. His positive theory is based on Pareto. Very noteworthy is his effort to find the source of the phenomenon of rent directly in the economic functions of private property.

A more useful work than either of these, is that of the Frenchman, Paul Frézouls,[27] who does not confine himself to a curt rejection of earlier theories, but endeavors rather to show genetically how the concept of rent develops from its narrow meaning with Ricardo to its present-day general shape. Frézouls himself understands by rent every derived earning that cannot be referred in the theory of distribution to cost of production. He distinguishes from "true" rent, which exists as well in a state of ideal economic equilibrium, "quasi rents," which exist only until this equilibrium has again been reached after some disturbance. With these ideas he departs somewhat from the strict Lausanne doctrine, and closely resembles Anglo-Saxon theorists. Frézouls works out especially well the concept of rent as depending on unusual personal abilities as well as that of consumer's rent. An analogous theory of rent is offered by Lavergne, who also stresses the importance of consumer's surplus. Other French writers are unable to familiarize themselves completely with this modern extension of the rent concept. Landry, for example, rejects it, as well as the idea of a special consumer's surplus and prefers to analyse rent in the traditional sense, as land rent.

The attempt to generalize the idea of rent reached its culmination in the bold attempt of Mario Calderoni, which remained unimitated, to outline the plan of a special new science, "proeretiks," or the science of exchange on the basis of the theory of rent.[28] According to this, there exists in the ethical world too a law of indifference by which we can judge the moral behavior of individuals only by means of an uniform, general standard, without regard to what it may have inwardly cost them. From this arises ethical rent. It would be enjoyed by somebody who accomplishes a good deed from an inner impulse, while he who could accomplish the same deed only through inner compulsion, would have no ethical rent. Calderoni considers these wide horizons as well as the social discords engendered by the general prevalence of the phenomenon of rent, which appears in so many different forms, sufficient to constitute a new and special branch of science.

6. *Consumer's Rent*

We have repeatedly mentioned writers who, partly in analysing the problems of price, partly in the extension of the concept of rent, arrive at a theory of consumer's rent. This theory becomes of marked importance in the French and Italian literatures of the last twenty-five years, and is enriched by many original discoveries. Gobbi states, in a noteworthy study of the subject, that every consumer's rent, in relation to the whole amount of consumption, reduces itself to zero, since one always spends the savings thus attained in buying other goods.[29] Graziani criticizes this theory with justice as being derived from a falsely objective attitude which looks upon consumer's rent as the difference between the amount of money paid and that which the individual would be willing to pay. In reality, consumer's rent is a purely subjective quantity; namely, that of the difference between the utility sacrificed and the utility received. Luigi Amoroso tries to deal mathematically with the interconnections between different consumer's rents and with their quantitative limits.[30] Umberto Ricci attempts to prove that, in the case of a change in the economic equilibrium as a result of changes in the price of a consumption-good, the users of this good receive a positive or a negative consumer's rent. This kind of rent is always dependent on changes in some condition of economic equilibrium. We may note the distinction which Ricci makes between natural and psychical consumer's rent.[31]

The Hungarian, Béla Ambrorovics, approaches consumer's rent through the problem of railway tariffs and customs duties.[32] He has some interesting things to say in the course of his mathematical analysis but nothing of the sensational importance which the author himself claims. Gino Borgatta has written a useful study, in which he analyses consumer's rent from the point of view of the Lausanne school and shows how this kind of rent can be made the object of taxation.[33]

In connection with the problem of consumer's rent, we have also the investigations of Del Vecchio on the relation between rent and consumption.[34] He tries, in connection with the well-known law of Engel, to state mathematically in what proportion the amount spent on means of livelihood stands to the whole amount of consumption. Some of the best works in Italian literature on the theory of consumption are that of Eugenio Slutsky,[35] a mathematical analysis, connected with the Lausanne doctrine of equilibrium, in a supposed consumer's balance, and that of Giovanni de Francisci Gerbino.[36] The latter confines himself to making a sharp logical distinction between the concept of rent and that of consumption. The Frenchman, Z. Georges Strat, offers an historical survey of the importance and the protection of the consumer in the economics of different epochs. In regard to the present epoch, he tends to glorify the idea of consumers' association.[37]

7. *The Attitude of the Lausanne School to the Problem of Interest and Theories of Savings*

In regard to the theory of interest, two main tendencies can be discerned in French and Italian economics of the past twenty-five years. The first is influenced by the Lausanne school and the second, which is more fruitful, starts with the teaching of Böhm-Bawerk and reaches its own theories of interest partly by relying on him and partly by differing from him.—To begin with the Lausanne school, it has really little to say about this problem. Like other kinds of income, it considers interest a compensation for co-operation in production, with its level determined according to the law of economic equilibrium by the supply and demand of capital. As concerns the problem of price, the question of interest has a special position only in so far as, according to Walras's theory, it is decided in a special market, that of the formation of capital, in which that part of income which is not immediately needed for consumption, is saved according to the level of the expected interest-rate, and placed as capital at the disposal of production or else again given over to consumption. An equilibrium reigns also in this market, which maintains itself by means of the changing levels of interest. When production needs more capital, the rate of interest rises and stimulates the formation of capital and therefore of savings. An over-supply of capital is naturally accompanied by a fall in the rate of interest, which diminishes savings and halts the further superfluous formation of capital.

Pareto himself seems to be embarrassed in explaining the real source of interest on capital. He is not satisfied with the mere idea of productivity, and so he looks eclectically for other principles; e. g., the main ideas of Böhm-Bawerk's agio theory. Interest then is a result of the cooperation of these different factors. The origin of interest, however, is of secondary importance with Pareto; only the problem of changing rates of interest absorbs him, and he makes this part of economics also accessible to the idea of equilibrium.

It was natural, with this theory of interest, that the adherents of the Lausanne school should gradually turn their attention from the actual problem of interest to that of capital formation and of savings, for in this they rightly perceived a suitable point of departure for applying the idea of equilibrium.

Walras assumed that, in the course of creating capital, the application of savings to some branch of production is determined only by the level of pure income which is expected therefrom. Pareto agrees with this in theory but emphasizes in his applied economics the fact that the various possible applications of savings may have the same relations to each other in certain cases as goods of different qualities and therefore the level of pure income which can be obtained is not the only decisive factor. Consequently in these cases Walras's theory of an equalization of the average of all pure incomes is also invalid. Felice Vinci points out, in a short but interesting study,[38] the fact that individual tastes play as a rule an important role in the application of savings, and that the supply of new capital is not directed to the various branches of capital only by the interest rate. Naturally, we can talk even less of a tendency toward a general equalization of the average incomes from capital.

Charles Rist, who is in general well disposed to the mathematical tendency, offers some noteworthy studies on the problem of savings.[39] He distinguishes first between reserves of savings which remain for purpose of consumption and productive savings which are meant to become sources of income for the individual and an increase in wealth for society. He then examines these productive savings according to the manner of their appearance, their composition and the general importance of their role in the mechanism of economics, by analysing their relation to the other factors in production. In conformity with his theory of savings,

Rist attacked in an earlier essay the view that capital originates only in labor.[40] In this connection we may also mention the recent studies of Charles Bodin in which he discusses the internal connections between the concepts of capital and income from original points of view, which also present stimulating ideas for the theory of interest.[41] Mourre tries to ascertain with the help of mathematics the causes for the fluctuations in the rates of interest but reaches only mediocre conclusions.[42] Recently he has gone back to the problem of the formation of capital and tries to discover, with the help of the mathematical method, the manifold relations in which the supply of savings is dependent on all elements of the equilibrium in the economics of the consumer.[43] The equilibrium, then, in which the entire supply of and the entire demand for savings meet determines—in the sense of the general Lausanne theory—the rate of interest.

The best theory of capital in French and Italian economics of the first quarter of the 20th century, is that of Ricci,[44] who criticizes all the modern views on the subject in his survey, which also embraces the general theory of production and consumption. G. H. Bousquet, in a clever criticism, is convinced that the theory which is based on equilibrium and developed on psychological lines can interpret interest for an hypothetical static economics but is inadequate to explain the actual social phenomenon of interest in dynamic economics.[45] Amoroso is not content with analysing the concept of capital, but also examines the accuracy of the modern theories of interest, in which matter the standard of value of his criticism is the eclectic attitude toward the problem of interest adopted by Pareto.[46] In his positive exposition he approaches most nearly Cassel's theory of interest.

Del Vecchio also starts with a basic criticism of the prevailing theories of interest but reaches more independent positive conclusions than Amoroso. In the main, his attitude is also somewhat eclectic but he manages very cleverly to combine elements from different doctrines into a new and independent theory. He works out especially the extra-economic, the social and psychological, relations of interest and tries to prove that a satisfactory solution of this problem can be achieved only by constantly considering these aspects. Del Vecchio attributes a decisive role to custom in the origin of savings and consequently in the formation of capital and in the fixing of the interest rate and considers that its importance in economics is too often underrated. Besides this, he also draws upon ideas of the dynamic theory and of the agio theory.[47]

8. *The Influence of Böhm's Agio Theory in the Romance Countries*

The views of del Vecchio, and partly also those of Bousquet and Amoroso, lead us to the second main group of theories of interest in recent Italian literature, which are based on the theory of Böhm-Bawerk. While the Lausanne school gave only partial and eclectic consideration to this doctrine, it here comes to the front. Among the economists who most closely resemble Böhm, we must first mention Graziani who, following the lead of Ricca-Salerno, appropriates the main ideas of the agio theory and makes only formal changes. He tries to reduce Böhm's "absolute" difference of value between present and future goods to a relative one by referring it to the different evaluations of the capitalist on one side and of the employer on the other. The capitalist who is sufficiently provided with present goods values future goods more than the employer who needs present goods for production, but hopes to have a surplus of future goods. It is by means of this relative difference of the two evaluations that Graziani and his adherents explain the interest on capital.[48] The theory of interest propounded by Tangorra [49] at the beginning of the century is also in its essence founded on the time element, but relies on the ideas of Ferrara rather than on those of Böhm. His attempt to justify interest on ethical and socio-economic grounds strikes one as rather futile.

Böhm's theory of interest also had a great deal of influence on French economics in the first quarter of the twentieth century. Landry, who has undoubtedly been responsible for the finest contribution, makes a desperate attempt to rid himself of Böhm's thoughts,[50] but is able to criticize him only for insisting on the derivation of interest from a single source. He himself is more inclined to return to the productivity theory of the classical school, which has remained unchanged to the present day among most French economists; formally, however, he tries to treat the question of interest as purely a problem of price. He starts by analysing the demand and supply of capital. The former he refers, in addition to the productivity of capital, especially to psychological reasons which bring about a higher evaluation of present goods in comparison with future goods. Most of this is taken from Böhm-Bawerk. The factors in the supply of capital are, on the one hand the desire to counterbalance the sacrifice made in the formation of capital by a corresponding enjoyment of its fruition, and on the other hand the fear of a future depreciation of goods. These factors in the demand and the supply of capital have many complicated relations to each other, from which result the two curves, the intersection of which represents the actual level of the rate of interest. To be more precise, this intersection takes place with Landry at the point where the marginal surplus value expected from the application of capital to production meets the marginal sacrifice of capitalization.

9. *Partial Weakening of the Theory of Interest*

Not even in France did the clever, but unusually complicated theory of Landry find favor. More attention was paid to those writers who try to explain interest as simply as possible. An example of the latter is Ansiaux, who sharply criticizes Böhm's doctrine in his text-book, and reproaches it with being too complex and artificial. In his positive exposition on interest, Ansiaux develops a productivity theory of a classical kind, in which his attempt to merge the whole question of interest with the problem of value justly incurs the charge of superficiality.—A much more primitive explanation of the income from capital is concealed behind the brilliant dress which Lavergne gives to his own peculiar theory of interest. According to him, there is no immediate productivity belonging to monied capital; nevertheless, the entrepreneur needs it in order to acquire the immediate means of production. In the case where this monied capital is placed at his disposal by others, we have the consent of economics to individual production; a consent for which the entrepreneur has to pay a price: interest. It does not take much study to show that Lavergne, on the whole, discusses nothing more than the appearance of loan interest and consequently explains nothing more than the theory of interest was able to do in its very beginnings.

10. *Socio-ethical Wage Theories in Italy*

The Lausanne school has devoted considerably less attention to the theory of wages than to the theory of interest. Whatever can be said about wages from the point of view of pure theory has been said by Pareto and his followers in their general theory of distribution. The special socio-ethical aspects, however, which come into consideration with wages are not amenable to the mathematical attitude. Consequently, Italian economists of the first quarter of our century have contributed relatively little on this point. Those who stood outside the Lausanne school and who devoted more attention to the problem of wages tried, with few exceptions, to work out principally its socio-ethical side, thus neglecting more or less its purely economic aspects.

Supino has made some noteworthy attempts to comprehend the essence of the classical wage-fund theory.[51] He wishes to develop this doctrine from the point of view of a dynamic conception of economics; and therefore he not only derives wages from the wage fund but also studies the relations by which the wage fund itself in the course of economic development originates in the produce of labor, grows and completes itself. Supino then enters upon a consideration of social ethics, laments the discord that prevails in consequence of the present organization of labor as between production and consumption and permeates his theory of wages with the ideas of social-reform.—Guiseppe Ricca-Salerno also published his great work on the theory of wages at the turn of the century.[52] The chief value of this is its unusual wealth of statistical and historical material. In his theoretical exposition, he endeavors to connect the theory of wages directly with that of value; he flirts with the wage-fund theory, and devotes much attention to the ideas of productivity. He considers the difference in the value between present and future goods the basis for determining the level of wages. The main characteristics of the book, however, are its compassion for the socially oppressed classes and its socio-ethical demand for the improvement of the economic condition of the working man. Ricca-Salerno's disciple, Graziani, accepts this doctrine with slight alterations,[53] and attacks in his text-book chiefly the iron law of wages and the application of the principle of marginal productivity to the theory of wages.

Considerations of social ethics are paramount in the wage theory of Loria.[54] He starts from the main principles of his well-known doctrine of land-reform. In consequence of private property in land, the worker is robbed of his economic independence and capitalists are in a position to force wages down to the minimum necessary for existence. This is the old, well-known attitude which socialist theorists have always shown toward wages.—Here we may point out that Antonio Graziadei has recently made Marx's wage theory the object of a thorough examination, in connection with his criticism of the doctrine of surplus value.[55] On the whole, he reaches the conclusion that a sound and lasting rise of wages is possible only on the basis of a corresponding increase in production. Frederico Chessa, on the other hand, studies the influence which trade unions exert on settling the wage level.[56]

11. The Realistic Explanations of Wages by Levasseur, Cornélissen and Simiand

The theory of wages is one of the few fields of economic theory in which the French have contributed more than the Italians in the first quarter of our century. The reason for this is that while Italian economics lost here its best men through the indifferent standpoint of the Lausanne school, French economists found in the theory of wages a set of problems which were especially suited to their constant interest in economic and social conflicts. At first the writers who dealt with this subject were those who reject the mathematical method. Levasseur, Cornélissen, and Simiand all three published their works at about the same time and represent, with certain different shadings, a decidedly social and realistic tendency.

Émile Levasseur was the last to publish his book on the wage theory; but, in the course of his long and fruitful scientific career, he often treated the question of wages, years earlier and in approximately the same way. His work [57] can best be compared with Ricca-Salerno's, which we have just mentioned. He deals with a great deal more than with the actual question of wages, touches upon nearly all the problems of social policy, and exhibits strong socio-ethical traits—even though he attacks all utopistic social reform. He considers wages the result of the cooperation of six different factors: the productivity of labor, the general wealth of the country, the cost of maintenance of the workers, their mutual competition, state regulations and custom, should all be taken into consideration, if we seek to discover the origins of wages. We can reduce these different factors to a common denominator: the law of supply and demand, and can consequently solve the problem of wages from one comprehensive point of view.[58] Cornélissen also derives wages from similarly manifold sources,[59] but especially emphasizes the importance of the social environment. His principle is to solve the problem of the wage theory in a purely inductive way, by minutely studying individual cases; but he also tries, in evident contradiction to this, to offer a general and complete explanation of wages by utilizing his theories of value and of price, which we have already mentioned. According to this, the price of labor, wages, results from the combination between cost of production and the use value of the labor, approaching now the one now the other limit according to the particular case. In dealing with the level of the production cost of labor, we must also consider the cost of subsistence of the laborers with the lowest standard of life, who are still employed by the entrepreneur. Cornélissen has nothing very new to say in this stressing of the marginal factor, since the idea of the origin of the real wage level as midway between use value and cost value had already been expressed much earlier by German writers. We may notice, however, the large mass of inductive material that Cornélissen has marshalled in his work.

Simiand's investigations cover a narrower field,[60] but are all the more independent. He tries above all to offer a concrete application of Durkheim's positive method. The object of his study is the fluctuations in the wage level in the French coal mines. Simiand utilizes a mass of statistical material covering fifty years in order to work out certain regularities in the fluctuation of wages. These he refers to the actions of individuals and groups motivated by certain tendencies. The actions of employers as well as employees revolve around profit and effort and on both sides we notice the effort to maintain both factors at the level already attained. The tendency to increase profits and to diminish effort is of a secondary character. Out of the conflict between these different and contrary forces there result the relations between changes in the price of the product on one side and the wage level on the other which also throw much light on the nature of wages. In the main Simiand's subtle investigations resolve themselves into a theory of wages of which the chief explanatory principles are the productivity of labor and the conflict between employer and workmen.

12. The Marginal Principle and Socio-ethical Viewpoints in the French Theory of Wages

Landry and Lavergne build their theories of wages on the principle of marginal productivity. For the latter, this principle is sufficient to explain wages in its entirety since, according to him, labor has no cost price of production. It cannot be increased at will: the present generation of workers always enjoys a monopoly, since the next one will not attain the working age for from twenty to twenty-five years. Landry, on the other hand, thinks that the theory of marginal productivity of labor throws light on only one side of the problem of wages; namely, demand. The other side, supply, is of equal importance in the labor market, and represents a pure problem of population. Landry refers the main ideas of this wage theory, expounded in his *Manuel*, in a special work [61] to Cantillon and to Effertz.

In the French literature of the first quarter of our century, too, we meet with many studies which deal with their subject from the socio-ethical aspect. For instance, Léon Polier published a book,[62] at the beginning of the century, in which he sharply criticized in parts the Christian and socialistic doctrines of a "fair wage," and tries to derive them from the sentimental postulate of the socio-ethical idea of equality, which has nothing to do with science. Barthélemy Raynaud proposes, in his thoroughly well grounded study,[63] a minimum wage, settled by the state, and tries to justify it and prove its necessity. Max Lazard, who is also inspired by social ethics, tries to show the flaws in all deductive theories of wages.[64] Relying partly, but always with a critical spirit, on the American, Clark, he works out the manifold individual relations of the problems of labor and of wages, and complains finally of the great injustice of the prevalent distribution of wealth. Charles

Gide tries, in a recent work, to point out the difficulties which would attend the abolition of wage labor.[65]

13. *Monopoly Theories and Eclectic Explanations of Profits*

French and Italian science of the first quarter of our century, has brought forth no essentially new and creative thoughts on the theory of profits. The reason probably is that the Lausanne school has hitherto paid no particular attention to this problem, although their method was better adapted to it than to the problem of wages. The other writers offer first of all a few monopoly theories of profits. Etocle Lorini [66] tries to give his theory too broad a basis, with which his final conclusions do not agree. He reaches the problem of entrepreneurship by way of the principles of economy and of diminishing returns, as well as of Malthus's law of population. He sees in the problem of the entrepreneur the kernel of the whole social problem. The big industrialist abuses his paramount position in modern economic society and exploits even the capitalist because of his exaggerated profits. According to Lorini, socialists as well as liberals are wrong since the fundamental social evil is to be sought not in capitalism but in modern large scale industry. —The theory of Loria, which contains an original idea, appears more plausible. First of all men produced in isolation; then, under the compulsion of want, when the means of production, especially land, had been seized by a few powerful individuals, they had united themselves for combined production. That portion of the surplus produced by this combined labor which falls as profit to the entrepreneur is to be considered in its origin as a monopoly profit caused by social power.

Landry too proposes what is essentially a monopoly theory of profit, which sees the basis of the entrepreneur's monopoly not only in the social conditions of power but also in the relatively infrequent union of capital and administrative ability in one person. Landry underestimates the importance of the numerous cases in which modern entrepreneurs have neither their own capital nor especial abilities when he says that they are only exceptions, which may be neglected. Emilio Cossa sees the source of profits in the intellectual capacities as well as in the special aptitude of the entrepreneur, but at the time relies upon the chief principles of the theory of economic friction.[67] Christian Cornélissen has recently offered an even more eclectic monopoly theory of the entrepreneur's profit,[68] in which he also strongly emphasizes the idea of social force. The entrepreneur can dispose of natural, legal or material monopolies, which assure him a profit. The exploitation of human labor comes then into consideration as a factor of social force. The efficient organization and direction of the business; that is to say, the personal activity of the entrepreneur, also plays an important role; finally the element of risk, the speculative management of the competitive relationships, should also be regarded as a source of the entrepreneur's profit. Since for Cornélissen profit is a residual income, he lets its level be determined by the state of the other branches of income.—Whereas this theory is primarily based on induction, and does not take much of the literature on the subject into consideration, a young Frenchman, François Perroux, starts with an extremely careful examination of all previous theories of profit.[69] In his positive solution of the problem, he too reaches an eclectic conclusion: risk, personal activity and economic power are the three most important sources of profit.

Guido Sensini is of the opinion that the problems which Perroux sets himself can be solved more accurately and clearly by using the mathematical method.[70]—Gustavo del Vecchio, a master of this method, stresses, besides the dynamic character of the entrepreneur's profit, especially its element of risk according to its different forms of appearance.[71]—Frederico Chessa throws much light on the general importance of the element of risk in economic life.[72]

14. Differential Profits

At the beginning of the century, Costantino Ottolenghi published a theory of profits, which differs from those which we have already mentioned.[73] He too makes much of the element of ability in the entrepreneur, but gives it a somewhat different treatment. There is for Ottolenghi no absolute profit, but only a differential one, which—somewhat like Ricardo's differential rent—exists in the difference between the income of any one entrepreneur and that of the marginal entrepreneur in the same branch of production. Indeed, a certain ability is necessary to achieve a profit beyond that which replaces costs of production. Such a profit, however, can arise in certain circumstances through a more favorable general external condition of the entrepreneur. Nevertheless, there is, according to Ottolenghi, also an absolute upper limit of profit, which is dependent on the "law of definite proportions." On this assumption of the most favorable coordination of the elements required for production, he relies upon Valenti's theory of production which we have already mentioned. A special value is attached to Ottolenghi's theory by the inclusive statistical material, taken from different countries, upon which it is built.—Profits possess a similar differential character in the works of Lavergne, who treats them in the same manner as rent in general. Whether entrepreneurs are capable or not, the means of production are at their disposal for equal prices. It depends upon the business ability as well as upon the business condition of the individual entrepreneur if and to what extent he will be able to use these means of production for profit. Lavergne calls the special personal capacity, which assures the entrepreneur of profit, "the idea of production" (*l'idée de production*).—This theory of differential profits offers no essentially new doctrine: its main ideas are expressed with great clarity by earlier German authors, such as Mangoldt and Schäffle.

PART FOUR

THE DEVELOPMENT IN THE ANGLO-SAXON COUNTRIES

CHAPTER I

METHOD

1. The Mathematical Procedure

The conditions under which economics developed in England and in America in the twentieth century differ widely. In spite of a common language the difference between French and American economists at the turn of the century was about as marked as that which we noticed between German and Austrian theorists. In England at this time the "theoretical investigation" founded by Jevons reached its highest development and the scientific success of the mathematical method had assured it a leadership which it has retained. On the other hand, American political economy was almost revolutionized around 1900. The doctrines of Carey, Walker and George were falling into oblivion, making way for an energetic generation of young American economists who had been trained in German universities by such men as Roscher, Knies, Held, Schmoller, Wagner, Cohn, Knapp and Conrad. The scientific method which they imported from Germany was of course historical. But as early as the late eighties these young men were turning their eyes with steadily increasing interest toward the Austrian school. They brought the deductive method into prominence and were able effectively to develop the mathematical theories of England and Italy. In the year 1899 there appeared the most important result of this movement—the publication of Clark's work on distribution, by which the deductive method was assured of its position in modern American economics. The years which follow, however, witness a strong reaction: the practical business mind of the American harks gradually back to realism. And the post-war generation of economists seems to be turning away from the abstract deductive method.

While in America, the discussion of method was a lively one in the first quarter of the century, in England it caused no commotion. The authority of the Cambridge school—founded by Marshall and directed by him for many years—was practically unquestioned, and its moderate mathematical procedure is even today the authoritative force in British economics. In the present century leadership passed from Marshall, who devoted his latest energies to a literary solution of practical economic problems, to Francis Y. Edgeworth who had always busied himself with methodological questions. Edgeworth has recently died, but his works on method seemed assured of lasting influence in his country.

Notwithstanding a similarity in their attitudes toward method, there is a marked difference between the uses which Marshall and Edgeworth made of mathematical procedure. Marshall employs mathematical analysis with prudence and moderation. He is always especially concerned with the practical phenomena of economic life and he does not employ mathematics until the position which he has taken has been firmly buttressed by "realistic" considerations. Even then he is unwilling to become absorbed in his mathematics and returns as quickly as he can to the *practical* problems—which, indeed, he has never abandoned. Marshall's advice on the use of the mathematical method is characteristic: one should use mathematical formulas as an abbreviated language, not as a means of research, but as soon as one has attained the expected results, one should translate the mathematical formulae into ordinary language, and then burn them.[1] Edgeworth's attitude is quite different. Allowing full scope to his mathematical tastes, he is passionately fond of the wildest abstractions, which he develops for their own sake, forgetting that they are merely a means toward a better understanding of practical economic affairs. At times he is too far removed from genuine economic experience, but at other times he is capable of most fruitful ideas which he could not have attained without this use of mathematical procedure. An example is the important results which have been reached by his application of the reckoning of probability to economic problems. Marshall uses mathematical research unwillingly and as a last resort; for Edgeworth it is an end in itself.

It would be an error to conclude that Edgeworth, in his enthusiasm for mathematical procedure, exaggerates its importance. On the contrary: he never forgets its limitations and he repeatedly says, in his methodological works, that we should not expect too much from its application. The most important discussions in which he champions these views have been republished in the second volume of his complete works.[2]

Between these two extremes, represented by Marshall and Edgeworth, we have all the other more recent adherents of mathematical economics in England. The most successful of these are A. C. Pigou and J. M. Keynes.

At the beginning of the century, H. Cunynghame made a spirited attempt to express the most important economic theories in the form of geometrical figures.[3] More recently, Arthur L. Bowley has developed the main tenets of modern mathematical economics in a clear and penetrating sketch.[4] It is characteristic that special text books [5] have recently been published in England, for the purpose of familiarizing students with the mathematical method.

In America, the mathematical method, in its original purity, has had comparatively few adherents. Nevertheless, some valuable contributions to this procedure have been made. Its two most important practical exponents have been Irving Fisher and Henry L. Moore. These have also taken an occasional part in methodological discussion. Moore gives an excellent exposition of the connection between statistical research and deductive mathematical theory.[6] Thomas Nixon Carver makes an interesting attempt toward an improved quantitative conception of economic phenomena,[7] whereas Willard C. Brinton, following Cunynghame, give a broad and graphic description of economic principles, without introducing the language of mathematics.[8] Also worthy of mention is the older treatise of Frederick Kellog Blue,[9] which attempts to cover the psychological principles of economics with a cloak of mathematics.

2. *Logical Attempts*

The next of kin to the adherents of the mathematical method in England and America are those writers who seek to improve our science by means of logic. The concrete points of view from which they start vary widely.

At first we find a return to classicism and an attempt to borrow logical unity from the standpoints of natural science. Charles A. Tuttle studies the relations which emerge out of man's physical needs and his dependence on the physical environment and tries to rest the entire structure of economics on these relations.[10] Arthur H. Gibson, who published at the beginning of the century the first part of an ambitious system of economics which he never completed,[11] makes the physical laws of production and consumption the bases of his abstract speculations. More recently, Julius Davidson [12] and L. Southern [13] have come to somewhat similar conclusions, with reference to the problems of the law of profits and especially to the abstinence theory of interest. Southern works symbolically with the concept of independent economic substances and tries by this means to reach a coherent solution of certain problems. Of more importance than these almost forgotten attempts are the works of the Englishmen W. W. Carlile [14] and James Bonar.[15] They demand a system of economics that is logically flawless and sharply attack the lack of coherence and the logical mistakes which appear even in the most practicable economic theories. Bonar's achievements are especially illuminating. Leverett S. Lyon, an American, follows the example of German scientists when he tries to view economic factors as functional relationships.[16] In this direction he has recently been followed by an increasing number of American economists. Lyon first devotes himself to a thorough study of a few elementary factors, and hopes to probe by degrees the more complex phenomena of the science. John A. Hobson, the Englishman, in one of his recent studies, opposes the traditional classical and neo-classical attitude with an entirely new critical philosophy.[17] After having analysed the behavior of the economic man, he comes to the conclusion that æsthetic interests play a more important part in economic affairs than has hitherto been supposed. Consequently, this viewpoint must be taken into account in theoretical investigations.

3. *The Quarrel over Psychological Principles*

Hobson's attempt leads us to the recent movement in American literature to revise the principles of economics from the point of view of psychology. The exponents of this movement rely on the "new American psychology," which originated at the end of the nineteenth century out of a union of associationist psychology, Spencerian evolution and German experimental psychology, and which rejects the abstract deductive system of traditional hedonistic and utilitarian economics. Among the most polemical adherents of this movement are Charles H. Parker,[18] Carl E. Parry [19] and O. Fred Boucke.[20] These three are of the opinion that deductive economics, founded on marginal analysis, has been superseded by the latest findings in psychology. They therefore demand a return to the psychological origins of man's needs, in the light of which can best be recognized the real connections between economic behavior and the social-economic environment. Similar ideas have been advanced, more succintly, by L. K. Frank [21] and A. J. Snow.[22] The latter attacks the doctrines of Z. C. Dickinson.

As Carver [23] had done more concisely, Dickinson [24] tries to prove that, notwithstanding the new developments of psychology, the old hedonistic doctrine is still essentially suited to our needs, since it considers the phenomena of mental life in the only aspect that is possible from the point of view of the economist. Proceeding from this conviction, he subtly analyses the psychological motives of economic behavior, around which revolves the whole machinery of production and consumption. He follows Irving Fisher in his conceptions of saving, capital and interest and in his consistent adherence to a subjective theory of value. F. A. Fetter also attacks the psychological arguments of the institutionalists, and tries to show that hedonistic assumptions are not at all the foundations of modern economic theory. They had been included in the theory of marginal utility only through faulty English translation.[25] Somewhat similar to the attitude of Fetter is that of the Englishman P. S. Florence, who studied in the United States and who thinks that economic theory should be independent of all difference of opinion in the realm of psychology. As long as this was not the case, traditional economics was on the wrong track; institutionalism, too, is just as mistaken when it unites its fate with that of the new American psychology. Nevertheless, Florence expects much from the new statistical and realistic methods of research.[26]

It seems unlikely that the efforts of Dickinson and Fetter, or the attempts of some of the older orthodox leaders to alter or to consolidate the psychological foundations of their system by a thorough analysis of the concept of wants and its relations to the primary objects of economic life, will be able to withstand the onslaughts of their young opponents.

4. *The Realistic Current in America*

As we have already remarked, the Institutionalists start their plan of positive reform by investigating economic institutions in their essence, their growth and their interactions with the economic behavior of man. Their methodology is marked by meticulousness of description, and by a wealth of historical and statistical data; while their general work is characterized by a retention of the "veil of money." It is partly owing to these efforts that the study of business cycles has come into such prominence in the last fifteen years. During the first quarter of the century there has been a parallel movement toward greater realism; so that most of the younger American economists, including many who are not specially interested in psychology, agree, as did the English in their development of the mathematical method, upon the necessity of a social and practical orientation of economic theory. This is the reason that America has not seen those disputes over method, such as were experienced in Germany. Whereas the English are always conscious of the limitations of their mathematical procedure, the new American realists—with the exception of the left wing institutionalists—recognize the rights of abstract research: their proposals, therefore, all tend toward a realistic interpretation of economic theory. The necessity of a "division of labor" between more abstract and more realistic investigations, is as a rule not disputed in the economic literature of English-speaking people. But while most English economists are especially interested in abstract procedure, the Americans are more and more showing signs of realism in their conceptions of method.

A balance is found in Allyn A. Young—to mention but one of the foremost defenders of the classical tradition.[27] To him, the question of deduction or induction is quite futile. Jacob Viner tried, in one of his earlier articles, to show the logical necessity of using both methods.[28] Compare these two with one of the leaders of institutionalism, for example Lionel D. Edie: [29] with him, the various currents of economic investigation, which differ so widely in their methodology, are beautifully harmonized. He tries to show that the chief positive viewpoints of Institutionalism are present in the works of some of the modern leaders in abstract theory. Paul T. Homan is, on the whole, sceptical of the future of American economics; nevertheless, his most recent researches in the history of theory [30] show signs of methodological reconciliation.

5. *Methodological Discussions among American Economists*

This development becomes clear, if we examine the yearly Records of Meetings of the American Economic Association. This leading association of American economists was founded about the middle of the eighties, with a program which clearly reflected the main principles of the historical school, that had been learned in Germany. A change soon became noticeable in favor of the modern abstract theoretical attitude. At about the turn of the century the adherents of this tendency predominated in influence if not in numbers. Yet a gradual reaction, and a partial return to the original program, set in.

Edwin R. A. Seligman, who is one of the leading American figures in economic research and public finance and who has also made some valuable contributions to theory, exemplifies this reaction. In a report made before the Association at the beginning of the century, he stressed the importance for theoretical as well as practical investigators of taking into consideration the leading social, political and ethical attitudes in economic life, if they wish to keep on the right track.[31] This thought appears in other works of Seligman, in which he interests himself especially in the relations between social life and economic phenomena. He arrives, thus, at a thoughtful, moderate and considered defence of historical materialism.[32]

Two years after Seligman, Jacob H. Hollander discussed, in the association, with much penetration the practical references in the predominating theories of distribution and emphatically demanded that economists should return from the "metaphysical speculations" of pure theory to economic reality. He therefore recommends a more realistic tendency in the development of the theory of distribution.[33] In the discussion which followed Hollander's report, Victor Rosewater and David Kinley were among those who seconded him, whereas J. B. Clark and H. R. Seager (who as a matter of fact has recently shown leanings toward a social attitude) try to show that every economic theory, however abstract, is in the long run a means toward the clarification of practical reality. Opposed to this moderate position, we have the attitude of Frank Albert Fetter, who rejects Hollander's attack, and seeks to justify abstract theory. It should be mentioned here that Fetter himself has recently reverted to a more realistic conception of economic theory through his "ideal of welfare," which he enthusiastically advanced as destined to take the place of the problem of price at the center of theoretical economics. We shall deal with this more fully below.

In a somewhat later report, Simon Nelson Patten defended the view that economic theory would win much by greater simplicity of diction and clarity of exposition.[34] This would easily be attained if economists used moderation in abstractions, and adhered more closely to the phenomena of economic life. He believed that this procedure would not injure the scientific character of our theoretical studies. Some years earlier Patten had adopted a similarly unfriendly attitude toward ultra-abstract research in his discussion of the criticism which Charles W. MacFarlane made of J. B. Clark's theory of distribution.[35] He tried to show that it was impossible to reach any really new conclusions in economic theory by the mathematical method. He expressed similar opinions in a discussion by the society of the theory of distribution.[36] At this time, in a small special treatise on methodology, Patten demanded a reconstruction of economic theory on realistic, inductive and statistical foundations, instead of the earlier deductive doctrines, which to him were already obsolete.[37]

In a paper before the association, David R. Dewey favored, in more moderate tones, the construction of economic theories only on the carefully proven results of practical observation; he does not, however, deny all right to deductive procedure.[38] During the war, Hollander appeared again upon the scene, and in some interesting discussions of method, voiced the opinion that economics had made no progress in the last thirty years, owing to the plethora of abstract theories.[39] According to him, abstract speculations could be really productive only when they are balanced by a parallel development of factual investigations. In the colloquy, even Irving Fisher felt bound to agree with Hollander's main thesis, and ventured only modestly to show the other side of the picture: the dangers which attend an untheoretical gathering of undigested facts. If Hollander judged with pessimism the recent past of our science, Thorstein Veblen, whom we have mentioned as the leader of Institutionalism, and one of the most profound thinkers of modern American economics, has more recently prophesied, no less dismally, its calculable future. In his report to the association, at its 37th session, held in Chicago in December 1924, he pointed out the flaws in the inner structure of present-day economic theory, and prophesied that, before long, the specialized investigation of facts would develop into the viewpoints of private economics and the devouring spirit of commerce, while economic theory itself would become ossified in a scholastic traditionalism.[40] John Maurice Clark and Raymond Taylor Bye are right in contrasting with this depressing picture first of all the original and profound researches which have been made in recent years, especially in the very workshop of Veblen himself. Although they realize that the fears of their older colleague are partially justified, they believe that the vital force of our science conceals its further developments. Of much importance for the change which has taken place in American economics to the advantage of realism is the fact that, at the last two methodological discussions of the association at St. Louis, December 1926,[41] and at Washington, December 1927,[42] the disposition of the parties was the opposite of what had taken place hitherto. From the beginning of the century the attacks had been made, as we have seen, against the ruling abstract-theoretical tendency, in behalf of a more realistic attitude. Now that the realists have become the leaders, they can in turn adopt a comfortable position of defence. For instance, Hollander, who had always spoken against the exaggerations of the deductive method, strikes us today as rather defending it against the overflow of realism. Similar is the standpoint of F. W. Taussig and John D. Black, F. H. Knight and T. S. Adams. Although they follow the golden mean, the last two stress the dangers which may result from an incautious use of the statistical method. Only the two Chicago professors, Jacob Viner and Henry Schultz, take up the cudgels in defence of deduction. Viner says that without it one cannot dream of a fruitful application of statistics for the further development of economics; while Schultz quotes the works of Cournot, Walras, Auspitz and Lieben, to prove the necessity of a mathematical theory of economics. Their voices, however, do not attract much attention, for the leading personality in both these discussions was Wesley Clair Mitchell, a champion of Institutionalism. We shall come back to a consideration of his views later. He is supported in his defence of statistical economics by several writers, including Frederic C. Mills, Horace Secrist, Kemper Simpson and Carl Snyder. John Candler Cobb, in his papers on the subject [43] has some fine distinctions to make with regard to the use of statistics in solving economic problems. In this he follows Marshall, and stresses the means whereby the result of quantitative analysis may be developed in theory.

Out of all these discussions of the American Economic Association, held in the last few decades, there emerges the effort to bring economic theory back into more realistic and practical paths, and to restore the balance between deductive speculation and inductive research, which was almost lost before the war. The same idea is at the bottom of the reform attempted by the Institutionalists. Whenever their demands became too reactionary, the adherents of pure theory would enter a protest; these are, however, becoming more and more timid and are making more and more concessions to the new realistic trend.

6. "*Young America*"

This gradual retreat of pure abstract method is most evident in the compilation [44] recently published by Rexford Guy Tugwell, in which the "younger generation [45] of American economists" offer their methodological ideas in a general manifesto. The attitudes which they represent vary considerably: from natural science to purest relativity, through every intermediate stage. The result, however, and the main tenor of the book, is a settling of accounts with exaggeratedly abstract and purely theoretical investigation.

R. T. Bye,[46] alone, comes to the rescue in an energetic attempt to make of pure theory a scientific end in itself. He tries to prove, by the results of the recent doctrines of value and distribution, that only by this means can our science in the long run contribute to the welfare of society. Frank Hyneman Knight [47] is more moderate. By means of a thorough-going logical and psychological study, he arrives at the conclusion that the laws of exchange and price allow for a narrow realm in which economic relations may be studied deductively. He does not wish to be blind to the realistic reforms, but he thinks that their justification must be thoroughly proved before we give up the theoretical doctrines which have been won by so much intellectual labor. Knight belongs to those American writers who are especially interested in the ethical aspect of economics. He considers Ethics and Economics axiologic sciences and submits the connection between them to psychological analysis. He has also made interesting researches on the role and importance of ethical viewpoints in practical economic life, especially in the origin and progress of competition.[48] Knight holds himself aloof from the school which relies on the new psychology and set forth his view before Parry and Clark Jr. in the discussion of the American Economic Association of December 1920.[49] In his latest writings, he has even sharply attacked radical innovators. They pay him back in his own coin: Morris Albert Copeland especially has recently tried to destroy Knight's arguments systematically.[50]

A strongly realistic tone is shown, in the Tugwell collection, by Albert Benedict Wolfe, who upholds the opposite of Bye's thesis.[51] For him, pure economic theory, as an end in itself, is nonsense, for our knowledge becomes such only through its relation to some sphere of human interests. The only true science is that which is causal; nevertheless a teleological viewpoint lies at the back of its sphere of activity. Therefore either economics should deal with problems which concern practical or ethical relations or it should be approached from a ready-made ethical viewpoint. From this springs the only valid system of thought, which Wolfe calls "functional economics" and which has an ethical and practical tinge even in its theory. John Maurice Clark follows the golden mean, and develops the work of his famous father more realistically. In his report at the 31st annual meeting of the American Economic Association at Richmond in December 1918, he warned against the two extreme tendencies in economic theory. He recommended for the future a realistic theory; this was, above all, to be a theory, and not a mere collection of facts. In the same year, he published a study [52] in which he advocated the necessity of economic theory being based on the results of the new psychology. Two years later, at a meeting of the association at Atlantic City, he showed clearly his sympathy with the doctrines of Veblen.[53] The same spirit can be felt in his logically well-constructed contribution to Tugwell's collection,[54] in which he develops a notable dialectical theory of the history of economic doctrines. His recent investigations into the relation between the static and dynamic attitudes have led to conciliatory results: the more inductive advantages of the latter are offset by the deductive explanations of the former, to make a perfect picture of the process of economic life.[55]

Tugwell,[56] who edited the collection, and Sumner Huber Slichter [57] take a decided stand against abstract economic theory. The former especially attacks the concept of natural economic laws, and tries to show in general terms that all dogmatism in our science contains logical contradictions. Therefore, we should endeavor to know—as far as we can—real economic relations through practical observation, in the experimental way. In an earlier work,[58] Tugwell brings the argument to bear against the narrowness of hedonistic political economy but declares himself opposed to the radical exaggerations of some of the institutionalists. Schlichter is no less zealous in denouncing hasty deductive generalization and tries to show the falsity of some widespread doctrines, based on unsound induction. F. Cecil Mills attempts to prove in his contribution [59] the concrete possibilities of adapting the statistical method to economic research. The places where, following Marshall, he treats economic laws as mere tendencies and conceives of them from a statistical point of view as the expression of average relationships, and his great statistical work [60] in which he expounds more fully his leading thoughts may be read with profit by all economists. Similar researches are those of William Ernest Weld,[61] in which he studies the foundations of general welfare statistically. Passing over the other essays in the collection, we shall only mention the leading article of Wesley Clair Mitchell.[62] In some of his earlier works he made important contributions to contemporary economic theory and in a more recent article [63] he has compared the relative value of realistic research, directed by statistics, and the attitude of Marshall. Here, however, he takes hold of the fundamental principles of all modern economic theory. Continuing the trend of ideas exhibited in some of his earlier investigations,[64] he appears here as a radical adherent of Veblen. He attacks without mercy the leading hedonistic and utilitarian economic theories, his arguments culminating in the one reproach that its first principles have been superseded by the new psychology. Consequently, all our theories of value and distribution of which we are so proud are just so much junk. A new theory should take into consideration the latest results of psychology and, instead of being historical or mere propaganda, should be founded upon a "scientific," theoretical study of the development of economic institutions, such as has been done in England by Webb, in Germany by Sombart and in America by Veblen. This is what Mitchell means by the "institutional" method.

We see then that American economics on the whole tends to go back to the methodological program of the nineteenth century historical school in Germany. One can argue that the Tugwell collection is not a methodological manifesto of the younger generation. As a matter of fact, the number of open adherents of institutionalism is small. A short survey, however, of economic results in America since the world war, will unmistakably show the great influence of the new tendency and the importance of its results as compared to those of the abstract-deductive method. Moreover, institutionalists are responsible for the remarkable work that is being carried on in New York by the National Bureau of Economic Research, in Washington by the Institute of Economics, in Chicago by the Institute for Research in Land Economics and Public Utilities, and in the many other American institutes of scientific research. These scholars will often not admit that they are flirting with the historical school, especially with its older branch, and they endeavor to give their methodological views the air of a "modern acquisition" by employing a glittering exterior and a newfangled name. The essence of the movement, however, is old and familiar to us.

7. *The Legal, Historical and Socio-ethical Attitudes*

It is in John R. Commons that we see most clearly the return to a realistic viewpoint. With reference to his work on the theory of distribution, published some thirty years ago, he now says that he then tried to "mix" things which could not be mixed. Now he is a staunch supporter of the new behaviorism. He does not, however, follow the example of some of its adherents who lose themselves in methodological disputes. He follows rather the path of positive investigation for which he chooses a legal and historical attitude. He buries himself in an historical study of Anglo-American legal procedure in its connection with social and economic problems, and tries to distil from this the concepts which may illuminate modern economics more truly than do the traditional theories based on abstract-deduction.[65]

The open adherents of the historical school also give expression now and then to their methodological views in Anglo-American literature.

W. J. Ashley, who was perhaps the most distinguished representative of the historical school in England, recognized in his studies of the modern development of economics,[66] the importance of the new theoretical movements but recommended a more frequent return to historical and practical economic research. In advising the building of a new science: "Business Economics," from a development and elaboration of private economics, of which he stresses the importance, Ashley came into contact with some corresponding currents in modern German and American economics. One of the well known historians of economic doctrine in America is Lewis H. Haney, whose researches in method should be mentioned here. Starting from an eclectic set of principles, derived in part from organic, in part from individualistic sociology, he considers a social point of view the only correct one for judging economic phenomena. He endeavors to prove that the concept of economic value as well as the phenomena of price and distribution form essentially social categories and that a study of these will produce satisfactory results only when it is attempted from the outset from a social point of view.[67]

In modern English literature, comparatively little is said on the ethical aspect of methodology.

Besides the studies of Hawtrey, and others, which we have already mentioned, or upon which we shall touch later, the only names worthy of mention are John G. Murdock [68] whose book was published before the war and J. A. R. Marriot [69] whose treatise appeared a few years ago. The former bases himself on Marxian historical materialism, tries to show the dependence of traditional ethical views on economic premises and sharply criticizes the system of capitalistic profit by drawing upon anthropological, biological, psychological and sociological viewpoints. Marriot endeavors to explain the connections, as well as the contradictions, between classic economic theory and Christian ethics. Apart from the result he reaches, that the two do not get along well together, he presents some stimulating reflections; but from the point of view of method he has nothing essentially new to say.

8. The Problem of Value Judgments

English and American economists have on the whole been little worried by the problem of the possibility of forming scientific value judgments in economics. Some of them have had only an occasional interest in the quarrel which was waged so bitterly in German literature. Of these, Marshall and his school were for, while Shield Nicholson was against, value judgments. At the turn of the century, however, a stimulating and methodologically important discussion of the subject took place in the American Economic Association. Only socio-economical arguments were used, and epistemological depths were avoided.

Arthur T. Hadley, as reporter, contended that the real end of economics was the promotion of the welfare of the community, and that consequently the economist should be above all factional interests and furnish a bright, fixed light in the darkness of social and economic strife.[70] In the discussion, both Seligman and Mayo-Smith agreed with

Hadley. J. R. Commons tried to prove that, in general, scientific disagreements between economists could be reduced to differences of party or of class, for man can think in social questions only according to his political party. The ideal then is the "associated economist" who stands in the midst of the social fray and not the "individual economist" who spends his life in lonely and contemplative seclusion. In the long run the factional politician works for the good of the community which is a result of the contest between different political views.

In this debate not only Commons but also his opponents based themselves upon value judgments, since they too were fighting for the general welfare. Nevertheless, this contact helped to clarify opinions concerning the attitudes of economists to this question. Later on, the result of the German methodological dispute over the possibility of scientific value judgments gradually reached America. Although the younger generation in America does not worry much over such epistemological questions, they are leaning more or less toward the attitude of Max Weber. This became clear in the discussion which took place on the relations between economic theory and ethics at the meetings of the American Economic Association at Pittsburgh, in December 1921.[71]

F. H. Knight, the president, and to a certain extent H. G. Hayes, G. A. Kleene and W. J. King, desired a sharp separation between the ascertainment of facts and the expression of value judgments in economics. Only a small minority—A. B. Wolfe and, to a certain extent, J. Viner—were sceptical of the possibility of such a distinction.

9. *Business Economics, Science of Management, and the Economics of War*

The first quarter of the twentieth century saw no greater changes in the systematization of our science in England and America than it did in France or Italy, and consequently no discussion worthy of mention on related topics. The literature of the new branch called "Business Economics," which corresponds approximately to German private economics, has grown considerably in importance within the last few years, without arousing any counter-attacks on its independence.

We may mention here, as newer and more significant contributions to this field, the works of the Englishman James Stephenson [72] and of the American H. B. Vanderblue.[73] They both exhibit a sound knowledge of their subject and try to explain the relation of private to political economy by practical description rather than by criticism. Especially noteworthy is what Vanderblue has to say on the relation of the problems of business cycles and crises to private economics.

Frederick Winslow Taylor's Science of Management, a branch of business economics, has enjoyed an undisturbed development and today, especially in America, it is a mature and independent science with a vast library of books at its disposal. Its bible is Taylor's famous work [74] which appeared in 1911 and in which he expounds, with literary skill, the fundamental ideas of his system, based upon clearly defined rules and principles and applicable to every kind of human activity. This new science, which teaches the promotion of productivity in general business, but especially in technical industry, has been adopted and elaborated with much success even in the old world. In its broader aspect Taylor's system tends to absorb the whole of private economics.

English and American economists have been spared all discussion as to the necessity of a special doctrine of war economics.

Soon after the outbreak of the World War, studies were made—especially in England—of war economics, which were far-reaching in theory. Of these, we need only mention F. W. Hirst's study,[75] and a smaller work of R. A. Lehfeldt.[76] Even distinguished economists such as Seligman,[77] Edgeworth,[78] Keynes,[79] Pigou,[80] and Allyn A. Young,[81] did not disdain interesting themselves in the economic problems of the war, especially of the peace treaties. All these writers, however, as well as many others who dealt with similar subjects, were content to note the transient changes to which general economic phenomena were subject during and following the war. Not one of them attempts a basic and comprehensive study, such as Pigou's work, with the idea of founding an independent science of the economics of war. The appearance of such a tendency must accordingly be considered an especial characteristic of German literature.

CHAPTER II

ATTEMPTS TO CREATE SYSTEMS

1. The Cambridge School, and Other Abstract Theoretical Systems in England

In no country has economic theory in the first quarter of our century developed so straightforwardly as in England. While German science is in a state of flux and in Italy the doctrines of the Lausanne school penetrate with difficulty; while France shows marked changes in the direction of the modern theory and in America, as we shall see later, a contrary change is taking place in the direction of greater realism, English economics continues the same traditions handed down from Adam Smith through Ricardo, Mill and Jevons. We can clearly notice here the sure and gradual progress, the dislike of sudden and radical change, the appreciation of tradition, which are such characteristic traits of English culture.

The influence of the historical trend, which made its appearance only during the transition from the old to the new theory, has left slight traces in the development of English economics. The few English scholars who belonged to the historical school did not practice an exaggerated relativism, but tried to keep as close as possible to the achievements of the classical school. Ashley himself, in 1909, provided a new edition of John Stuart Mill's *Principles*. Consequently, it was comparatively easy to overcome this temporary reaction against theoretical investigation. The strong personality of William Stanley Jevons has had a direct influence in England, even up to the beginning of the present century.

In 1911 his son, Herbert Stanley Jevons, issued the fourth edition of his father's chief economic work,[1] and tried to defend the latter's theory of interest against Marshall's criticism in a supplement which contains some interesting historical facts. Six years earlier, at the same time that a long-awaited fragment of his father, embracing all economic theory, appeared under the editorship of Henry Higgs,[2] the younger Jevons published a largely methodological work which was on the whole very favorably received. In this he tries to develop the method by his father from the psychological aspect and to apply it in this shape to the study of a few phenomena of production, marketing and the distribution of goods.[3]

The most famous and valuable economic system in modern English literature is contained in Alfred Marshall's *Principles*, first published in 1890. For maturity of thought and logical presentation, it can be compared only with Mill's *Principles*, the scientific position of which it inherited and assumed also far beyond England's boundaries. Jevons's contribution was soon overshadowed by that of Marshall, though the former was undoubtedly the first one in English literature to work out the main principles of modern economic theory; he also deserves credit for greater originality. Marshall, however, saw more widely and had a more systematic mind. He was the first to accomplish the much imitated synthesis between modern and classical economics and at the same time he did not neglect the ideas of the historical school. It is to this summarizing of the results of different tendencies and also to the important new solutions which it contains that Marshall's *Principles* owes its great scientific and literary success. This is best illustrated by the numerous editions and translations which have so far appeared.

Inasmuch as, according to its first publication, Marshall's great work belongs to the last century, we shall not deal with it more fully here. We shall merely mention the fifth edition,[4] which falls within the period covered by this book. This contains some important revisions concerning the arrangement of the material and some of the more outstanding theories such as that of marginal costs in the explanation of value. What should be especially noted is the clever and successful use made by Marshall in this edition of the time element in the theory of distribution. He thereby shed much light on the difficult concepts of rent and quasi-rent and helped notably to clarify all those incomes which are based on the possession of material means of production. He also developed more lucidly the concept of a "national dividend," which is closely connected with the element of time, and which had remained somewhat unclear in the first editions of his work. In this new form he understands by that term the amount of economic goods and productive services which are made available each year and he is able to draw from this central concept important conclusions for economic and social policy. The growth of a nation's income depends above all on the perfection of production; this is carried on by technical discoveries which almost always originate in private initiative and are only seldom due to a common activity. According to Marshall, this should never be forgotten when we discuss the advantages and disadvantages of equalitarian social reform, such as the abolition of private property, which is the life-source of all private initiative.

The *Principles*, as they appear even in the latest edition, are meant only as the first and theoretical part of a more comprehensive system. Marshall's spiritual conflict over the continuation of his work may perhaps be compared with that of Goethe over the second part of Faust. Marshall was perpetually concerned with the completion of his work, but other writings, teaching and his participation in practical economic policy took up his time. Like Goethe, he was constantly changing the formal plan of his continuation, and more than thirty years elapsed before parts of it were published. Meanwhile Marshall had reached the age of eighty, and so the two recent volumes of his work [5] show in increasing degrees the stamp of age. Marshall was aware of the gradual loss of his spiritual energy, and consequently limited himself chiefly to a summary and repetition of his earlier essays, some of which had appeared almost a half century before, dealing with practical problems of economics. The gaps are almost entirely filled with descriptive data and the theoretical spirit which animated the *Principles* is visible here only in sparks. Nevertheless the aged scholar succeeded in offering to the public in one unified system most of his ideas on the organization of economic life, his theory of money and especially his theory of foreign trade. Fighting tirelessly against advancing age, Marshall worked up to the end on another volume which was to be published under the title *Progress: its Economic Conditions*. In the summer of 1924 he died, and the work remained unfinished.

The other leader, next to Marshall, of English economic theory in the first quarter of our century, Edgeworth, did not succeed during his long life in publishing a unified system of his principles. Separate investigations, methodological studies and his astonishing activity as a critic made too many demands on his energy. The three-volume edition of his collected essays, published by the English Royal Economic Society shortly before the author's death, contains a rich fund of new ideas which Edgeworth sought away from the main current of theoretical investigation and in the study of apparently unrelated details. It is scarcely possible, however, to construct from them a closed and unified system.

Among other eminent British economists of this generation, the recently deceased Joseph Shield Nicholson started to publish, in the nineties, a comprehensive system of which the last volume appeared in the present century.[6] Theoretically Nicholson closely resembles Marshall. This is especially noticeable in the development of the concept of consumer's surplus. With reference to his theory of quasi-rent, Nicholson himself admits that it is identically the same as Marshall's. The theories of the classical school are even more prominent in Nicholson than in Marshall; he makes use of much historical material and is in general well disposed to the ideas of the historical school. He lost no opportunity of attacking the stagnation of our science through theoretical dogmatism.[7] He could not accept the mathematical method which he even sharply criticized on occasions.[8]

Nicholson's chief work is eclectic in the best sense of the word. He takes for his model John Stuart Mill's *Principles* which he follows even in the formal distribution of his material; he is thus attracted to the historical viewpoint but cannot escape the influence of modern tendencies. Although he succeeds in uniting these different points of view in a more or less unified system, his work did not meet with the literary success which many had expected. Nicholson published also an excerpt of his great work in the shape of a one-volume text book.[9] In this he tried to give a simpler and clearer exposition and made some important changes in the arrangement of his material; but the treatment of the theory of distribution before that of exchange does not seem to be very successful and did not help the author's didactic aim.

A. W. Flux makes considerable use of the mathematical method in his concise system.[10] The subtitle of the book, "An Introductory Study," does not correspond to the contents, for his ideas are difficult to grasp and presuppose much technical knowledge, so that it is useful only for those who are somewhat advanced in the study of economics. Flux follows a strict plan of composition. The starting point of his system, and the central idea which is always kept in sight, is the problem of value which he tries to solve according to the principles of marginal utility. Other economic problems interest him only in so far as they are directly related to value. Consequently he treats the theory of price and distribution, money, international trade, as well as a few questions of public finance, equally from the point of view of the problem of value and tries to give them all a single explanation based on the marginal principle. He is able thereby to offer some useful ideas for the unification and extension of the theory of marginal utility. Without entering into discussions with other authors Flux considers the most recent discoveries of theoretical investigation and is strongly influenced by Marshall. In the second edition of his work which was published after the world war the only chapters which he revised and developed were those on the theory of money and on international trade. In both, Flux devotes his attention especially to changes in the general price level, their causes and consequences. He brings his theory of money into direct connection with them and rejects his earlier use of the term "quantity theory."

In spite of the works of Nicholson and Flux, and the prestige enjoyed by Marshall's system, the English, at the beginning of the century, seemed to be still looking for a substitute for Mill's *Principles*. Foreign literatures were scanned and a translation was finally made of N. G. Pierson's famous *Leerboek der Staathuishoudkunde*, whereby the work was made available for the international reading public. The various volumes of this work were published in the original Dutch from 1884 to 1902, and A. A. Wolzel's English translation in two volumes, owing to unfortunate circumstances, took ten years to appear.[11] Since this work also belongs, according to the date of its first publication, to the last century, we shall deal with it very briefly here. We have already stated that Nicholson kept closer to the theories of the classical school than did Marshall, and this is still more the case with Pierson. The foundation of Pierson's work is taken entirely from classical economics and the ideas of marginal utility are added as an element of secondary consideration.

Of importance are Pierson's independent theoretical solutions of problems, among which we draw attention only to the close union of the theory of distribution with the formation of price as well as to the subtle analysis of profit and its arrangement in three parts: the entrepreneur's compensation for his risk, the reward for his activity and a surplus income, which is often present, resembling rent. Many of the most successful young economists, as we shall see later, have adopted these ideas. A special charm is lent to Pierson's work by its close contact with actual economic life, with the smallest details of which the author, who has had much practical experience, was well acquainted. His criticism of socialistic theorists is unusually penetrating: he claims to find astonishing mistakes of logic in Lassalle and denies to Marx the title of a serious scientific thinker. His sympathies with the classical school are especially visible in his enthusiastic defense of free trade against protectionism.

Contrary to Nicholson and Pierson who, though they accepted the principles of marginal utility, remained adherents of classical theory, Philip Henry Wicksteed, like Flux, belongs to modern theory. He devotes himself above all to a logical study of the theory of marginal utility, in order to clear up certain ambiguities which generally obscure its principles. He also pursues other vague concepts and logical contradictions which are scattered over economic theory and will allow only those principles which are immediately intelligible. The thick volume which he dedicated to this purpose [12] offers no closed system of economics, but treats its problems in so many different cases that it seems fitting to discuss it here. No adherent of marginal utility should neglect to read the passages in which Wicksteed tries to show its central ideas in the elementary phenomena of daily life. Perhaps no one has possessed to a more perfect degree than Wicksteed the gift of expounding abstract theories, such as that of the "equilibrium of marginal values," in a fascinatingly simple style, as a truth which is obvious to common sense. With reference to marginal utility, he stresses the fact that it is not the special characteristic of a last unit, but merely a differential concept or one of relationship which expresses what is the importance of the last unit with reference to the whole homogeneous stock. In order to correct the numerous errors which result from confused concepts on this point, he proposed instead of the ambiguous expression "marginal utility," that of "proportional utility." [13] Besides this analysis of the fundamentals of modern economic theory, Wicksteed's large work contains valuable ideas on distribution, which he considers a pure problem of value, on the theory of money, and against the ideal of free trade.

While Nicholson and Flux, in so far as they based themselves on Marshall, were content to simplify his ideas and Wicksteed took a more radical path to modern theory, A. C. Pigou's work represents a direct continuation of Marshall. As Marshall's pupil and successor in the Cambridge chair, Pigou sees his chief scientific duty in a further development of the master's doctrines and is the worthy leader of the literary movement which is devoted to the care of the Marshall traditions.[14] His system (first published before the war, then eight years later under a new title and twice as large, and again recently in a shorter form),[15] shows the most mature results of the Cambridge school and is at the same time one of the outstanding works of modern economic theory. In its method, the work follows the same paths as Marshall's *Principles*. Although Pigou attempts to build his theory as far as possible on actual facts, he is not as successful as Marshall in creating a harmony between theory and reality. In places his work creates too abstract an impression. He makes no greater use than did his master of the mathematical method and in the last edition most of the mathematical exposition is given at the end of the text as addenda.

Pigou's main ideas are directly related to Marshall's doctrine of a connection between national income and general welfare. The manner in which he treats his fundamental postulate of general welfare is strongly reminiscent of modern English utilitarianism, especially that of Henry Sidgwick. Satisfaction and dissatisfaction are also Pigou's two psychological bases, the mutual relation of which determines individual welfare, and each additional individual welfare increases that of the community. Pigou's underlying fundamental principle is the well-known utilitarian postulate of the greatest possible welfare of the greatest possible number. This concept of welfare is entirely measurable, for on the one hand the sum of individual welfares, upon which general welfare depends, is measurable and on the other hand the relation between satisfactions and dissatisfactions can be treated quantitatively for each person. Like Sidgwick, Pigou avoids the reproach of materialism by referring the concept of welfare to a psychic state, and not to the disposal of material goods.

The amount of the general welfare depends for Pigou on the size of the national income. Here he adopts the concept of a "national dividend," which Marshall had introduced in the first edition of his *Principles*, and further developed in the subsequent editions. This concept has nothing to do with those dividends which are paid by joint stock companies. In choosing this rather unfortunate expression, Marshall's idea was that a nation's yearly income is divided, just as are the earnings of a company. With Pigou, too, "national dividend" is merely a metaphorical expression for national income. Of what does this consist? Pigou defines it, like Marshall, as the sum of objective services which are offered partly indirectly, through economic goods, and partly directly. These must be expressible in money value, just as the economic welfare depending on national income represents only the balance-sheet of satisfactions and dissatisfactions which can be valued either directly or indirectly in terms of money. Considering this conception, those who, like Cannan and Knight, criticize Pigou and see at the center of his system only the category of exchange value or, more generally expressed, the traditional problem of value, do not seem to be entirely wrong.

General welfare, however, depends not on the size of the national income but on the manner in which it is distributed among the various members of the community. Pigou is, like Sidgwick, of the opinion that a decrease of the inequalities in distribution is necessarily connected with an increase of general welfare.

After discussing the relation between welfare and national income, and the problem of the size of the national income, he studies its distribution in the third part of his system. Originally the fourth part dealt with the question of changes in the national income, since he considers that general welfare increases with a diminution in the temporal inequalities of distribution. In the revised edition, which appeared after the war, the two first parts were considerably enlarged and two new parts were added on national income and labor and on national income and public finance. In the third edition of his work, the last mentioned part, of which the essence had appeared in his *Political Economy of War*, was omitted, as well as the original fourth part on the changes in the national income, of which Pigou had included the main ideas in his recent work on business crises.[16] In this new system, which centers on the concept of welfare, Pigou introduces his individual contributions to the study of marginal utility, especially his ideas on price and distribution. We shall return to these later. Pigou has also published a small volume of collected essays on various problems of practical economic life.[17]

On no other system in the Anglo-American literature of the last twenty-five years has criticism waxed so intensive as on Pigou's work. Edgeworth recognizes its great originality and objects to only a few minor characteristics such as his use of the mathematical method, his disregard of scientific authorities and a few unimportant theoretical errors.[18] Shield Nicholson misses the actual relationship between Pigou's abstractions and the phenomena of practical economic life,[19] while Edwin Cannan, the worthy historian of distribution theories, objects especially to Pigou's concept of national income and tries to show its obscurities and inconsistencies.[20] Among the Americans, Allyn A. Young [21] points out mistakes in his theory of rent. In the latest edition of his work the distinguished English scholar took account of these criticisms, especially of Young's suggestion in his theory of diminishing returns. Frank H. Knight, who criticizes especially the ethical and psychological principles of Pigou's system, adopts a tone of the greatest appreciation.[22]

Pigou's colleague, S. J. Chapman, shows less originality. Although he refers partly to Walras and to Jevons, he bases himself chiefly on Marshall, but tries to express Marshall's ideas without the help of the mathematical method. He has new ideas to offer only in secondary matters, such as in some subtle distinctions in his theory of returns and rent. His system, which has been published in several forms,[23] is marked by much profundity of thought but, because of its difficult abstractions, is useful only for advanced students. In his more recent editions, however, Chapman attempts to give his system a more realistic aspect by introducing more factual data.

Professor L. V. Birck, of Copenhagen, published a more independent system, which enriched the theories of the Austrian and Cambridge schools with some stimulating ideas.[24] Starting from Marshall's theory of value, he develops in succession all the more important ideas which have been produced by the theory of marginal utility and unites them into a good, compact, systematic survey. The only fault is that Birck neglects almost entirely the latest achievements of American economics.

We mention only in passing the work of W. A. Robson [25] who makes a noteworthy attempt to extend the concept of welfare as the central point of economic theory. According to Robson scientists should notice that not only wealth, but also health, art, education, etc., are parts of welfare.

2. *Clark's School in America*

Unlike the English literature of the first quarter of our century which produced only one really satisfactory, new and up-to-date system of economic theory (that of Pigou), American economists have produced a long list of excellent systems, based upon the most recent theoretical discoveries. Modern American economics comes of age with the new century and, conscious of its vigor, tries to free itself from European science and literature. The teaching of economics in the universities has assumed undreamed of proportions and more text books are needed each year, so that nearly all the leading economists have been compelled to impart their doctrines to their pupils and to the public in succinct summaries of the whole field of economics.

John Bates Clark's study [26] is not one of the most popular of American text books. Nevertheless, because of the great reputation which it enjoys even outside of his own country, it should be mentioned here first. Clark's importance lies in the fact that he stands in the middle of the two extremes which we have noted above: between Jevons on the one hand and Marshall on the other. He may be compared with Jevons in respect of his creative genius, which led him to discern the fundamental principles of contemporary economic theory, at the same time as, but independently of, the European scholars. Like Marshall, he has the greatest respect for classical political economy, as well as for the systematic methods which have enabled him to create a thorough and coherent structure out of his various theories. He was considerably helped in this by the fact that he was a conscious admirer of classical tradition and was, to a certain extent, filling old bottles with new wine. There is little in Clark's text book which is not already contained in his famous work on the theory of distribution, at the end of the nineteenth century. Here too, distribution is the important thing, and the whole book is colored by Clark's characteristic theories: a conscious union of the subjective and objective attitudes, and the consequent distinction between static and dynamic economics.

The widely-read treatise of Seligman,[27] which is well-known to European economists also, is partially dependent on Clark's teachings. In solving problems of theory he is also indebted to Böhm-Bawerk, and he gives an attractive and well-rounded exposition to the theory of marginal utility. Unlike Clark, however, who is apt to play with the idea of the economic man and even to dally with "Robinsonades," Seligman discloses a decided trend toward realism. He shows a thorough familiarity with the German historical school, especially that of Karl Bücher and is inclined, therefore, to stress the social aspect of economic problems. The comprehensive economic and sociological introduction of his work is full of excellent ideas, and the chief didactic value of his system lies in the rich collection of facts, which he has illustrated with numerous tables and diagrams. Of especial importance is the vast amount of explanatory data and remarks on the economic life of America which lends his book a typically American flavor. In the same way, in his latest work on installment selling,[28] he is able, with true American optimism, to regard this practice, which Europeans still distrust, as a source of further prosperity for his nation. Seligman also shows his Americanism in dealing with social problems in an individualistic, equalitarian and democratic manner. His dislike of socialism is just as pronounced.

Although Seligman's work was received with considerable favor by critics, including those in foreign countries, Frank W. Taussig made a series of strong objections.[29] He criticized in part the general arrangement of the material, and blamed his colleague for a lack of theoretical acumen and for a partly superficial presentation of the facts. For these reasons he thought that the work did not meet the demands of a text book. The discussion [30] which followed between the two remained, as usual, fruitless. Taussig's criticism was justified only in so far as his own text book, which appeared a few years later [31] proved to be a fine piece of work. It is not only a broad survey of modern economic thought, but it is entitled to rank among the best American text books from the point of view of exposition and structure. The work takes only a general knowledge for granted in the reader, and demands no technical familiarity with economics at all. One is led, step by step, through the fundamental phenomena to the most complicated situations. The difficult task has scarcely ever been accomplished with so much success. Taussig's general theoretical outlook most closely resembles that of Marshall: as a rule he derives his views directly from John Stuart Mill, and manages to maintain a complete independence of Clark. He makes considerable use of the mathematical method, and the distinction which he draws between static and dynamic economics is remarkable. When he adopts the usual hedonistic and utilitarian views, his psychology is not always so sound, and we need not look for new light from him on the problem of marginal utility. His strength lies in another direction: in an accurate grasp of the complicated relations of modern industry with reference to the theory of distribution. This is his most valuable contribution to economics. His quantitative theory of money and his conservative views on public finance fall far below the level of the rest of the work. In the third edition, published in 1921, Taussig is compelled to make concessions to the realistic current which had, in the meantime, grown so strong in America. He therefore now stresses the practical facts of economic life and their relation to society. Twenty years have passed since his attack on Seligman's book; Seligman, however, seems to remember it with some degree of sensitiveness. At least we may so infer from his recent remark that the *Principles* of Taussig is not distinguished by the same originality which is found in some of the other American treatises.[32]

In contrast to Taussig, we may mention Henry Rogers Seager's text book.[33] This was intended to supplement the author's lectures; consequently it is not very elementary, and does not attempt to give so much a complete explanation of economic phenomena as an introduction to the problem of the various viewpoints by which these may be judged. Seager does not try to impress his own opinions on his readers; he endeavors to stimulate them to think for themselves on economic questions. In this respect he is successful. He gives a good review of the development of modern industry in England and the United States, discusses consumption, production, exchange and distribution, and finally presents his theories of money and credit. It is clear that Seager's plan is to start from practical questions and to move, through the more simple, to the more complicated problems of theory. More than any other writer today, he stresses the importance of human wants as the fundamental motive of all economic activity. What the consumer thinks good, then, becomes the most important fact in economic life: Production, exchange and distribution are all dependent upon the important fact of consumption. In his methodology and theoretical views, Seager is often influenced by Clark, but he also makes considerable use of the idea of static economics, developed by the Lausanne school. In his political views, he steers a middle course between liberalism and government interference.

A subsequent presentation of his doctrine shows a return to realism. The abstract traits of his former theories of value and distribution are abandoned; the influence of Patten is often visible and his whole mental attitude turns more towards practical economic life. Consequently he devotes considerably more attention to social problems, social politics and socialism. Besides his larger work, Seager has also written a short summary of his economic views.[34]

3. *Fisher on Money and Interest*

Undoubtedly the best known contemporary American student of mathematical problems in economics is Irving Fisher. Before the war, he published a system of political economy [34a] which differed considerably from other works with the same title. First of all, Fisher believes that it is impossible to compress the whole of economic theory into one coherent system, since every author has, to some extent, his own pet standpoint from which he regards economic relations. In accordance with this view he shapes his own expositions; as a result some portions of his work are overburdened, while others receive only inadequate treatment. He considers the common American idea of a central theory of distribution as a mistake, since this cannot possibly give a complete explanation of all economic phenomena. He therefore picks out the problem of the value of money and of interest, and thinks that he can thus construct a theory of modern social and economic life. In interest he sees a much more general phenomenon than one is accustomed to admit, and in the variations in the value of money he finds one of the worst evils of our economic organization, to be attacked with every possible weapon. These thoughts he developed more thoroughly in his earlier works, which we shall mention below, so that he offers nothing essentially new in his *Elementary Principles*. As a representative of the mathematical school, Fisher naturally based this work on their principles.

4. Davenport and the Point of View of the Entrepreneur

Like Fisher, Herbert Joseph Davenport[35] built his system on his own peculiar view of the economic process. His chief effort is directed to an analysis of fundamental contrasts and differences between the desire for gain of the individual entrepreneur, and the economic interests of the group. The result of his discussion is to show what latitude may be allowed to the individual quest for profits, without injury to economic life. Developing this idea on an extremely profound theoretical and psychological basis, he proceeds to analyse the fundamental principles of economic theory, and to subject its chief doctrines to an acute criticism. He is especially opposed to the prevailing concept of the marginal utility theory which he tries to improve; and he points out some questionable practices in the common mathematical explanation of the theory of price. Like Fisher, he is not in favor of a general independent theory of distribution, for he identifies the theory of distribution with an analysis of market phenomena.

Alvin Saunders Johnson correctly notes Davenport's close relation to the classical school in general structure and method, and especially in his emphasis on the point of view of the entrepreneur and the importance of exchange.[36] Johnson, too, shows great regard for the classical attitude in his system, which appeared several years earlier,[37] by stressing the importance of the element of cost for the theory of price and distribution. In this respect he is greatly influenced by Clark, while in his theory of value he relies on the Austrian school. His eclecticism provides a bridge between the pure theory of marginal utility and later American doctrines. His system is, on the whole, very abstract, but logical and concise. In the later edition of his work (published under a different title),[38] apart from merely formal changes he tried to improve his exposition by the addition of numerous examples drawn from practical economic life.

5. *Fetter's Development*

All the American systems of the pre-war period which we have mentioned have, with the exception of some definite individual traits, followed more or less parallel lines. Sometimes they lean more to classicism, sometimes to Clark, sometimes to modern European theories. Frank Albert Fetter, however, stands alone in the history of modern American economics. He has a most independent mind and for originality of thought may perhaps be best compared with Othmar Spann among his contemporaries. Like him, Fetter objects to the increasing materialism and "chrematistics" of economics, and draws attention to the fact that our science is but a means to help man to his goal. As to the contents of his views, he is really more closely related to Liefmann, Spann's bitterest enemy, since he attacks, with him, the present structure of economic theory which he desires to replace by a new one founded on psychologically reformed bans. The object of his attacks is the utilitarian and somewhat hedonistic attitude which goes back to Bentham. According to him voluntaristic psychology provides the proper foundation upon which a theory of value and consequently the whole of economic theory, may be securely built.

At the beginning of the century, a report which he read at a meeting of the American Economic Association caused quite a stir. He predicted radical changes in the future development of the science and gave a sketch of his own theories.[39] Soon afterward, he developed this more systematically and published it in the form of a book, which has since become deservedly famous.[40]

Fetter accuses modern American economic theory of floundering uncertainly between the Austrian theory of marginal utility and the older classical view. It remains, therefore, eclectic and imperfect. He also accuses the Austrians of lacking the courage to follow their fundamentally correct principles to their logical conclusion. According to him, they became afraid of the vast vista before them and reverted mid-way to classical thought. In this he finds the cause of the discord which exists between their separate theories and of the lack of harmony in their whole doctrine. Fetter's next attempt was to develop psychologically some of the doctrines of the Vienna school. In this way he proposed a theory of value which he considers entirely original and self-sufficing and which provides the background for his theory of distribution. Even his opponents cannot deny the logical unity which pervades his whole economic system.

Fetter had always realized that the criticisms levelled against the narrow hedonism of the marginal utility theory were due to a misinterpretation of certain verbal expressions. Nevertheless, he has never been an adherent of the Austrian school. He accepts the views of voluntaristic psychology, in the light of which the entire theory of utility seems outworn.[41] To him the most elementary activity in economic life is the free choice among the means at one's disposal. This is the basis of his theory. Later on he lays more stress on the distinction between static and dynamic economics and grows more interested in problems of welfare. According to him Adam Smith was right in studying the relation between wealth and welfare. Emphasis on the problem of price was due to the chrematistically-inclined mind of Ricardo, and economics has not yet recovered from this disease. A more reasonable attitude was indeed introduced by Mill; but only the future can show whether economists will return to the correct and original path. Fetter asks: shall we have a price economics or a welfare economics? In recent years, he has ceaselessly emphasized the fact that an economics which is built upon the concept of price can serve only to clarify the economic problems of private property. Against this it should set up a concept of social wellbeing if it wishes to attain its highest ends. Therefore the problem of welfare should be put at the center of our science.[42] We see here the points of resemblance between Fetter and Pigou.

6. *Carver and Other Theoretical Systems in Post-War America*

Thomas Nixon Carver [43] deserves without doubt the most eminent place in the construction of economic systems that have appeared in America since the war. Like his colleague, Fetter, he was at the beginning of the century one of the keenest champions of abstract theory, being considerably influenced by Clark. Unlike the latter, however, he retains the Austrian theory of marginal utility and tries to explain through it all the phenemona of economic life. How far Carver succeeded in his aim we shall see later. The theories which he developed at this period are worthy of notice from a methodological point of view and provide considerable support for the abstract-deductive procedure.[44] At the beginning of the World War he devoted himself to a study of the ethical problems of economics.[45] Taking also into account the examples of social ethics and folk biology which the war afforded, he related the results of these studies to his earlier economic theories. The outcome was an all-embracing synthesis, which he published under the title of *Principles.* His relation to Fetter appears even in the dedication: "To all those who care to see their country grow strong and great." His chief aim is the nation's welfare. He perceives the way to this in a harmony between the lowest possible cost of living and the greatest possible productivity. He is preoccupied with problems of religion and ethics, devotes his attention to the moral and spiritual qualities of the population, as well as to the geography of the country and tries to show how dependent economic welfare is on all these factors. Nevertheless, in the theoretical parts of his work Carver retains the essential results of his earlier investigations. He devotes much space to refuting the various forms of socialism, as to which he shows a moderately liberal attitude based upon typically American optimism. He also takes stock of the advantages of the co-operative movement, in so far as it deals with production.

Apart from a simple outline of his system,[46] Carver has recently published a more or less prophetic work [47] in which he expounds the ideal of an intensive transformation of forces into human energy. For this he demands an increase in general spiritual and material wellbeing through a continual growth of population. This growth, considering the room for food, he deems possible for still a long while. He is most optimistic when dealing with the present and future prosperity of his own country. Even though Carver hardly ever rises to an historical attitude, the use which he makes of his factual material is worthy of notice.

Carver's leanings towards protectionism are attacked by Harry Gunnison Brown, who tries to show how Carver confuses economics with business.[48] The short treatise which Brown himself published has a misleading title,[49] since he does not make economic welfare the center of his investigation but devotes himself rather to an analysis of the objective phenomena of price to which he co-relates distribution. His psychological analysis of the problem of value is fruitful, since he is able to derive from the principle of marginal utility not only utility but also cost.

John Roscoe Turner [50] also explains distribution in terms of market prices and reduces the separate shares of income to one common denominator. He follows Fetter in his solution of the problem of value but also takes into consideration the traditional theory of marginal utility. Being moreover convinced of the importance of the historical attitude in economics he devotes four chapters of his treatise to the development of economic life from the earliest times to modern industrial capitalism, with the evident intent of making concessions to modern institutionalism. Notwithstanding his eclecticism Turner has some independent theories of his own; especially the law of proportion, which is offered as the most important foundation of modern economics.

In the system of Fred Manville Taylor,[51] we find a markedly abstract-deductive procedure. He is an enthusiastic and learned champion of the mathematical method which he uses with great skill in order to explain the process of price formation. It is on this, with the help of the marginal principle, that he bases his whole system which extends into every sphere of economics. Although Taylor's work is the result of care, erudition and long practical experience as a teacher, it is too technical to be used as a text-book by any but advanced students.

Besides Taylor, Fred Rogers Fairchild [52] has also come under the influence of Irving Fisher. On the whole, however, he may be called an admirer of Marshall. He is a devoted adherent of the theory of marginal utility; nevertheless a classical strain is recognizable in all his works. His finalistic attitude strikes a new note in American literature and even the arrangement of his material has a certain originality.

Although he uses the deductive method, Fairchild knows how to give his work an attractive appearance by the use of historical and practical examples. The comprehensive text books which Fairchild has recently published with Edgar Stevenson Furniss and Norman Sidney Buck [53] also contain inductive points. Mention should likewise be made here of Raymond T. Bye,[54] another outstanding young American theorist. He dwells especially on questions of organization and deals particularly well with monopolies and corporations. In pure theory his work is characterized by the supremacy of the marginal theory. There are useful ideas in his doctrine of price in which his analysis of demand is principally used to explain market prices, whereas "normal prices" are made dependent on costs and supply. The idea of welfare is at the center of the economics, the principles of which he learnedly expounded together with W. W. Hewett, his colleague in Philadelphia.[55] The latter too has given a good example of the prevailing economic theory in America.[56]

7. *Realistic and Ethically Religious Systems, and Those Devoted to Social Reform*

The English and American systems which we have hitherto mentioned have been predominantly theoretical, while an emphasis on the realistic social attitude has been comparatively rare. In America the Institutionalists, when they have not been absorbed in methodological disputes, have devoted themselves to special branches of research. It is only recently that O. Fred Boucke [57] and Lionel D. Edie [58] have published two treatises, which illustrate the general critical attitude of the new movement.

Boucke's chief aim is to give a description of the social background of economic phenomena, with much stress on psychological and biological factors. In his endeavors to avoid mathematical and mechanical explanations he neglects the problem of price and distribution but emphasizes production. The physical factors of this are dealt with thoroughly, but perhaps his most useful contribution is his description of the alternation between productivity and business cycles. Edie tries harder to remain traditional, takes stock of the most important results of classical economics and willingly applies the modern marginal principle. He endeavors to view the forces which are active in economic life, in their real diversity; thus diluting the so-called economic laws and showing an entirely realistic attitude. He stresses, for instance, the fact that all the elements which play a part in the formation of prices do not aim in the long run at an equilibrium between supply and demand. Edie uses a great mass of historical and statistical data on our economic institutions as a basis for this relativistic attitude. The introduction for beginners [59] in which Rexford Guy Tugwell, Thomas Munro and Roy E. Stryker attempt to show the paths to economic welfare, with especial reference to American conditions, is entirely institutionalistic.

Among the few English economists who are realists, only Edwin Cannan has published in the new century a worthwhile treatise.[60]

This is chiefly historical; Cannan tries to explain socio-economic phenomena in terms of economic history, and stresses the social and legal aspects of our science. Especially noteworthy is the way in which he refers differences in income to the laws of inheritance, and his researches on the economic relationships of private property. Every page reminds one of Schmoller; likewise, the two volumes in which Cannan has published his collected essays.[61]

A most original treatise is that of the Hindu Radhamakal Mukerjee,[62] who studies the relationships with economic theory and social sciences as psychology, biology and sociology. Although he is not fully acquainted with the latest theories, many of his criticisms are worthy of notice. In the main, he reaches a relativistic conclusion, which corresponds to the historical attitude. In economics, certain categories and types correspond to the changing conditions of psychology, biology and social science. He criticizes European individualism, with a certain amount of prejudice, and tries to show the ethical and social advantages of a peculiar system of communalism for the Orient. The whole second volume of his work is an encomium of Hindu communalism. His two most recent works,[63] of which the latter deals especially with Indian affairs, present the same ideas but show the influence of the latest American tendencies, especially in his criticism of the theory of marginal utility, in which the arguments of the Institutionalists are repeated word for word.

During the war, and under the influence of the Paris economic conference, there appeared a book from the pen of J. Taylor Peddies,[64] which promised much but offered little. It is not worth our while to waste time over the author of a national system of economics who chanced upon the works of Friedrich List only after the completion of his book and who is not acquainted with the principal works of classical or modern economics. The rest of his criticism of economic principles is entirely worthless, as is also his demand to replace by a nationalistic policy the international and liberalistic principle of laissez-faire. Considerably more scientific are the attacks which Cannan made on every mention of nationalism in economics.

Henry Clay is influenced by the social and ethical idealism of Carlyle and Ruskin. As every one knows, these philosophers are practical rather than speculative. They mingle religion and idealistic metaphysics to form an attitude which is akin to Christian socialism. Thus, Clay too is opposed to all chrematistic attempts in economics, a tendency which he shows especially in his theory of distribution. His treatise [65] is based upon the results of modern theory, which he tries to popularize. Although he is much indebted to Marshall, he does not overlook Marx, of whom he gives a notable criticism. The clarity of its thought is not the least of qualities which justified the publication in the United States of Clay's work, with the necessary alterations.[66]

Recently, another Englishman, R. G. Hawtrey, has published an original systematic survey,[67] which is entirely inspired by social and ethical considerations. Notwithstanding all that has been said about the matter, especially in Germany, Hawtrey is still of the opinion that economics cannot be divorced from ethics. The general welfare is the highest aim of economics, before which all abstract theorems must give way. The individualistic idea of free competition should be discarded and the chief aim of the future should be to abolish war and economic crises.

There are a few satisfactory economic treatises in modern English literature which are based on religion.

Charles S. Devas [68] finds his inspiration in the teachings of the Catholic Church and attacks liberalism and materialism in economics. On the whole, he clings to the well-known critical arguments and makes some curious theoretical mistakes. For instance, in his theory of productivity, he confuses the ideas of real income and money income. The theories of the American E. J. Burke,[69] are even more insecure. The moral law, in the Catholic sense, is for him the only solution of economic problems. Since he means by this the economic law as well, his system resolves itself into chaos. Although he is somewhat bewildered by the law of marginal utility, he has a few original ideas on the subject.

Simon Nelson Patten's doctrines are a curious mixture of respectable theory and utopian speculation. His genius was too unruly for him to produce a coherent system. He devoted himself to special studies, of which the results have been published in one volume.[70] He touched upon nearly all the problems of economics in his famous work,[71] published at the beginning of the century, in which he expressed his unusually optimistic view of society. On the whole, he is critical toward the modern abstract and hedonistic attitude and more indulgent towards realistic ones. He even accepts the principle of marginal utility in a corresponding social environment. He concludes that a great deal of labor cannot be accounted as cost, since it is an outlet for our superfluous energy and is, therefore, a pleasure in itself. In the course of economic development the element of pleasure finally absorbs all necessary economic labor so that the concept of cost is entirely eliminated. Patten finds a similarly optimistic state of equilibrium in the mechanism of exchange of commercial life, in the antithesis of supply and demand and in the continuous reproduction of capital. The harmonious ordering of society which is approaching, despite capitalism and the systems of rents and wages, is at present considerably hindered by "heredity": the bonds placed on the individual by race and the natural conditions of life. The obstacles, however, will soon be removed by the forces of American economic life. We can not here discuss the plan for social reform which Patten develops.

Charles Lee Raper [72] is another social reformer. He starts from the utopian premise that every factor in production plays a role in distribution which exactly corresponds to its productivity. He does not succeed in explaining how this ideal may be made practicable but tries to build on it his entire system. This is only one of the reasons which have prevented his work from appealing either to students or to the public. The Englishman John Atkinson Hobson is a more zealous social reformer. His outline of modern industry,[73] which is directed against profit making can hardly be called thorough, since it deals principally with distribution. We shall deal with him more fully later on.

8. Text books

One cannot overlook the number of text books in English which have appeared in the first quarter of the century, which contain no new discoveries and do not even lay claim to any special scientific value. The lion's share of these belongs to the United States where, owing to the development of economic teaching, they have been appearing by the score. We shall take a few examples of each kind in order to show the main characteristics of this type of literature. To avoid misunderstanding, however, we wish again to stress the fact that these text books play no part in the actual development of our science. Nevertheless, we find, in England as well as in America, valuable compilations of the leading economic theories. Even when they come from the pen of eminent authors, however, their value is chiefly didactic.

For instance, the Englishman James Bonar has written an excellent introduction to economics [74] in which he deals with both theoretical and practical problems.

This book may be compared with the famous *Outlines* of Richard T. Ely, which appeared in America in the last century. The chief characteristic of this work is its historical and ethical attitude toward economic phenomena. Its theoretical parts, where the theories of consumption and production are placed in the foreground, are also valuable, especially in the way he contrasts value with utility and develops the theory of price. Ely had the help of his students for the later editions of his work. He secured the aid of George Ray Wicker for a shorter version,[75] and later published, with Thomas S. Adams, Max O. Lorenz, and Allyn A. Young, a comprehensive and more penetrating account of his system.[76] After Ely, we should notice especially C. J. Bullock,[77] whose text books are marked by clarity and a valuable account of distribution, and Charles M. Thompson.[78] The latter owes much to Ely and Bullock, but makes use of the thoughts of Fetter, Fisher, Seligman, Seager and Taussig in his text book which is supplied with a wealth of factual data. James Dyart Magee's *Introduction* has valuable qualities from a didactic point of view.[79] At the end of each chapter, there are some well chosen questions, which make the discussions easier for the student to grasp. In his theory, Magee is very much under the influence of Turner. As a rule he is more successful when describing socio-economic conditions than when dealing critically with scientific problems. The influence of Fetter and Turner is also strongly felt in the noteworthy text book of A. L. Faubel.[80]

We may now deal with the more theoretical text books. Before the war there appeared an optimistic work by Frank Watson and Scott

Nearing,[81] written under the influence of Patten, and to a lesser degree of Clark. It is primarily descriptive, and well suited to the needs of the beginners. Nearing also wrote an original work in conjunction with H. R. Burch,[82] in which the authors create unnecessary theoretical difficulties for themselves. Both works are illustrated with numerous examples taken from American life. Mabel Atkinson's and Margaret McKillop's introductory text-book [83] contains the most modern theoretical developments but avoids complex matters. The best part of it is the treatment of the problem of value. The first part of Sir T. Henry Penson's text-book has an illuminating account of distribution; and the second part, published after the war, consists of theoretical analysis, well done even if a little too abstract.[84]

After the war there appeared the book of W. M. W. Splawn and W. B. Bizzel,[85] which consists of a somewhat eclectic collection of classical and modern theories. J. H. Todd's book,[86] and Robert Jones's,[87] are both popularizations of Marshall's theory, although the latter lays more emphasis on marginal utility and has tiresome classifications, e. g., the five advantages and the six disadvantages of the division of labor. We find the same defect in the text-book of S. Evelyn Thomas,[88] which contains, however, a lucid exposition of the theory of marginal utility in its particularly Anglo-Saxon form. Although it is occasionally dogmatic, the author's vigorous personality is felt throughout. M. Brigg's work,[89] which also discusses the theory of marginal utility, is valuable for its historical and dogmatic side. Among the followers of Jevons and Marshall we may mention R. G. Richards; [90] whereas C. A. Fay,[91] R. E. Curtis,[92] and L. A. Rufener [93] come under the influence of Clark. The last named makes much out of Taussig's idea of marginal vendibility. While these text books are intended for students, Henry P. Shearman addresses the practical man.[94] He makes full use of charts and tables of statistics, is opposed to monopolies and is devoted to the interests of the working man. George W. Gough, the son of a railroad man, is without a rival in explaining the most difficult problems in the simplest words.[95] He even succeeds in bringing the theory of marginal utility directly home to the lay reader.

Of all the text books which deal primarily with the practical problems of economics, the best is undoubtedly that of L. C. Marshall, C. W. Wright, and J. A. Field, published before the war, in which the wealth of material is matched only by the depth of knowledge.[96] Another excellent book is that of H. G. Hayes,[97] which is basically institutionalistic. Of less value is the book of E. S. Meade,[98] which is rather superficial in its treatment of the problems of production, organizations of labor and of exchange, as well as prices and distribution. A similar attempt of C. J. Melrose, also intended for the lay reader, is scarcely more satisfactory.[99] He tries to lift the money veil and to recognize the real economic activities behind it. His material is rather well arranged. J. M. Robertson's book [100] consists of lectures delivered before the National Liberal Club. Its chief emphasis is on the question of population, and it is full of errors and theoretical inaccuracies. There is a better and more practical work by James E. Le Rossignol,[101] who is especially interested in questions of organization which he always considers in their actual social and historical settings. This is also the attitude of T. R. Williamson,[102] who deals more thoroughly with theoretical problems. We may also mention here a book translated from the Russian of A. Bogdanoff,[103] which has had much success in communistic Russia, which also emphasizes problems of organization and answers them in a Marxian sense.

Finally, there are a few elementary books which deserve to be mentioned. J. Johnston promises much but accomplishes little.[104] He is especially interested in Irish conditions. More stimulating is the booklet of Henry Higgs,[105] which is predominantly nationalistic and takes into consideration the changes brought about by the world war. Miss M. C. Buer,[106] A. R. and Mrs. E. M. Burns,[107] and J. Cunnison,[108] have popularized the theories of Marshall. The Burnses deal merely with production and distribution. Cunnison goes back to Ricardo, and devotes some space to Pigou's idea of welfare. Frank Tracy Carlton [109] has an almost uncanny ability to touch upon nearly all the problems, both practical and theoretical, of economics, in an astonishingly small space. He has some stimulating ideas on the problem of the organization of labor. This theme is successfully treated by J. Harry Jones in his realistic introduction to economic theory,[110] which is however more practical than theoretical. John Lee is a moralist in his short survey: [111] fair value, fair price, and similar expressions, are perpetually recurring.

CHAPTER III

VALUE

1. The Prevalent Tendency Toward Compromise in the Anglo-Saxon Theory of Value

THE GREAT discussions which took place in English-speaking scientific circles during the eighties and nineties over the concept of value seem to have reached a standstill around the turn of the century. In England the debate between Jevons and Marshall was decided in favor of the latter. Marshall successfully refuted Jevons's attack on Ricardo's doctrine of value by combining the real essence of the classical objective theory of value with the modern subjective doctrine. He also managed to show that the chasm between the old and the new theories of value is not so wide as the founders of the theory of marginal utility had assumed and that the idea of cost can be used as a practical principle to complete the subjective explanation of value. In the main, his attitude was accepted by Edgeworth, who did pioneer work for the perfection of the mathematical conception of the modern theory of value in his *Mathematical Physics* (1886), through the development of his so-called curves of indifference which we have already mentioned in connection with Pareto. With very few exceptions, the whole present-day generation of English economists accepts a theory of value in which marginal utility and cost stand together in harmony.

Under the leadership of Clark, American economics had reached a similar state of compromise. Here, however, the element of cost was patterned to suit the hedonistic taste of the modern theory of value and no longer formed a foreign part of its structure. This was accomplished by a clever subjectivistic conception of the objective idea of cost: it was opposed to utility as disutility, the element of displeasure or pain, which appears especially as labor and as sacrifice, i. e., as renunciation of all other applications. Practical experience shows us that every additional increment of the sacrifice is felt more deeply than all previous increments, and that therefore the entire sacrifice—insofar as it is divisible with its increments susceptible of substitution—is valued on the basis of the final unit which has been sacrificed. Or, in other words: it is recognized that disutility or sacrifice of utility is also subjected to the marginal principle, and that it works in the opposite direction to marginal utility. For, as the Americans teach, the greater the sacrifice, the more economic good can be produced. If the quantity increases, the marginal utility decreases, just as the marginal utility increases when the quantity of goods diminishes, that is, when only moderate sacrifices are made for their production. In this case increasing marginal utility is accompanied by decreasing marginal sacrifice. In the course of their contrary motions, utility and sacrifice must meet somewhere, and it is at this meeting point that value arises.

2. *Developments of the Theory of Disutility, especially in a Social Direction*

We have sketched above the main outlines of the American disutility theory which attained pre-eminence at the turn of the century, and has maintained its position ever since. The younger generation calls it today the "orthodox" theory of value. Clark had suggested it in his earlier works, but gave it a more mature and classical development in his *Essentials,* which we have already mentioned. After him, Irving Fisher, Taussig, Seager and Seligman are the most distinguished adherents of this direction of the theory of value. Fisher has recently proposed to substitute for "utility" the more appropriate expression of "wantability," which corresponds to the concept of "marginal vendibility" recently introduced by Taussig, which we shall mention later, and which is supposed to remove the ambiguities of the modern doctrine of value.[1] Fisher has also recently published a new edition of his work [2] written on the mathematical basis of the modern theory of value, which at one time influenced even Pareto. In his most recent writings, Seager tried to provide a realistic and social foundation for the theory of value, by excluding as far as possible all abstract isolating ideas. Seligman took the same direction considerably earlier, and attacked with great vigor the ordinary Robinson Crusoe fables used in founding the theory of value.

If a wealthy fool, says Seligman, takes it into his head to give a thousand dollars for an ordinary spoon which can be had for five cents, his subjective evaluation would have no influence on the value of the spoon. For in the formation of value, it is a question not of individual but of social utility, and not of individual but of social costs, just as individual welfare and individual ethics can be referred only to social welfare and to social ethics.[8] Seligman has also in his well-known textbook made notable attempts to develop the social relationships of the theory of value.

Hannah Robie Sewall, apparently stimulated by Seligman's ideas, will hear, in her dogmatically historical work,[4] only of a division between social and individual value. In a discussion with the Cambridge school, and especially with Henderson, L. T. Hobhouse has recently emphasized the social aspect of the real problem of value, whereby his attitude strongly resembles that of modern American Institutionalism.[5]

On the basis of similar considerations, Charles E. Persons has come to the conclusion that neither the element of utility nor the element of cost can in their individualistic garbs afford a positive standard of value, since the great social and economic divisions of the prevailing socal order make such an assumption from the first impossible.[6] A similar idea already appears in Taussig's doctrine of "non-competing groups," and Davenport,[7] with whom we shall deal later, is partly in the same vein. Nevertheless, Davenport severely criticizes Seligman's theory of social value.

Patten too gives his theory of value, in which he develops Clark's doctrine, an entirely social character. We have mentioned in an earlier connection, how he brings the element of cost first to the same level as that of utility, by which he then lets it be partially absorbed. In this way, according to Patten, there results a perpetual surplus of social utility, i. e., of usable goods since, through the satisfaction of our natural desire to work, that is, through a productive activity, which provides pleasure in itself without causing any costs at all, that amount of goods can always be produced, through the consumption of which a new desire to labor is reborn in constant rotation. The fact that in the modern economic organization we procure the greater part of our need for goods not directly in the way of production but by giving away other goods, by exchange, does not alter the level of the social surplus, since only individual surpluses are there interchanged. The fact that goods in spite of this constant surplus have a value is because our wants increase in intensity and variety more rapidly than our power to produce.

Like this doctrine of Patten, the noteworthy studies of Ludwig Kotany,[8] and of Lindley M. Keasbey,[9] date from the beginning of the new century. The former analyses fruitfully the "productive capacity," on the basis of which goods of the second order are valued, while Keasbey tries to insert between use value and exchange value the new concept of "prestige value." This does not result from the satisfaction of our wants which are connected directly or indirectly with consumption, as do use and exchange values, but spring from our desire "to become a proprietor," which plays an important part in our practical economic life. Little attention was paid in scientific circles to this proposal. Since the war Fairchild has continued Clark's theory of value in his text book which we have already mentioned. Instead of value of goods he proposes the not very happily chosen expression "intrinsic value."

More useful appear the attempts of those students who, instead of a further dismembering of the abstract concept of value, investigate the possibility of a practical measurement of value. Thus Irving Fisher, in a mathematical study of marginal utility conducted along these lines, comes to the conclusion that progressive taxation is justified from the point of view of the theory of values.[10]

Other Americans try to investigate the question of the measurement of value with relation to various problems of public industries, railways, tariff policy, etc. A one-sided, but stimulating, attempt has been made by the engineer David Atkins,[11] to treat value on the basis of purely scientific and technological considerations and thereby to solve the problem of its measurement. He lets value itself result from the mechanical interworkings between forces and opposing forces. In this respect he is not far from the ideas of Pareto. He suggests as the best unit for measuring this value the man-acre-hour, a peculiar combination of units of land, population and time. The use of gold to measure value leads, according to Atkins, to economic crises and to other social evils.

In accordance with the attitude of Böhm-Bawerk, Fetter, etc., James G. Smith tries to do justice to the element of time in the formation of value.[12] G. P. Watkins refers the problem of the difference between the valuation of the present and future goods rather to the theory of price.[13]

3. Efforts to Save the Labor Theory of Value

The large work of Logan G. McPherson,[14] which attempts to offer a picture of the historical development of the formation of value within the frame of the distribution of goods, is sadly confused. As far as one can judge through the mist of his new-fangled nomenclature, McPherson tries to refer the theory of disutility back to the idea of the labor theory of value. In their jointly written work,[15] Percy and Albert Wallis decide that only a constant recognition of labor as the source of value can lead to an amelioration of the prevailing social ills. Obvious reminiscences of the labor theory of value can be found in the Scandinavian Birck, an adherent of the doctrine of marginal utility. In his fundamental principles, he bases himself entirely on Marshall's theory of value, since he assumes in the elementary economic activity, in the process of dedication, that is, in the application of goods to the satisfaction of our wants, a state of equilibrium between use and sacrifice. Here he has a few subtle and successful analyses, e. g., the differentiation between use and utility. In studying the element of cost, he lays too much stress on the pain of labor, so that his thought approaches, if not in form at least in substance, the labor theory of value. This theory has been thoroughly rejected by the American, Albert C. Whitaker.[16] While Whitaker defends the modern theory of value against the conceptions of earlier English writers, the Englishman H. W. B. Joseph [17] defends it against the Marxian labor theory, which he tries to prove untenable with convincing arguments. In this he bases himself largely on the critical views of Böhm-Bawerk.

4. Davenport's Pseudo-objective Theory of Value

Davenport occupies a peculiar position in the modern American theory of value. He started from the theory of disutility, which he tries to bring in closer contact with practical economic life. In the course of his investigations he came to the conclusion that the whole theory of marginal utility is based on a false conception of real economic relationships. The marginal principle in itself is correct, since value and price actually arise on the level of marginal utility or of marginal sacrifice; but they are by no means decided thereby. The fundamental mistake of the theory of marginal utility and of all the erroneous calculations of the mathematical school built on it lies in the assumption of such a causal relationship.

Going back to the attitude of MacVane, Davenport is rather of the opinion that the determination of marginal utility is accomplished on the ground of considerations of value and price. Therefore he devotes his attention to a direct analysis of these subjects, translates them immediately with a certain realism into the language of money, and tries to solve their problem especially by means of a corresponding change in the traditional concept of cost. In using a commodity to satisfy a certain want, or in using our labor and time for a certain productive activity, it is not, according to Davenport, the absolute cost of manufacture of the commodity used which comes into consideration, but only the sacrifice which is incurred by a refusal of the eternal second-best possibility of use. He calls this sacrifice—using an expression taken from the literature of the last century—"opportunity cost." From the point of view of the entrepreneur, which is always the leading one with Davenport, the costs of production do not consist of the sums expended for raw materials, wages of labor, etc., but are the same as the income which the entrepreneur could have obtained by the second-best expenditure of his knowledge, his power and his capital. Davenport claims, by referring this marginal utility to the relative marginal sacrifice, to have solved the problem of value in an entirely new fashion which has nothing in common with the old cost theory of value.[18]

Davenport's studies have left a deep imprint on the science of English speaking countries, and especially on those writers who cling even today more or less to the modern subjective theory of value in its original form, owe him a great deal of recognition. Among these we may mention Wicksteed,[19] undoubtedly the most important follower of Jevons and Menger,[20] who had reached the idea of "opportunity cost" even before Davenport; Alvin S. Johnson, whose criticism of Davenport we have mentioned above, and Carver.[21] The last-mentioned author pays, indeed, some attention to the ideas of Marshall and Clark but at the bottom he belongs to the pure marginal utility school.

In this connection we should also mention the work of W. E. Johnson,[22] who tries, with much elegance, to place the subjective theory of value on a more profound mathematical basis, the merit of which was recognized by the master of this tendency, Edgeworth himself.[23] Recently A. E. Moore has interested himself in working out the relations between entrepreneur's cost and the formation of value.[24]

5. *Fetter, Anderson and the Struggle against the Marginal Utility Theory of Value*

Fetter's theory of value, especially as he expounded it in the early period of his scientific development, is based on purely subjective foundations. He would have suffered little loss of his own attitude if he had accepted the teaching of the Austrian school on value in its entirety. But Fetter is, in what concerns science, a revolutionary spirit—approximately what Liefmann is in the most modern German economics—and so he goes his own peculiar way in solving the problem of value. First he works out the concept of "psychic income," which tries to treat economic utility, free from all materialistic connotations, on a purely psychic basis. Value therefore arises only from the capacity of goods to satisfy our wants. Fetter's thought then follows more or less the path of the Austrian theory of value: his conclusions are also the result of the law of diminishing marginal utility and of the element of scarcity. The element of cost is important in Fetter's explanation of value only insofar as the quantity of goods to be disposed of is brought into connection with the costs of producing them. But even in this point, to which we shall return later, he agrees mainly with Wieser. Only gradually did Fetter succeed in making the fundamental principles of his economics more or less independent of those of the Austrian school. In this more recent stage of his development, he bases his theory of value on the free choice which in the course of human development becomes even more perfect among the means at our disposal, which in their turn are subjected to the principle of scarcity. In this way Fetter arrives at the concept of "marginal valuation" which, according to him, represents a different category from marginal utility. For the rest, he clings to most of the superstructure of his earlier theory of value, and only emphasizes rather more strongly the element of cost. Economic value appears to him only as a derivation, or a special form of the general concept of value in the axiological sense.

In this point Fetter resembles a group of young American economists whose efforts are directed toward an extension of the economic concept of value. In this they go back especially to the doctrines of the elder Clark and of Seligman, in whom—as we have just seen—the socio-organic attitude is strongly emphasized. B. M. Anderson Jr., is at the head of this group and teaches that value as a general fundamental concept of all social sciences cannot be limited to serving as a standard of economic relationships of exchange.[25] Relying upon some ideas of the social psychologist C. H. Cooley, he here speaks of an absolute social value, which he opposes to the narrower, relative concept of value of leading economic theory, and which he considers the only correct basis for the future development of our science.

An interesting discussion took place on this theme between Anderson and the younger Clark.[26] On Anderson's side, Ralph Barton Perry,[27] and Abbott Payson Usher,[28] offer modest contributions toward explaining the difference between the concepts of the general "axiological," or the ethical and economic value. The Englishman George Binney Dibblee also comes under the influence of Anderson and has recently attempted a thorough analysis of the problem of value resting upon comprehensive practical economic experience.[29] In this he has succeeded in pointing out a few social psychological elements, such as the attempt to awake from within the appearance of welfare, which generally remains unnoticed as a source of value. His ideas on the subject resemble in part the theory of prestige value sketched by Keasbey, which we have mentioned above.

For Correa Moylan Walsh, who attempts to keep the four different kinds of use value, esteem value, cost value, and exchange value strictly separated,[30] there can be no greater retrogression in economic theory than the effort of Anderson and his followers to integrate and to unify the concept of value.

Dickinson has recently opposed with great vehemence all these attempts to build a value theory on a new psychological basis; he tries, as we have already seen, to come to terms with the traditional hedonistic attitude and acknowledges himself as the psychological defender of the leading American theory of value according to Clark. In this he has against him the whole army of the institutionalists who devote their criticisms especially to the overthrow of the marginal utility theory of value. Their leader is Veblen [31] and E. H. Downey [32] follows him enthusiastically. Walton H. Hamilton tries to prove on the ground of dogmatic historical studies that not only the idea of utility, but also the whole theory of value, has at most only a formal importance in modern economics: their former central positions are to be considered taken by the problems of institutionalism.[33] The other adherents of the new tendency also seize every opportunity of giving a kick to marginalism in value theory. Knight is a critic of institutionalism, but always opposes a value theory based upon marginal utility from another point of view: that of his socio-ethical ideals.[34] Thus it is that David Friday could, in view of this concentrated attack and relying upon parallel phenomena in European science, talk of a "moribund" value theory,[35] the resurrection of which he awaits, like Anderson, only from an extension of the concept of value.

Fetter's peculiar position is to be seen in the fact that, in spite of rejecting hedonistic and utilitarian psychology and starting from a voluntaristic attitude, he reaches a solution of the value problem which closely resembles the essential conclusions of the marginal utility theory. It is to this synthesis that he owes the influence which he exerts on modern American writers. Thus J. R. Turner completely acknowledges Fetter's theory of value, and H. G. Brown, on more independent grounds, tries to achieve a connection between it and Davenport's views.

6. Gradual Retreat of the Whole Value Theory in Anglo-Saxon Economics

In view of the powerful support which the value theory based on marginal utility found, especially in Fetter's earlier work and in his followers, its position still seemed fairly strong in America a few years ago. One was justified in assuming that the combined forces of Clark and Fetter would be successful in defeating the ever increasing opposition manifested from different sides against marginal utility and in being able to continue their theory of value. Another situation, however, was brought about by the fact that a gradual change took place in the interests of Fetter himself. As a result of this change he brought the idea of welfare into the center of economic theory and the whole theory of value was, so to speak, dethroned by him. He now thinks that the historical task of marginal utility was only to conquer at last the Marxian labor theory of value.[36] But he is forced to add: "A solar-plexus knockout is no less decisive because both boxers were weak in their foot-work." For even the position of the conquerer, marginal utility, does not seem particularly secure in Fetter's eyes. He himself now teaches that this theory can explain economic phenomena only in a narrow radius, and even then only hypothetically. For the explanation of welfare, which is not only an economic but also a socio-ethical problem, the utility theory of value and the money theory of price based upon it are no longer sufficient. Fetter still holds to a value theory which is closely related in its results with that of marginal utility, but he relegates it in importance to economic problems of the second class.

The theory of value fares the same way with the other English-speaking economists who wish to put the problem of welfare at the center of our science. Thus value theory has less importance with Marshall than with Jevons, and even less with Pigou. The idea of welfare is built by these authors principally upon the satisfaction of wants, on utility, and so the value theory based on marginal utility is able here—as Jacob Viner[37] has recently pointed out—to maintain itself as an intermediate organ of secondary importance. This cannot conceal the fact that it has lost its former central position even in Pigou's system, and that its star is beginning to set in the most recent development of English economics, too. In the long run the idea of welfare will scarcely be compatible with the theory of marginal utility. This is best shown by the American example where, in the criticism of modern value theory, especially with Knight, arguments are advanced that are based upon the idea of welfare as the central point of economic theory. A similar note was struck by Young even before the World War.[38]

CHAPTER IV

PRICE

1. Marshall's Theory of Price, and its Developments

On the whole, the development of price theory in the economics of the English-speaking world in the first quarter of our century presents a more quiet picture than that of value theory. For although all changes in value theory necessarily influenced the price theory based on it, the eagerness of the reformers generally gave way here. With few exceptions, the scholars were content with a criticism of the prevailing price theory derived from value theory, and offered no new positive solutions of the price problem. The expenditure of energy was therefore less and a detailed and gradual development of the heritage of the last century can be more clearly noticed in this field.

Most writers in England to the present day are, as far as regards the price theory, under the mighty influence of Marshall's studies. After he had accepted the fundamental principle of the subjective doctrine of price based on the marginal idea, he devoted all his attention to the classical doctrine and wove its objective aspects into the price theory of marginal utility. He enlarges the doctrine of minimum and maximum costs as price determining factors by the laws of constant returns, which operates as soon as equally strong tendencies of diminishing and increasing costs meet in the same branch of production. Marshall considers marginal costs of prime importance for the determination of price, but only in agricultural commodities. In those products which are subject to the law of constant or increasing returns, he lets market price result from the usual average cost. The final price on the market is influenced by subjective considerations of utility. It is upon this that the equilibrium in the price mechanism rests, the play of which, influenced by many secondary factors, determines the point at which the price will finally be settled. Edgeworth also reached the same conclusion; a coincidence to which Loria draws attention.[1] In general, Marshall is more interested in the problem of the free formation of price, whereas Edgeworth prefers the study of monopoly prices.

Pigou continued Marshall's analysis of the factors which operate on the market, and convincingly proved the necessity of a separate investigation of the various sources from which the individual elements of supply and demand spring.[2] He also tries to develop further Marshall's studies of the relations between the costs of an enterprise and the price formation on the market.[3] Lionel Robbins criticizes these results of Marshall unfavorably.[4]

In contrast to the mathematical and schematic studies of Cunynghame, mentioned above, Chapman [5] stresses the fact that within the costs of production of many articles of industry there are manifold heterogeneous tendencies which all work together in the formation of their supply on the market. Noteworthy too are Pigou's investigations, in which he tries to determine mathematically the elasticity of demand in the most important articles of consumption, on the basis of a few household budgets of workmen's families.[5a]

In the American literature, Carver accepts Marshall's doctrine of an equilibrium between supply and demand. Patten is especially successful in developing it. He makes the objective equilibrium in the mechanism of market price result from the meeting of two further subjective equilibria which exist on the one hand with the buyer and on the other with the seller, between marginal utility and marginal expenditure and which are connected with exchange. In his judgment of this mechanism of price Patten's well known optimism reappears: he teaches that the whole formation of price is dependent only on the attitude of the consumers, that in most cases they are at liberty to replace the object of their consumption by other goods, and can then exercise a decisive influence on the shaping of the market. According to him even monopolies can do little to counteract this for, in the course of modern economic development, they show a tendency of mutual compensation.

2. *The Explanation of Price from the Point of View of Demand. Fetter*

Patten's idea of the supremacy of the buyer in the market is especially stressed in English literature by Wicksteed. Wicksteed's studies, however, do not have the optimistic social background which we find in the works of the American. In close connection with the Austrian school, the idea is worked out that the real source of price formation is to be found on the side of demand. Fetter's price theory, especially in his earlier years, is characterized by a marked dependence on the Austrian theory. In his analysis of supply and demand, he is always emphasizing the sovereign role of subjective evaluations, and derives price only from these. Nevertheless, as Robert F. Hoxie has shown [6]—the objective element of cost also has a certain importance in his theory. Nature furnishes the goods which we need to satisfy our wants only in limited quantities, and we must exert ourselves, and work, in order to increase this quantity. Here Fetter makes use of his general law of diminishing returns and subjects the labor sacrifice to the marginal principle to which, on the other side of the process of valuation, the law of diminishing marginal utility corresponds. Therefore, according to Fetter, the objective element of cost is already contained in the purely subjective evaluations which the parties bring to the market.

Fetter has done much to clarify the concept of price by his thorough dogmatic historical studies, which result in a comparison of 177 price theories of old and new economists, especially from the point of view of their subjective or objective characters.[7] An interesting dispute took place at the Washington meeting of the American Economic Association in December 1911, following Fetter's report on definitions of price.[8] Of late the principle of marginal utility has played a minor role in Fetter's theory of price, and the whole doctrine of price has somewhat given way in importance as compared to the idea of welfare. Nevertheless, Fetter has still produced some notable works on the subject, although their tendency is more practical. Thus he reaches the conclusion that the geographical boundaries between various market areas which compete with respect to the same kind of goods, have the shape of hyperbolas.[9]

3. *Clark's Theory of Price, and the Analysis of Price Boundaries*

Fetter's contribution of showing how considerations of scarcity in the process of valuation bring the element of cost into the otherwise purely subjective price theory is the link with the main tendency of modern American price theory. Like Marshall, the elder Clark strove above all for a synthesis between the new subjective and the old objective solution of the problem of price. He attains this by strongly emphasizing the quantitative proportions of the goods produced among those factors which co-operate to cause supply. These, he teaches, depend in turn on market demand, for it is that which first of all decides the level of the price that can be obtained. A quantitative extension of production can proceed only as far as production costs remain within the price which is to be expected for the goods on the market. Nevertheless, Clark is able to give the quantitative element in supply a partially independent character whereby the cost element is again lifted into the rank of a direct, effective factor of price formation. The second most important characteristic of Clark's price theory is the emphasis on the social relationships which determine the formation of price. In this direction, Seligman especially continued his researches and produced important new results for economics. Whereas the theory of marginal pairs, as developed by the Austrian school and especially by Böhm-Bawerk, mentioned only individual marginal buyers and marginal sellers, who arrived at an exchange in a given state of the market, this idea was now applied by Seligman to the social levels which are really present in practical economic life and should always be considered. The various social classes appear on the market as divers classes of buyers and sellers who are capable of exchanging. The level of supply arises in the main from advantages or disadvantages in the technique of production, but in demand what is of prime importance is the nature of the social condition of the purchasing public. Since demand has the deciding word in the market, price will have to correspond to the purchasing power of the marginal level which demands, i. e., of that social class which can just reach an exchange under the given conditions of supply. In this way the law of price of the marginal utility school, which was constructed with special reference to individual economic conditions, is translated by Seligman into the language of social reality.

Seager offers us a "social" theory of price, built upon similar lines. He draws attention in addition to the fact that price can reach different levels in the market owing to the eventual interaction of the last effective demand with the last effective supply and that within this range technical market factors are always in the long run decisive. John A. Hobson built his "Bargain Theory of Wages" which appeared at the end of the last century on the idea that between the lowest wage which a laborer will accept and the highest wage that the entrepreneur is ready to pay there is generally a fairly large difference which theory should not neglect. According to Hobson the question as to who will profit most from this broad difference is decided not by supply and demand but by the skill with which both parties act in the labor market. Hobson later generalized this idea [10] and extended it to cover all cases of price formation. For the shares which the exchanging parties are able to secure for themselves from the variation between the "marginal demand price" and the "marginal supply price," he coins the expression "forced gains," and makes their level depend on the market knowledge and the bargaining skill of the parties.

E. W. Kemmerer expresses the idea more concisely when he says that price will arise at that point between the two limits in which the disadvantages connected with further bargaining seems greater to both of the exchanging parties than the advantages expected therefrom.[11] The Englishman Flux on the other hand holds that an appreciable range between the level of marginal demand and of marginal supply occurs much less frequently in practical economic life than Hobson and other writers assume.[12] For this reason alone we should not attach too much importance to Hobson's solution of the problem of price. Moreover Flux blames him for falling into the error of attributing activity to the condition of the marginal pairs in exchange, qualities which in reality belong only to the other parties to the exchange and not to the marginal pairs. For the marginal level of the marginal pairs can have no other meaning but that they have no further range of activity in the formation of prices. In the mathematical exposition of price theory which he offers in his text book Flux keeps close to Marshall's attitude.

In American post-war literature F. M. Taylor's studies, which deal with the most abstruse points of price mechanism, deserve especial attention. Unfortunately he is unable to escape the danger of exaggerated abstraction and his mathematical explanation of price formation in the text-book mentioned above is often inflexible, too schematic, and therefore artificial. Nevertheless, his distinctions, in which he feels bound to assume an "extra-marginal" supply and an "extra-marginal" demand by the side of marginal supply and demand, remain stimulating and instructive for every theorist. It is in the interplay of these four factors that Taylor looks for an explanation of price fluctuations. Frank H. Knight takes a somewhat opposite path and instead of working out further distinctions proposes a simplification of traditional price theory.[13] He tries to prove that the idea of utility and the theory of cost are incompatible in price theory since, for example, in the cost explanation of diminishing returns the idea of marginal utility is already implicit; therefore it is useless to continue arguing about this so-called problem since the scholars have long ago agreed as to the essential explanation of the phenomenon of price.

American price theory has recently received a marked impulse from the contributions of those writers who make a study of the quantitative analysis of the factors in price formation. One group of these writers is influenced by the Lausanne school and lays most stress on the mathematically deductive continuation of their results, whereas the others are more realistic and devote their attention rather to a statistical and descriptive point of view. At the head of the first group are the Columbia professor, Henry Ludwell Moore, and his pupil, Henry Schultz; the second is led by Frederick C. Mills, also of Columbia, while James W. Angell now also at Columbia and a few others stand somewhere in the middle between these two tendencies.

Moore studies the question of elasticity of supply and demand. He applies his conclusions to the problem of price fluctuations, and works out, somewhat in the sense of the Lausanne doctrine, the concept of a moving equilibrium between both price-forming factors.[14] Schultz joins himself to Moore's investigations of the problem of elasticity, makes a thorough statistical analysis of the price of sugar in the United States during the last quarter of the nineteenth century and thus arrives at his mathematical laws as to the formation of supply and demand. These laws he tries to defend especially against institutionalism and endeavors to show that he is dealing with objective facts, which are independent of the entire psychological foundation of economic theory.[15] C. F. Ross, one of Schultz's pupils, endeavors to develop dynamically his theory of price.[16] Norman J. Silberling tries to give an exact mathematical explanation of price formation with the help at times of three dimensional curves. On the whole, he keeps close to Marshall's views.[17]

Mills has recently published, with the help of the New York National Bureau of Economic Research, a most noteworthy work in the field of a statistical-descriptive investigation of price.[18] He is especially interested in prices from 1890 to 1925 and compares the development in the United States to America with that of other countries. The result of this is to be an inductively planned outline of a great system of price. Jacob Viner is not entirely wrong when he objects that Mills's theoretical results stand in no relation to his broad statistical foundation.[19] G. F. Warren and F. A. Pearson, the agricultural experts of Cornell University, make use of Mills's idea in the investigation of the interactions between land produce and the movement of prices with respect to a few agricultural products.[20] They too throw much light on the elasticity of supply and demand. Frank M. Surface tries to examine theoretically the effects of the American government's control over the price of wheat in the years 1917–19.[21] In these matters Warren and Pearson, as well as Surface, follow the lead taken by the South African R. A. Lehfeldt immediately before the war.[22] Holbrook Working tries to determine by statistics the differences which exist between demand caused by consumption and that caused by speculation.[23] E. J. Working,[24] R. S. Merriam [25] and Mordecai Ezekiel of Washington [26] should also be mentioned among those who devote themselves to an analysis, partly theoretical and partly statistical, of supply and demand.

Both these methods are united in the comprehensive studies which James W. Angell has made of the international relationships of price formation.[27] He makes a wide use of points of view taken from theories of money, banking, credit and commerce, which he treats institutionally, and is able too, as a pupil of Taussig, to make notable contributions to the development of pure theory: he expounds, for instance, with success, the connections between wants and demand.[28] The theory of dumping has been recently expounded by Jacob Viner of Chicago; [29] that of comparative costs especially by F. W. Taussig,[30] followed by Frank D. Graham,[31] with whom the following entered into a discussion: F. H. Knight,[32] Kemper Simpson,[33] Edward S. Mason,[34] etc.

4. The Point of View of Costs

Contrary to Fetter, who strongly emphasized the subjective element in his theory of price, all these American scholars lay a more or less equal weight on the subjective and objective elements in explaining price. We can distinguish a further group of writers who, systematically renewing the classical theory, devote their attention especially to costs of production in price theory, which they develop analytically. The most important member of this group is Davenport, who lets his price theory spring directly from his original explanation of value.[35] The level of production costs, which represents the lower limit of the evaluation placed by the seller on the commodities brought to the market by him, is accordingly equal to the utility which he could achieve by the second best employment of his productive activity. But since this utility can be realized only on the market, and is in this way dependent on the demand represented by every other product, the seller's marginal evaluation, or the supply curve, can also be in the last analysis referred to a demand curve. This has the same function in the formation of price as the direct and primary market demand curve. Davenport accordingly considers it superficial and misleading to seek price at the intersection point of supply and demand curves.

The theory of opportunity—cost, touched upon by Wicksteed, but first developed by Davenport, has recently been taken up by the Englishman Hubert D. Henderson, who tries to inject it into the theory of equilibrium between supply and demand, and thus to put new life into the price theory of the Cambridge school.[36] Another younger member of this school, D. H. Robertson, stresses the importance of supply as well as of production costs in the formation of price.[37]

Before the World War, John Maurice Clark, then at Chicago, made a praiseworthy attempt to bring the element of time into the theory of production costs and, by taking stock of the various lengths of the production and business periods, reached the conclusion that in dynamic economics price does not necessarily have to remain on the same level as production costs.[38]

He devoted himself later even more completely to this type of problem, and finally published his work on the theory of production,[39] which is perhaps the most valuable contribution of recent American economic theory. While most theories which assign both a subjective and an objective origin to price lose themselves in deductive abstractions, Clark attacks inductively the question of what are the concrete roles played by production costs from the point of view of price formation. He distinguishes two main classes of goods according as their market prices are determined by production costs or by subjective evaluations. In the first class are all those branches of production the price of which, because of their great public importance, is subject to government control as well as those which produce staple commodities. In the second class are those commodities which are intended to satisfy higher wants and in which individual style, taste and artistic finish are of more consequence. Since the first class is by far the more important, costs of production become the central economic problem in price formation. Within these the constant costs, or "overhead costs" are especially prominent. These cannot be referred to the unit of production, since within definite periods of production they are independent of the amount of units produced. The vitality and success of productive branches depend on the relationship into which these constant costs are brought with regard to the variable ones: on the question whether producers can make full or only partial use of the capacity contained in their "overheads," or constant costs. The changes in this ratio exert a decisive influence on the price formation of products. Since, however, according to Clark, in the most important economic relationships all labor belongs more or less, from a social point of view, to the "overhead"—for laborers must eat, whether they work or not—it is not only the obvious interest of each individual, but also the social duty of every enterprise, to make the most of its capacity, even with temporary sacrifices, in order to check unemployment. In this way Clark gradually enlarges the scope of his problem, until he touches upon most of the important questions of economics, which he illumines with social and ethical viewpoints.[40] His main contribution lies in the advice which he gives to the industries for the full development of their capacity, by means of which he brings the concept of private business into economic theory. He is especially fond of drawing his examples from the management of American railways.

Other American economists have also devoted their attention since the war to a study of the practical relationship between production costs and the price level, and make use especially of the experiences of wartime industry. Thus Taussig [41] explains how right it was that during the war the official fixing of prices was made on the level of the cost of the marginal producer. Although he acknowledges here that the law of supply and demand is in most cases overruled by compulsory regulations, he admits elsewhere [42] that in view of the manifold variety of practical economic phenomena neither this law nor the general construction of supply and demand curves should be interpreted too rigidly. In the third edition of his text book, which appeared after the war, Taussig introduced the idea of marginal vendibility, hoping to free the theory of price from the disturbance of one-sided, subjective interpretations. Philip G. Wright points out the close connection between Taussig's ideas and the neo-classical theory of price in America (Walker).[43] Kemper Simpson's investigations ran parallel with those of Taussig. He points out especially, with the help of statistics, the tension which might have resulted during the war from the abnormal market conditions between the level of the average costs of production and the prices which were actually attained.[44]

Raymond T. Bye has recently given us what appears to be a useful analysis of production costs. All costs may be referred, according to him, to compensations for the following eight elements: effort, ability, waiting or saving, uncertainty-bearing, land-space, natural materials, production goods naturally fixed in supply, and monopolies for excess profits on goods under their control. Out of these elements are formed wages, interest, rent, losses, insurance-premiums, taxes, and profits, as well as any sums which are considered by the entrepreneur as costs.[45]

5. *Monopoly Price*

While Americans have distinguished themselves in the study of costs, Englishmen have taken the lead in continuing to develop the theory of monopoly price. This field is especially well suited to the mathematical procedure, and Edgeworth could give his keen intellect full play here. In refutation of Cournot's doctrine, he concludes that the economic equilibrium is indeterminate if two or more monopolists are pitted against freely competing groups. In consequence of this Edgeworth emphasizes that in a system of monopoly which comprises all fields of economics, abstract theorists must forfeit their occupation, since here there are purely economic conditions which can be approached only by empirical investigation. Of prime importance is his statement that a seller's monopoly, which generally includes only slight sacrifices on the part of the monopolist, is not necessarily associated with detriment to the buying public, which often fares even better in this situation than under free competition. For instance, the classification of prices, often adopted by monopolists in contrast to the uniform prices of free competition, possesses advantages for the public which should not be underestimated. This is best exemplified in the monopolistic fixing of railroad and shipping rates.

As a practical consequence of Edgeworth's ideas, Pigou has recently drawn attention to the fact that a disruption of big business combinations would lead, not to free competition, but merely to the indeterminateness of many monopolies.[46] Edgeworth's successful analyses of the laws of price formation in the presence of monopolies were worthily continued by Pigou who by means of his mathematical analysis was able to grasp with accuracy the case of bilateral monopoly.[47] A. L. Bowley has recently made a useful contribution to this subject.[48]

On the basis of Edgeworth's and Pigou's optimistic conception, F. Lavington tries to prove that, with reasonable behavior on the part of the monopolist, monopolies can lead not only to a permanent insurance against the instability of labor and to a lowering of the costs of production but also to a strengthening of the equilibrium in business life.[49]

We have already mentioned, in American literature, Patten's theory of monopoly. His doctrine that monopolies fight against and offset one another is accepted by Frank T. Carlton, who sees in it a weakening of "absolute intensive rents," the origin of which he traces to the formation of price by a monopoly.[50] Ely is less optimistic,[51] and depicts the clashings between monopolists and consumers in rather dark colors. Alvin S. Johnson agrees in his text book with the main principle of Ely's theory of price: that in the long run prices tend in the direction of the cost level of those who produce under the most favorable circumstances. In his theory of monopoly Johnson distinguishes especially between temporary and permanent monopolies, according as they have their origin in the commercial situation or in the conditions of production.[52] He also asks for a different politico-economic treatment of the two kinds of monopolies. Harry Gunnison Brown tries to bring the theory of competition and that of monopolistic price formation under the same single principle, and to find identical mathematical formulas for both.[53] John R. Commons objects to the absence of social viewpoints in Brown's theory of price,[54] and attempts to show that the real difference between the two kinds of price formation lies in the discontinuance of production on the part of the monopolist when a higher marginal utility is reached than that with which the producer under free competition must be satisfied.

6. Normal Price and Price Fluctuations

The idea of a normal price seems to have undergone a renaissance in recent American literature. Knight draws an interesting parallel between Marshall's concept of normal price and Clark's doctrine of a static condition.[55] He sees in market price a simplified picture of the market condition prevailing at a given period of time, while in normal price he sees a cross-section of the whole industrial system in a continual process of development. Knight considers the attitudes of Marshall and Clark too narrow and artificial, since they try to expel from their "purely economic" views on mechanical economic equilibrium the social and "ethical" elements of normal price, generally considered extra-economic. But without these elements our author thinks that we can get but a caricature of the concept of normal price.

E. G. Nourse keeps closer to Marshall's theory, and directs his attention, in addition to the distributive functions of normal price, especially to the equilibrium which occurs here between production and consumption.[56] The Englishman, G. B. Dibblee, outlines a picture of the mechanism of price,[57] from the point of view of the practical business man, in which we find precise knowledge of the system of big business before the war and some accurate psychological analyses, but also exaggerated and somewhat unscholarly criticism of the prevailing abstract theories.

It is chiefly the influence of the modern institutional tendency that has brought the problem of price fluctuation since the war to the front in American economics. Wesley Clair Mitchell laid the foundations for this even before the war.[58] We have already drawn attention to the works of his followers which are more closely related to the static theory of price. Among those whose studies are more theoretical, the most important, for the problems of price fluctuations, is Irving Fisher.[59] In regard to details, we must refer the reader to the extremly voluminous new literature on the theory of business cycles.

CHAPTER V

DISTRIBUTION

1. The Problem of Distribution in Modern English Theory

THE CHIEF emphasis in the economic theory of English-speaking countries lies in the doctrine of distribution. The tendency to re-introduce the idea of welfare at the apex of economic theory, begun by Marshall, and apparently fast winning ground in the United States, implies a decided advance of the theory of distribution at the expense of the other divisions of economics. Modern American theory is derived, not like European, from the doctrine of value but from a study of the problem of distribution; consequently the American trend of development is only further confirmed by the movement in English economics toward distribution.

In Marshall's theory of distribution we find, closely connected, the two points of view which have proved most fruitful in the more recent phases of our science for solving that problem. On the one hand he makes a clever use of the marginal principle, whereby he comes close to the American theory of marginal productivity to be dealt with later, and on the other hand he brings the process of distribution at times into immediate connection with the formation of price, somewhat in the same manner as Pierson did at the same time and with more consistency. At times Marshall's doctrine of distribution springs directly from his theory of value, in which he especially resembles Wicksteed who holds that the solution of this problem is possible only on the basis of the new analysis of value. Edgeworth deals with distribution entirely from the viewpoint of price [1] and is interested not so much in the general equilibrium problem of distribution as in the influences which the various limitations of free competition and the one and two sided monopolies exert on the distribution of goods. The practical consequences which he draws as a result of his theoretical analyses of questions of economic policy, especially of wage-policy, are of great value. Pigou, who keeps closer to Marshall, brings the problem of distribution consciously into the center of all economic theory. The national "welfare," which he considers the highest aim of economic life, depends according to him not only on the absolute size of the national income but also on its most equable distribution. For the shaping of this whole process he attributes decisive importance to the economic regulations by the state. Henry Clay tries to prove, by means of the most recent English economic legislation, that state regulation of the distribution of incomes could materially increase the welfare of the community, without endangering to any extent the principle of business freedom. [2]

We may mention here a few of the less successful attempts at a theory of distribution in recent English literature. Rossington Stanton tries to explain the process by the somewhat unsuitable expedient of going back to the historical origins of economics, and explaining thus "rationalistically" the nature of the various kinds of incomes.[3] The collected essays of T. Lloyd, also published before the war under a misleading title,[4] do not deserve consideration from the point of view of theory, but contain some noteworthy ideas with relation to the practical side of the problem. M. A. Kirkaldy offers a pure productivity theory of distribution, when the "law of fungibility," according to which the producer bring the factors of production into the most favorable relation to each other, also becomes the foundation of the distribution of wealth.[5]

2. *The American Theory of Marginal Productivity*

The leading theory of distribution in America today is still that of marginal productivity, propounded by Clark at the end of the last century. According to this, in a state of perfectly free competition, each of the three factors of production, land, capital and labor, receives a share of the whole production, measured according to that increase in production which can be brought about by a slight increase in one factor, the others remaining the same. This is essentially but a generalization and logical development of theories worked out by earlier investigators. His most important independent contribution is undoubtedly the extension of the theory of diminishing return on land to all factors of production, through which their marginal contributions first became decisive for the whole of distribution. We shall come back to this later. Fifty years before, von Thünen had applied the marginal principle to the theory of distribution; with some restrictions in the case of the theory of wages. Walras and Marshall continued his work. Clark, however, hit upon his theories of distribution independently of these authors and did not know that others had previously followed the same path until after he had developed them. He then tried to defend his priority against von Thünen by giving his theory of marginal productivity an ethical aspect which he found lacking in the doctrine of the great German. In marginal productivity we should see, according to him, not only a mechanistic principle of distribution but also the principle of justice. That which the separate factors of production get from the whole produce on the basis of their marginal productivity is, Clark teaches, their equitable share. Here we see a marked strain of American optimism which, as we have already stated, is surpassed only by the optimism of Patten's theory of distribution. The historian of dogmas must, however, point out that for Thünen the "natural wage" is also the "just" wage. The social strain, which is present in Clark's marginal productivity, is especially emphasized by Seligman and Seager, who see in it the expression of the social valuation of the productive services of land, labor and capital. Whereas Seligman lays the greatest emphasis only on this social aspect of distribution, Seager devotes his attention also to the equilibrium concepts of the Lausanne school. Important contributions to the theory of distribution have been made by Taussig who, taking into consideration the experiences of modern industrial capitalism, gives a more prominent position to social ethics. Carver has gone even further in this direction. He agrees with the general principle of marginal productivity (*cf.* also his earlier works) but criticizes certain parts of Clark's doctrines.[6] His own theory of distribution,[7] which makes successful use of some of the ideas of Marshall and the Austrian school, is one of the best synthetic works that have appeared in American economic theory in the first quarter of our century.

Charles W. MacFarlane points out, like Carver, certain flaws and contradictions in the logical structure of Clark's theory of distribution.[8] In the discussion which ensued, in the American Economic Association, Alvin Saunders Johnson successfully defended the theory of marginal productivity, and adopted it later in his text book. R. S. Paden sharply criticized Clark's *Distribution*, and tried to prove that all the phenomena of distribution are dynamic, and as such explicable by the eternally fluctuating forces of business life, and not abstractly of universal application.[9] A more recent criticism, by Walter M. Adriance, is similar in tendency. He rejects the theory of specific productivity, which Clark attributes to the various factors of production, and directs attention to the fact that distribution is not merely a problem of value, but also one of social power.[10] Thorstein Veblen also is opposed to the sharp definition of specific productivity, and doubts whether a direct physical relationship necessarily exists between the increase of one factor of production and the consequent increase in the amount produced.[11] This argument is part of his general attack of the hedonistic and utilitarian substructure of Clark's entire system. Paul H. Douglas on the other hand, who is on the whole well disposed toward Veblen's institutionalism, accepts the chief conclusions of Clark's theory of distribution, and contents himself with saying that they should be founded also on induction and rendered more concrete.[12] Noel Morss even attempts a mathematical treatment of specific productivity with reference to distribution.[13] A stimulating discussion has recently taken place on the problem of marginal productivity [14] between Knight, a critic of Veblen's institutionalism, and the younger Clark, who is undertaking an original mathematical exposition of his father's teachings.

3. Distribution of Wealth and the Social Conflict over Prices

The Englishman Hobson touches the weakest spot of Clark's distribution when he blames the American for having too mechanistic a view of the process of production. Hobson sees in it an organic cooperation, in which there can be no question of a specific productivity that can be formulated in figures. The central idea of Hobson's distribution is a broad generalization of the concept of "forced gains," which we have already mentioned in connection with his theory of price. Rent, interest and wages are thereby brought down to a common denominator and the whole process of distribution is seen as the direct result of the social conflict over price. Another eminent English economist, Cannan, who also stands outside of the Cambridge school, assigns an important place to social views especially as to the unequal distribution of property in his theory of distribution.[15] Cannan is also noted for his excellent theoretical history of distribution, published at the end of the last century.[16]

The theories of Hobson and Cannan lead us to Davenport. Here too we find an emphasis on extra-economic elements which influence distribution, e. g., the difference in law between property in land and capital. Davenport also derives his theory of distribution directly from the process of price formation. Whereas Hobson finds a special explanatory principle for distribution in his three fold law of rent, Davenport will have nothing to do with this and lets the simple market law rule. He thinks that the origin of the various branches of income can be explained by the well-known experimental fact that the factors of production can to a certain extent replace each other. Just as the entrepreneur is able to evaluate the marginal importance of each factor which he uses in relation to the others and with reference to the market price of the product, the whole process of distribution in economics works on the same principle.

The disciple of the Cambridge school, Henderson, who was apparently influenced by Davenport in his works on the theory of price, mentioned above, also explains distribution as a direct consequence of the mechanism of the market, thus resembling Hobson to some extent. The problem is treated in the same way in Turner's text book. Most institutionalists, e. g., Boucke and Edie, derive the distribution of income directly from the process of price formation and emphasize especially the social factors of this relationship. The theory of marginal productivity still plays a certain role with Edie, e. g., in his theory of wages, but Boucke rejects it completely.

4. Development of the Austrian Theory of Imputation

In contrast to these attempts to make of the process of distribution a pure problem of price, Fetter goes back to the viewpoints of the Austrian school and subordinates distribution to the general theory of value. Here we find a repetition of what we saw in his theories of value and of price: although his theoretical foundation appears different and he works with what seem to be original concepts, Fetter comes in last analysis very close to the conclusions of Menger, Böhm-Bawerk and Wieser. He accuses the Austrians of having committed the great mistake, after developing correct ideas on the theories of value and of price, of remaining stuck in the strait jacket of rent, interest and wages. This three fold division contradicts in every way their general theoretical ideas which he, Fetter, intends to apply with greater precision to the theory of distribution. He teaches first of all that only consumption goods are amenable to a direct evaluation resting on the principle of marginal utility, since only they come into consideration for the direct satisfaction of wants. With reference to instrumental goods, these consumption goods may be considered as their fruit. Since the law of diminishing returns is universally valid for all production and since moreover the expression rents is traditional for the fruits which result from the use of production factors that are subject to this law, we can perceive in every consumption good a rent which is yielded by the production goods. Their value is determined by the value of their rents or, in other words, by the value of their usufruct. In this way, the value of production goods is referred to the value of consumption goods. From this point Fetter takes a course which lies somewhere between the Austrian theory of imputation and the American theory of marginal productivity. Since much instrumental capital is needed to produce goods for consumption, a key is needed by means of which the productive contributions in a consumption good may be attributed to each one of those factors which help to produce it. This key is found, according to Fetter, in the principle of marginal productivity which is the basis for the entire distribution of wealth. There is a formal distinction between rent in the narrow sense on one side and wages and profit on the other: the first springs from tangible instrumental goods, the other two from personal services. Nevertheless all are branches of income—with the exception of interest on capital—and subject to the one universal law of rent, which rests upon marginal productivity.

Is not the main idea of the Austrian theory of imputation the attribution, with the help of the principle of marginal utility, of the value of goods of a higher order to that of goods of the first order? Did not Clark stress the general character of the law of diminishing returns and the principle of marginal productivity which rests upon it? Finally, did not Hobson propose a general law of rent? Fetter himself sees the chief value of his theory of distribution in his new and original terminology. When he proposed this to the American Economic Association,[17] he was greeted with some sharp criticisms. Carver, Hollander and MacFarlane saw no reason for abandoning Clark's terminology, and W. G. Langworthy Taylor and Ely even voted to retain the expressions coined by Ricardo. Nevertheless, Fetter still clings to the main traits of his earlier theory of distribution. Instead of "evaluation according to marginal utility," he now says "marginal evaluation"—and thinks that he thus avoids the principle of hedonism. In general, he is trying nowadays to give, if possible, an even more uniform picture of distribution, by distinguishing the factors of production which come into consideration in distribution only according to their economic peculiarities, and not according to their physical natures.

During the World War, George Pendleton Watkins made a notable attempt to perfect the Austrian theory of imputation. With much subtle psychological analysis, he reaches the conclusion that Wieser's concept of imputation is too narrow; he therefore contrasts with it what appears to be a more perfect transputation.[18] Starting from the consideration that every instrumental good would be quite valueless if it stood alone, he draws attention, in valuing a production good, to all the goods which are directly connected with the production. In this way he comes to the concept of transputed utility which is supposed to be decisive for distribution also.

In determining the productivity of goods he makes use of a neglected element, the load factor.[19] Watkins took this expression from electrical theory and means by it the ratio which exists between the average demand for a good within a certain period and the maximum demand for it at any moment of the same period. Unfortunately, we cannot here enter more deeply into this noteworthy idea, which Watkins has also illustrated with practical examples.

Watkins also made successful investigations in variability in the distribution of goods, and in the problem of measuring it statistically and mathematically. Especially interesting is his discussion on this subject with Warren M. Persons.[20] Wilford J. King deals with a kindred subject when he points out the fundamental difficulties which lie in the way of an exact measurement of income and private wealth.[21] Here we may also note that Clark Warburton has explained the changes which have taken place in the latest development of the American theory of distribution in an analytical discussion,[22] while Irving Fisher tries to give a clearer concept of income principally from the standpoint of taxation.[23]

5. *The Passing of the Narrower Conception of Rent and the Problem of Returns*

If the studies of Marshall have been of great importance for the general development of modern economics, they have been practically decisive for the modern form of the theory of rent. The revolution started with the important realization on the part of the great English economist that the origin of rent like income of rent is not a phenomenon restricted to agricultural land. Marshall himself proceeds carefully from this point. First he studies the role of capital used in agricultural industry, and only gradually does he come to the concept of quasi-rent.[24] By this he means the income of the producer, which comes to him through an increased application of capital. The influence of this on price will be felt only in a certain period of time; in the interval the producer enjoys, in consequence of his diminished costs of production, a rent which is similar in structure to the differential income based on the possession of better lands.

Thus was the classical theory of land rent as a branch of income subject to special rules wrecked in its foundations. The blow dealt by Marshall was followed up by the American theorists and they were able to prove that the fundamental fact which led the classicists to a particular attitude concerning land rent and which they conceived as the law of diminishing returns was a much broader and more general phenomenon which touches upon all forms of productive activity. Marshall speaks of three different laws of returns, which run parallel to each other: the laws of diminishing, increasing and constant returns. The other leading English theorists keeps more or less close to this distinction: Edgeworth plays it off against Seligman's teaching; [25] Chapman [26] receives it from Edgeworth, and it is also retained by Pigou, whom it led to an interesting methodological discussion with J. H. Clapham.[27] A similar idea is at the bottom of G. F. Shore's notable analysis of costs.[28]

The Americans at first follow the same course, but ascribe much greater importance to Marshall's first-mentioned law of returns and grant the validity of the others only within the framework of the broadened general law of diminishing returns. According to them, increasing and constant returns can exist only in a narrow field. Beyond a certain limit, an extension of productive activity will everywhere cause a diminishing tendency to appear in the proportional returns. We find in Clark, but especially in Seligman the idea that we are dealing here only with a variation of the general modern law of value: in the case of increasing increments in a consumption good following upon each other, the marginal utility decreases and in consequence of the same law, the returns which correspond to the increases in the means of production, decrease proportionally. In his *Distribution of Wealth,* which appeared in 1893, John Rogers Commons gives a still more general and uniform shape to this assumption by referring the importance of diminishing returns directly to the diminishing marginal utility brought about by increased production. Fetter then criticizes with great severity all the known narrower concepts of rent, which he rejects,[29] and assigns the highest place in his "Principles" to the generalization of the law of diminishing returns, in which he perceives one of the first principles of economics.

Charles J. Bullock has written a sketch of this whole development, which is interesting from an historical point of view,[30] in which he goes back to the principal works of the classical school, and finally reaches the conclusion that it is futile to extend the law of diminishing returns unchanged from agriculture to business since some different tendencies are at work here. Besides Charles W. Mixter,[31] who later entered the lists for the supremacy of the law of diminishing returns in industry,[32] the Englishman Flux has also criticized Bullock's attitude and accused him of having misinterpreted Marshall's position,[33] whereas Carver, one of the leaders of the generalized theory of diminishing returns, defended it against Bullock in a sharp counter attack.[34] Taussig brings weighty arguments to bear against the unification of the laws of returns and, continuing the famous discussion between Clark and Böhm-Bawerk, points out the manifold limitations and the very special character of capital returns.[35] The view, held especially by Fetter and Carver, that the diminishing returns of productive goods are but a special case of diminishing marginal utility, Taussig considers a gross error. Davenport recognizes the existence of a general law of diminishing returns, but refers it to imperfections in production, and opposes to it a law of proportions, dealing with the correct distribution and arrangement of the various factors in production.[36] In post-war literature, E. Dane questions the validity of the law of diminishing returns, not only for industry but also for agriculture.[37] His ideas run very much in the same lines as Patten's and Carey's optimism, as well as Bastiat's doctrine of economic harmony. He considers human reason and inventive power the inexhaustible sources of new technical progress, from which must spring ever increasing returns in all branches of industry. The joint work of W. J. Spillman and E. Lang is more realistic. They accept the general law of diminishing returns, but distinguish sharply within it between the purely technical aspect of productivity and the business aspect of remunerativeness.[38] They are also careful not to put their law in the same category with the law of diminishing marginal utility, with the Weber-Fechner psychological law or with the decrease in atmospherical pressure that accompanies an increase in height.

Greater attention has recently been devoted in America to the other questions of production, in connection with the problem of returns. Thus Allyn A. Young works out the somewhat neglected relationships between industrial returns on one side and distribution of labor and extension of the market on the other.[39] Charles W. Cobb and Paul H.

Douglas study from an historical and statistical point of view, the interconnections of the various factors in production, and especially the problems of marginal productivity of capital and of labor.[40] J. M. Clark agrees with their chief points of view.[41] In his work on the theory of cost he tries to prove that considerable distances or changes in time can exist between the maximum intensity of consumption and that of production. In the large volume on private economics by John D. Black,[42] questions of agricultural production are treated with thoroughness. The studies of the Englishman Dennis Holme Robertson are largely of an industrial nature,[43] while the theory of production advanced by the Norwegian banker P. H. Castberg before the world war [44] throws light on the practical aspects of the problem, but makes no new contribution to theory.

6. *Newly Recognized Incomes Resembling Rent*

In spite of all the conflicts which have opposed the attempts to generalize the law of returns, the concept of rent in Anglo-Saxon science has gradually lost its special aspect as limited to land and has been step by step enlarged. Here again Marshall's leadership must be stressed. His theory of consumer's surplus, to which we have often referred, quickly triumphed to an unusual degree in international literature. This theory was developed, and the venerable scholar even lived long enough to be corrected in it and taught by others.

In the work of his old age, *Money, Credit and Commerce,* he applies his theory to international trade and adds the surpluses of the same consumer to each other. We have already mentioned how the Italian Gobbi had meanwhile noticed the canceling tendency of positive and negative rents, i. e., of savings and expenditures. Loria does not miss the opportunity of correcting Marshall's ideas from this point of view,[45] and the same course is taken, independently of the Italians, by the American Young,[46] who had formerly criticized Pigou with success. In the further development of the theory of consumer's surplus, Pigou is chiefly to be noted after Edgeworth. On the same subject we have the less important discussion between Edwin Cannan [47] on one side, and D. H. MacGregor,[48] and A. L. Bowley,[49] on the other. The American Harry E. Miller tries to prove that Marshall's theory of consumer's surplus contradicts the meaning of the marginal theory,[50] while Joseph Mayer [51] and G. W. Terbourgh,[52] consider the whole theory illogical.

During the World War, the American Philip G. Wright approached the conclusions of Young, but subsequently departed from this direction. He explains how consumer's surplus can stimulate the production of goods to satisfy higher needs, which would never find a demand if incomes were equally divided.[53] Miss Hazel Kirk has recently made a noteworthy contribution to this set of problems.[54] She works out clearly the relationships between income and consumption, and shows how much the consumer's needs, which are the preliminary conditions of production, are influenced by the general state of society and by the whole environment. In this way she builds on the principles of the modern institutional tendency and explains economic activity as the result, not of an innate hedonistic urge, but of social influence. The text book on consumption of W. C. Waite is also behavioristic.[55] He stresses especially the application of individual income in private business.

Extending the concept of rent, there has been talk in recent American literature of a rent of business ability. By this A. B. Wolfe means the special income beyond the usual rate of profits which accrues to the entrepreneur because of his special business ability. He considers this a monopoly profit, by means of which the traditional ideal of perfectly free competition is exploded.[56] His attempts, in connection with the studies of Silberling mentioned above, to illustrate certain questions of the generalized theory of rent by means of three-dimensional curves,[57] have been attacked by the younger Clark, who considers this procedure much too complicated, obscure and inadequate.[58]

The generalization of the law of diminishing returns led American economists at the end of the last century to oppose to Marshall's consumer's surplus a general producer's surplus. The elder Clark makes a parallel use of both concepts, understanding by consumer's surplus the differential income which, as a consequence of the uniform market price, accrues in varying degrees to all producers except the marginal ones. In spite of the adverse criticism which this interpretation received, especially from Veblen, it spread quickly among Clark's followers.

Alvin S. Johnson's theory of rent [59] is, in the main, built upon this foundation, although he has some noteworthy original ideas when he criticizes other theories. We have already drawn attention to the extreme generalization which Fetter's consumer's surplus underwent. The idea of rent is somewhat narrower in Turner's text book. By rent he means remuneration for the use of lasting production-goods, but excepts human labor. Turner also presents a good survey of the history of the theory of rent in earlier American writings.[60]

In England a similar tendency is represented principally by Hobson. With reference to price formation, both interest and wages seem to him to be but variations of rent in general, and it is only gradually that he recognizes in them certain definite characteristics. Since he bases himself partly on the studies of the American Commons, he assigns prominence to the element of restriction of free competition in producer's surplus, and thus gives it the appearance of a monopoly-rent. Although lacking the socio-ethical framework given it by Hobson, the concept of producer's surplus has acquired a decidedly monopolistic tinge, not only with American but also with some English economists, e. g., Pigou [61] and D. H. MacGregor.[62] The former continues to use his mathematical analysis in this application, whereas the latter draws attention to the manifold logical difficulties in such theoretical discussions.

7. *The Classical Differential Rent*

In view of this widespread tendency to broaden the concept of rent, we find scarcely any attempts in the modern literature of the English-speaking countries to keep to the narrower field of the classical theory. We may note the work of Henry C. Taylor, who tries to show the influence of the cultural environment as well as of the farmer's knowledge on the level of the land rent in farming; [63] and we also have the investigation of Lewis Cecil Gray into the connection between the rate of interest and agricultural rent, in which he goes back directly to Ricardo but is also well disposed on the whole to the broader concept of rent.[64] Lewis H. Haney tries to revivify Ricardo's theory of rent with the aid of a few of the ideas of modern value theory,[65] but is contradicted by Frank T. Carlton [66] who accepts the new tendency entirely.[67] A reform of the old theory of rent has been recently attempted by Harry Gunnison Brown in his text book, and it receives a new foundation in the shape of Davenport's theory of production costs. The latter is still influenced by the old differential idea when he tries to show the justification and the social advantages of the increment tax on land.[68] On the other hand, Richard T. Ely, an old connoisseur of these matters, points out the fact that "unearned" or easy, and especially quick, profits from movable capital are in fact usually larger than those from property in land.[69] Other adherents of Ricardo's attitude are Fairchild, Furniss and Buck, who are severely criticized by H. Gordon Hayes.[70] At the end of a good historical survey of theories, the Indian J. Gosh declares himself decidedly against the broadening of the concept of rent, and tries to strengthen his position by a thorough exposition of the special characteristics of land rent.[71] His ideas are not novel, but they are clearly and systematically arranged. The American F. L. Patton has recently thrown light on the law of diminishing returns from the technological side, as well as in its practical workings.[72]

8. No New Theories of Interest in England

It is useless to look for a new interest theory in English economics in the first quarter of our century. Marshall himself took a somewhat eclectic attitude toward this problem, joining the idea of productivity to the mathematical theory of equilibrium, and making use of other explanatory principles. The whole interest theory of the Cambridge school moves along these lines, and their attitude here is very close to that of the Lausanne school. Edgeworth assigns a greater role to the marginal principle, while Pigou is more interested in the social aspect of the problem. In the systems of both writers, however, the theory of interest is treated with neglect.

F. Lavington bases himself on Pigou, but stresses more strongly the uncertainty of future events and its effects on interest.[73]

Of the Americans, Clarence Gilbert Hoag stands closest to the Cambridge theory.[74] He tries to solve the problem of interest from the point of view of Marshall's conception of normal price, and with the help of an assumption of equilibrium between the supply of land and demand for capital. At the same time he takes stock of Irving Fisher's ideas on income, which we shall mention later. F. H. Knight resembles Hoag in his criticism of Böhm-Bawerk's theory, and also stresses the ideas of normal interest and of equilibrium; [75] but on the whole he tries to develop a pure productivity theory of interest. To illustrate his abstract ideas he makes use of three-dimensional curves, but even then he is fully conscious of the hypothetical nature of this procedure.

Among the English economists who are above all interested in social questions Hobson stepped forward at the turn of the century with a well-grounded theory of interest. First he subordinates it to his general theory of rent and continues, with a sure instinct, to trace the specific sources of capital income. In the foreground he places the idea of abstinence, and considers interest principally a reward of thrift, which incites to the formation of new capital. In this point he resembles Cassel who first published his income theory, which we have already mentioned, in English.[76]

Whereas Hobson derives all kinds of income from the formation of prices, and consequently does not consider interest a price forming factor, the American Clinton H. Scovell has recently written a book to prove that interest is an active element in cost.[77] He attacks the contrary opinion, and draws especial attention to the private economic aspects of the problem. Raymond T. Bye tries to justify Scovell's results in so far as in social economics, and therefore in respect to the formation of value and of price, interest is a part of costs, while the contrary is the case in private economics where in accounting income is contrasted with the losses or gains of the enterprise.[78] Interest is also treated as an element of cost by Waldo F. Mitchell,[79] who, partly in a discussion with Carl Snyder,[80] considers the level of the interest rate an important factor in the fluctuations of the business cycle.

9. The Idea of Productivity and the Theory of Interest in America

In spite of the great influence of Böhm-Bawerk's ideas on modern American economics, the leading theory of interest is still based on the principle of marginal productivity. In the idea of interest as a return, subject to the marginal principle for the power of capital in production, we find the full expression of the seductively simple uniformity of the theory of distribution, as expressed by Clark. Most American economists accept this doctrine unreservedly. Seligman is one of its principal adherents; Seager defends it against the attacks of Irving Fisher,[81] and H. G. Brown tries to bring about a synthesis between the principles of productivity and of impatience.[82] His doctrine that all production which is based on the co-operation of capital requires a longer time and that therefore the element of waiting, or of impatience, is already contained in the concept of capital, seems to effect the union of both explanatory principles in a more satisfactory manner than does Ely in his textbook, who sees in the productivity of capital only the possible, in the impatience of the capitalist the necessary, source of interest. To this class belongs also Davenport's well-founded interest theory. In the main it is built on the idea of productivity but concedes much importance to the element of time, in the sense of Böhm-Bawerk.[83]

On the basis of factual research, L. Kotany has offered an independent theory of productivity, which is built on the assumption that production costs can be diminished in all cases by a corresponding application of capital.[84] The foundation which Kotany gives to these ideas from the point of view of production technique is noteworthy. Fabian Franklin also tries to offset Cassel's theory of interest with the idea of productivity.[85]

10. The Conflict over the Concept of Capital

The pure agio theory of Böhm-Bawerk was enthusiastically received in America and numbered many adherents at the close of the last century. A quarrel soon broke out between them and the supporters of the theory of marginal productivity. Since both sides soon realized that the real source of the different interpretations of the interest problem was to be found in the different meanings given to the concept of capital, the discussion gradually centered upon this difference. The most important phase of this conflict is the long and famous duel, mentioned above, between the leaders, Böhm-Bawerk and Clark, which is the most important discussion that has taken place in modern economic theory after the methodological dispute in Germany over value judgments.

We shall here briefly summarize the object of the dispute. For the Austrian capital is a material concept, by which he means a group of concrete production-goods. The American sees in capital an immaterial financial expression of production goods, that is to say, a productive force and calls the concrete production goods capital goods. Not to mention the complications which arose over the further distinction of a concept of social capital, both causes were fought with an unusual amount of polemical skill. Toward the end of the last century it seemed as if a draw had been reached: each side approached the other and came near to realizing that they were disputing only over the outward form although their attitudes were in essence closely similar. After a few years the dispute started again by the skirmishes between the adherents of both sides, broke out even more acrimoniously [86] and up to the time of Böhm's death no agreement could be reached between the two eminent scientists who had both formerly studied with Knies at Heidelberg. A meeting between the two at Geneva was unable to clarify the situation.

To mention only the three most important writers who continued the discussion in the present century, Fetter [87] and Charles A. Tuttle [88] recognize Clark's immaterial concept of capital with reservations, whereas Irving Fisher,[89] approaching Böhm's concept, attempts a reconciliation. Fetter sees a capital in concrete wealth only in so far as its quantity is expressed in the general unit of value. Tuttle stresses the element of superfluous wealth as property in the immaterial capital concept; whereas Fisher considers the total amount of goods in stock at a given moment capital. This definition of Fisher's is accepted by Fairchild and his collaborators in their text book. Although Veblen criticizes Fisher's attitude,[90] he takes a mediating position in the discussion. In his careful and profound exposition, he goes his own way, and sees the essence of capital in the relationships between creative human intelligence and material goods.[91] A related attitude is that of Frederick B. Hawley who, following a purely deductive method, comes to the conclusion that the main aspect of the capital concept lies in the productive activity of the capitalist or of the entrepreneur.[92]

11. The Reception of Böhm's Interest Theory in America

The best result of the discovery over the capital concept in America is the interest theory of Irving Fisher. Above all he makes a meticulously planned distinction, according to the accounting practice of private economics, between capital and income.[93] Harking back to the theory of Newcomb, he perceives the essential difference between these two concepts in the element of time. Whereas, as we have just seen, capital is, according to Fisher, the amount of goods in stock at a given time, income is the perpetually accruing stream of services and is therefore to be sharply distinguished from capital. Consequently he separates the increase of capital, i. e., savings, from income and defends this procedure in a stimulating discussion [94] in the American Economic Association against Daniels, Maurice H. Robinson, etc., who count savings as income. The Englishman Flux took a mediating part in the discussion; his objections to Fisher's theory [95] have been generally made from the standpoint of terminology. Fisher has treated the objection that his concept of income is sufficient only for the process of production but not for the physical product of capital, with as much attention [96] as he devoted to Commons's criticism,[97] that in his theory he did not sufficiently distinguish the aspects of private economics from those of political economy. Fisher's theory of interest is directly connected with his studies of capital and income, is marked by the same prominence given to the element of time, and rests upon the assumption that present income is generally valued more highly than future income.[98] Although Fisher took this central idea of his theory from Böhm-Bawerk, he criticizes some of the Austrian's ideas, e. g., the doctrine of the productivity of round about production, and makes use of other elements, e. g., changes in market mechanism and in individual incomes, as factors in generating and determining interest. Two of the chief characteristics of Fisher's interest theory are its clear and logically concise structure and the many examples which he employs to illustrate interest as a phenomenon of actual economic life.

Fetter disagrees with Fisher's concept of income and disapproves of the way in which his colleague exaggerates the importance of the process of price formation in the growth of interest. He considers that Böhm had the right idea of interest but fell back into the old errors of productivity theories through his theory of round about production.[99] His main objection to modern theories of interest is their unfruitful eclecticism. This led him into a somewhat sharp controversy with H. G. Brown, against whom he had directed this accusation.[100] In answer to this, Fetter himself tries to give an explanation of interest which rests upon a single uniform principle.

According to him, only rent, as a fundamental category of value, has anything to do with the concept of productivity. Quite independent of this is the time value—another, purely psychological, fundamental principle of all economic theory, which expresses the universal distinction between the valuation of present and that of future "psychic income," i. e., utility. Interest arises only from this time value, as the difference between the present value of capital at two different periods and is seen in the fact that, in the purchase of future goods for present ones, it is already discounted in the price. Thus Fetter's theory is essentially the purest theory, based only on psychology which has nothing to do with the idea of productivity which even Böhm employed.

As a consequence of the great importance which Fetter attributes to time value for the whole field of economics, he has recently tried to show the relations which exist between interest on one side and price formation, the general price system, and fluctuations in price due to the business cycle, on the other. He attempted to prove before the American Economic Association that these relations are best understood on the basis of his purely psychological conception of interest.[101] The discussion which followed,[102] and in which Irving Fisher, Wesley C. Mitchell, Waldo F. Mitchell, Frank H. Knight and others took part, centered more on questions of the theory of business cycles than on actual interest. W. F. Mitchell again expounded the ideas which we have mentioned above in connection with his discussion with Carl Snyder.

Besides Fetter, both Taussig and Patten have accepted Böhm's interest theory, in their systems which we have frequently mentioned. The former makes the level of the interest rate depend on the outcome of the conflict between accumulation and ameliorations in the process of production and tries to connect the theory with the principle of marginal productivity as well as with the idea of abstinence. Patten makes an interesting and original contribution to Böhm's theory in trying to find the yield of round about production in the multiplicity of products. This multiplicity makes possible the satisfaction of various wants, whereby the marginal utility of the goods is increased: an increase which can be bought by the consumer only by a payment for the capital which makes time-consuming round about production possible. R. S. Padan is of the opinion that interest represents a substantial economic category and therefore cannot possibly spring from value, which is only a relationship, an idea and at most an explanatory principle. From this standpoint he subjects Böhm-Bawerk's theory to a sharp criticism.[103] In spite of other attacks, equally well-founded, the agio theory of the Austrian scholar has enjoyed great popularity in the new world and to it are due many new minor branches of investigation. To take but one example, there is the slight practical study of George R. Davies, in which he investigates the causes of the movements in the bank rate in post-war inflation.[104]

12. Abstinence, Risk, and the Residual Principle in the American Theory of Interest

Carver's theory of interest stands apart in American economics. He adversely criticizes Clark's theories of capital and interest [105] and at the same time separates himself from Böhm-Bawerk in certain main principles. Eleven years before the publication of his *Theory of Distribution,* in an essay which appeared in the *Quarterly Journal,* he adopted an abstinence theory of interest somewhat like those of Senior or of MacVane. In this way, he approached the theory which we have already mentioned of Hobson, Ely and Brown. Later on, in the face of Böhm's criticism, Carver lost no occasion to defend his doctrine against the Austrian.[106] Nevertheless, he agrees with Böhm, in so far as he closely connects the idea of abstinence with the agio principle and derives interest from a cooperation of the two factors. Carver has recently also given prominence to the idea of productivity and tries to base his theory of interest likewise on a foundation of social ethics.[107]

A. F. McGoun is directly related to Carver, but devotes more attention to a productivity theory, stressing the labor-saving role of capital.[108] Besides C. W. Mixter, in an article which appeared at the end of the last century,[109] both E. C. K. Gonner,[110] and A. B. Wolfe,[111] develop Carver's ideas that interest should be considered in part as a reward of saving. The former, after an analysis of the psychological and economic motives of saving, emphasizes the element of risk as a factor in the creation of interest, while the latter, who is able to make use of the latest experiences of war economics, ends by recommending the social expropriation of the saver's surplus. The Englishman F. P. Ramsey has recently tried to build a complicated mathematical formula according to which the rate of saving multiplied by the marginal utility of money should always be equal to the amount by which the total net rate of enjoyment of utility falls short of the maximum possible rate of satisfaction.[112]

Neither the agio nor the abstinence nor the productivity theories of interest satisfies G. A. Kleene, who tries to prove that they are all fallacious, and who finally offers a residual theory of capital interest.[113] He considers wages a fixed quantity independent of capitalistic production, assigns a relatively fixed origin to rent and profits and finds the interest on capital in what remains of the result of production.

13. The Problem of Wages in English Literature

The development of the theory of wages in the English-speaking countries in the first quarter of our century, like that of the theory of interest, has been carried on chiefly in America. The Cambridge school followed the old path which led, between Ricardo and Jevons, to a synthesis of apparently dissimilar viewpoints. From the classics they learned to appreciate the supply aspect of wages formation which finds expression in the costs of maintenance of the laborer at his accustomed standard of living; from Jevons they took the demand aspect of labor which is determined by its productivity. Between these two general price-forming factors they let the actual wage arise. Consequently, socio-ethical tendencies already appear in Marshall and are even more pronounced in Pigou.

Although the abstract theory of wages has led to no new results in England, important contributions have been made toward an understanding of the practical side of the problem. Among the authors who have especially distinguished themselves in this direction are Ashley, the leader of the English historical school, who offered valuable socio-ethical suggestions in a special study,[114] Arthur L. Bowley, whose statistical and historical studies of wages are among the best,[115] and Sidney J. Chapman who, continuing the works of Lord Brassey that were published in the seventies, constructs a monumental system of practical economics around the central problem of wages.[116]

14. The Modern American Productivity Theory of Wages

In the United States the doctrine which is based on the principle of marginal productivity reigns supreme in the theory of wages. Starting from the fact that labor and capital must be united to proceed to production, Clark perceives that, where few groups of workers are employed, their productive importance would be very great in view of the large sums of capital apportioned to each one. If additional groups of workers are employed, the existing capital is divided among more hands, and so their relative importance in the whole results of production correspondingly diminishes. Since each of these groups can be substituted for the other, the productive importance of each is equal to that of the last one employed. This importance is the marginal productivity of labor and only when wages are measured on this basis can the requisite amount of labor be at the disposal of capital. As there are limits to the increase of labor, while the capital which is socially available always increases more rapidly, the mutual relationship changes from the point of view of production to the gradual advantage of labor; its marginal productivity increases and consequently the average wage in a dynamic social development must show a tendency constantly to rise.

This idea, the optimism of which closely resembles that of Patten's theory of wages, published at about the same time, was outlined by Clark in a report made to the American Economic Association [117] and gave rise to a stimulating discussion. His chief opponent was Hobson, who pointed out that wages did not originate so simply but were much more the result of severe social conflicts. Hobson also stresses the element of social power in his other works [118] and teaches that under our present industrial system everything is to the advantage of the capitalist, through whose various unearned incomes wages are diminished and held far below the level of their marginal productivity. Society should not tolerate this since labor should not be considered from the simple angle of production costs, as are raw materials. Behind it are human values and the welfare of our fellow men depends upon wages, a consideration which, for its social and ethical aspects, should dominate all others in economics.

In this connection it is interesting to note that the younger Clark, in his work on overhead costs mentioned above, partly through considerations similar to those of Hobson, also reaches the conclusion that, under perfectly free competition and especially under a limited use of the capacity of labor—even if only temporary,—wages have a tendency to sink below the level of marginal productivity.

Carver defended the productivity theory of wages against Hobson's attacks and supported Clark's optimism with a telling argument. According to him, human labor is being more and more replaced by machinery and removed to higher technical regions where its marginal productivity must also be greater. If labor succeeds in always remaining a step ahead of the machine, wages and the laborer's standard of life will have a tendency perpetually to increase. In the system which he published after the World War, Carver generalized this idea into the thesis that the raising of the general level of labor causes a decrease of unskilled labor and consequently a rise of wages.

More recently H. Gordon Hayes has approached Carver's conception, and has attempted, in opposition to Seager, Cassel, Fetter and others to prove that in modern economics wages will increase at the same time that the use of machinery becomes more prevalent.[119] He starts from a consideration of the actual fact of rising wages which, through the greater purchasing power of the masses, have made possible a general increase of price and consequently the ability of the entrepreneur to use new and costly machines. On the other hand the assumption that the entreprenuer has been moved to introduce machines directly by the rise of wages is false. Thereupon a discussion ensued, in the course of which Clyde Olin Fisher,[120] L. A. Morrison,[121] Martin A. Gearhart,[122] and Willis Wissler [123] offered various objections to Hayes's views, while Frank D. Graham [124] and George E. Bigge [125] try rather to complete them and to perfect their theory. Graham's contribution is especially useful. He points out that in the relation between increased use of machinery and wage level what is decisive is the level of the whole share of labor in the distribution of the social results of production. George E. Barnett takes an inductive view of the matter and shows that the consequences of the increased use of machinery for the formation of wages differ in the various branches of industry according to time and place.[126] The Englishman E. Dane is optimistic as to the spread of machinery. Like

Carver he sees in this a change from the physical labor to the advantage of intellectual work and consequently a general rise of wages.[127]

Most modern American theorists accept, like Carver, the main principles of the wage theory based on marginal productivity, with the addition of more or less individual points of view, e. g., Fetter, for whom earned income comes under the general law of rent but who had little luck in trying to balance the idea of productivity with the discounting effect of time in his wage theory. Besides emphasizing the principle of productivity, Seligman devotes even greater attention to the supply aspect of the wage question and stresses the laborer's accustomed standard of living as a decisive factor. The Englishman W. T. Layton also tries to solve the wage problem from the point of view of marginal productivity[128] but goes off too soon into technical and social fields, in which he recommends scientific management and profit-sharing of the laborers respectively. H. A. Silverman has published a wage theory based on marginal productivity, practical in character, in which he evinces sympathy for modern tradeunionism.[129] On the other hand, Solomon Blum rejects Clark's theory of wages somewhat in the manner of Hobson, and sees in wages the expression of the social relationship of power and force.[130]

A noteworthy criticism of Clark's wage theories has recently been made by the Dutchman Willem L. Valk. He accepts the principle of marginal productivity as a passable explanation of the formation of value, but rejects it for the price formation of the factors of productivity. His reason is that if every factor of production were rewarded according to its marginal productivity the sum of incomes thus secured would exceed the amount ready for distribution. Valk therefore turns to Walras's theory of equilibrium, especially as simplified by Cassel's equations, and tries to build upon it a wage theory adapted to static economics. He considers another factor in the formation of wages to be the appraising choice which the entrepreneur makes between the various labor forces which can be substituted for each other and other kinds of production factors.[131]

15. The Wage Fund Theory

Taussig is more successful than Fetter in combining the element of time with the theory of productivity. He starts from the fact that, in the hands of the entrepreneur, labor is a future good that can be realized only later but for which he must give present goods, in the form of wages. Since the amount of these present goods is a fixed sum, depending on the work which has been previously done, it is for the time given a definitely limited cash discount so that only a restricted amount of future goods can be afforded and out of which only a limited amount of new labor can be paid. In this idea of Taussig we see the spirit of the classical wage-fund theory. He first expressed this thought in his famous *Wages and Capital,* published at the end of the last century, and offered it later with slight changes (e. g., greater emphasis placed on the principle of marginal productivity) to the American Economics Association.[132] In the discussion which followed, Hollander attacked this principle and demanded a return to the more realistic theory of Ricardo, in which the picture of the practical conflict of wages, not dependent upon marginal productivity, is more vividly delineated. As we have just seen, Hobson had advanced similar objections to Clark's theory a few years previously. J. G. Thompson attacks Taussig's statement that the laborers depend for their subsistence only upon the results of the period of production which has just passed, i. e., on the contemporary wage fund. He points out, with the help of statistical data, the very important savings at the disposal of the present-day working classes.[133] To this Taussig could give only an embarrassed reply.[134]

Perhaps it is because of other criticisms also that Taussig has upheld his theory, first propounded more than a generation ago, with continually more timidity. Thus he gradually discards the expression "loan fund" and when Kleene, inspired probably by Taussig's own *Wages and Capital,* brought out during the war a wage fund theory, logically elaborated in all its details and based on the results of the most recent theoretical investigations, Taussig was unable, in the criticism which he wrote, to agree entirely with Kleene.[135] For the latter, the supply price of labor is today determined by its own production costs only in economically backward countries. In America this supply price is to be found in the standard of living attained by the lowest class of the latest immigrants. Kleene himself had to retire, however, before Taussig's very just objection that this does not hold for England, Germany, etc., which are no less advanced economically.[136] At the meeting of the American Economic Association in December 1925 in New York, Kleene abandoned still more of his earlier loan fund theory but showed, in opposition to Richard S. Meriam and Raymond T. Bye, the defects of the loan theory which is based on the principle of marginal productivity. In the same discussion,[137] this theory was also sharply criticized by Sumner H. Slichter and A. B. Wolfe.

Besides the theories of Taussig and Kleene, we find in the works of other American theorists echoes of the old wage fund theory, e. g., in the favorite idea of Davenport that wages are diminished through every kind of parasitism.[138] Formally, however, he criticizes the wage fund theory.

Elements of the classical wage fund theory lie behind the thoughts of all those who await a lasting general wage increase only from a corresponding increase of labor productivity, and not from the conflict of wages determined by power. Such thinkers are quite numerous in modern Anglo-Saxon literature. A good example is to be found in the Englishman Lionel Robbins.[139] The attempt of Nora Milnes [140] is logical and well founded historically, but otherwise is built chiefly on Marshall's wage theory. A similar idea, based on induction, appears in the work of J. D. Cox Jr. who tries to explain wages as a residual income.[141] Among other authors who have treated the subject we may mention S. S. Garrett, who points out especially the economic dangers which may attend forced increases of wages not based on production, through collective bargaining.[142]

16. Moore's Inductive Explanation of Wages

Unlike the more or less deductive investigators which we have thus far mentioned, Henry Ludwell Moore treats the problem of wages inductively, and offers through the mathematical handling of comprehensive statistical data a universally recognized contribution[143] which can be worthily compared with the work of the Frenchman Simiand that appeared a few years earlier. His studies lead him to verify by statistics the productivity theory of wages, a verification the importance of which Moore stresses [144] in opposition to the contrary attitude of Edgeworth.[145] In spite of this general conclusion, Moore pointed out in an earlier work [146] the limited value from the standpoint of knowledge of the principle of productivity in certain special cases of wages. Accordingly labor is not rewarded on the basis of its marginal produce not only in those branches of industry where the law of increasing returns prevails but especially in those in which there are complete or partial monopolies. In this conception the question obviously is how broad the idea of monopoly is. The more we extend its meaning, the more illusory becomes the whole productivity theory of wages and the more are we forced to accept the idea which Hobson and Hollander opposed to it: namely, that wages are the result of the social conflict between the entrepreneur and the laborer.

17. The Problem of the Wage Level

The social conflict is the chief subject of the branch of investigation in recent Anglo-Saxon literature which aims to discover the ways and means whereby wages can in general be increased. At the beginning of the century the American John Augustine Ryan worked out on religious grounds the social and ethical demands of the wage level.[147] Walton H. Hamilton offers a noteworthy study. Viewing the problem institutionally he reaches the conclusion that we should not proceed along rigid general principles, but should work for a wage increase flexibly, through the means which best suit the particular case.[148] Robert W. Woodbury thinks that the development of popular education and the resultingly greater intelligence of the laboring classes is the surest way to increase the general rate of wages.[149] With the help of practical arguments Edward A. Filene favors a law of minimum wages, and expects from this a marked increase of the general productivity of labor.[150] On the other hand, both Mrs. E. M. Burns [151] and J. H. Richardson [152] display much more caution in their detailed studies of the subject. Mrs. Burns keeps entirely to the productivity theory, which explains it rather in the American sense,[153] while Richardson tries to treat wages on the basis of the general formation of price. Alvin S. Johnson is not able to speak entirely in favor of a governmental determination of the minimum wage,[154] while Commons again demands a vigorous governmental policy of wages.[155] Bertram Austin and W. Francis Lloyd, two young English engineers, through their studies of the American wage system [156] see the solution of the social question in a general extension of profit-sharing.[157] Of more scientific value is the attitude of Paul H. Douglas, based upon institutional practice, in favor of family subsidies for workmen.[158] Douglas points out a not inconsiderable increase of American real wages in the last generation.[159] The same conclusion is reached for the period from 1914 to 1920 by David Friday,[160] and for the years after the war by Alvin H. Hansen.[161] Friday stresses especially the change in the whole distribution of income to the advantage of wages; Hansen proposes a special consumption index to measure real wages.[162] In his statistical study of the average rate of industrial wages in the American distribution of income for the years 1904–1925, Jürgen Kuczynski[163] reaches few definite theoretical conclusions. We may note, however, his discovery that wages tend to fall lower beneath the average level of the whole costs of production than they are accustomed to rise above it. George Soule uses the actual development of American real wages as a weapon against the productivity theory and tries to prove that the recent marked increases of wages cannot possibly be referred only to the increase in productivity of labor.[164]

18. The After-effects of the Classical Idea of Productivity in the Theory of Profits

In regard to the theory of profits the English have not been able to rid themselves completely of the classical traditions. They still tend to neglect the sharp distinction between interest and profits and to treat these two kinds of income from the same angle. Like the classical economists Marshall sees in profits a pure element of cost, which is the entrepreneur's reward for his activity in the conduct of production. Edgeworth points out correctly that profit cannot be measured on the basis of marginal productivity, since there is no factor in economics which could prescribe such a measurement. Matters are different in the productive contributions of other factors, since the entrepreneur himself rewards them on the basis of their marginal productivity. Moreover the salaried managing director renders about the same services as the independent entrepreneur and yet their incomes are generally widely different. Edgeworth also makes use of this argument, in order to prove that profit cannot possibly correspond exactly to marginal productivity.[165] Chapman reaches the same conclusion.[166] In order to repair the loss of exactitude caused by this deficiency of the marginal principle, recent English writers have, like the Dutchman Pierson or the Scot Nicholson, made use of other well-known principles besides the element of productivity to explain profits. These we shall discuss later. The same attempt is apparent in the works of R. A. Lehfeldt [167] and D. H. MacGregor,[168] who try to unite in an eclectic manner the idea of productivity with the element of risk. Both of them draw a careful distinction between the concepts of profits and interest.

Among recent American theorists who come nearest to the old classical conception with its uniform theory, in which interest and profit are closely united, are Taussig and Kleene. Like most of their contemporaries they emphasize the element of risk as the most important source of profits. In his studies published immediately after the war, C. J. Foreman distinguishes earned from unearned profits, meaning by the former an income covered entirely by the principle of productivity, and by the latter a monopoly gain which is to be reprobated from the viewpoints of social ethics.[169] He refers the first kind of profit to the knowledge and business ability of the entrepreneur, as well as to the new and better technical methods by which he makes production more intensive and productive. Ely, who even talks of wages of management, and Bullock, who treats the wages of labor and enterprise under the same headings, both see in profit a reward for this personal activity. Fetter views profits only as a special form of the general rent resulting from marginal productivity, while Carver skillfully introduces into the theory of profit the marginal principle neglected by Englishmen in this connection. According to him, the entrepreneur enjoys the results of the work of variously productive laborers. Since these receive only the wage of the marginal worker, the differential productivity of all the other workers is to the advantage of the entrepreneur. F. M. Taylor explains profits eclectically in his text book and stresses, in addition to the idea of productivity as the source of profit, the responsibility which the entrepreneur has to bear in the management of production.

19. Risk and Profit

About a generation ago the idea of risk was predominant in the American literature on profit. Discussions upon this subject were rekindled at the turn of the century. H. C. Emery, in a report of the American Economic Association, referred speculators' profit to the risk which the speculator assumes on the market.[170] This he considers a special kind of risk based upon proprietary right, which should be sharply distinguished from the risk assumed by the capitalistic employer in the management of production. The validity of this distinction was disputed by Carver, Hadley and Commons in the discussion which followed. These tried to treat the profits of the speculator as well as of the employer in the same way. Thereupon Frederick B. Hawley, who had expounded a noteworthy risk theory of profits in his earlier writings, again came upon the scene and in a debate with Carver [171] worked out the concept of a special entrepreneur's risk distinct from pure speculation and tried to make of his theory on the subject the positive basis of all economics.[172] The entirely deductive and apodictic system which he built on this [173] has met with little approval in scientific circles.[174]

The risk theory of profit propounded by F. H. Knight leads to similar broad perspectives.[175] Although he derives profit from the risk of the entrepreneur, yet he distinguishes risk in the narrower sense of the word from the concept of uncertainty. Whereas risk, according to Knight, is a factor that can be measured quantitatively and which can, if necessary, be eliminated by insurance or by reducing it to the average—that is, by self-insurance—the element of uncertainty in its undeniable complexity can be grasped only by the clear judgment of the business man. This judgment can be trained and developed by practice, but it is due essentially to an inborn disposition, the capacity to be an employer, which is the real source of profit. Knight builds a whole theoretical system around this idea and the subtle distinctions which it contains reach from the first aspects of economics to an analysis of modern big business. In this he makes full use of those methodological and socio-ethical views upon which we have often dwelt.

Charles O. Hardy's work on the general economic relations between the bearing and the elimination of risk in production and distribution [176] is inferior to the more recent investigations of the Italian Chessa. More useful are the solutions which Hardy proposes for the problem from the point of view of private economics.

20. *The Residual Principle and the Dynamic Element in Profits*

Although all the Anglo-Saxon theories of profits which we have already mentioned attribute an independent origin to this branch of income in the process of distribution, Clark, as Hollander had remarked,[177] treats it merely as a residual income. Given a state of perfect, undisturbed, free competition in a static economic system the result of social production would be divided on the basis of the principle of marginal productivity between land, capital and labor without any remainder. But actual modern economic life is not static, nor can free competition develop undisturbed. Thus it happens that, in the distribution of wealth, after the three above mentioned factors of production have been rewarded, there is a remainder which the entrepreneur appropriates. This had already been realized by the Lausanne school, but Clark stresses the dynamic character of modern economic development and sees its leader in the entrepreneur. According to him the constantly new shaping of the production process bring forth all the more easily the distribution residues, which are to be considered the source of profits. This is the dynamic theory of profits which was introduced into German science by Schumpeter, as we have mentioned in the appropriate place.

This theory was clearly and logically developed by Seligman, who sees in profits only the results of the fluctuations of the market prices and correspondingly allows no profit at all in a normal state of equilibrium. Patten also explains profits entirely from the fact of economic development, from the perfection of the process of production. According to Seager, perfectly free competition would absorb only one part, the dynamic element, of profits, which include, however, other ingredients, based upon the principles of productivity and monopoly. A similar view is held by A. S. Johnson, who thinks it quite obvious that profits should contain an element of wage besides the interest on the capital invested by the entrepreneur. When this is withdrawn there still remains in the entrepreneur's hands a residue, a "surplus," which is to be considered the "pure profit." Turner offers a consistent residual theory of profits.

Clark's theory of profits has recently undergone a thorough overhauling, but also a development at the hands of Charles A. Tuttle.[178] Clark had already seen a source of profits in productivity under perfectly free competition and with the use of new and more productive methods, but Tuttle develops this idea to a logical application of the theory of marginal productivity for the formation of price. Therefore he admits profits even in a static economic condition: they come from the "supra-marginal" use of the units of labor (Carver!) and capital united for production, and also from a unique activity, as the functional income of the entrepreneur. Ideas of margin, productivity and friction are blended here into a happy synthesis.

21. *Profits as a Monopoly Income*

Hobson is the only Englishman who has developed the dynamic theory of profits, illustrating the problem with aspects of modern industrial investigations. But he holds that, in the present day economic situation, only a relatively small part of the profits earned can be really ascribed to the imaginative, dynamic leadership of the entrepreneur. The greater part of profits consists of a monopoly-like income derived from the formation of prices which, according to the social reform that Hobson advocates, should be eliminated.

Maurice Dobb, a young writer who belongs to the London School of Economics, treats profits entirely as a monopoly income. While it is customary to deal with this branch of income from the aspect of demand, Dobb continues the analysis of supply begun by Marshall, which stressed the activity of the entrepreneur as a factor of production on the market and thus reaches noteworthy theoretical conclusions.[179] Unlike Hobson, however, Dobb does not see in the entrepreneur's monopoly a necessary social evil. This is also the attitude of the Americans William T. Foster and Waddill Catchings, who, in the work which they published jointly [180] on the practical origin and importance of profits in economics, assign paramount importance to the study of free and monopolistic formation of income. They try to found, principally by means of the theory of the business cycle, the principle that saving leads to disturbances of the equilibrium in modern market economy. This idea has given rise to an extensive discussion.

SUMMARY AND PROSPECTS

SUMMARY AND PROSPECTS

In the three main divisions into which we have thought fit to separate the development of economic theory in the first quarter of the twentieth century according to the three chief linguistic groups, we pointed out the individual trees of the forest and in some cases made them the object of detailed study. Now in conclusion, we shall endeavor to outline a comprehensive picture of the forest itself and try to point out the most general tendencies of economics for the period in question.

First of all we must notice the fact that, in spite of the general isolation which exists in the German, Romance and English speaking divisions, there are certain points of contact and of correspondence. In time certain revolutionary theories filter through into the science of the other countries and before the World War there was an occasional direct discussion on the more important newer theories between the scholars of different nations. One need only mention the famous debate between Böhm-Bawerk and Clark on the problem of capital and interest. The war and the immediately ensuing years caused a great interruption; it is only since 1924 and 1925 that the former international relations have been gradually renewed. A few theorists seized the opportunity even earlier to expound their views in foreign languages. Thus we find before the World War Italian works by Edgeworth, French and English ones by Loria, English publications by Schumpeter, etc., and recently G. H. Bousquet, Mentor Bounatian, Robert Michels, etc., have done the same thing. Translations have served the international exchange of scientific thoughts since as before the war. The period of revival in the last three or four years has witnessed German translations of the works of Cournot, Gide, Cornélissen, Loria, Barone, Graziadei, Seligman and Henderson; English translations of the books of Cournot, Wieser and Max Weber; Italian translations of the works of Karl

Menger, and Sombart; and French translations of the books of Seligman, Schwiedland, etc. The greatest contribution toward an international *rapprochement* has, perhaps, been made by the theoretically inclined economic periodicals and in their reports, often thorough, of the more important foreign publications. German periodicals lead here; but foreign writers, too, occasionally publish detailed accounts of a few important German works.

To mention only isolated examples, Thorstein Veblen tested his economic ideas, based on modern American psychology, on the viewpoints expressed by Schmoller in his *Grundriss*.[1] Rist disposes of Schumpeter's *Hauptinhalt* in one and a half pages, remarking that the book would be more stimulating if reduced to half its size and that the author is not sufficiently sparing of his reader's time.[2] The American R. C. McCrea, on the other hand, makes a thorough analysis of Schumpeter's system and praises the Austrian scholar for having given an agreeable, mature and logical form to his theories, which are derived in the main from America.[3] R. S. Meriam has correctly understood and developed the main ideas of Karl Diehl's *Theoretische Nationalökonomie*.[4] Liefmann was dissatisfied with the detailed, but adverse, criticism of G. A. Kleene,[5] and tried to answer his arguments, claiming that his own teachings have penetrated not only into Germany but also into Switzerland, Holland and Japan.[6] A. B. Wolfe,[7] Fabian Franklin,[8] and F. H. Knight [9] discuss in detail the German publications of Cassel, and studies are made of the ideas of Sombart by Wesley C. Mitchell,[10] John R. Commons and Selig Perlman,[11] as well as by Talcott Parsons.[12]

On the whole we see that the interest in new foreign economic doctrines, both in recent years and at present, is strongest in America. Italy, Germany and Austria come next, while England and France seem to concern themselves the least with the economic achievements of foreign countries and, in the last few years, especially little with those of German-speaking countries. It was typical of the American Economic Association to have started their own discussion,[13] before the war, on the dynamic economic theory of the absent Pantaleoni in which important figures such as Clark, Patten, and Fetter took part. It could only promote the uniform development of international science to point out that the dynamic ideas of Pantaleoni are essentially identical with those which have prevailed in American economic theory since Carey.

Besides these various forms of a deliberate connection with foreign doctrines, we may notice numerous cases where scholars of various nationalities, starting from different premises independently of each other and often at the same time, have reached the same or similar conclusions. The classical example of this is the temporal coincidence, so often discussed, of the investigations of Menger, Jevons and Walras, from which came the renaissance of economic theory in the seventies. Similar, though less complete and less important, parallelisms have also appeared in the modern history of economics. Although we have touched upon some of them in the course of our narrative, we shall try to summarize their most general traits.

First with regard to the philosophical foundations of contemporary economic theory, coincidences which appear at first sight accidental can be in most cases easily referred to common sources. We have already shown how the ideas of the modern theory of value, then the theory of economic equilibrium, and in general the modern mathematical view of economics spring more or less from the same philosophical sources. Nevertheless, coincidences occur in these fundamental philosophical ideas which cannot possibly be referred to a common intellectual influence. The Austrian Spann and the American Fetter differ widely in their general philosophies; yet they agree in devoting their attention in economic theory always to the primary values and ends of life and consider the economic system only as a subordinate means. Both are sworn enemies of the materialistic interpretation of economics and Fetter is anxious, like Spann, to substitute a teleological attitude for the purely empirical and causal one in our science. Both, therefore, are partly opposed to the prevailing doctrines and both are able to defend their views of reform with a talent for propaganda. If both Fetter and Spann appear in their latest development to have come strongly under the influence of the most recent social and economic changes, the *Économie Nouvelle* of the Frenchman Valois is due entirely to the post-war mentality. Although his booklet, which is of slight scientific value, cannot be compared with that of Spann, we think it necessary to point out the close relationship of their thoughts, which interpret the cultural development of mankind in a thoroughly idealistic way, and combat all materialism, liberalism and socialism. In this way both come to a rejection of mechanistic, individualistic and subjective economic theories. While Spann replaces these with constructive ideas, Valois's contribution to theory is weaker than his critical activity. We have noticed above the points of contact between Spann and another Frenchman, Tarde, and the partial relationship which exists between the former's universalistic and the latter's interpsychological conceptions.

While Tarde, on the basis of his interpsychological sociology, arrives at a generalization of the value theory, in which the economic value concept appears to him only as a partial problem of the great phenomenon of value which embraces all the social sciences, the American Anderson, under the influence of Clark and Seligman, works his way to a similar broad extension of value. In this he starts chiefly from the new American psychological and voluntaristic sociology, as represented by Ward, Giddings and especially by Cooley. A conscious agreement exists between the fundamental ideas of Tarde and Hobson, for the English socialist borrows from the French sociologist the ideas of repetition and invention and tries to use them as a key to the practical achievement of the whole social reform. Hobson wishes, namely, to deliver that part of production which relies on an essentially repeating activity into the hands of the community, while productive activity, in which invention plays a relatively large role, should be entrusted to private initiative, that is, to free enterprise. Relying upon Tarde's sociological doctrine, Hobson hopes that such a dual apportionment of production can be worked out in practice. There are also points of contact in the ideas of social reform in the systems of Oppenheimer and Loria. In both the project of land reform runs through their whole sociological and economic doctrines. Both try to prove historically that the root of all social ills has always been private property on land, and both expect a general social renaissance from its abolition. What interests us most is that both Loria and Oppenheimer interweave this idea of land reform throughout their economic systems and formulate its premises in a corresponding manner. In spite of this relationship, each scholar developed his system independently.

From the methodological point of view, the most important agreement has been that of Max Weber, Croce and Simiand in demanding a "value-less" economics. All three start from different philosophical principles and all three make use of different expressions,—but essentially they agree in thinking that one can and must separate "scientific" doctrines, limited by pure causality, from the ethical or any teleological ideas in economic theory. Another Italian, Emanuele Sella, arrives at the same methodological conclusion, apparently uninfluenced by Croce. Durkheim's method of "concomitant variations," successfully applied by Simiand to economic problems, which deals with a comparative study of economic phenomena under various conditions of environment and which is meant to replace the directly experimental procedure that is not applicable to economics, is closely connected in its contents with the methodological principles of Ehrenberg. The Rostock scholar also desired to recognize as the conditions of his thinking the typical causal relationships of economics through the arbitrary grouping of precise and measurable units of comparison. Both the exact-comparative procedure and the comparison of concomitant variations proceed along the lines of induction but expect to reach the causal rulings of economic phenomena through their experimental nature from within and thus to understand them more perfectly than is possible with the help of the equally inductive historical method.

Ehrenberg studies first of all the management of single private enterprises, and tries to reach a comprehension of economic conditions in this way. The Italian Zorli brings a similar viewpoint of private business to bear on economic theory. He sees in economics a collection of many enterprises, of which the private appearances, the aspects of assets and liabilities are in the last analysis decisive. This subjective comparison of profit and loss is related to the fundamental principles of Liefmann's theory of returns. Liefmann places at the center of his system the difference between utility and costs and tries to explain the important phenomena of economic life by means of this point of view. As a matter of fact, Liefmann speaks of a purely psychic yield which arises from the comparison of pleasure and pain while Zorli's idea, applied externally, is to be taken quantitatively and materialistically. The entrepreneur's interpretation of economic conditions appears to Liefmann in various connections. No one has worked out this entrepreneur aspect more completely than the American Davenport. He too makes use of socio-ethical considerations and tries to show the limits up to which free play can be accorded to private desire for gain without harming the community. Liefmann shares his purely psychic economic theory with another American, Fetter. The latter also endeavors to explain all the phenomena of economic life on a psychic basis. His concept of "psychic income" is related to Liefmann's doctrine of "psychic yield." While the German makes equal use of the elements of cost and of utility, the American considers merely utility—even though he avoids the term—and assigns only a subordinate and indirect importance to the element of cost.

A similarity can be seen in the starting points of the systems of the German Diehl and of the Frenchman Brouilhet. Both think it false to derive economic theory from an abstract study of individual enterprises, since in this way we can obtain only an incorrect picture which does not correspond to real economic life. Economic theory should begin by considering the social, and especially the legal, conditions of economic life, since these form an essential element of the simple, actual economic phenomena. Although both scholars make common use of this general attitude, they differ in the further development of the doctrines. Diehl endeavors to build a theoretical system on his socio-legal foundation, while Brouilhet takes an entirely relativistic direction and, somewhat like the younger historical school, turns his back on all theory. The American Commons and the Hungarian Balas are related to Diehl and Brouilhet through their attempts to explain economic conditions with the aid of legal points of view.

The next connecting link which we should like to point out between the economic theories of different countries has been deliberately forged by means of detailed literary studies. Schumpeter gave himself an exact account of his plan to act as an intermediary, before he transplanted one of the chief viewpoints of modern American theory into German economics. We refer here to the idea of the distinction between static and dynamic economics, which predominates in all of Clark's school and which Schumpeter made the central idea of his whole system. It is from this that he derives the explanation which he gives of the phenomena of interest and profit. Schumpeter also imported ideas from the Romance countries. He takes the theory of equilibrium and his mathematical attitude from the stock in trade of the Lausanne school. His chief merit in transplanting foreign theories is that he gave them an individual and partly original shape by his logical revision.

The teachings of Cassel, which were published partly in English and partly in German, show a union similar to that in Schumpeter's system between American and Romance economic theories on the one hand and German science on the other. Cassel's whole intellectual background is essentially English. He shows certain points of contact with modern German philosophy, but here too he allows full rein to his English empiricism. His whole system is based on one idea: the justification of individualistic liberalism as handed down to him by English political economy. His whole theory of the mechanism of price, his theory of saving and of interest, and finally his solution of the problem of crises are in the service of this idea. The skillful and uniform liberalism of all these theories, to which Cassel owes his great success, is a traditional characteristic of English political economy and even the Swede learnt it here. The English themselves, especially Edgeworth,[14] have recognized and stressed the role of Cassel as an intermediary between English and German economic theories.

At the turn of the century, Cassel published a sharp criticism of the theory of marginal utility. He finds fault with it in the main because a direct comparison as well as a measurement of different needs, as well with one and the same person as among several persons (one of the fundamental assumptions of this theory), is impossible because of the lack of a common unit of measure. The theory of marginal utility also rests upon the fallacy that consumption goods can be shared at will and that our valuations are continual functions of the amount which has been previously possessed. About the same time, Graziadei subjected the theory of marginal utility to a similar criticism. While the Swede rejects it completely, the Italian enters into its main idea and tries to show its deficiencies from within. In spite of this difference of content, the resemblance between these two critics is very great. Both aroused international interest in scientific circles within a short time.

Cassel not only rejects the theory of marginal utility but also believes that he can expel with it the whole theory of value from economics. Although they start from different considerations, Dietzel, Gottl-Ottlilienfeld, and Liefmann agree with Cassel on this point, while Amonn and, in his latest development, Spann, by his emphasis on the theory of price, reach an essentially related position. A similar, if weaker, tendency is to be noted in the Romance countries. Brouilhet considers the whole theory of value a mistake of artificial, abstract speculation, and the Italians Gobbi and Zorli think that they can do without it in their systems. We must not overlook the fact, however, that the idea of value is in its essence contained, in spite of this formal rejection, in Cassel's concept of valuation and in the theory of "economic convenience" of the two last-mentioned authors. In American economics the institutionalists direct their attacks especially against the theory of marginal utility; parallel with this is the tendency to oust the theory of value even further from the central position which it formerly occupied in economic theory. The same result is obtained by the increasing promience of the idea of welfare, which we notice especially in Fetter, and partly in modern English literature. As a result of all these tendencies, the American Friday expressed the idea in 1921 that the whole theory of value was "moribund," and German scientists such as Gottl, Diehl, etc., have reechoed his thought in speaking ever more often of a "dying" theory of value.

Besides these parallelisms in the method and general structure of economic theory, numerous points of contact exist between the various countries in the solutions of individual problems. We may mention first those new theories which have succeeded in spreading beyond the frontiers of language and have taken root in foreign science. We shall, however, refrain from treating anew the spread of those theories, such as the Austrian theory of value and price, Böhm's theory of interest, the Lausanne theory of economic equilibrium, Marshall's theory of value and the extension of the theory of rent, or the American theory of marginal productivity. Our concern here is not so much with the connection that is made by simply accepting foreign ideas, as with the parallel and more or less independent appearance of new and creative theoretical thoughts, so closely related as to justify our belief in a uniform development of economics as a whole.

The first important point of contact of this kind is to be found in the theory of value and price. With the development of their new economic theory, the Americans endeavor to make equal use of the element of utility and of the idea of cost in explaining the phenomenon of value and price. Costs are viewed as a loss of utility, as displeasure, as economic pain, as contrasted with the element of utility, and are also reduced to the common denominator of the marginal principle. In European science, this reconciliation between the subjective and objective theories of value is even more apparent; in the Romance and German countries it is generally accompanied by a more or less sharp criticism of the theory of marginal utility. In Romance science we may remind the reader only of the theory of Cornélissen, which is perhaps the most typical example of these views. In German literature, Otto Conrad's value theory especially is oriented in a similar direction and resembles the American attitude in his new subjective interpretation of the concept of costs. In Liefmann's theory of price we again find a union of the subjective and objective viewpoints, since the elements of both utility and cost appear in his principle of returns.

In his final conclusions, his purely "psychic" interpretation leads him into the close neighborhood of the price theory of marginal utility.

Colson, one of the foremost contemporary French theorists, works out a theory of price in which, while retaining the principles of the classical theory of supply and demand, he is able cleverly to unite objectivism and subjectivism. The fact that an Englishman called Marshall, or whatever his name may have been, appeared with exactly the same theory twelve years earlier, does not appear to perturb the French in their joy over the achievement of their compatriot. Colson claims that he did not know Marshall's theory of price when he planned his own—this should suffice for anyone. The French are only too prone to chide the customary German practice, which has been accepted by many Italians since Cossa, of discussing the more important native and foreign theories before expounding their own. This kind of scientific writing may have its drawbacks, but a prominent German or Italian theorist could scarcely fare as unhappily as did Colson with his theory of price. Other French economists, such as Gide, have adopted Marshall's theory of value and price but do not pretend to have created a new and independent one.

While most American economists and their German analogues manage to unite the objective and the subjective viewpoints in the theory of price by dealing with the element of cost, which is in itself objective, from the subjective side, Davenport takes the contrary direction in his theory of "opportunity" costs. He projects the subjective element of utility on to costs, which are the sacrifice that results from a rejection of the second-best possibility of application and also reaches in this way a union between the subjective and objective attitudes. This idea was suggested earlier by the Englishman Wicksteed. The Frenchman Bodin has offered in his recently published text book a solution of the price problem which is similar to, but independent of, those of Davenport and Wicksteed. Contrary to Davenport, he tries to obtain his results without the foundation of a real value theory. This is perhaps also the place to point out that the distinction between "processus satisfactoire" and "processus présatisfactoire," which Bodin makes in his theory of production, has a certain relationship with Spann's "maturity grades in economics."

When Spann, in his latest stage of development, reaches the concept of a just price through his universalistic theory of equal importance, he approaches the Frenchman Valois who, starting from similar ideals, also dreams of a "single just normal price." Theoretically, however, Valois is superficial, and simply explains the level of the just price as identical with that of production costs. We have often mentioned how closely related another Frenchman, Tarde, is to Spann with his concept of a normal price. Along somewhat parallel lines, we have the recent investigations of the American F. H. Knight, who sharply contrasts the socio-ethical postulates of actual economics, which are operative in the formation of price, with the purely mechanistic theory of a normal price such as we find in modern economics, and especially in Marshall.

Out of the mass of similar points of contact we shall take only one more, which relates to the theory of returns and which is of fundamental importance for the recent development of the theory of rent. At the turn of the century, the Italian Jannacone devoted himself to an analysis of the question of returns in production and worked out the various factors which contribute towards diminishing production costs and at the same time increasing returns. A few years later, Richard Schüller followed the same path. While the Italian pointed out the general difficulties in production technique which hinder the factors for increasing returns being brought into harmony with each other, the Austrian believes that such a harmony is quite possible up to a certain limit. It is only when production is extended beyond this absolute limit that industries which have been producing under favorable conditions lose their technical advantages. Alfred Weber's famous theory of the localization of industries contains essentially the same thought. Starting from partly different premises, both Jannacone and Schüller arrive at a generalization of the law of diminishing returns on land and thus provide further arguments for the broad, international stream of theory which arose at the end of the preceding century, especially with the Englishman Marshall, and which is directed toward an extension of the traditional theory of rent.

It is to be assumed that neither Jannacone nor Schüller knew of each other, although their investigations took them along the same paths. The same is probably true of the other theoretical ideas which have made parallel and often simultaneous appearances in various countries. Although we have touched upon some of them, the list could be continued for a long time. In reply to the question whether these parallelisms have been quite fortuitous, we must answer, with reference to the personalities of the different scholars, undoubtedly yes. With reference to the general development of our science, these very coincidences point to the element of a great international unity. Under this condition, the web of more or less fortuitous parallelisms was bound to spread over all the details of economic investigation or at least over its most important conclusions. In the most recent development of economic theory, however, the situation is different. Points of contact occur quite frequently, but as a rule they have no reference to the leading ideas. They are detached and do not form part of a unified picture of parallel development. On the whole, we may say that these parallel phenomena can break through the great cultural barriers that exist between the various language groups, even in economics, only in isolated points and are unable to destroy them entirely.

The barriers between the great cultural groups are on the whole higher today than ever, and within them political economy follows along different directions. Apart from some sporadic exceptions, these directions are determined by the general cultural and spiritual condition of the various peoples and groups. The first quarter of the twentieth century has seen no change in this rule, if we consider the main lines of theoretical development.

The Romance countries are those which have least felt the traces left by the social, economic and cultural changes caused by the World War. Italian economics, which had in former times always been strongly marked by social ethics, was decisively influenced by the new abstract theory, especially by the achievements of the Lausanne school. Toward the end of the last century all other tendencies were being pushed aside in Italy by the mathematical method, and since then this has been still more the case. In France, traditional classical and liberal economics has survived only in the hot-house atmosphere provided by the *Académie des Sciences Morales et Politiques*. This academy, which was founded at a time when the classical theory was in full bloom, replaces each of its eight members on his decease by its own free election. Since it was founded on the crest of the classical theory, it is easy to understand that the same spirit continues, for only those scholars are elected who are acceptable to the old members, i. e., who represent the same economic theories. Because of the high repute in which the academy is held in France, not only do those who desire to become members or to receive one of its numerous prizes try to remain modern guardians of classical doctrine, but larger circles too revere traditional theory. This contains a motto which has a fascinating appeal for the French: "liberté." Liberty is the Frenchman's first and highest political and social requirement, which can be limited only by coming into opposition with the postulate of "égalité" and "fraternité."

In the present century, however, one can notice in France, in addition to the classical liberal school, a decided *rapprochement* with the Lausanne theory. While those economists who are outside of the academy—and among them we find some of the best brains—were formerly more occupied with historical and socio-political ideas, they have been leaning, since the turn of the century, more decidedly to the Lausanne theories. After the war of 1870–71, the spiritual influence of Germany was introduced by the prestige of Prussian arms; but this gradually disappeared in the different cultural environment and gave way to a new theoretical tendency which was more in harmony with the French spirit. It would have been surprising if the mathematical doctrine of the Frenchman Walras had long remained unnoticed in his country. The French recognize in this theory their own attitude to life and begins to speak of a new "positive" scientific method, meaning thereby the mechanistic and mathematical tendency, and not the earlier historical positive method.

The outcome of the World War was of course favorable to this development in the Romance countries. The flush of victory was at its highest here, and we are always prone to attribute success in war to the original forces which are innate in our own traditional and national brand of culture. This had always been directed in France to a belief in great, universal laws, to the treatment of materialistic and mechanistic relationships and to a mathematically exact method of expression. The Lausanne doctrine contains all these qualities and thus it is easy to understand that it should have become ever more popular in France. It is probable that this will continue to be the tendency of development in the immediate future.

The Anglo-Saxons treated the World War and its outcome much more realistically. The outbreak of national feeling, caused by the victory, was quickly overcome, and with their soberness and empirical training scholars began to utilize the experiences of the war and of the social and economic conditions which it had caused for the benefit of science and especially for political economy.

With reference to England, a firmly rooted and sane conservatism prevails even in the most recent development of our science. In the theories of the Cambridge school, the chief thoughts of modern theory have been brought most successfully into harmony with the specifically English tendencies of epistemological empiricism, ethical utilitarianism and economic liberalism. This synthetic system conquered economic science in the Island Kingdom with astonishing speed, and everything seems to point to the probability that its supremacy will remain undisputed for some time. The change in the points of view of economic theory, which appeared as a consequence of the World War, took place in England within the narrow limits of the Cambridge school and did not at all affect its leading position. While formerly a more or less abstractly conceived price theory formed its center, which gave the whole system a certain chrematistic appearance, recent social and economic events, with their profound changes, have brought about a closer realization of social reality. The Englishman's traditional practical sense discounted these events in their socio-ethical relationship, and so the utilitarian trait of the Cambridge theory became more prominent. Shortly before the war, the utilitarian idea of welfare played an important part in the system of Marshall and of his pupil Pigou; but at that time it had to contend with other principles. As a consequence of the experiences of the World War, it has triumphed over its competitors and the system of its expounder, Pigou, has been lifted to the summit of contemporary English economics.

This change took place in a more radical form in American economics. The American is above all a soberly calculating, ever active, practical man: once he recognizes the superiority of one practical method or of one theoretical idea over another, he rejects the latter—however, reputed and traditional it may be—and looks toward the better and more profitable one. Consequently American science is much more amenable to revolutionary reforms than is the English. This trait can be seen in two different tendencies of the most recent development of American economics.

Fetter has had a special position in the economic theory of his country ever since the beginning of the century. First he worked out his own theory of value on a new and purely psychological basis and then attempted to build an independent system on its foundation. In his conclusions he came nearer than any of his compatriots to the ideas of the pure theory of marginal utility. In his more recent development he constantly lays more emphasis on the idea of social welfare and now he realizes clearly that a study which is limited to the theory of value and price can solve only a relatively small part of economic problems. The central question of the production and safeguarding of the nation's welfare, which cannot be treated by a purely monetary attitude, Fetter tries to consider in its living social conditions, avoiding atomistic abstraction.

The other, much more important, reform movement in American economic theory can perhaps be best illustrated by a parallelism between the older and the younger Clark. The former belongs to that great generation of American economists who, full of enthusiasm for the scientific ideals borrowed from Germany, founded the American Economic Association in 1886 and, without having published much previously, without material means, and without important academic chairs, determined to breathe a new spirit into the economic theory of their country. This bold attempt was crowned with success, and in a few years they had everywhere conquered: through them American economics entered upon its classical age. The older Clark is at the head of this movement. He considered the widest perspectives of economic phenomena, dealt with them from the deductive side and produced thereby a pleasing, optimistic, and abstract-deductive system. His son, who entered upon his scientific career with the purpose of further developing his father's thoughts, could not free himself from the influence of a new tendency which had meanwhile arisen and had to admit that economic theory should be based on the results of the "new psychology." The first quarter of the twentieth century begins in American economics with the great work on distribution of the older Clark, and closes with his son's work on the theory of production, which is perhaps of no less importance. The great change which has taken place since then in the science of the new world, is clearly reflected in the general spirit of these two books. At the present moment scholars are again devoting their attention to the investigation of facts: the younger Clark starts again with an exact investigation of the most minute relationships of real economic life, as it appears in present-day questions of economics and sociology, and from here arrives, by means of gradual induction, at the knowledge of more general truths. The radical wing of young institutionalism rejects all theory that is based on deduction, and especially the whole hedonistic and utilitarian structure of classical American economics which the older Clark and his group took such pains to build, and proceeds to investigate the laws of historical development of economic institutions and their complicated and constantly changing relationships to the practical economic behavior of mankind.

A clear trait has recently become noticeable, even within the American classical group, of transplanting more realistic, social, and ethical viewpoints into their theory. Seligman had made these demands at an earlier date, while Carver, Seager, etc., have recently shown a somewhat similar disposition. The World War has led American economics from its abstract deductive heights down to sober, realistic study. Here we have a plastic representation of the great wave motions in the general development of thought. Wonderfully speculative systems, dealing with only the broadest conditions, are always followed by a period of realistic investigation of details: in the modern development of American economics, the older Clark is on the crest of the first wave, while the second, realistic one may be characterized by the recent activity of his son. America is the country of quick and sudden progress; therefore it is not impossible that the present wave will soon be followed by another one, of new deductive speculation.

The main courses which we have mapped of the most recent development in the economic theory of the Romance and English-speaking countries are crossed and surrounded by a whole network of smaller streams. These, however, are phenomena of lesser importance, which are unable to disturb to any appreciable degree the picture of a straight and uniform development.

In the German-speaking countries, we can discover in the first quarter of our century, no trace of a uniform development, directed according to central thoughts. The World War found the scholars already in a state of indecision, in which one was on the verge of a period of transition. After the historical school had finally passed away, there was an interregnum and the struggle between the various claimants to the position of leadership wavered with varying luck in all directions. The Austrian abstract theoretical school seemed to have the greatest prospects of winning out, and it reached its highest point in 1914 with the publication of Wieser's *Theorie der gesellschaftlichen Wirtschaft*. The socio-legal tendency of Stammler, Stolzmann and Diehl was helped by its close relationship to the historical school, and the Marxist theory in its revised form also had some chances. Little attention was paid to Ehrenberg's exact comparative method; and Liefmann's purely psychic system was only just beginning to appear.

All of a sudden the alarum of war was heard in economic circles. The first impulse to found a special theory of the economics of war was soon overcome, but demands were all the more insistent for a new direction, an "entirely new doctrine" in economic theory, and the defeat in the war acted like oil on the fire of this new tendency. It was much harder to answer the question as to what positive new directions should be taken. The Germans lost their great leaders, Schmoller and Wagner, Böhm-Bawerk and Philippovich during the war, and since then Max Weber and Knapp, Karl Menger and Wieser have died. The Italians and the English have also lost their leading economists since the war: Pareto, Pantaleoni and Barone, Marshall, Edgeworth, Wicksteed and Nicholson. While a strong group of the younger generation continues in those countries the development along the traditional lines of the Lausanne and the Cambridge schools, this does not exist in the German-speaking countries. The inheritance of the illustrious departed is rather the cause of debilitating conflicts.

As regards the socialistic theory, this seems to have lost a great deal of its remaining strength as a consequence of the disappointments undergone with respect to socialism in the practical economic life of the post-war period. At the same time there seems to be a confusion over the traditional ideals of German culture, and we notice more attention paid to foreign tendencies. Despondency seems to have taken hold even in scientific circles and the Germans are inclined to view the defeat in war as a defeat of their own cultural and scientific fundamental ideas. The general disenchantment which was bound to follow as a reaction to the war-time enthusiasm contributed to paving the way for realism. This appears in economic theory in markedly pragmatic tendencies which are directed toward building up positive systems rather than toward "fruitless" methodological disputes, and toward the rejection of all theories which do not immediately serve the elucidation of economic phenomena. Cassel's profound system unites all these traits and has the added advantage of coming from a foreign author schooled in a foreign culture. His wide success in Germany is an eloquent, and perhaps the most characteristic, phenomenon in post-war German economics.

Liefmann's purely psychic system, which reached its final form after the war, is similarly realistic and pragmatic and, in order to make a greater appeal, contains many of the aspects of the theory of marginal utility. Nevertheless: *nemo propheta in patria sua.* Liefmann is a German and perhaps that is the reason why he does not today enjoy in his own country the reputation which he deserves. The sharp tone of his criticism has earned for him many enmities and the spread of his economic ideas naturally suffers in consequence. The socio-legal tendency has not found much greater favor since the World War, although some excellent minds direct it. Perhaps the large text book of Diehl, which it is to be hoped will soon be concluded, will succeed in spreading the ideas of this tendency which is so close to the German spirit into wider circles.

Spann's universalistic system appears almost as a reaction to the individualistic, material, mechanistic and empirical currents which—although they are rather of western European origin—have been becoming ever more predominant in modern German economics. In its structure it attempts especially to carry on the great traditions in which German culture has been perhaps most successfully represented: it deals with totality, and has therefore an universalistic as well as an idealistic, teleological and romantic stamp. In a certain way the post-war period seems to be favorable to this tendency as well. He who has once stood for years in the field, as the majority of the present-day German generation has done, in trenches, where it was no longer a question of earnings and gain or material loss, but of life and death, is forced, even unwillingly, to consider the problems of human existence. The great political and social upheavals of the years after the war are also conducive to leading economic investigators to the deepest foundation of their science, where it is bound up with the large, general questions of social life. Spann's universalistic social philosophy and his economic theory which is built upon it seem, on this plane, to be able to maintain their right to exist from the point of view of cultural history. The radical reforms which the Austrian scholar has demanded in the most recent stage of his development in economic theory have aroused widespread opposition. His attempt to make his universalistic thoughts absolutely predominant in economic theory and to replace the most fundamental discoveries of scientific development with entirely new theories has rendered his position difficult. This is especially so in the case of the Romance and Anglo-Saxon countries in which economists generally have a different intellectual background: even the attempts to understand Spann's new and over-complicated concepts often involve considerable difficulties for them. Any further development of Spann's tendency will have to take this fact into account.

And the theory of marginal utility? Since this problem has stood for over a half century in the foreground of economic discussions, we think that we should devote a few words here to a consideration of its course, its rise and gradual decline.

The theory of marginal utility as an economic system was created and developed principally by Austrian economists in the last three decades of the nineteenth century. Its historical contribution consists in the fact that it raised German economics out of the decline into which it had been brought by the one-sided exaggerations of the younger historical school and led it back into sound theoretical paths. It succeeded in giving convincing explanations of several economic phenomena, but it was never able to find a secure bridge to economic policy out of its own self and without the help of other, unrelated, viewpoints. Various attempts have been made to answer a few applied economic questions from the point of view of the law of marginal utility; but a uniform and unambiguous position toward the whole complex of problems of economic policy cannot be reached simply by the theory of marginal utility, both on the basis of previous historical experiences and for purely logical reasons. The great conflict over the possibility of a "value-less" economics has shown that most, and especially the most important, economic problems contain socio-ethical and other uneconomic elements. Nothing can be expected toward their solution from a theory which tries above all to be "purely economic." All properly conceived economic systems are more or less purely economic in the sense that they try to discover only the formal relations of economic means and say little or nothing directly about the nature of the ends which animate economic life. The objectivism of most leading economists, however, offers in itself a favorable foundation for applied economic theory. This is not the case with the essentially subjective aspect of a theory which is based only on the ideas of marginal utility: its subjective, individualistic and atomistic abstractions afford in themselves alone no key to explain organic social economic conditions. There are from the ethical point of view hedonistic, and from the sociological point of view, individualistic elements in the theory of marginal utility. Relying upon these, some have tried, especially its opponents, to read economic liberalism into it. In reality, however, these uneconomic elements are found in an entirely different field: they are contained only in the psychological analysis of isolated private economics, and consequently are much too weak to unite with it a definite attitude toward questions of applied economic theory. Practical experience has also shown by many examples that men who theoretically accept marginal utility can be enthusiastic liberals as well as radical socialists. The end of all scientific research is pure knowledge. An abstract economic theory, however, which affords no unified basis toward applied economic theory has failed in its purpose.[15]

This failure to form a unified connection with economic policy was the first element which was in time to shake the pure theory of marginal utility. We have several times pointed out the numerous other objections that have been made against it. We shall here only recall the surprising fact that the idea of marginal utility has been received with applause in nearly all the fields of western European culture, whereas in Germany itself it has met with little favor. At the outset we must emphasize that every schematic attempt to explain this phenomenon must necessarily be clumsy. In practical reality the various cultures cannot be divided into categories. On the whole, however, we may nevertheless distinguish certain traits, according to which the theory of marginal utility does not harmonize with the whole traditional and specific cultural history of Germany. The German mind is first of all synthetic, then idealistic to the verge of mysticism, organic and historical, while the theory of marginal utility is above all analytical, and inclined, through its hedonism, to a materialistic conception. It is soberly calculating, individualistic and unhistorical. It seems to be no mere coincidence that this theory originated, among the German-speaking countries, in Vienna and reached a really high state of development only in Vienna. For centuries the various peoples under the domination of the Hapsburgs have been streaming into this city, and conglomerate there in a German-speaking but extremely heterogeneous mixture of races. Oswald Spengler exaggerates when he states that, in consequence of the long reign of the Hapsburgs, Vienna still bears the stamp of a Spanish court. We may agree with him in so far as strong characteristics which are not of German origin are contained in the highly developed cultural life of this city. In this environment the theory of marginal utility could reach a high degree of development. Foreigners quickly adopted some of its elements, but in Germany itself it encountered suspicion.

Even there, however, it enjoyed a partial success. It triumphed in the great dispute over method at the end of last century. Its opponent, the historical school, tried to maintain an untenably rigid standpoint, and so the victory was fairly easy to obtain. Since the turn of the century, however, critics have attacked the theory of marginal utility on its own ground, that of abstract theory, and have joined in part those economists who still combat marginal utility from the methodological point of view. It still possessed a firm stronghold in Vienna and its situation did not become critical until recently, when Spann, one of the leading Viennese economists, attacked it. Amonn, another prominent disciple of the old Vienna school, rejects the atomistic elements in the theory of marginal utility, a fact that has also contributed to the weakening of its position in the German-speaking countries.

Even in other countries the pure theory of marginal utility was unable to lift itself to the position of a predominant, unified doctrine, productive of systems. Walras made use of it in his system, and since then it has become a part of the Lausanne theory of economics, which is increasingly influential in Italy and in France. But at the center of this is another theory: that of economic equilibrium, which has no necessary connection with the idea of marginal utility. The latter is no essential part, but merely an accessory of the Lausanne doctrine, and could be replaced at any time by another explanation of the phenomena of value and price without necessarily causing any essential change in the mathematical theory of economic equilibrium. This is best illustrated by the attitude of Cassel. The Lausanne school recognizes the validity of the law of marginal utility but in no way bases its system upon it. It would be false, therefore, to call their theory one of marginal utility in the sense that one uses this expression to designate the system of the old Vienna school.

The situation is very much the same today in England. The original form of Jevons's theory, in which the principle of marginal utility played an important role, though not such a decisive one as with Menger, was more or less supplanted by the appearance of Marshall's *Principles* not quite two decades later. In Marshall the supremacy of the idea of marginal utility seemed to be undermined and limited in two different directions. First he makes full use of the historical inductive method by the side of deductive theory, and secondly he places within the theory of price and value the objective element of cost in an equal position by the side of the subjective principle of marginal utility. In the foreground of his whole economic theory stands the doctrine of economic equilibrium, which is independent of the theory of marginal utility. Recently Pigou has placed the socio-ethical viewpoints contained in Marshall at the center of the Cambridge theory, and the idea of marginal utility is thereby removed one step further toward the background in its system. Under the present conditions of things in English economics, we think it safe to predict that it will continue to retreat in the near future.

The position of the theory of marginal utility is even worse in America. The older Clark and his adherents placed much importance on the general marginal principle, and in their theory of value and price the principle of subjective marginal utility has the deciding word by the side of the objective element of cost. Fetter emphasized this theory still more in the early stages of his development, and tried to base his whole economic system on a purely subjective theory of value. It is true that he started from different psychological premises, but his conclusions closely resembled the Vienna theory. In his more recent development he decidedly rejects the hedonistic foundation of marginal utility and, as we have often pointed out, places the whole value theory which is connected with it in the class of economic problems of secondary importance. On the other side, the classical theory of the older Clark is being attacked by institutionalism. This tendency rejects all theories based on abstract deduction, and especially that of marginal utility. It cannot be denied that this new movement has had an appreciable effect on the development of American economics since the World War. This represents a corresponding retreat of the theory of marginal utility.

Thus, in the countries of western European culture, the theory of marginal utility either is on the decline or else plays a subordinate role in the prevailing economic systems. Nevertheless, a few scholars try further to develop the marginal idea in these countries or to bring it into harmony with the old classical doctrine. For instance, the Americans F. M. Taylor and Tuttle, and the Italian Empoli have recently worked successfully with the concept of extra-, supra-, and ultra-marginality respectively.

The last few years have seen renewed attempts on the part of the old Vienna school to regain their former influence. They answer new editions or translations of the works of Cournot and Walras with the similar new editions of Gossen and Karl Menger. At the same time two other important literary events have favored their resuscitation. Both events rely upon the personal prestige of Wieser, the last member (who has recently died) of the great Viennese triumvirate. First of all Wieser was, with Ludwig Elster and Adolf Weber, one of the editors of the fourth edition of the *Handwörterbuch der Staatswissenschaften*, and as such he was in a position to have most of the articles that were of importance for economic theory written by his pupils and adherents. Consequently this edition of the *Handwörterbuch*, which will probably be in every one's hands for another decade, is stamped by the theory of marginal utility. Moreover, the adherents of this theory published in Vienna the collection on *Die Wirtshaftstheorie der Gegenwart*, which we have often mentioned, which was originally planned to be a birthday offering for Wieser's seventy-fifth anniversary and in which the intention was to give a picture of the present condition of economic theory with the help of numerous contributions from distinguished foreign economists. The history of the theory of marginal utility in the second quarter of our century begins with these two achievements. Will it succeed in giving a new birth to the old Austrian school? In all likelihood, as little as the large, important work of Letrosne or Schmoller's survey succeeded in reviving the decaying prestige of the physiocratic or of the historical school respectively. The age of the pure theory of marginal utility, as an economic system built entirely on the principle of marginal utility, seems to be irrevocably gone.

Those who fear a weakening in the international position of German economic theory from this loss seem to start from false assumptions. It is undoubtedly true that the history of economics shows only two tendencies, the historical and that of marginal utility, both of which, starting from German-speaking countries, have been widely adopted abroad. The success of these two tendencies has a fundamentally different character. While the ideas of the historical school, trained in the social philosophy of German idealism, were adopted abroad under the influence of the political and cultural prestige which Germany had then attained, the theory of marginal utility was able to spread in foreign countries since it was originally more or less in accord with their fundamental ideas. Today, when Germanic prestige is generally at a low ebb, it would be useless to expect that any economic system which breathes a German spirit would find much approval in western Europe. Does this imply the small value of systems such as those of Stammler and Diehl, of Stolzmann, Amonn or Spann? Are the spread and reputation which an idea finds among contemporaries the right standard for its real cultural value? The whole history of the human mind seems to prove with hundreds of examples that this is not so.

The outward success of an economic system depends only on whether it is able more or less to suit the mental disposition prevailing in the respective scientific circles. Schumpeter's system, for instance, was from the first attuned to the western European spirit and thus met with much favor where this spirit prevails. Ten years later, the partly similar system of Cassel was quickly adopted in Germany, where a great cultural change had in the meantime taken place. The ideas of socio-legal, of teleological or of universalistic economics are meant for entirely different minds and only among these will they find acceptance. The mechanistic and mathematical, realistic and empirical tendencies are related to these somewhat in the same way as modern aviation is related to the ascension of a saint into heaven. For the majority of men, the former is the only sensible and possible method; but there will always be souls to whom it is given to see a deeper truth in the latter.

In spite of its gradual retreat, the theory of marginal utility remains one of the most brilliant achievements that economic theory has created in the course of its development. It can be compared in its whole course with Ricardo's profound doctrine. Just as many of the ideas of the latter survived the collapse of the classical school, the real essence of the theory of marginal utility is preserved in the Lausanne and Cambridge theories, in Clark's school as well as in other modern economic tendencies, and it must henceforth be reckoned among the positive contributions to the development of science.

It is not the theory of marginal utility that has outlived itself, but only the attempt to found upon it alone the entire system of economic theory. This fact will do no damage to the international importance of German economics. For the moment it loses the leadership in a certain tendency which was not native, and into which it fell rather by chance. What matters in the development of economics as a whole is not the supremacy of this or that cultural group, but rather the most complete distribution and coordination of work that is possible. This happens when one strives in the various great linguistic divisions to direct the main stream of economic investigation into the channels of one's own spiritual and cultural gifts. It is probably in this way that one can make the most valuable contributions to science. The boundaries here are indeed often vague: it is proved by many examples that various cultural circles are able to exploit with great success certain fields of knowledge which are generally better suited to the spiritual traits of other cultural groups. We can speak here of only average and approximate tendencies. In the Romance countries economic phenomena are most perfectly viewed from the rationalistic and mathematical, materialistic and mechanistic side; the Anglo-Saxon probably sees best when he is soberly empirical, individualistic and interested in immediately practical relationships; the German is usually superior when he studies the historical background, the broad organic relations, and the idealistic philosophical superstructure of social economic life and tries to discover its laws from these points of view. It is through this division of work that the one and supreme economic truth will be most completely recognized from different angles.

A further development of all economic theory will result only when a coordination of work takes place at the same time as this distribution: as soon as the theoretical results attained in different ways are analysed in discussion and thus gradually clarified. Of equal importance for the development of our science are: the thesis, theoretical investigation in itself; then the antithesis, theoretical investigation from another point of view; and finally, the synthesis, which can result only from the conflict between different economic attitudes. We have, accordingly, no reason for despairing of the future of our science in view of the numerous cleavages and the bitter theoretical disputes. The more the battles rage, the surer are we that the dialectical development will produce a more unified and positive economic doctrine. For this it is above all necessary that economists should maintain constant intellectual contacts with those of alien tongues.

ABBREVIATIONS OF PERIODICALS

Am. Ec. Rev.: The American Economic Review, New York.
Ann. d. Ec.: Annali de Economia, Milan.
Arch. f. ex. Wirtschaftsforsch.: Archiv für exakte Wirtschaftsforschung (Thünen-Archiv), Jena.
Arch. f. Rechts- u. Wirtschaftsphil.: Archiv für Rechts- und Wirtschaftsphilosophie, Berlin.
Arch. f. Sozwiss.: Archiv für Sozialwissenschaft und Sozialpolitik, Tübingen.
Crit. Soc.: Critica Sociale, Milan.
Ec.: Economica, London.
Ec. Journ.: The Economic Journal, London.
Ec. Rev.: The Economic Review, London.
Giorn. d. Ec.: Giornale degli Economisti e Rivista di Statistica, Rome.
Jahrb. f. Nat. u. Stat.: Jahrbücher für Nationalökonomie und Statistik, Jena.
Journ. d'Ec.: Le Journal des Économistes, Paris.
Journ. of Pol. Ec.: The Journal of Political Economy, Chicago.
Logos: Logos. Internationale Zeitschrift für Philosophie und Kultur, Tübingen.
Nationalwirtschaft: Nationalwirtschaft, Blätter für organischen Wirtschaftsaufbau, Berlin.
Pol. Sci. Quart.: Political Science Quarterly, New York.
Publ. of the Am. Ec. Ass.: Publications of the American Economic Association, Baltimore.
Quart. Rev.: The Quarterly Review, London.
Quart. Journ. of Ec.: The Quarterly Journal of Economics, Cambridge, Mass.
Rev. d'Ec. Pol.: Revue d'Économie Politique, Paris.
Rev. de Mét.; Revue de Métaphysique et de Morale, Paris.
Rif. Soc.: La Riforma Sociale, Turin.
Riv. d. Scienza: Rivista di Scienza, Bologna.
Schmollers Jahrb.: Jahrbuch für Gesetzebung, Verwaltung und Volkswirtschaft im Deutschen Reich, Leipsic.
Weltw. Arch.: Weltwirtschaftliches Archiv, Jena.

Ztschr. f. Pol.: Zeitschrift für Politik, Berlin.
Ztschr. f. Schweiz. Stat. u. Volksw.: Zeitschrift für Schweizerische Statistik und Volkswirtschaft, Bern.
Ztschr. f. Sozwiss.: Zeitschrift für Sozialwissenschaft, Leipsic.
Ztschr. f. Volksw.: Zeitschrift für Volkswirtschaft und Sozialpolitik, Vienna.

NOTES

THE AUTHOR'S PREFACE

[1] *Grundprobleme der volkswirtschaftlichen Theorie*, 3rd ed. Leipsic, 1928.

[2] *Die Haupttheorien der Volkswirtschaftslehre*, 18th ed., 90th thousand. Leipsic, 1928. English translation as *The History of Economics*, by Eden and Cedar Paul. New York, 1930.

[3] "Geschichte der Nationalökonomie," in the collection: *Grundrisse zum Studium der Nationalökonomie*, vol. 2. Jena, 1927.

[4] *Histoire des doctrines économiques depuis les physiocrates jusqu'à nos jours*, 5th ed. Paris, 1926. English transl. by R. Richards. New York, n.d.

[5] *Essai sur l'évolution de la pensée économique.* Paris, 1927.

[6] *History of Economic Thought*, rev. ed. New York, 1920.

[7] "Epochen der Dogmen- und Methodengeschichte," in *Grundriss der Sozialökonomik*, vol. I, 2nd. ed., Tübingen, 1924.

[8] *Geschichte der Volkswirtschaftslehre.* Berlin, 1923.

[9] *Die Krisis der heutigen Nationalökonomie.* Jena, 1925.

[10] *Die Ausgangspunkte der Wirtschaftswissenschaft.* Jena, 1923.

[11] *Volkswirtschaftliche Gedankenströmungen, Systeme und Theorien der Gegenwart, besonders in Deutschland.* Karlsruhe, 1925.

[12] *The Development of Economics.* New York, 1921.

[13] *Contemporary Economic Thought.* New York, 1928.

[14] The following collections give the best accounts of recent developments which I have not treated in the present volume, as well as of the status of those economic problems which I have omitted: *Die Wirtschaftswissenschaft nach dem Kriege. Festgabe für Lujo Brentano zum 80. Geburtstag*, Munich and Leipsic, 1925, and *Die Wirtschaftstheorie der Gegenwart*, ed. by Hans Mayer, Frank A. Fetter and Richard Reisch, 4 vols. Vienna, 1927–28.

INTRODUCTION

[1] *Cf. Les Allemands et la science.* Paris, 1916.

[2] *Cf. La science et les savants Allemands.* Paris, 1917. Préface by Raphael Georges Lévy.

[3] *Cf.* "Teaching the Introductory Course in Economics," *Quart. Journ. of Ec.*, vol. 31 (1916–1917), pp. 86 *et seq.*

[4] *Cf.* Yves Guyot: "Le manifeste der Kulturkrieger et M. Lujo Brentano," *Journ. des Ec.*, Sér. 6, vol. 64 (1919), pp. 59 *et seq. Cf.* also Hans Wehberg: *Wider den Aufruf der* 93, Berlin, 1920.

PART ONE

[1] "Économie optimiste et économie scientifique." *Rev. de Mét*, vol. 15, 1907, p. 610.

PART TWO

CHAPTER I

[1] *Zur Erkenntnislehre der volkswirtschaftlichen Erscheinungen*, Leipsic, 1900.

[2] "Naturrechtliche und realistische Betrachtungsweise in den Staatswissenschaften," *Schmollers Jahrb.* N.F., vol. 27, 1903, p. 863.

[3] *Zur Methode der Volkswirtschaftslehre*. Karlsruhe, 1907.

[4] "Zur Grundlegung der Wirtschaftswissenschaft," *Jahrb. f. Nat. u. Stat.*, 3 F., vol. 64, 1922, p. 465, and "Methodik der Volkswirtschaftslehre," *Schmollers Jahrb.* N.F., vol. 52, 1928, p. 219.

[5] "Wirtschaftswissenschaft als Wissenschaft," *Schmollers Jahrb.* N.F., vol. 50, 1926, p. 389.

[6] "Zur Methode der exakten und historischen Nationalökonomie," *Schmollers Jahrb.* N.F., vol. 52, 1928, p. 611.

[7] "Mit welcher Methode wurden die Gesetze der theoretischen Nationalökonomie gefunden?" *Jahrb. f. Nat. u. Stat.*, 3 F., vol. 27, 1904, p. 289.

[8] "Die Beziehungen der politischen Oekonomie zu den anderen Socialwissenschaften," *Jahrb. f. Nat. u. Stat.*, 3 F., vol. 26, 1903, p. 433.

[9] "Sozialwissenschaft, Geschichte und Naturwissenschaft," *Jahrb. f. Nat. u. Stat.*, 3 F., vol. 28, 1904, p. 592.

[10] *Güterverzehrung und Güterhervorbringung*. Jena, 1906.

[11] "Die Wirtschaftstheorie bei Sombart," *Jahrb. f. Nat. u. Stat.*, 3 F. vol. 72, 1927, p. 161.

[12] *Untersuchungen über die Methodologie der Wirtschaftswissenschaft*. Leipsic, 1909; *Die historische Schüle der Wirtschaftswissenschaft*. Bern, 1914.

[13] *Recht und Macht*. Leipsic, 1910.

[14] "Macht oder Oekonomisches Gesetz?" *Zeit. f. Volksw.*, vol. 23, 1914, p. 205.

[15] *Das Gesetz der Macht*. Vienna, 1926.

[16] *Objekt und Grundbegriffe der theoretischen Nationalökonomie*. Vienna and Leipsic, 1911; 2nd ed., Vienna, 1927.

[17] "Gustav Schmoller und die Probleme von Heute," *Schmollers Jahrb.* N.F., vol. 50, 1926, p. 337.

[18] "Wirtschaft und Recht. Ein Beitrag zur Theorie der sekundären wirtschaftlichen Erscheinungen," special reprint from the *Journal for Hungarian Public and Private Law*. Budapest, 1907.

[19] *Soziologische Nationalökonomie, Einleitungsheft*. Munich and Leipsic, 1917.

[20] *Uber das Verhältnis der Volkswirtschaftslehre zur Rechtswissenschaft und zur Politik. Ist die Volkswirtschaftslehre eine selbständige Wissenschaft?* Berlin and Leipsic, 1919. Arthur Wolfgang Cohn opposes Kaulla's attitude and similar ones, and tries to prove that only a small part of economics depends upon sociology or other social sciences. "Wirtschaftslehre oder Sozialwissenschaft? Zugleich ein Versuch zur Systematik der Wirtschaftswissenschaften," *Arch. f. Sozwiss.*, vol. 49, 1922, p. 170.

[21] "Macht oder Oekonomisches Gesetz," *Schmollers Jahrb.* N.F., vol. 49, 1925, p. 273.

[22] "Der Machtgedanke und das Produktionsproblem (Politik und Wirtschaft)," *Schmollers Jahrb.* N.F., vol. 49, 1925, p. 533.

[23] *Cf.* the first part of his work on *Grundprobleme der funktionellen Verteilung des wirtschaftlichen Wertes*. Jena, 1923.

[24] *Cf.* especially: *Die Herrschaft des Wortes. Untersuchungen zur Kritik des*

nationalökonomischen Denkens. Einleitende Sätze. Jena, 1901; "Zur socialwissenschaftlichen Begriffsbildung," *Arch. f. Sozwiss.*, vol. 23, 1906, p. 403, and vol. 24, 1907, p. 265; *Freiheit vom Worte. Ueber das Verhältniss einer Allwirtschaftslehre zur Soziologie.* Munich and Leipsic, 1923. The earlier works of Gottl have been recently published in the collection *Wirtschaft als Leben.* Jena, 1925.

25 *Die Logik der sozialwissenschaftlichen Begriffsbildung.* Tübingen, 1905, and "Der logische Aufbau der Nationalökonomie und ihr Verhältnis zur Psychologie und zu den Naturwissenschaften." *Ztschr. f. d. ges. Staatwiss.*, vol. 64, 1908, p. 1.

26 *Cf.* especially, *Materielle und Psychische Wirtschaftsführung. Versuch einer Begründung des Identitätprinzips der Wirtschaftstheorie.* Jena, 1921; "Die Kategorie der Funktion in der Nationalökonomie und ihre Anwendung auf die Kapitaltheorie," *Jahrb. f. Nat. u. Stat.*, 3 F., vol. 64, 1922, p. 193 *et seq.*

27 "Die Verkehrsgleichung," *Arch. f. Sozialwiss.*, vol. 52, 1924, p. 344.

28 *Das Prinzip der Causalität des seelischen und sozialen Geschehens, insbesondere des Wirtschaftens. Eine positive Untersuchung über die Grundlage der Socialwissenschaften.* Halberstadt, 1925; *Die Kausalität der Volkswirtschaft, Die volkswirtschaftliche Form des Grundprinzips der psychischen Kausalität.* Halle, 1925; "Vom Sachgut zur socialer Willensfunktion," *Jahrb. f. Nat. u. Stat.* 3 F., vol. 72, 1927, p. 577.

29 *Die ökonomischen Kategorien und die Organisation der Wirtschaft*, Jena, 1923.

30 *Die Logik der Sozialwissenschaftlichen Begriffsbildung.* Tübingen, 1905, and "Der logische Aufbau der Nationalökonomie und ihr Verhältnis zur Psychologie und zur den Naturwissenschaften," *Ztschr. f. d. ges. Staatswiss.*, vol. 64, 1908, p. 1.

31 "Aenderungen in den Daten der Wirtschaft," *Jahrb. f. Nat. u. Stat.*, 3 F., vol. 73, 1928, p. 641.

32 *Wirtschaftsformen. Grundzüge einer Morphologie der Wirtschaft.* Jena, 1927. *Cf.* also Horst Wagenfuhr: "Zur Frage einer Gestaltenkunde (Morphologie) der Wirtschaft." *Schmollers Jahrb.* N.F., vol. 52, 1918, p. 809.

33 "Uber die mathematische Methode in der theoretischen Oekonomie," *Ztschr. f. Volksw.*, vol. 5, 1906, pp. 30 *et seq.*

34 "Die graphische Methode in der theoretischen Oekonomie dargestellt in Anlehnung an das Tauschproblem," *Arch. f. Sozialwiss.*, vol. 39, 1914–1915, pp. 438 and 795.

35 "Uber die mathematische Methode in der deutschen theoretischen Nationalökonomie. Eine literarhistorisch-kritische Studie." *Jahrb. f. Nat. u. Stat.*, 3 F., vol. 68, 1925, p. 653.

36 "Mathematische Nationalökonomie," *Arch. f. Sozwiss.*, vol. 58, 1927, p. 252; also a critical discussion with the Englishman Bowley.

37 "Prolegomena zur Begründung der nationalökonomischen Kategorienlehre," *Ztschr. f. d. ges. Staatswiss*, vol. 80, 1925–26, p. 649.

38 "Nationalökonomie und phänomenologische Philosophie," *Jahrb. f. Nat. u. Stat.*, 3 F., vol. 71, 1927, p. 225.

39 *Statik und Dynamik in der theoretischen Nationalökonomie.* Leipsic, 1926; *Die Dynamik der theoretischen Nationalökonomie.* Tübingen, 1928.

40 "Statik und Dynamik als Grundprobleme der theoretischen Nationalökonomie," *Ztschr. f. d. ges. Staatswiss.*, vol. 84, 1928, p. 225.

41 "Naturgesetze und sociale Gesetze (Logische Untersuchungen)," *Arch. f. Socialwiss.*, vol. 31, 1910, p. 711 and vol. 32, 1911, p. 689; also: "Ueber Gesetzmässigkeiten in der Geschichte (Historische Gesetze)," *ibid.*, vol. 34, 1912, p. 299.

42 "Historische Kausalität und Soziale Gesetze," *Arch. f. Rechs. u. Wirtschaftsphil.*, vol. 4, 1910–1911, p. 448.

[43] *Geist und Freiheit, Allgemeine Kritik des Gesetzesbegriffes in Natur und Geisteswissenschaft.* Tübingen, 1914.

[44] *Die Logische Natur der Wirtschaftsgesetze.* Stuttgart, 1911.

[45] "Die Gesetzmässigkeit des sozialen Geschehens. Ein Beitrag zur Methodologie der Geisteswissenschaften," *Schmollers Jahrb.*, N.F., vol. 41, 1917, p. 1729.

[46] "Ueber die theoretische Nationalökonomie und ihre Methoden als Hilfsmittel pragmatischer Wirtschaftshistorik," *Jahrb. f. Nat. u. Stat.*, 3 F., vol. 53, 1917, p. 673.

[47] *Die Gesetzmässigkeit in der Wirtschaft.* Vienna, 1927.

[48] "Die Meinungsverschiedenheiten unter den Volkswirtschaftslehrern." *Cosmopolis*, April, 1896; reprinted as "Ueber Werturteile in der Volkswirtschaftslehre," *Archiv. f. Sozwiss.*, vol. 33, 1911, p. 695.

[49] *Cf.* the review in *Braun's Archiv* vol. 5, 1892, p. 490, "Ideale der Sozialpolitik," *ibid.*, vol. 10, 1897, p. 1; but especially in *Schriften des Vereins für Sozial-politik*, vol. 88, 1900, p. 253.

[50] "Ethik und Reaktion in der Volkswirtschaft," *Schmollers Jahrb.*, N.F., vol. 24, 1900, p. 839.

[51] *Arch. f. Sozwiss.*, vol. 19, 1904, p. 22.—It is interesting to note here that, not more than a decade before, Max Weber himself had seen the highest end of all political economy in the development of national power, a social and ethical ideal. This is the leading idea of his work: *Der Nationalstaat und die Volkswirtschaftspolitik* (Freiburg and Leipsic 1895). He mentions, it is true, in the preface that his ideas do not pretend to be those of absolute science.

[52] *Cf.* in this connection the very complete work of Alexander Schelting: "Die logische Theorie der historischen Kulturwissenschaft von Max Weber und insbesondere sein Begriff des Idealtyps," *Arch. f. Sozialwiss.*, vol. 44, 1922, p. 623; also Bernhard Pfister: *Die Entwicklung zum Idealtypus.* Tübingen, 1928. *Cf.* also the similar treatise of Max Weber, published just before his death: "Der Sinn der Wertfreiheit, der soziologischen und ökonomischen Wissenschaften," *Logos*, vol. 7, 1917–1918, p. 40.

[53] *Arch. f. Sozwiss.*, vol. 20, 1904, p. 479, note.

[54] *Sozialismus und soziale Bewegung*, 6th ed., Jena, 1908, p. 128.

[55] *Schriften des Vereins für Sozialpolitik*, vol. 132, p. 572.

[56] "Politik und Nationalökonomie," *Ztschr. f. Sozwiss.*, N.F., vol. 1, 1910, pp. 69, 170, 201, 280, 361, and *Die gegenwärtige Krisis der deutschen Volkswirtschaftslehre. Betrachtungen über das Verhältniss zwischen Politik und nationalökonomischer Wissenschaft.* Leipsic, 1911.

[57] "Gegen Gesinnungs–und Tendenzwissenschaft," *Ztschr. f. Sozwiss.*, N.F., vol. 3, 1912, p. 252.

[58] "Die Untauglichkeit der historischen Methode zur Lösung volkswirtschaftlicher Probleme," *Zeitsch. f. Sozwiss*, N.F., vol. 3, 1912, pp. 241, 311, 383 and "Teleologische und objektive Volkswirtschaftslehre," *ibid.*, vol. 4, 1913, pp. 521, 699, 758, 842.

[59] "Werturteile, Wertbegriffe und Werttheorien," *Ztschr. f. d. ges. Staatswiss.*, vol. 84, 1928, p. 22.

[60] "Grundbegriff, Aufgaben und Methode der Wissenschaft von der Volkswirtschaftslehre," *Ztschr. f. Sozwiss.*, N.F., vol. 5, 1914, pp. 30 and 71.

[61] *Die Aufgaben der Volkswirtschaftslehre als Wissenschaft.* Tübingen, 1909.

[62] "Zur gegenwärtigen Krisis in der deutschen Wissenschaft," *Arch. f. ex. Wirtschaftsforschung*, vol. 4, 1912, p. 4.

[63] "Ueber den wissenschaftlichen Charakter der Nationalökonomie," *Arch. f. Sozialwiss.*, vol. 70, 1905, p. 461.

[64] *Cf.* his above mentioned leading article in the 3rd ed. of the *Handb. d. Staatswiss.*

[65] *Grundriss der Politischen Oekonomie*, 7th ed. Tübingen, 1914.

[66] "Der Kampf um das sittliche Werturteil in der Nationalökonomie," *Schmollers Jahrb.*, N.F., vol. 36, 1914, p. 515.

[67] "Die Stellung der Werturteile in der Nationalökonomie," *Schmoller's Jahrb.*, N.F., vol. 38, 1914, p. 557.

[68] "Die Objektivität," *Schmollers Jahrb.*, N.F., vol. 39.

[69] "Die Erkenntniss des sittlich Richtigen und die Nationalökonomie," *Schmollers Jahrb.*, N.F., vol. 38, 1914, pp. 1509 and 1737.

[70] "Die Werturteile in der Nationalökonomie," *Jahrb. f. Nat. u. Stat.*, 3 F., vol. 43, 1912, p. 177.

[71] "Gegenstand und Aufgabe der Nationalökonomie" in the *Festschrift für Rudolf Stammler*, Berlin and Leipsic, 1926, also in the 12th ed. of Conrad's *Grundriss*, revised by Hesse. Part I, Jena, 1927.

[72] "Wissenschaft und Wirklichkeit, Betrachtungen zur Methode der realistischen Nationalökonomie," *Weltw. Arch.*, vol. 27, 1928, p. 49.

[73] "Das Geltungsproblem des sozialen Werturteils," *Jahrb. f. Nat. u. Stat.*, 3 F., vol. 64, 1922, p. 1.

[74] *Normative Wirtschaftswissenschaft. (Wissenschaftliche Wirtschaftsphilosophie). Systematische Darstellung, Erklärung . . . über "Politik als Wissenschaft," oder die "Werturteile," in der deutschen Volkswirtschaftslehre sowie selbständige Entscheidung der Frage: Normative Wirtschaftwissenschaft oder Keine? Berlin, 1920.* The first half appeared also in 1920 as a dissertation at Tübingen

[75] "Zur logischen Grundlegung der praktischen Wirtschaftswissenschaft," *Schmollers Jahrb.*, N.F., vol. 52, 1928, p. 53.

[76] "Ueber die Ausgangspunkte der Volkwirtschaftspolitik," *Schmollers Jahrb.*, N.F., vol. 52, 1928, p. 823, and "Le rôle de la méthode statistique dans l'économie politique," *Journal de la Société Hongroise de Statistique*, vol. 6, 1928, p. 1.

[77] "Die Pseudowertfreien," *Schmollers Jahrb.* N.F., vol. 49, 1925, p. 753, and "Die Nationalökonomie als Naturwissenschaft," *ibid.*, p. 1029. (Both works severely criticize the attitude of Pohle, who tried to fashion a weapon out of the methodological quarrel against the professorial socialists.) "Max Weber als Erkenntnis-kritiker der Sozialwissenschaften," *Ztschr. f. d. ges. Staatswiss.*, vol. 79, 1925, p. 583; *Das Problem der Volkswirtschaftspolitik*. Stuttgart, 1925; "Das Ende der historisch-ethischen Schule," *Weltw. Arch.*, vol. 24, 1926, pp. 73 and 228; "Die Wirtschaftstheorie als Grundlage der Politik," *Arch. f. Rechts. u. Wirtschaftsphil*, vol. 20, 1926–1927, p. 507. All these have been recently gathered together in one systematic work: *Der Volkswirt als Berater der Volkswirtschaft. Erkenntnis-theoretische und methodologische Grundlegung*. Stuttgart, 1928.

[78] Cf. here, amongst others, the attack of Karl Bücher: "Eine Schicksalsstunde der akademischen Nationalökonomie," *Ztschr. f. d. ges. Staatswiss.*, vol. 73, 1917, p. 255.

[79] *Cf.* amongst others: *Sozialreformer und Unternehmer. Unparteiische Betrachtungen.* Jena, 1904; *Terrorismus in der Wirtschaftswissenschaft.* Berlin, 1910; "In eigener Sache," *Arch. f. ex. Wirtschaftsforsch.*, vol. 9, 1918–1922, p. 170.

[80] *System der Rechts- und Wirtschaftsphilosophie.* Munich, 1904, 1907.

[81] "Sinn und Wert einer Wirtschaftsphilosophie," *Arch. f. Rechts-u. Wirtschaftsphil.*, vol. 1, 1907–08, p. 36.

[82] *Grundzüge einer Philosophie der Volkswirtschaft.* Jena, 1920; and the methodological addition to it, known as *Wesen und Ziele der Wirtschaftsphilosophie.* Jena, 1923. Both of them are united in the second edition (Jena, 1925).

[83] *Oekonomie. Ideen zu einer Philosophie und Soziologie der Wirtschaft.* Tübingen, 1920.

[84] *Cf.* the treatise published as a summary of a larger work in Russian, "Die naturphilosophischen Grundlagen der Wirtschaftstheorie." *Arch. f. Sozialwiss.*, vol. 36, 1913, p. 359.

[85] *Philosophie des Geldes.* Leipsic, 1900, 3rd ed. 1920.

[86] *Philosophie der Landwirtschaftslehre.* Stuttgart, 1919.

[87] *Grundlegung einer wissenschaftlichen Philosophie. Die geistige Natur, 3. Völkerpsychologische Erscheinungen,* vol. I. *Wirtschaft und Philosophie,* I. Abt. *Die Griechen,* 3rd ed., Zurich, 1915.

[88] *Die Bewertung der Wirtschaft im philosophischen Denken des 19 Jahrhunderts.* Leipsic, 1921.

[89] *Cf.* his treatise on the relation between economic theories and philosophical systems, published in various numbers of the *Arch. f. Rechts.-u. Wirtschaftsphil.*, vols. 1–8, 1907–1915.

[90] *Philosophie in der Volkswirtschaftslehre. Ein Beitrag zur Geschichte der Volkswirtschaftslehre.* 2 vols. Jena, 1923–1926.

[91] *Handelspolitik.* Jena, 1920.

[92] "Privatwirtschaftliche Untersuchungen." *Arch. f. ex. Wirtschaftsforsch.*, vol. 4, 1912, p. 28.

[93] *Begriff und Gliederung der Staatswissenschaften.* Tübingen, 1906.

[94] *Grundlegung und Systematik einer wissenschaftlichen Privatwirtschaftslehre und ihre Pflege an Universitäten und Fach-Hochschulen.* Karlsruhe, 1912.

[95] His *Allgemeine kaufmännische Betriebslehre* (Leipsic, 1912), attained six editions in ten years.

[96] *Allegemeine Handelsbetriebslehre.* Leipsic, 1919.

[97] *Betriebswissenschaft.* Munich and Leipsic, 1914.

[98] *Volkswirtschaft und Weltwirtschaft, Versuch der Begründung einer Wirtschaftslehre.* Jena, 1912.

[99] *Weltwirtschaft und Volkswirtschaft.* Dresden, 1900.

[100] *Die Grundlagen der Weltwirtschaft. Eine Einführung in das internationale Wirtschaftsleben.* Leipsic and Berlin, 1924.

[101] *Einführung in das Studium der Weltwirtschaft.* Füssen am Lech, 1923.

[102] *Die Weltwirtschaft und die staatlich geordneten Volkswirtschaften.* Leipsic, 1926, and *Weltwirtschaft und Weltanschauung.* Jena, 1927.

[103] "Handelsbetriebslehre oder Privatwirtschaftslehre," *Arch. f. Sozwiss.*, vol. 34, 1912, p. 905.

[104] "Der Streit um die Weltwirtschaftslehre," *Jahrb. f. Nat. u. Stat.*, 3 F., vol. 48, 1914, p. 486.

[105] "Ueber Begriff und Stufe der Weltwirtschaft," *Jahrb. f. Nat. u. Stat.*, 3 F., vol. 56, 1918, p. 385.

[106] "Privatwirtschaftslehre, Volkswirtschaftslehre, Weltwirtschaftslehre," *Jahrb. f. Nat. u. Stat.*, 3. F., vol. 46, 1913, p. 433.

[107] *Cf.* the above mentioned *Eine Schicksalstunde, etc.*

[108] *Cf.* his article on Weyermann-Schonitz, *Jahrb. f. Nat. u. Stat.*, 3 F., vol. 31, 1925, p. 658.

[109] "Eine neue Wissenschaft," *Arch. f. Sozwiss.*, vol. 33, 1911, p. 842, and "Das Wesen der Weltwirtschaft," *ibid.*, vol. 35, 1912, p. 797.

[110] *Schmoller's Jahrb.*, N.F., vol. 40, 1916, p. 1525.

[111] "Privatwirtschaftslehre und Nationalökonomisches Studium," *Jahrb. f. Nat. u. Stat.*, 3 F., vol. 61, 1921, p. 148.

[112] *Die deutsche Volkswirtschaft im Kriegsfall.* Leipsic, 1909.

[113] *Grundlagen der Kriegstheorie.* Berlin, 1912.

[114] "Versuch einer Bibliographie zur Kriegswirtschaftslehre," *Weltw. Arch.*, vol. 3, 1914, p. 506.

[115] *Der Krieg und die Volkswirtschaft.* Münster, I. W., 1915.

[116] *Cf.* his numerous essays, published especially during the war in *Arch. f. Sozwiss.*

[117] "Krieg und Weltwirtschaft," *Weltw. Arch.*, vol. 7, 1916, p. 225.

[118] "Weltwirtschaft und Weltkrieg," *Weltw. Arch.*, vol. 5, 1915, p. 292.

[119] "Volkswirtschaftliche Lehren des Weltkrieges," *Arch. f. Rechts. u Wirtschafts-phil.*, vol. 9, 1915–1916, p. 49.

[120] *Cf.* volumes 43, 45 and 48.

[121] Besides earlier treatises, *cf.* esp.: "Kriegswirtschaftslehre als Sonderdisziplin," *Weltw. Arch.*, vol. 1, 1913, pp. 342 *et seq.*; "Probleme der Kriegswirtschaftslehre," *Ztschr. f. d. ges. Staatswiss.*, vol. 69, 1913, p. 438; "Einführung in die Kriegswirtschaftslehre," from the *Mitteilungen aus dem Intendanzwesen.* Vienna, 1914.

[122] "Aufgabe, Methode und Leistungsfähigkeit der Kriegswirtschaftslehre," *Arch. f. Sozwiss.*, vol. 44, 1914, p. 760.

[123] *Kriegswirtschaftslehre.* Leipsic, 1915.

[124] "Volkswirtschaft, Weltwirtschaft, Kriegswirtschaft," *Arch. f. Rechts. u. Wirtschaftsphil.*, vol. 9, 1915–1916, pp. 38 and 188.

[125] "Zur Theorie der Kriegswirtschaft. Ein Versuch," *Arch. f. Sozwiss.*, vol. 43, 1916–1917, p. 349, and vol. 45, 1918–1919, p. 477; "Die wissenschaftliche Behandlung der Kriegswirtschaft," *ibid.*, vol. 44, 1917–1918, p. 775.

[126] "Die Theorie der Volkswirtschaftslehre und der Weltkrieg," *Ztschr. f. Volksw.*, N.F., vol. 2, 1922, p. 595.

[127] "Der Anteil Deutschlands an der nationalökonomischen Forschung seit dem Weltkrieg," in the *Festgabe für Lujo Brentano zum 80. Geburtstag.* Munich and Leipsic, 1925, vol. 2, p. 3.

[128] "Kriegswirtschaftslehre und Kriegswirtschaftspolitik" in the *Hdwb d. Staatwiss.*, 4th ed., vol. 5, Jena, 1923, p. 84.

CHAPTER II

[1] *Cf. Grundriss der allgemeinen Volkswirtschaftslehre.* Leipsic, Part I, 1900, Part II, 1904. Schmoller published a revised and enlarged edition before his death, in 1918.

[2] *E.g.*, Carl Brinkmann, "Schmollers Grundriss," *Weltw. Arch.*, vol. 17, 1921, p. 90.

[3] "Schmollers Volkswirtschaftslehre," *Ztschr. f. Volksw.*, vol. 15, 1906, p. 462.

[4] *Lehrbuch der Nationalökonomie.* Leipsic, 1902. New editions in 1909 and 1922.

[5] *System der politischen Oekonomie*, 3 vols., Berlin, 1903, 1906 and 1908.

[6] *Nationalökonomik des Gewerbefleisses und des Handels*, 8th enl. ed. reviewed by Wilhelm Stieda, Stuttgart, 1917, and *Grundlagen der Nationalökonomie*, 25th ed. pub. by Adolf Weber, Stuttgart and Berlin, 1918.

[7] *Die Nationalökonomie der Gegenwart und Zukunft und andere gesammelte Schriften*, pub. by Hans Gehrig, Jena, 1922.

[7a] Grundzüge der Volkswirtschaftslehre. Leipsic, 1925.

[8] "Theorie der gesellschaftlichen Wirtschaft," in *Grundriss der Sozialökonomik.* Tübingen, 1924; 2nd ed., Tübingen, 1924.

[9] 1st ed., p. 397.

[10] *Cf.* "Wieser's Theorie der gesellschaftlichen Wirtschaft," *Arch. f. Sozwiss.*, vol. 53, 1925, pp. 389 and 653.

[11] *Vorlesungen über Nationalökonomie auf Grundlage des Marginalprincips*, authorized trans by Margarethe Langfeldt, vol. 1, Jena, 1913.

[12] *Die Grundlagen der Volkswirtschaft*. Jena, 1923.

[13] *Volkswirtschaftslehre*, 1st vol.; *Theoretische Volkswirtschaftslehre*. Leipsic, 1927.

[14] *Grundzüge der ökonomischen Theorie, Eine Einführung*. Tübingen, 1922.

[15] *Cf.* "Emil Lederers Grundzüge der Ökonomischen Theorie," *Weltw. Arch.*, vol. 23, 1926, p. 160.

[16] *Grundzüge der Volkswirtschaftslehre*. Vienna, 1911.

[17] *Das Wesen und der Hauptinhalt der theoretischen Nationalökonomie*. Leipsic, 1908.

[18] *Theorie der wirtschaftlichen Entwicklung*. Leipsic, 1912; 2nd ed., Munich, 1926.

[19] *Jahrb. f. Nat. u. Stat.*, 3 F., vol. 37, 1909, p. 813; and recently *Theor. Nationalökonomie* to be mentioned later, vol. 1, p. 310.

[20] *Arch. f. Sozwiss.*, vol. 30, 1910, p. 786.

[21] *Schmoller's Jahrb.*, N.F., vol. 35, 1911, p. 909.

[22] *Ztschr. f. Volksw.*, vol. 20, 1911, p. 181.

[23] *Ztschr. f. Volksw.*, vol. 12, 1909, p. 332.

[24] *Jahrb. f. Nat. u. Stat.*, 3 F., vol. 46, 1913, p. 84.

[25] *Weltw. Arch.*, vol. 1, 1913, p. 442.

[26] *Ztschr. f. Volksw.*, N.F., vol. 4, 1924, p. 423.

[27] "Der Zusammenbruch der Grenznutzentheorie, eine Auseinandersetzung mit Joseph Schumpeter," *Jahrb. f. Nat. u. Stat.*, 3. F., vol. 74, 1928, p. 481.

[28] *Theorie der Geld–und Kreditwirthschaft*, Munich and Leipsic, 1914.

[29] *Theoretische Sozialökonomie*, Leipsic, 1918. Originally the first part of a *Lehrbuch der allgemeinen Volkswirtschaftslehre*, which he intended to publish together with Pohle, 4th ed., Leipsic, 1927. *Cf.* a short excerpt called *Grundgedanken der theoretischen Oekonomie*, 4 lectures, Leipsic and Erlangen, 1926.

[30] *Weltw. Arch.*, 1 vol. 15, 1919, p. 445.

[31] *Ztschr. f. Sozwiss.*, vol. 11, 1920, p. 618.

[32] *Schmoller's Jahrb.*, N.F., vol. 46, 1922, p. 517.

[33] *Arch. f. Sozwiss.*, vol. 51, 1923, pp. 1 and 322.

[34] *Ztschr. f. Volksw.*, N.F., vol. 1, 1921, p. 207.

[35] *Ztschr. f. Schweiz. Stat. u. Volksw.*, vol. 57, 1921.

[36] *Jahrb. f. Nat. u. Stat.*, 3. F., vol. 64, p. 369.

[37] "Ueber Cassels System der theoretischen Sozialökonomie," *Weltw. Arch.*, vol. 27, 1928, p. 207, and vol. 28, 1928, p. 144.

[38] "Cassels theoretische Sozialökonomik," *Schmollers Jahrb.*, N.F., vol. 51, 1927, p. 24.

[39] *Die Systemidee im Aufbau der Casselschen Theorie*, Leipsic, 1927.

[40] "Der Ausgangspunkt der theoretischen Nationalökonomie, Eine Auseinandersetzung mit Gustav Cassel," *Jahrb. f. Nat. u. Stat.*, 3 F., vol. 72, 1927, p. 1.

[41] "Die Casselschen Gleichungen und die mathematische Wirtschaftstheorie, *Jahrb. f. Nat. u. Stat.*, 3 F., vol. 72, 1927, p. 385.

[42] *Vorträge über wirtschaftliche Grundbegriffe*, Jena, 1905, 4th ed. 1925.

[43] *Grundzüge der theoretischen Nationalökonomie*, Jena, 1925.

[44] *Die nationalökonomische Theorie*, Breslau, 1924.

[45] *Allgemeine Volkswirtschaftslehre* (*Die Kultur der Gegenwart*, published by P. Hinneberg, Part II, vol. 10, 1) Berlin and Leipsic, 1910, 3rd ed., Leipsic, 1926.

[46] *Allgemeine Volkswirtschaftslehre. Eine Einführung.* Munich and Leipsic, 1928.

[47] *Grundzätze der Volkswirtschaftslehre,* 2 vols. Stuttgart and Berlin, 1917–1919; 3rd ed., 1923.

[48] *Cf.* Amonn: "Liefmanns neue Wirtschaftstheorie," *Arch. f. Sozwiss.*, vol. 46, 1918–19, p. 367; Liefmann: "Professor Amonn als Kritiker," *ibid.*, vol. 47, 1920–21, p. 500; Amonn: "Robert Liefmann als nationalökonomischer Schriftsteller," *ibid.*, p. 523; finally, Liefmann's "Erklärung," and Amonn's "Antwort," *ibid.*, vol. 49, 1922, p. 558.

[49] *Cf.* Esslen: "Nutzen und Kosten als Grundlage der reinen Wirtschaftstheorie," *Schmoller's Jahrb.*, N.F., vol. 42, 1918, p. 1075; and Liefmann's "Abwehr" and Esslen's "Erwiderung," *ibid.*, vol. 44, 1920, p. 299.

[50] "Die Krisis der theoretischen Nationalökonomie," *Ztschr. f. Pol.*, vol. 11, 1922, p. 475.

[51] "Zur Kritik der psychologischen Theorie von Liefmann," *Arch. f. Sozwiss.*, vol. 49, 1922, p. 800.

[52] *Ztschr. f. d. ges. Staatswiss.*, vol. 75, 1920, p. 514.

[53] "Liefmann's rein-psychisches System der Volkswirtschaft," *Jahrb. f. Nat. u. Stat.*, 3 F., vol. 63, 1922, p. 9.

[54] *Jahrb. f. Nat. u. Stat.*, 3 F., vol. 35, 1908, p. 400, and recently, *Theoretische Nationalökonomie*, vol. 1, p. 321.

[55] *Arch. f. Sozwiss.*, vol. 31, 1910, p. 125.

[56] "Das Liefmannsche Gesetz des Ausgleiches der Grenzerträge in der Konsumwirtschaft," *Jahrb. f. Nat. u. Stat.*, 3 F., vol. 54, 1917, p. 385.

[57] "Gibt es ein Gesetz des Ausgleichs der Grenzerträge? Kritisches und Positives zur Preistheorie," *Arch. f. Sozwiss.*, vol. 42, 1916, p. 119.

[58] *Jahrb. f. Nat. u. Stat.*, 3. f., vol. 57, 1919, p. 579.

[59] "Das theoretische System der kapitalistischen Wirtschaftsordnung," *Arch. f. Sozwiss.*, vol. 44, 1917–18, p. 1.

[60] "Die metaphysische Grundlage der Volkswirtschaftslehre," *Arch. f. Rechts. u. Wirtschaftsphil.*, vol. 12, 1918–19, p. 369.

[61] *Der Grenzausgleich bei Robert Liefmann und sein Zusammenhang mit der Grenznutzentheorie. Ein Versuch der Tiefergründung und Zusammenfügung der in ihren Wert–und Nutzenlehren von H. Gossen, W. St. Jevons, C. Menger, L. Walras und R. Liefmann gelieferten Bausteine zu einer einheitlichen Nutzenlehre.* Calw, 1921.

[62] *Fundament der Volkswirtschaftslehre.* Jena, 1918; 3rd ed., Jena, 1923. The philosophical and sociological foundations of this book are found chiefly in the following works of Spann: *Schöpfungsgang des Geistes. Die Wiederherstellung des Idealismus auf allen Gebieten der Philosophie.* 1st part, Jena, 1928; *Kategorienlehre.* Jena, 1927; *Gesellschaftsphilosophie.* Munich, 1928; *Gesellschaftslehre* 2nd ed. Leipsic, 1923; *Tote und lebendige Wissenchaft,* 2nd ed. Jena, 1925; *Der wahre Staat,* 2nd ed., Leipsic, 1923.

[63] One may note first the remarks of Nickel (*Ztschr. f. d. ges. Staatswiss.*, vol. 74, 1919, p. 279), Jahn (*Jahrb. f. Nat. u. Stat.*, 3. F., vol. 62, 1921, p. 73), and Köhne (*Arch. f. Rechts. u. Wirtschaftsphil.*, vol. 17, 1923–24, p. 68). Since then, scarcely a single economist has neglected to give his opinion of Spann.

[64] Karl Dunkmann, in *Der Kampf um Othmar Spann.* Leipzig, 1928, gives an account of the discussion of Spann's doctrine, which took place chiefly at the 5th Congress of German Sociology in Vienna, in 1926.

[65] *Jahrb. f. Nat. u. Stat.*, 3 F., vol. 57, 1919, p. 413; and more recently:

Die Krisis der heutigen Nationalökonomie. Jena, 1925, and "Die Ganzheitslehre O. Spanns," *Jahrb. f. Nat. u. Stat.*, 3. F., vol. 72, 1927, p. 881.

[66] "Das Werk Othmar Spanns," *Weltw. Arch.*, vol. 27, 1928, p. 143.

[67] *Cf. esp. Geschichte der Produktivitätstheorie.* Jena, 1926.

[68] *Cf. esp. Grundlagen einer universalistischen Krisenlehre.* Jena, 1928.

[69] *Cf. esp. Die Systemgedanken der sog. klassischen Volkswirtschaftslehre.* Jena, 1926.

[70] "Persönlichkeit und Entwicklung," *Schmoller's Jahrb.*, N.F., vol. 50, 1926, p. 283; *Moderne Arbeiterpolitik.* Leipsic, 1927.

[71] "Die Theorie des volkswirtschaftlichen Entwicklungsprozesses, etc.," *Jahrb. f. Nat. u. Stat.*, 3 F., vol. 73, 1928, p. 369.

[72] Methodik der Volkswirtschaftslehre," *Schmoller's Jahrb.* N.F. vol. 52, 1928, p. 219.

[73] "Teleologische und technologische Wirtschaftsauffassung," *Jahrb. f. Nat. u. Stat.*, 3 F., vol. 74, 1928, p. 321.

[74] "Zur 'facheigenen' und 'fachfremden' Begriffsbildung in der theoretischen Volkswirtschaftslehre, Eine verfahren-kundliche Betrachtung," *Jahrb. f. Nat. u. Stat.*, 3 F., vol. 73, 1927, p. 401; " 'Theoretische' und 'historische' Volkswirtschaftslehre vom heutigen Stand der Forschung," *Schmoller's Jahrb.*, N.F., vol. 52, 1928, p. 27.

[75] "Der Streit um das Wesen der Soziologie," *Jahrb. f. Nat. u. Stat.*, 3 F., vol. 69, 1926, p. 218.

[76] "Wirtschaftsgeschichte und Wirtschaftstheorie. Bemerkungen zur Lehre Othmar Spanns," *Ztschr. f. d. ges. Staatswiss.*, vol. 82, 1927, p. 45.

[77] "Das Fundament der Volkswirtschaftslehre," *Jahrb. f. Nat. u. Stat.*, 3 F., vol. 67, 1924, p. 577.

[78] *Einführung in die Methodenlehre der Nationalökonomie.* Vienna, 1925.

[79] *Volkswirtschaftliche Gedankenströmungen, Systeme und Theorien der Gegenwart, besonders in Deutschland.* Karlsruhe, 1925, p. 102.

[80] Othmar Spann's "Überwindung der individualistischen Gesellschaftsauffassung," *Arch. f. Sozwiss*, vol. 53, 1925, p. 11.

[81] "Universalismus und Wirtschaftstheorie," *Weltw. Arch.*, vol. 23, 1926, p. 31.

[82] *Aufriss der Politischen Oekonomie.* Stuttgart and Berlin, 1927.

[83] *Der Zweck in der Volkswirtschaft. Die Volkswirtschaft als sozial-ethisches Zweckgebilde. Versuch einer sozial-organischen Begründung der Volkswirtschaftslehre.* Berlin, 1909, in which he develops more fully the ideas of his earlier work, published in 1896: *Die soziale Kategorie in der Volkswirtschaftslehre.*

[84] *Cf.* Suranyi, *op. cit.*

[85] *Arch. f. Sozwiss*, vol. 31, 1910, p. 142.

[86] *Schmoller's Jahrb.*, N.F., vol. 36, 1912, p. 928.

[87] *Jahrb. f. Nat. u. Stat.*, 3 F., vol. 37, 1909, p. 826.

[88] *Grundlagen des wirtschaftlichen Denkens.* Brünn, 1925, and *Handbuch der Nationalökonomie.* Brünn and Leipsic, 1927.

[89] *Ztschr. f. d. ges. Staatswiss*, vol. 83, 1927, p. 350, and vol. 84, 1928, p. 578.

[90] *Prinzipien der Wirtschaft. Eine Grundlegung der Einkommenslehre.* Jena, 1925.

[91] *Theoretische Nationalökonomie*, vol. I, *Einleitung in die Nationalökonomie.* Jena, 1916, 2nd ed., 1922; vol. II: *Die Lehre von der Produktion.* Jena, 1924; vol. III: *Die Lehre von der Zirkulation.* Jena, 1927.

[92] *Cf.* Suranyi, *op. cit.*

[93] *Grundzüge der Volkswohlstandslehre*, 1st part: *Der Prozess der Wohlstandsbildung (Die Volkswirtschaft).*" Jena, 1926.

[94] "Volkswohlstandslehre und Volkswirtschaftslehre," *Ztschr. f. d. ges. Staatswiss.*, vol. 83, 1927, p. 241. *Cf.* also the answer of Amonn: "Gegenwartsaufgaben der Nationalökonomie," *ibid.*, vol. 84, 1928, p. 495.

[95] "Alfred Amonn's 'Objekt und Grundbegriffe,'" *Weltw. Arch.*, vol. 27, 1928, p. 167.

[96] *Arch. f. Recht-u. Wirtschaftsphil.*, vol. 21, 1928, p. 610.

[97] "Volkswirtschaftslehre als Organon. Eine Auseinandersetzung mit Alfred Amonn und dem Problem der volkswirtschaftlichen Objektbestimmung," *Schmoller's Jahrb.*, N.F. vol. 51, 1927, p. 881.

[98] "Objekt und Grundbegriffe der theoretischen Nationalökonomie," *Nationalwirtschaft*, vol. 1, 1928, p. 296.

[99] *Systematischer Grundriss der Volkswirtschaftslehre.* Berlin, 1925.

[100] *Grundlehren der Nationalökonomie. Kritische Einführung in die soziale Wirtschaftswissenschaft.* Berlin, 1903.

[101] *Volkswirtschaftliche Vorlesungen. Kurzgefasster Auszug, allgemeiner theoretischer Teil.* Tübingen, 1909.

[102] *Einführung in die Volkswirtschaftslehre.* 4 vols., Stuttgart, 1924–25, especially the 3rd vol.: *Theorie der Volkswirtschaft*, 1925.

[103] *Theorie der reinen und politischen Oekonomie. Ein Lehr-und Lesebuch für Studierende und Gebildete.* Berlin, 1910; 5th ed. published as the 3rd vol. of his *System der Soziologie*, Jena, 1923–4; an abridgment of it: *Grundriss der theoretischen Oekonomik*, 2 vols. Jena, 1924.

[104] "Oppenheimer's Theorie der reinen und politischen Ökonomie," *Arch. f. Sozwiss.*, vol. 59, 1928, p. 449, and vol. 60, 1928, p. 302.

[105] "Gesellschaft und Staat. Studie zur Gesellschaftstlehre von Franz Oppenheimer," *Arch. f. Sozwiss.*, vol. 56, 1926, p. 339, and also Oppenheimer's answer: "Gesellschaft und Staat. Studie zu der Methodologie Fritz Sanders," *ibid.*, vol. 57, 1927, p. 179; also Sander's rejoinder, *ibid.*, p. 186.

[106] "Sander contra Oppenheimer?" *ibid.*, vol. 60, 1920, p. 648, and Sander's reply, *ibid.*, p. 652.

[107] *Die Theorie der Volkswirtschaft. Einführung in die politische Oekonomie*, trans. into German by N. Nachimson. Leipsic, 1912.

[108] *Grundzüge der Volkswirtschaftslehre*, trans. into German by E. Altschul, Leipsic and Berlin, 1918, 2nd ed., Leipsic and Berlin, 1928.

[109] *Die Lehre von der bäuerlichen Wirtschaft. Versuch einer Theorie der Familiewirtschaft im Landbau*, trans. from the Russian. Berlin, 1923.

[110] *Lehrbuch der Nationalökonomie*," vol. I: *Grundlegung*, Freiburg i. Br., 1905; vol. II: *Allgemeine Volkswirtschaftslehre. I. Wesen und Ursachen des Volkswohlstandes*, *ibid.*, 1909; vol. III: *Allgemeine Volkswirtschaftslehre. II Die aktiven Ursachen im volkswirtschaftlichen Lebensprozess*, *ibid.*, 1913; vol. IV: *Allgemeine Volkswirtschaftslehre. III. Der volkswirtschaftliche Prozess, 1. Deckung des Volksbedarfs als volkswirtschaftliche Aufgabe. 2. Produktion*, *ibid.*, 1922; vol. V: *Allgemeine Volkswirtschaftslehre. IV. Der volkswirtschaftliche Prozess. 3. Tauschverkehr. 4. Einkommens-und Vermögensbildung. 5. Störungen des volkswirtschaftlichen Prozesses*, *ibid.*, 1923. A new edit. of the whole work, Freiburg i. Br., 1923–26.

[111] *Ethik und Volkswirtschaft.* Freiburgi. Br., 1918.

[112] *Grundriss der ethnologischen Volkswirtschaftslehre*, vol. I: *Die soziale Organisation der menschlichen Wirtschaft.* Stuttgart, 1920; vol. II: *Der soziale Wirtschaftsprozess der Menschheit*, *ibid.*, 1921.

[113] *Kultur und Volkswirtschaft.* Heidelberg, 1918.

[114] *Volkswirtschaftliche Betrachtungen.* Leipsic, 1903.

[115] *Entwicklungswerttheorie, Entwicklungsökonomie, Menschenökonomie. Eine Programmschrift.* Leipsic, 1908.

[116] *Die Wertungslehre. Versuch einer exakten Beschreibung der ökonomischen Grundbeziehungen,* Jena, 1923.

[117] *Wertänderungslehre.* Leipsic, 1925.

[118] *Nationalökonomie und Statistik. Eine Einführung in die empirische Nationalökonomie.* Berlin and Leipsic, 1925.

[119] *Das System der Verkehrswirtschaft.* Tübingen, 1903.

[120] "Das Begriffsgebaüde der Wirtschaftslehre und seine Grundlagen," *Ztschr. f. d. ges. Staatswiss.*, vol. 73, 1917–18, p. 484.

[121] *Einführung in die Volkswirtschaftslehre.* Leipsic, 1903.

[122] *Nationalökonomie als exakte Wissenschaft. Ein Grundriss.* Leipsic, 1908.

[123] *Die Volkswirtschaft der Gegenwart und Zukunft.* Leipsic, 1912.

[124] *Allgemeine Volkswirtschaftslehre.* Vienna, 1909; 7th ed. 1922.

[125] *Theorie der Volkswirtschaftslehre,* a revised ed. of the work published in 1918: *Wirtschaftliche Begriffe. Ein neuer Versuch zur wissenschaftlichen Klärung der in der Volkswirtschaft üblichen Ausdrücke.* Vienna and Leipsic, 1923.

[126] *Einführung in die Volkswirtschaftslehre.* Vienna, 1909.

[127] *Volkswirtschaftslehre. Vorlesungen an der Technischen Hochschule Wien.* Vienna and Leipsic, 1918. 3rd ed., 3 vols. Stuttgart, 1922–23.

[128] *Einführung in die Volkswirtschaftslehre.* Leipsic, 1917.

[129] *Grundzüge der Volkswirtschaftslehre.* Leipsic and Berlin, 1921.

CHAPTER III

[1] *Cf.* Wieser's *Theorie der gesellschaftlichen Wirtschaft,* mentioned above, and the latest edition, revised by the author, of Böhm-Bawerk's great work on *Kapital und Kapitalzins.* 3rd ed., Innsbruck, 1912–14.

[2] Among his latest works *cf.* esp. the article "Price" in *Handwörterb. d. Staatswiss.*, 3rd ed., vol. 6, 1910, p. 1130, and 4th ed., vol. 6, 1925, p. 994.

[3] "Die Lösungen des Zurechnungs-problems," *Ztschr. f. Volksw.*, vol. 20, 1911, p. 353.

[4] "Substitutionsprinzip und Substitutionsgesetz in der Nationalökonomie," *Ztschr. f. d. ges. Staatswiss.*, vol. 79, 1925, p. 395.

[5] "Untersuchung zu dem Grundgesetz der wirtschaftlichen Wertrechnung," *Ztschr. f. Volksw.*, N.F., vol. 1, 1921, p. 431, and vol. 2, 1922, p. 1.

[6] *Zur Theorie des Wertes. Eine Bentham-studie.* Halle a.d.S., 1901, p. 105.

[7] *Das Wesen und der Hauptinhalt der theoretischen Nationalökonomie.* Leipsic, 1908, p. 99.

[8] *Cf.* besides the *Hauptinhalt* esp.: "Bemerkungen über das Zurechnungsproblem," *Ztschr. f. Volksw.*, vol. 18, 1907, p. 79.

[9] "Bemerkungen zum Zurechnungsproblem," *Jahrb. f. Nat. u. Stat.*, 3 F., vol. 69, 1926, p. 1.

[10] "Die Frage der Zurechnung in der deutschen Volkswirtschaftslehre," *Jahrb. f. Nat. u. Stat.*, 3 F., vol. 73, 1928, p. 801.

[11] *Grenznutzen und Wirtschaftsrechnung,* parts I and II. Vienna, 1924; also "Nutzen und Wirtschaftsrechnung," *Ztschr. f. Volksw.*, N.F., vol. 3, 1923, p. 636.

[12] "Der Meinungstreit zwischen Böhm-Bawerk und Wieser über die Grundsätze der Zurechnungslehre," *Arch. für Sozwiss.*, vol. 46, 1918–19, p. 449.

[13] *Grundprobleme der funktionellen Verteilung des wirtschaftlichen Wertes.* Jena, 1923, and "Theorie der Verteilung," in the collection *Die Wirtschaftstheorie der Gegenwart*, ed. by Hans Mayer, Richard Reisch, and Frank A. Fetter, vol. 3, Vienna, 1928, p. 1.

[14] "Grentznutzentheorie und Grenzwertlehre. Fragmentarische Bemerkungen," *Jahrb. f. Nat. u. Stat.*, 3. F., vol. 27, 1904, pp. 1 and 145.

[15] "Zur Frage der Bewertung der wirtschaftlichen Güter," *Ztschr. f. Volksw.*, vol. 20, 1911, p. 622.

[16] "Über Arbeitswert und Arbeitsleid (Eine wertkritische Studie)," *Ztschr. f. Volksw.*, vol. 20, 1911, p. 289; and "Der Begriff der 'Elastizität' in der theoretischen Nationalökonomie," *Arch. f. Sozwiss.*, vol. 57, 1927, p. 336.

[17] "Zur Theorie der Arbeitsbewertung," *Arch. f. Sozwiss.*, vol. 55, 1926, p. 681, and vol. 56, 1926, p. 129.

[18] "Bemerkungen zum Grundproblem der subjektivistischen Wertlehre," *Arch. f. Sozwiss.*, vol. 59, 1928, p. 32.

[19] *Die Grenznutzenschule.* Halberstadt, 1926.

[20] *Zur Lehre von den Bedürfnissen. Theoretische Untersuchungen über das Grenzgebiet der Ökonomik und Psychologie.* Innsbruck, 1907.

[21] "Der Begriff des Bedürfnisses. Seine psychologische Grundlage und seine Bedeutung für die Wirtschaftswissenschaft," *Jahrb. f. Nat. u. Stat.*, 3 F., vol. 48, 1914, p. 721.

[22] "Die Wertungstheorie der Steuer," *Ztschr. f. Volksw.*, N.F., vol. 4, 1924–25, pp. 191.—Compare also Hans Ritschl's criticism "Zum Abschluss der Saxschen Steuerwertlehre," *Schmoller's Jahrb.*, N.F. vol. 50, 1926, p. 111.

[23] "Zur Kritik der Wertlehre. Beiträge zur Beurteilung ihrer Aufgaben im Rahmen der reinen Wirtschaftslehre," *Ztschr. f. Volksw.* N.F., vol. 3, 1923, p. 500.

[24] "Gleichwichtigkeit und Grenznutzen. Grundlegung der Preis und Verteilungslehre," *Jahrb. f. Nat. u. Stat.*, 3. F., vol. 68, 1925, p. 289.

[25] *Supra*, p. 30 and p. 104.

[26] "Die Grenznutzenlehre und die Werttheorie Othmar Spanns," *Jahrb. f. Nat. u. Stat.*, 3 F., vol. 74, 1928, p. 641.

[27] "Die Ganzheitslehre O. Spanns," *Jahrb. f. Nat. u. Stat.*, 3 F., vol. 72, 1927, p. 881.

[28] "Kritik der Grenznutzenlehre," *Jahrb. f. Nat. u. Stat.*, 3 F., vol. 23, 1902, p. 227.

[29] *Ertrag und Einkommen auf der Grundlage einer rein subjektiven Wertlehre.* Jena, 1907.

[30] *Die Lehre vom subjektiven Wert als Grundlage der Preistheorie.* Leipsic and Vienna, 1912.

[31] *Wert und Geld. Grundzüge einer Wirtschaftslehre, Tübingen*, 1918; and "Zur Grundlegung der Wirtschaftswissenschaft," *Jahrb. f. Nat. u. Stat.*, 3 F., vol. 64, 1922, p. 465, which treats of Hänel's book.

[32] *Wertbeinflussung und Unternehmertätigkeit. Grundzüge einer organischen Theorie der ökonomischen Wertrelationen und ihrer dynamischen Rückwirkungen.* Jena, 1922.

[33] "Beiträge zur Theorie des wirtschaftlichen Güterwerts," *Ztschr. f. d. ges. Staatswiss.*, vol. 78, 1924, p. 71.

[34] *Cf.* besides his above mentioned *Theorie der reinen und politischen Oekonomie*, esp.: *Wert und Kapitalprofit. Neubegründung der objektiven Wertlehre.* Jena, 1916, 3rd ed. 1926.

[35] "Objektivismus und Subjektivismus in der Preistheorie. Eine Kritik der

Wertlehre Oppenheimers," *Ztschr. f. d. ges. Staatswiss.* vol. 77, 1922–23, pp. 115 and 328.

[36] "Franz Oppenheimers Neubegründung der objektiven Wertlehre," *Ztschr. f. Volkswiss.*, N.F., vol. 4, 1924–25, p. 1.

[37] *Cf. ibid.*, vol. 5, 1925–26, pp. 108, 125, 556, and 585. This discussion is essentially continued in Oppenheimer's criticism of Amonn's system, as well as in Amonn's above mentioned attitude toward Oppenheimer.

[38] *Das Ende der Grenznutzentheorie? Eine Auseinandersetzung mit Franz Oppenheimer.* Stuttgart, 1925. *Cf.* also Oppenheimer's guarded answer in *Weltw. Arch.*, vol. 28, 1928, p. 188**.

[39] "Methodologisches zu den Problemen des Wertes und des wirtschaftlichen Princips," *Arch. f. Sozwiss.*, vol. 37, 1913, p. 758.

[40] *Wert und Preis. Eine theoretische Untersuchung nach realistischer Methode.* Munich and Leipsic, 1914.

[41] *Die Wert- und Preistheorie mit Berücksichtigung ihrer dogmengeschichtlichen Entwicklung.* Leipsic, 1908.

[42] "Die Lehre vom Grenznutzen und das sogenannte Zurechnungsproblem der Wiener nationalökonomischen Schule," *Jahrb. f. Nat. u. Stat.*, 3 F., vol. 59, 1920, p. 97.

[43] *Dogmengeschichte der Zurechnungslehre*, Jena, 1914.

[44] *Wertphilosophie eines Outsiders.* Leipsic, 1922.

[45] "Die Bewegung der Werte," *Ztschr. f. Volksw.*, vol. 19, 1901, p. 257.

[46] *Der wirtschaftliche Wert vom Standpunkte der geschichtlichen Forschung. Versuch einer Morphologie des wirtschaftlichen Wertes.* Berlin, 1900.

[47] *Neue Feststellung des Wertbegriffes und ihre Bedeutung für die Volkswirtschaft.* Darmstadt, 1906.

[48] *Das Werturteil als Grundlage der Lehre vom Wert.* Munich and Leipsic, 1913.

[49] Dietzel: *Vom Lehrwert der Wertlehre und vom Grundfehler der Marxschen Verteilungslehre.* Leipsic and Erlangen (1921), and Cassel's *Theoretische Sozialökonomie*, already mentioned.

[50] *Die wirtschaftliche Dimension. Eine Abrechnung mit der sterbenden Wertlehre*, Jena, 1923.

[51] "Vom Bedarf und von den Grundlagen seiner Deckung," *Weltw. Arch.* vol. 27, 1928, pp. 1 and 174; also: *Bedarf und Deckung*, Jena, 1928.

[52] "Zur Verteidigung der Grenznutzenlehre," *Ztschr. f. d. ges. Staatswiss.*, vol. 56, 1900, p. 577; and "Professor Cassels nationalökonomisches System," *Schmollers Jahrb.* N.F. vol. 52, 1928, p. 771 (published in Sweden in 1919).

[53] "Nationalökonomie und Wertlehre, eine systematische Untersuchung," *Ztschr. f. Volksw.*, vol. 20, 1911, p. 52.

[54] *Cf.* esp. *Die sozialökonomische Kategorie des Wertes.* Leipsic and Vienna, 1922, and his earlier treatise: "Zur Frage der 'Objektivität' des wirtschaftlichen Prinzips," *Arch. f. Sozwiss.*, vol. 44, 1920–21, pp. 154 and 418.

[55] "Von der sterbenden Wertlehre," *Schmollers Jahrb.* N.F., vol. 49, 1925, p. 1269, also the 3rd vol. of his text book.

[56] "Werturteile, Wertbegriffe und Werttheorien," *Ztschr. f. d. ges. Staatswiss.*, vol. 84, 1928, p. 22.

[57] "'Wert' oder 'Wirtschaftliche Dimension'?" *Arch. f. Sozwiss.*, vol. 59, 1928, p. 225.

[58] "Die 'wertlose' Nationalökonomie, eine Auseinandersetzung mit Fr. von. Gottl-Ottlilienfeld," *Jahrb. f. Nat. u. Stat.*, 3 F., vol. 74, 1928, p. 801.

[59] *Der Streit um die nationalökonomische Wertlehre mit besonderer Berücksichtigung Gottls*, Jena, 1926.

[60] *Die geschichtliche Entwicklung der modernen Werttheorien*, Tübingen, 1906.

[61] "Das Objekt des Tauschwerts," in the *Festschrift* for Brentano (in honor of his 70th birthday). Munich and Leipsic, 1916, p. 297.

CHAPTER IV

[1] *Cf.* the article "Preis," in *Handwörterb. d. Staatswiss.*, 4th ed., vol. 6, 1925, p. 994.

[2] *Cf.* the article "Der Monopolpreis," *ibid.*, p. 1026.

[3] "Das intertemporale Gleichgewichtsystem der Preise und die Bewegungen des 'Geldwertes,'" *Weltw. Arch.*, vol. 28, 1928, p. 33.

[4] "Kritische Beleuchtung der modernen Wert- und Preistheorie," *Ztschr. f. d. ges. Staatswiss.*, vol. 68, 912, p. 397.

[5] *Cf. supra*, p. 73; *cf.* also the controversy between Liefmann and Conrad in the *Jahrb. f. Nat. u. Stat.*, 3 F., vol. 45, 1913, pp. 94, 362 and 676. Liefmann also defends his price theory in animated controversies with Cassel, Oppenheimer, and others. Cf.: "Subjektivismus und Objektivismus in der neueren Wirtschaftstheorie." *Ztschr. f. d. ges. Staatswiss.*, vol. 80, 1925–26, pp. 38 and 222.

[6] "Zur Kritik der Preistheorie," *Jahrb. f. Nat. u. Stat.*, 3 F., vol. 72, 1927, p. 32.

[7] "Grundriss einer elementaren Preislehre," *Ztschr. f. d. ges. Staatswiss.*, vol. 55, 1899, p. 395. This also contains Cassel's much discussed criticism of marginal utility.

[8] "Kritisches und Positives zur Preislehre," *Ztschr. f. d. ges. Staatswiss.*, vol. 64, 1908, p. 587; and vol. 65, 1909, p. 78.

[9] "Über den Subjektivismus in der Preislehre. Ueberlegungen im Anschluss an Liefmanns Preistheorie," *Arch f. Sozwiss.*, vol. 38, 1914, p. 1.

[10] "Preislehre und Konjunkturforschung," *Ztschr. f. d. ges. Staatswiss.*, vol. 82, 1927, p. 255.

[11] "Der Stand der reinen Theorie," in *Festgabe für Lujo Brentano zum 80 Geburtstag*. Munich and Leipsic, 1925, vol. 2, p. 309; also in part his *Volkswohlstandslehre*, in which he borrows Cassel's equations.

[12] *Bestimmungsgründe des Preises*. Reichenberg, 1921.

[13] For the resemblances and differences between Engländer and Cassel, *cf.* Andreas Predöhl: "Zur Preislehre Oskar Engländers," *Jahrb. f. Nat. u. Stat.*, 3 F., vol. 66, 1923, p. 345.

[14] "O. Engländers Bestimmungsgründe des Preises," *Schmoller's Jahrb.*, N.F., vol. 49, 1925, p. 457.

[15] *Supra*. p. 85.

[16] *Grundlagen des wirtschaftlichen Denkens*. Brünn, 1925.

[17] "Grundlagen der Preis- und Lohnbildung," *Jahrb. f. Nat. u. Stat.*, 3 F., vol. 119, 1922, p. 290, and vol. 120 (1923), p. 123.

[18] *Cf.* p. 104.

CHAPTER V

[1] *Versuch einer Theorie der Produktion*. Munich and Leipsic, 1915.

[2] *Cf.* the article "Produktion," in *Handwtb. d. Staatswiss.*, 4th ed., vol. 6, 1925, p. 1108.

[3] *Cf.* "Zur Produktionslehre," *Schmollers Jahrb.* N.F., vol. 49, 1925, p. 1231.—Also his posthumous: "Weitere Beiträge zur Produktionslehre," *Schmollers Jahrb.* N.F., vol. 52, 1928, p. 961.

[4] *Tote und lebendige Wissenschaft. Abhandlungen zur Auseinandersetzung mit Individualismus und Marxismus.* 2nd ed. Jena, 1925.

[5] *Geschichte der Produktivitätstheorie.* Jena, 1926.

[6] *Allgemeine Theorie der gesellschaftlichen Produktion.* Munich, 1901.

[7] *Produktivität.* Jena, 1926.

[8] "Produktivität," *Weltw. Arch.*, vol. 28, 1928, p. 1.

[9] *Über den natürlichen Ursprung der Kategorien Rente, Zins und Arbeitslohn.* Berlin and Leipsic, 1906.

[10] *Ertrag und Einkommen auf der Grundlage einer rein subjektiven Wertlehre.* Jena, 1907; "Zurechnung und Verteilung," *Schmollers Jahrb.*, N.F. 1 vol. 48, 1924, p. 439. *Cf.* also his *Grundsätze*, which we have often mentioned.

[11] *Cf.* Landauer: "Wert, Preis und Zurechnung. Betrachtungen zu Robert Liefmanns Aufsatz: Zurechnung und Verteilung," *Schmollers Jahrb.*, N.F., vol. 49, 1925, pp. 805; Liefmann: "Nutzen und Kosten, Wert und Preis" *ibid.*, p. 993.

[12] *Cf.* Schumpeter: "Das Grundprinzip der Verteilungstheorie," *Arch. f. Sozwiss.*, vol. 42, 1916, p. 1; Oppenheimer: "Das Bodenmonopol, usw.," *ibid.*, vol. 44, 1917–18, p. 487; Schumpeter: "Entgegnung," *ibid.*, p. 495; Oppenheimer: "Das Bodenmonopol usw.," *ibid.*, vol. 47, 1920, p. 866.

[13] *Das Einkommen. Eine kritische Studie.* Tübingen, 1927.

[14] *Soziale Theorie der Verteilung.* Berlin, 1913.

[15] Der Preis als Grundlage der Verteilungstheorie," *Ztschr. f. d. ges. Staatswiss.*, vol. 71, 1915, p. 588.

[16] "Zur sozialen Theorie der Verteilung," *Jahrb. f. Nat. u. Stat.*, 3 F., vol. 47, 1914, p. 71.

[17] "Die soziale Theorie der Verteilung und des Wertes," *Jahrb. f. Nat. u. Stat.*, 3 F., vol. 55, 1918, pp. 1, 145 and 273.

[18] *Der Einfluss der gegenwärtigen Wirtschaftsordnung auf die Einkommens- und Besitzverteilung. Untersuchungen zur theoretischen Nationalökonomie.* Jena, 1928.

[19] *Theorie der Einkommen- und Zahlungsmachtverteilung.* Vienna, 1928.

[20] *Cf.* besides Eduard Lukas' parallelisms between the theories of distribution of Ricardo and Cassel, mentioned above: W. Robeck, "Das Bodengesetz als mathematisches Gleichungssystem," *Jahrb. f. Nat. u. Stat.*, 3 F., vol. 64, 1922, p. 136; and "Das Bodengesetz und das Substitutionsprinzip," *ibid.*, p. 495.

[21] *Lohn und Rente.* Leipsic and Vienna, 1909.

[22] Besides his two important works already mentioned, *cf.* esp., "Das Rentenprinzip in der Verteilungslehre," *Schmollers Jahrb.* N.F. vol. 31, 1907, pp. 31 and 590; also: "Das Grundprinzip der Verteilungslehre," *Arch. f. Sozwiss.*, vol. 42, 1916, p. 1.

[23] *Schutzzoll und Freihandel.* Vienna and Leipsic, 1905.

[24] *Theorie des Ertrages*, Jena, 1927; "Entsprechung als Grundlage der Ertragstheorie," *Jahrb. f. Nat. u. Stat.*, 3. F., vol. 72, 1927, p. 597; "Ertragstheorie und Verteilungstheorie," *ibid.*, vol. 73, 1928, p. 1.—*Cf.* also Weddigen's discussion with Franz Oppenheimer, *Schmollers Jahrb.*, N. F., vol. 52, 1928, pp. 249 and 883.

[25] "Die tatsächliche Bedeutung des Gesetzes des abnehmenden Bodenertrages," *Thiels Landw. Jahrb.*, vol. 38, 1909, Suppl. vol. 5, p. 491.

[26] "Kritische Beiträge zur Grundrententheorie," *Ztschr. f. d. ges. Staatswiss.*, 1. vol. 67, 1911, p. 474.

[27] *Beiträge zur Wirtschaftslehre des Landbaues,* Berlin, 1905, and "Ursachen und Formen wechselnder Betriebsintensität in der Landwirtschaft," *Arch. f. ex. Wirtschaftsforsch.*, vol. 2, 1908, p. 363.

[28] *Das Gesetz des abnehmenden Bodenertrages seit Justus Liebig. Eine dogmengeschichtliche Untersuchung.* Munich, 1905, and "Das Gesetz des abnehmenden Bodenertrages im landwirtschaftlichen Betriebe," *Arch. f. Sozwiss.*, vol. 30, 1910, pp. 333 and 721.

[29] "Noch Einiges zur Verifikation des Bodengesetzes," *Arch. f. ex. Wirtschaftsforsch.*, vol. 2, 1908, p. 568 (a discussion with Waterstradt).

[30] "Das Gesetz vom abnehmenden Bodenertrag und die wirtschaftliche Entwicklung," *Arch. f. Sozwiss.*, vol. 49, 1922, p. 421.

[31] "Das Ertragsgesetz in der Industrie," *Arch. f. Sozwiss.*, vol. 42, 1912, p. 761.

[32] "Gibt es ein allgemeines Ertragsgesetz für alle Gebiete des Wirtschaftslebens?" *Jahrb. f. Nat. u. Stat.*, 3 F., vol. 65, 1923, p. 1.—In the second volume of his *Theoretische Nationalökonomie,* Diehl gives a comprehensive survey of all the old and new literature on the discussion.

[33] "Gibt es ein allgemeines Ertragsgesetz für alle Gebiete des Wirtschaftslebens?" *Jahrb f. Nat. u. Stat.*, 3 F., vol. 68, 1925, p. 638.

[34] "Die Grundrente im System der Nutzwertlehre," in the collection *Die Wirtschaftstheorie der Gegenwart,* ed. by Hans Meyer, Frank A. Fetter, and Richard Reisch, vol. 3. Vienna, 1928, p. 210.

[35] *Ueber Bodenrente und Bodenspekulation in der modernen Stadt.* Leipsic, 1904; *cf.* also "Die städtische Grundrente," in the collection: *Die Wirtschaftstheorie der Gegenwart,* ed. by Hans Meyer, Frank A. Fetter, and Richard Reisch., vol. 3, Vienna, 1928, p. 235, which contains a defense of the old attitude of v. Thünen.

[36] *Kleinhaus und Mietkaserne,* in collab. with Paul Geldner, Berlin, 1905.

[37] *Die Theorie der städtischen Grundrente.* Vienna and Leipsic, 1909.

[38] *Das Wesen der städtischen Grundrente.* Leipsic, 1912.

[39] "Böhm-Bawerks These von der Mehrergiebigkeit der kapitalistischen Produktionsumwege," *Jahrb. f. Nat. u. Stat.*, 3. F., vol. 41, 1911, p. 223; "Der subjektive Wert als Grundlage der Zinstheorie Böhm-Bawerks," *ibid.*, vol. 46, 1913, p. 289; "Böhm-Bawerks Kritik der sozialistischen Zinstheorie," *Ztschr. f. Volksw.*, vol. 20, 1911, p. 699.

[40] *Jahrb. f. Nat. u. Stat.*, 3. F., vol. 21, 1901, p. 833, and vol. 50, 1915, p. 584.

[41] *Der Kapitalzins. Kritische Studien.* Berlin, 1916.

[42] "Eugen v. Böhm-Bawerk und Emil Sax über den Kapitalzins," *Ztschr. f. Volksw.*, vol. 26, 1917, p. 265, and *Ist der Kapitalzins berechtigt? Voraussetzungen und Grenzen des Sozialismus.* Leipsic and Vienna, 1919.

[43] "Der Kardinalfehler der Böhm-Bawerkschen Zinstheorie," *Schmollers Jahrb.*, N.F., vol. 30, 1906, p. 942. *Cf.* also Hans Oswalt: "Zur Zinstheorie," and Bortkiewicz's "Entgegnung," *ibid.*, vol. 31, 1907, p. 1280.

[44] Ueber das Wesen des Kapitals," and Böhm's "Gegenbemerkungen," *Ztschr. f. Volksw.*, vol. 16, 1907, p. 426. What directly precipitated this debate was Böhm's article: "Zur neuesten Literatur über Kapital und Kapitalzins," *ibid.*, vol. 15, 1906, p. 443, and vol. 16, 1907, p. 1.

[45] "Die Böhm-Bawerksche Kapitalzinstheorie," *Jahrb. f. Nat. u. Stat.*, 3 F., vol. 33, 1907, p. 433.

[46] "v. Böhm-Bawerks kapitalistischer Produktionsprozess," *Jahrb. f. Nat. u. Stat.*, 3 F., vol. 38, 1909, p. 176.

[47] "Zur Zinstheorie," in the collection: *Die Wirtschaftstheorie der Gegenwart,* ed. by Hans Mayer, etc., vol. 3, Vienna, 1928, p. 199.

[48] "Moderne Scholastik. Eine kritische Darstellung der Böhm-Bawerkschen Theorie," *Weltw. Arch.*, vol. 24, 1926, p. 198.

[49] *Cf.* besides the "Exkurse" to the 3rd ed. of his *Positive Theorie des Kapitals,* esp: *Einige strittige Fragen der Kapitalstheorie. Drei Abhandlungen.* Vienna and Leipsic, 1900.

[50] *Cf.* as condensation of earlier writings: "Produktionsumwege und Kapitalzins," *Ztschr. f. Volksw.*, N.F., vol. 1, 1921, p. 493.

[51] "Zur Problemstellung der Zinstheorie," *Arch. f. Sozwiss.*, vol. 58, 1927, p. 517.

[52] *Die Zinstheorie Eugen v. Böhm-Bawerks im Lichte der deutschen Kritik.* Jena, 1924.

[53] *Cf.* Böhm-Bawerk: "Eine 'dynamische' Theorie des Kapitalzinses," *Ztschr. f. Volksw.*, vol. 22, 1913, pp. 1; also Schumpeter's "Entgegnung," and Böhm-Bawerk's "Schlussbemerkungen," *ibid.*, p. 599.

[54] "Das Reinökonomische im System der Volkswirtschaft," *Jahrb. f. Nat. u. Stat.*, 3 F., vol. 57, 1919, pp. 257 and 385.

[55] "Schumpeters Theorie der wirtschaftlichen Entwicklung," *Jahrb. f. Nat. u. Stat.*, 3 F., vol. 72, 1927, p. 126. *Cf.* also: "Das Zinsproblem am Geld- und Kapitalmarkt," *ibid.*, vol. 70, 1926, pp. 1 and 97.

[56] "Kapitalzins und wirtschaftliche Entwicklung," *Ztschr. f. d. ges. Staatswiss.*, vol. 84, 1928, p. 102.

[57] *Statische und dynamische Zinstheorie.* Leipsic, 1928.

[58] *Begriff und Funktion des Kapitals. Kritik und Neubegründung der Kapital- und Zinstheorie.* Jena, 1919.

[59] "Die Bewegung des Kapitalzinses unter dem Einflusse der Entwicklung," *Ztschr. f. d. ges. Staatswiss.*, vol. 72, 1916, p. 143.

[60] *Cf.* besides *Lohn und Rente* mentioned above, the essay: "Kapitalzins," *Jahrb. f. Nat. u. Stat.*, 3 F., vol. 90, 1908, p. 325.

[61] *Warenwert und Kapitalprofit,* Paderborn, 1902.

[62] *Der Kapitalprofit. Eine kritische Untersuchung unter besonderer Berücksichtigung Franz Oppenheimers.* Jena, 1920.

[63] "Der Kapitalzins als Residual-Rente," *Arch. f. Sozwiss.*, vol. 47, 1920–21, p. 833; *cf.* also Fr. X. Weiss: "Eine Residualtheorie des Kapitalzinses," *ibid.*, vol. 49, 1922, p. 198.

[64] *Das Wesen des Kapitalzinses und die Zinstheorie v. Böhm-Bawerks.* Breslau, 1904.

[65] *Zur Theorie des Produktivkapitalzinses.* Halle a. d. S., 1908.

[66] *Untersuchungen zur klassischen Nationalökonomie. Mit besonderer Berücksichtigung des Problems der Durchschnittsprofitrate.* Jena, 1915.

[67] *Weltw. Archiv.*, vol. 8, 1916, p. 142, Briefs "Entgegnung," Wicksell's "Replik," *ibid.*, vol. 9, 1917, p. 78.

[68] *Beiträge zur Geschichte und Kritik der Lohnfondstheorie.* Stuttgart, 1905.

[69] "Grundsätze einer Theorie vom Arbeitslohn," in the collection *Die Wirtschaftstheorie der Gegenwart,* ed. by Hans. Mayer, etc., vol. 3., Vienna, 1928, p. 40.

[70] *Lohngesetz und Lohntarif,* Frankfurt a. M., 1926.

[71] *Lohnpolitik und Lohntheorie mit besonderer Berücksichtigung des Minimallohnes.* Leipsic, 1900. For his most recent works on the subject *cf.* the article: "Lohntheorie und Lohnpolitik" in *Handwb. d. Staatswiss.*, 4th ed., vol. 6, 1925, p. 396; also: "Die Lohnpreisbildung," *Grundriss der Sozialökonomik,* part IV, 1st. div., Tübingen, 1925, p. 316.

[72] *Minimallohn und Arbeiterbeamtentum.* Jena, 1902.

[73] *Verkaufspreis und Arbeitslohn.* Berlin, 1913.

[74] *Cf.* his two lesser known, but important, essays: "Die Nachfrage nach Arbeitskräften," *Arch. f. Sozwiss.*, vol. 37, 1911, pp. 37 and 715, and "Die Ansprüche der Arbeiter," *ibid.*, vol. 39, 1915, pp. 33 and 385.

[75] *Zur Lohntheorie der Gewerkvereine.* Berlin, 1917.

[76] *Angewandte Lohntheorie. Untersuchungen über die wirtschaftlichen Grundlagen der Sozialpolitik.* Leipsic and Vienna, 1926.

[77] *Cf.* besides his *Grundlagen der Volkswirtschaft* mentioned above, also: "Die Grundlagen der Lohnbestimmung," *Ztschr. f. Volksw.*, N.F., vol. 2, 1922, p. 377.

[78] *Der Arbeitslohn. Kritische Studie.* Jena, 1926.

[79] *Der Arbeitslohn und die soziale Entwicklung.* Berlin, 1913.

[80] "Theorie der Lohnsteigerung," *Schmollers Jahrb.*, N.F., vol. 45, 1921, pp. 396 and 1111.

[81] *Die Stellung der Machttheorie des Lohnes in der sozialökonomischen Wissenschaft.* Greifswald, 1927.

[82] "Theorie der Verteilung," *Ztschr. f. d. ges. Staatswiss.*, vol. 68, 1912, p. 658.

[83] "Schumpeters System und die Ausgestaltung der Verteilungslehre," *Jahrb. f. Nat. u. Stat.*, 3 F., vol. 121, 1923, pp. 417 and 513.

[84] "Unternehmergewinn," in *Hdwb. d. Staatswiss.*, 4th ed., vol. 8, Jena, 1928.

[85] *Die Dynamik der theoretischen Nationalökonomie.* Tübingen, 1928, and "Zur Lehre vom Unternehmergewinn." *Schmollers Jahrb.* vol. 50, 1926, p. 161.

[86] "Die Diskrepanz zwischen Leistung und Einkommen im modernen Wirtschaftsleben," *Ztschr. f. d. ges. Staatswiss.*, vol. 81, 1926, p. 482, and "Unternehmergewinn und Arbeitslohn," *ibid.*, vol. 84, 1928, p. 280.

[87] *Der Unternehmerstand.* Dresden, 1910.

[88] "Das Persönliche im modernen Unternehmertum," *Schmollers Jahrb.*, N.F., vol. 34, 1910, pp. 223 and 577; also published separately: 2nd ed. Munich and Leipsic, 1920.

[89] "Die Bewegung des Unternehmereinkommens unter dem Einflusse der Entwicklung," *Ztschr. f. d. ges. Staatswiss.*, vol. 74, 1919, p. 1.

PART THREE

CHAPTER I

[1] These were first published in collections (1904, 1910 and 1923); finally as *Erotemi di economia*, of which 2 vols. have thus far appeared, Bari, 1925.—On Pantaleoni esp. Gaëtan Pirou, "M. Pantaleoni et la théorie économique." *Rev. d'Ec. Pol.*, vol. 40, 1926, p. 1144.

[2] Esp. "Le nuove teorie economiche. Appunti," *Giorn. d. Ec.*, vol. 23, 1901, p. 235; "Di un nuovo errore nello interpretare le teorie dell'economia matematica.", *ibid.* vol. 25, 1902, p. 401; "Applicazioni della matematica all'economia politica.", *ibid.*, vol. 33, 1906, p. 429, which appeared earlier in the *Encyclopädie der mathematischen Wissenschaften*; "L'interpolazione per la ricerca delle leggi economiche," *ibid.*, vol. 34, 1907, p. 366 and vol. 36, 1908, p. 423; "Economia sperimentale.", *ibid.*, vol. 57, 1918, p. 1; "L'économie et la sociologie au point de vue scientifique.", *Riv. d. Scienza*, vol. 1, 1907, p. 293.

[3] *Fatti e Teorie.* Florence, 1920.

[4] "Die sozialökonomische Literatur in Frankreich seit dem Beginn dieses Jahr-

hunderts" in the *Festgabe für Lujo Brentano*. Munich and Leipsic (1925), vol. 2, p. 31.

[5] Rist—as he has personally assured the author—does not share the attitude of his collaborator, and stresses the success of the recent mathematical school in France.

[6] *La méthode mathématique en économie politique*. Paris, 1901. This appeared previously in the *Rev. d'Ec. Pol.*, vol. 15, 1901, p. 819 and 1031.

[7] "Economie optimiste et économie scientifique," *Rev. de Mét.*, vol. 12, 1904, p. 643 and vol. 15, 1907, p. 596.

[8] *Les applications mathématiques à l'économie politique*. Lausanne, 1912.

[9] *Les mathématiques appliquées à l'économie politique*. Paris, 1914.

[10] *L'emploi des mathématiques en économie politique*. Paris, 1915.

[11] *Valeur de l'enseignement économique*. Paris, 1912.

[12] *Mécanique sociale*. Paris, 1911.

[13] Among his treatises, "L'applicazione della matematica alla economia politica.", *Giorn. d. Ec.*, vol. 40, 1910, p. 56; "L'applicazione della matematica allo studio dei fenomeni economici e sociali," *ibid.*, vol. 42, 1911, p. 349.; "La meccanica economica," *ibid.*, vol. 64, 1924, p. 45; Ciò che è scienza e ciò che e fede nel campo della dottrina economica," *ibid.*, vol. 67, 1926, p. 365; "W. S. Jevons e la economia pura," *Ann. d. Ec.*, vol. 2, 1925–26, p. 83.

[14] "Il Paretaio.", *Rif. Soc.*, vol. 23, 1912.

[15] "Paretaio e spirito paretiano," *Giorn. d. Ec.*, vol. 45, 1912, p. 76.

[16] "Sui tentativi di applicazione delle matematiche alle scienze biologiche e sociali," *Giorn. d. Es.*, vol. 23, 1901, p. 436.

[17] "Il metodo dell'economia pura nell'etica," *Rivista filosofica*, vol. 10, 1907, p. 577.

[18] "Sulla dottrina matematica della dipendenza riciproca dei fatti economici," *Giorn. d. Ec.*, vol. 47, 1913, p. 205.

[19] "Correlazioni e causalità nei fatti economici," *Giorn. d. Ec.*, vol. 35, 1907, p. 1029.

[20] *Les causes et les conséquences de la guerre*. Paris, 1915. Cf. also "La guerre et les lois économiques," *Journ. d. Ec.*, ser. 6, vol. 50, 1916, p. 3 and "La doctrine de l'utile," *ibid.*, vol. 54, 1917, p. 3.

[21] *L'Economie politique et les économistes*. Paris, 1916.

[22] The minutes of the conference in the *Journ. d. Ec.*, Ser. 6, vol. 13, 1907, p. 106.

[23] "La loi de la distribution," *Journ. d. Éc.*, ser. 5. vol. 41, 1900, p. 36.

[24] "Le droit dans l'économie sociale," *Rev. d'Ec. Pol.*, vol. 27, 1913, p. 290.

[25] "La loi économique," *Rev. d'Éc., Pol.*, vol. 38, 1924, p. 635.

[26] *Cf.* esp. his important historico-dogmatic essay, *L'individualisme économique et social. Ses origines. Son évolution. Ses formes contemporaines*. Paris, 1907.

[27] "La libertà nell'economia. Forli, 1907.

[28] "L'idée de la loi naturelle dans la science économique," *Rev. d'Éc. Pol.*, vol. 35, 1921, p. 294 and 463. A French translation of a chapter from his work on price theory which appeared in Russian.

[29] *Cf.* esp. "Il carattere delle leggi economiche," *Riv. di Scienza*, vol. 1, 1907, p. 99.

[30] *Degli indirizzi oggettivo e soggettivo dell'economia politica*. Rome, 1900.

[31] "Il coefficiente psicologico dell'economia politica," *Rif. Soc.*, vol. 39, 1928, p. 403.

[32] *Cf.* esp. his inaugural speech at Padua, "Il valore pratico delle dottrine economiche," *Giorn. d. Ec.*, vol. 26, 1903, p. 300.

[33] *La méthode positive en science économique.* Paris, 1912.

[34] "Della natura logica dei problemi terminali dell'economia politica." *Giorn. d. Ec.*, vol. 28, 1904, p. 401.

[35] "L'entropia economica elementare," *Giorn. d. Ec.*, vol. 41, 1910, p. 153.

[36] "Sulla necessità di una riforma nelle dottrine logiche della scienza economica," *Giorn. d. Ec.*, vol. 42, 1911, p. 139 and "L'economia e la meccanica," *ibid.*, p. 218.

[37] "Esquisse d'une conception et d'une ordonnance scientifique de l'économie," *Rev. d'Ec. Pol.*, vol. 34, 1920, pp. 22 and 189.

[38] *Introduction générale à l'économie politique.* Paris, 1911.

[39] "La méthode et la science économique," *Journ. d. Éc.*, Ser. 6, vol. 37, 1913, p. 177.

[40] *Introduction mathématique à l'étude de l'économie politique.* Paris, 1911.

[41] "Sull'uso delle formole empiriche nell'economia applicata." *Giorn. d. Ec.*, vol. 35, 1907, p. 1053 and "Una possibile creazione del metodo statistico. L'economia politica induttiva," Entrance speech, *ibid.*, vol. 36, 1908, p. 11.

[42] "La méthode statistique en économie politique," in the collection: *Problèmes actuels de l'économique*, par *March, Moret, etc.* A special number of the *Revue de Métaphysique et de Morale.* Paris, 1921.

[43] "L'économie politique, science statistique," *Rev. d. Mét.*, vol. 32, 1925, p. 475.

[44] *La méthode dans les sciences sociales.* Louvain, 1913.

[45] "L'applicazione dei procedimenti matematici alle scienze sociali nel momento attuale," *Giorn. d. Ec.*, vol. 51, 1915, p. 221.

[46] "Critique de l'économie pure." *Rev. d'Éc. Pol.*, vol. 40, 1926, p. 1166, *Essai sur l'évolution de la pensée économique.* Paris, 1927.

[47] "La dottrina dell'egoismo di H. Spencer come interpretazione dell'economia politica e delle forme storiche degli istituti industriali," *Giorn. d. Ec.*, vol. 33, 1906. pp. 133 and 279; "Della obiettività dell'economia politica come scienza," *ibid.*, p. 345; "L'economia politica e il sistema delle scienze," *ibid.*, vol. 35, 1907, p. 1047.

[48] *Cf.* esp. "Le basi economiche della costituzione sociale," 4th ed. Turin-Milan-Rome, 1913.

[49] *Cf.* his famous speech for the opening of the academic year, 1907–08 at the university of Turin: *La crisi della scienza*, published in an enlarged edition: Turin, 1908.

[50] *Cf.* "L'indirizzo storico nella scienza economica," *Riv. di scienza*, vol. 3, 1908, p. 107, also a few other essays, in the collection which has often been republished: *Verso la giustizia sociale (idee, battaglie ed apostoli)*. Milan, 1904.

[51] *La méthode historique appliquée aux sciences sociales.* Paris, 1901.

[52] They have now all been collected under the title, *La nouvelle orientation économique.* Paris, 1924.

[53] *L'économie sociale d'après la méthode historique et au point de vue sociologique.* Bruxelles, 1921.

[54] *Il valore della scienza economica. Introduzione e una critica dell'economia politica.* Naples, 1922.—University lectures, delivered 15 years previously, and published with only slight changes.

[55] *L'économie politique et la sociologie.* Paris, 1910.

[56] *Les lois de la sociologie économique.* Paris, 1913.

[57] *Cf.* his great work, in 3 vols.: *Philosophie des sciences sociales.* Paris, 1903–07, esp. the 2nd vol. *Méthode des sciences sociales*, Paris, 1904.

[58] *La méthode d'enseignement en économie politique.* Paris, 1907.

[59] *Materialismo storico ed economia marxistica.* Palermo, 1900. A collection of previously published essays. 3rd ed., Bari, 1918.

[60] *Riduzione della filosofia del diritto alla filosofia dell'economia.* Naples, 1907.

[61] *Cf.* Giovanni Carano-Donvito: "Economia e Ragioneria," *Giorn. d. Ec.*, vols. 62–63, 1922, p. 173 and also the partly repudiating remarks of Vincenzo Vianello, *ibid.*, p. 335.

[62] *Principii di economia commerciale.* Milan, 1917.

[63] *Manuel d'économie commerciale.* Paris, 1919; 2nd ed., Paris, 1925.

[64] *Economia industriale.* Milan, 1920.

CHAPTER II

[1] *Trattato di sociologia generale.* Florence, 1916. Also the slightly different French edition entitled *Traité de sociologie générale.* Paris and Lausanne, 1919.

[2] Full title: *Manuale di economia politica con una introduzione alla scienza sociale.* Milan, 1906.—In the French edition: *Manuel d'économie politique.* Paris, 1909, the mathematical supplement of the work has been remodeled.

[3] "La teoria dell'equilibro economico secondo il prof. V. Pareto," *Giorn. d. Ec.*, vol. 39, 1909, p. 353.

[4] "L'economia matematica ed il nuovo manuale del prof. Pareto," *Giorn. d. Ec.*, vol. 32, 1906, p. 296.—As an answer to it, Pareto's "L'ofelimità nei cicli non chiusi," *ibid.*, vol. 33, 1906, p. 15.

[5] *Précis de sociologie d'après V. Pareto,* Paris, 1925; "Vilfredo Pareto, seine Bedeutung für die österreichische Schule," *Ztschr. f. Volks.*, N.F., vol. 5, 1925–26, p. 342; *Introduction à l'étude du manuel de V. Pareto,* Paris, 1927; "Vilfredo Pareto, sa vie et son oeuvre," Paris, 1928.

[7] *Principii di economia politica.* Florence, 1911.

[6] "Vilfredo Pareto." Roma, 1928.

[8] *Sommario di lezioni di economia politica.* Florence, 1911.

[9] *Leçons d'économie politique suivant la doctrine de l'école de Lausanne,* édition française par Pierre Boven. Paris, 1920.

[10] *Lezioni di economia matematica.* Bologna, 1921.

[11] The *Economic Journal,* vol. 32, 1922, p. 400.

[12] *Giorn. d. Ec.*, vol. 65, 1925, pp. 38 and 498.

[13] *Elementi di economica: introduzione all'economica, economica statica generale.* Ascoli Piceno, 1925.

[14] *Lezioni di economia politica.* Padua, 1925; the second ed. appeared in 2 parts: *Lezioni di economia pura.* Padua, 1927, and *Lezioni di economia applicata.* Padua, 1928.

[15] *Petit traité d'économie politique mathématique.* Paris, 1902.

[16] "Un nuovo trattato d'economia matematica," *Giorn. d. Ec.*, vol. 26, 1903, p. 327.

[17] *Précis d'économie politique.* Paris, 1909.

[18] *Traité d'économie politique.* Lausanne, 1925.

[19] *Principes d'économie politique pure. La théorie de l'échange sous le régime de la libre concurrance.* Paris, 1910.

[20] *Traité d'économie politique.* Paris, 1927.

[21] *Economie rationelle.* Paris, 1927.

[22] *La théorie des marchés économiques.* Paris, 1910.

[23] *Cours d'économie politique,* 6 vols. Paris, 1901–07; final edition, Paris, 1915–1924.

[24] *Organisation économique et désorde social.* Paris, 1912.

[25] *Istituzioni di economia politica.* Turin, 1904; 4th ed., Turin, 1925.

[26] *Principii di economia politica.* Naples, 1904; 6th ed., Milan, 1923.

[27] *Principii di scienza economica.* Florence, 1906.

[28] "Osservazioni critiche su un nuovo libro del prof. Valenti," *Giorn. d. Ec.*, vol. 32, 1906, p. 440.

[29] *Cours d'économie pure.* Paris, 1928.

[30] *Traité théorique et pratique d'économie politique*, 4 vols., Paris, 1895, 5th ed., Paris, 1910.

[31] *La science économique.* Paris, 1881, 6th ed., Paris, 1928.

[32] *Ultima verba. Mon dernier ouvrage.* Paris, 1911.

[33] *Gli ideali di un economista.* Florence, 1921; *Le lotte del lavoro*, Turin, 1924.

[34] *Principes d'économie politique et sociale*, 2 vols. Paris, 1912–1913.

[35] *Cours d'économie politique*, 2 vols. Paris, 1920–1921; 2nd ed. of the 2nd vol. 1927; a short abridgment of the work: *Précis élémentaire d'économie politique.* Paris, 1926.

[36] *Traité d'économie politique*, 3 vols. Paris, 1920–1926.

[37] *Primi principii di economia sociale descrittiva e teoretica.* Turin, 1902.

[38] *Trattato di economia.* Milan, 1919. 2nd ed., 2 vols., Milan, 1923–24.

[39] *Principes de science économique*, 1 vol.: *Cours élémentaire d'économie simple*, Paris, 1925.

[40] *Cours d'économie politique*, 2 vols. Paris, 1914–16; 3rd ed., Paris, 1925.

[41] *Eléments d'économie politique. Production, circulation.* Paris, 1913; 2nd ed., under the title: *Traité élémentaire d'économie politique*, Paris, 1921; also an abridgement: *La vie économique (cours pratique d'économie politique)*, Paris, 1928.

[42] *Précis d'économie politique.* Paris-Lyon, 1912.

[43] *Le conflit des doctrines dans l'économie politique contemporaine.* Paris, 1910.

[44] *Psychologie économique*, 2 vols. Paris, 1902.

[45] "L'économie politique et M. Tarde," *Rev. d'Ec. Pol.*, vol. 17, 1913, p. 1.

[46] *Gabriel Tarde et l'économie politique. Un essai d'introduction du point de vue psychologique dans le domaine économique.* Paris, 1910.

[47] *Tarde et l'économie psychologique.* Paris, 1926.

[48] *Principes d'économie politique.* Paris, 1883.

[49] *Cours d'économie politique.* Paris, 1909; 7th ed., 2 vols. Paris, 1923.—also his short introduction: *Premières notions d'économie politique.* Paris, 1922.

[50] *L'économie nouvelle.* Paris, 1919.

[51] "L'Économie nouvelle. A propos d'un livre récent," *Rev. d'Éc. Pol.*, vol. 35, 1921, p. 60.

[52] *L'économie politique et la doctrine catholique.* Paris, 1923.

[53] *Corso di economia politica svolto sui principi della "Carta di lavoro."* Rome, 1928.

[54] *Les grandes lignes de l'économie politique.* Louvain, 1901.

[55] *Catéchisme d'économie sociale.* Liège, 1901.

[56] *Principes d'economie sociale non matérialiste.* Paris, 1927.

[57] *Trattato di economia sociale*, vol. 1: *Introduzione*, Florence, 1907; vol. 2: *La produzione*, Florence, 1909.—A new edition of the 1st vol. appeared in 1915.

[58] *Lezioni di economia politica.* 2 vols. Padua, 1923 and 1924.

[59] *Studii sulla teoria del valore nel cambio intorno.* Turin, 1890.

[60] *Eléments d'économie politique.* 2 vols., Toulouse, 1923–27.

[61] *Corso di economia politica.* Turin, 1910; 3rd ed. Turin, 1927.

[62] *Manuel d'économique.* Paris, 1908.

[63] *Antagonismes économiques.* Paris, 1906. The chief ideas of this work are already found in *Arbeit und Boden,* which was published in 1889.

[64] *L'utilité sociale de la propriété individuelle. Étude d'économie politique.* Paris, 1901.

[65] *Cf.* also Landry's essay: "*Un économiste méconnu: Otto Effertz,*" *Rev. d'Éc. Pol.,* vol. 20, 1906, p. 601.

[66] *Lineamenti di economia politica.* Rome, 1919; 2nd ed. in 2 vols. Bologna, 1920–25.

[67] *Manuale di economia politica.* Naples, 1919.

[68] *L'economia matematica.* Senigellia, 1914.

[69] *Lezioni di scienza economica razionale e sperimentale.* Rovigo, 1921; a French translation of the 3rd Italian edition: *Traité d'économie rationelle,* Paris, 1927.

[70] *Corso elementare di economia politica.* Milan, 1926.

[71] *L'économie de la vie sociale.* Paris, 1902.

[72] *Cours d'économie politique.* Paris, 1908.

[73] *Cours d'économie politique.* 2 vols., Paris, 1909–10; the 1st vol. of the 2nd ed., which consists of more than 1000 pages appeared in 1921.

[74] *Précis d'économie politique,* 2 vols. Paris, 1927.

[75] *Principi di économia politica,* 2 vols. Catania, 1926–27.

[76] *Précis d'économie politique.* Paris, 1921; 2nd ed., Paris, 1924, almost 900 large pages!

[77] *Lezioni di economia politica.* Parma, 1903.

CHAPTER III

[1] "Curve crescenti di ofelimità elementare e di domanda," *Giorn. d. Ec.,* vol. 29, 1904, p. 112.

[2] "La misurabilità del piacere a del dolore," *Giorn d. Ec.,* vol. 30, 1905, p. 15.

[3] *Théorie mathématique de l'échange.* Paris, 1913.

[4] "Alcune considerazioni sulla teoria matematica dell'equilibrio economico," *Giorn. d. Ec.,* vol. 69, 1928, p. 99.

[5] "Cenni sua una generalizzazione del concetto di ofelimità," *Giorn. d. Ec.,* vol. 37, 1908, p. 259.

[6] *L'ammontare e la composizione della ricchezza delle nazioni.* Turin, 1914, and "Sul concetto di utilità economica," *Giorn. d. Ec.,* vol. 52, 1916, p. 113.

[7] "Perchè e come il concetto dell'utilità economica è obbiettivamente indefinible," *Giorn. d. Ec.,* vol. 52, 1916, p. 1.

[8] *La teoria dei bisogni.* Turin, 1900.

[9] "La notion de valeur. Essai de psychologie économique," *Rev. d'Éc. Pol.,* vol. 28, 1914, p. 39.

[10] *Intorno alla legge del godimento decrescente ed al principio del grado finale di utilita.* Valparaiso, 1901.

[11] "La teoria moderna del valore economico," a special reprint from the *Atti e Memorie* of the Accademia Virgiliana di Mantova, nuova serie, vol. 8, 1916, p. 3.

[12] *La psychologie économique chez les Anglo-Américains.* Paris, 1918, and: *Etude bibliographique des sources de la psychologie économique chez les Anglo-Américains.* Paris, 1919.

[13] *Cf.* besides his writings on distribution to be mentioned later: "Les théories dominantes du change, étude critique," *Rev. d'Éc. Pol.,* vol. 40, 1926, p. 769;

"Théorie psychologique du change," *ibid.*, p. 945; *Monnaie, prix et change.* Paris, 1927.

[14] Ch.-H. Turgeon: *La valeur d'aprés les économistes anglais depuis Adam Smith jusqu'à nos jours.* Rennes, 1913; Ch. Turgeon: "Critique de l'utilité finale," *Rev. d'Éc. Pol.*, vol. 39, 1925, 74, 713, 876, and 1032; Ch. and Ch.-H. Turgeon: *Études sur la valeur*, 3 vols. Paris, 1925–27. The first vol. is a third edition of the above mentioned historical work of Ch.-H. Turgeon, the second vol. is critical, and the third contains their positive theory.

[15] "La théorie de la valeur, d'après un livre récent," *Rev. d'Éc. Pol.*, vol. 41, 1927, p. 1175.

[16] *Théorie de la Valeur. Réfutation des théories de Rodbertus, Karl Marx, Stanley Jevons et Böhm-Bawerk.* Paris, 1903; 2nd ed. Paris, 1913.

[17] *Cf.* besides his text-book: *Problemi speciali di valore di scambio.* Naples, 1910, a collection of several essays.

[18] *Il principio del valore e la misura quantitativa del lavoro*, Palermo, 1906.

[19] "Introduzione ad una teoria sociologica del valore," *Giorn. d. Ec.*, vol. 67, 1926; "Il problema del valore," *ibid.*, pp. 537 and 606.

[20] *Utilità limite e costo di riproduzione.* Bologna, 1901.

[21] *Saggi critici di economia politica.* Turin, 1901.

[22] "*La teoria del valore di Francesco Ferrara*," *Rif. Soc.*, 1901, 3rd no. of 15. July.

[23] "Su una critica ed un libro di critica," *Giorn. d. Ec.*, vol. 23, 1901, p. 402.

[24] "Appunti critici alla teoria del costo di riproduzione," *Giorn. d. Ec.*, vol. 32, 1906, p. 218.

[25] "La critica di Achille Loria alla teoria del valore di Francesco Ferrara," *Giorn d. Ec.*, vol. 32, 1906, p. 392.

[26] "La teoria del costo di riproduzione e la critica," *Giorn. d. Ec.*, vol. 32, 1906, p. 502, and vol. 33, 1906, p. 318.

[27] *Legge di valore. Grado finale di utilità. Costo di reproduzione.* Roma, 1928.

[28] "La teoria dell'astinenza," *Giorn. d. Ec.*, vol. 37, 1908, pp. 295 and 511.

[29] *Prezzo e sovraprezzo nella economia capitalistica.* Milan, 1923; *La concezione del sovralavoro e la teoria del valore.* Rome, 1925; *Il prezzo e il sovraprezzo in rapporto ai consumatori ed ai lavoratori.* Rome, 1925; *Le teorie del valore ed il problema del capitale 'costante' (tecnico).* Rome, 1926.

[30] *Il costo di produzione.* Turin, 1901.

[31] "La valeur et les prix," *Journ. d. Éc.*, Sér. 6, vol. 78, 1924, p. 221, an extract of his speech before the Paris Statistical Society.

[32] *De quelques théories sur la valeur en économie politique.* Paris, 1924.

[33] "Memorie sul Principio della convenienza economica e la scienza delle quantità," *Giorn. d. Ec.*, vol. 22, 1901, p. 470.

[34] "Osservazioni ad una memoria del. Prof. Gobbi sul principio della convenienza economica," *Atti dell'Accademia Pontiana*, Gennaio, 1901.

[35] *Crit. Soc.*, 1. Febr. 1901.

[36] "Il principio della convenienza economica e la scienza delle quantatà," *Giorn. d. Ec.*, vol. 22, 1901, p. 470.

[37] *Giorn. d. Ec.*, vol. 23, 1901, p. 62.

CHAPTER IV

[1] "Osservazioni sulla teoria del baratto secondo il prof. Walras," *Giorn. d. Ec.*, vol. 24, 1902, p. 282; "Osservazioni su alcune teorie di economia pura," *ibid.*, vol. 25, 1902, p. 503; "A proposito del massimo di ofelimità dato dalla libera concorrenza," *ibid.*, vol. 26, 1903, p. 41.

[2] *Cf.* besides the work which we have already mentioned: "Curve piane di offerta dei prodotti," *Giorn. d. Ec.*, vol. 33, 1906, p. 223 and "Elasticità dei bisogni, della domanda e dell'offerta," *ibid.*, vol. 65, 1924, p. 413 and 509.

[3] "Tentativi di ricerca sulle funzioni di domanda e di offerta nel caso del baratto, supposte le ofelimità elementari linearii," *Giorn. d. Ec.*, vol. 29, 1904, p. 210.

[4] *Quantità e prezzi di equilibro per domanda ed offerta in condizioni di concorrenza, di monopolio e di sindacato fra imprendatori (con particolari applicazioni all'industria del nitrato sodico)*. Rome, 1918.

[5] "Considerazioni sulle proprietà di un sistema di prezzi politici," *Giorn. d. Ec.*, vol. 42, 1911, pp. 9 and 114.

[6] "La teoria matematica del monopolio trattata geometricamente," *Giorn. d. Ec.*, vol. 43, 1911, p. 207.

[7] *Contributo alla teoria dell'offerta a costi giunti.* Rome, 1914.

[8] *Contributo alla teoria economica dei beni succedanei.* Milan, 1926.

[9] "Prezzi e consumi," *Giorn. d. Ec.*, vol. 40, 1910, pp. 99 and 235.

[10] "Di alcune relazioni fra prezzi presenti e prezzi futuri nel mercato dei prodotti," *Giorn. d. Ec.*, vol. 50, 1915, p. 311.

[11] "Problemi d'economia politica visti da un statistico," *Ann. d. Ec.*, vol. 1, Milan, 1924, p. 217.

[12] "La dinamica dei prezzi decrescenti e il riordinamento della circolazione," *Giorn. d. Ec.*, vol. 66, 1925, p. 30.

[13] "Sulle relazioni fra costo e quantità prodotta," *Ann. d. Ec.*, vol. 2, Milan, 1925.

[14] "Il costo quale elemento della teoria economica," *Giorn. d. Ec.*, vol. 67, 1926, p. 167.

[15] *Sul costo di produzione nei cicli economici.* Rome, 1926.

[16] *Riflessioni sull'equilibrio economico. Teoria del duplice costo di produzione. Costo marginale e costo ultramarginale.* Reggio-Calabria, 1926.

[17] The French translation by José d'Almada from the Portuguese: *Théorie mathématique de l'échange.* Paris, 1913.

[18] *Etudes sur la formation et le mouvement des prix.* Paris, 1913.

[19] *Sur les prix et la théorie générale de l'équilibre,* in the collection which we have mentioned above: *Problèmes actuels de l'économique.* Paris, 1921.

[20] *La théorie des prix de monopole.* Paris, 1927.

[21] "La valeur mathématico-économique de la loi de King," *Rev. d'Éc. Pol.*, vol. 37, 1923, p. 481.

[22] *La loi de la variation de la valeur et les mouvements généraux des prix.* Paris, 1927.

[23] "Prix-valeur. Énoncés fondamentaux," *Rev. d'Éc. Pol.*, vol. 36, 1922, p. 181.

[24] "Hausses et baisses générales des prix," *Rev. d'Éc. Pol.*, vol. 26, 1912, p. 452.

[25] *Le prix des produits à frais croissants et celui des produits reproductibles à gré.* Brussels, 1926.

[26] "Il prezzo come strumento di lotta fra organismi." *Giorn. d. Ec.*, vol. 40, 1910, p. 171.

[27] *Les prix de monopole d'après les doctrines et dans les faits,* Paris, 1926.

[28] *L'idée du juste prix: Essai de psychologie économique.* Paris, 1907.

[29] "A la recherche du "juste prix," *Journ. d. Éc.*, Sér. 6, vol. 77, 1924, p. 299 and vol. 78, 1924, p. 18.

[30] "Etude critique de la loi le l'offre et de la demande," *Journ. d. Éc.*, Sér. 6, vol. 82, 1925, p. 25.

CHAPTER V

[1] "Dell'influenza delle condizioni economiche sulla forma della curva dei redditi," *Giorn. d. Ec.*, vol. 31, 1925, p. 115.

[2] "Sulla curva di distribuzione dei redditi," *Giorn. d. Ec.* vol. 38, 1909, p. 557.

[3] "Note sulla curva Paretiana dei redditi," *Giorn. d. Ec.*, vol. 37, 1909, p. 695.

[4] "Note di economia induttiva. Sulla distribuzione dei redditi," *Giorn. d. Ec.*, vol. 42, 1911, p. 455.

[5] "Che cosa è il reddito?" *Giorn. d. Ec.*, vol. 47, 1913, p. 93.

[6] "L'indice di variabilità e la curva dei redditi," *Giorn. d. Ec.*, vol. 53, 1916, p. 177.

[7] "Economie optimiste et économie scientifique. II. Distribution des richesses," *Rev. de Mét.*, vol. 15, 1907, p. 596.

[8] "Les trois notions de la productivité et les revenus." *Rev. d'Éc. Pol.*, vol. 25, 1911, pp. 145 and 345.

[9] "Les expériences monétaires récentes et la théorie du revenu," *Rev. d'Éc. Pol.*, vol. 39, 1925, p. 813.

[10] "Une nouvelle théorie de la répartition de la richesse," *Journ d. Éc. Sér.* 6, vol. 18, 1908, p. 329.

[11] "La loi de la distribution," *Journ. d. Éc.*, Sér. 5, vol. 41, 1900, p. 36.

[12] *De l'influence de la baisse du taux de l'intérêt sur la baisse des salaires*, Paris, 1899.

[13] "Deux sophismes économiques. La théorie de la répartition proportionelle chez Bastiat et Rodbertus," *Rev. d'Éc. Pol.*, vol. 19, 1905, p. 223.

[14] *La sintesi economica, studio delle leggi del reddito.* Turin, 1909.

[15] *La sintesi economica, analisi dell'opera di A. Loria.* Turin, 1911.

[16] *Distribuzione del dividende e produttività marginali*, Naples, 1900.

[17] *Le leggi della distribuzione moderna.* Palermo, 1907.

[18] "Note sur la loi du rendement non proportionnel," *Rev. d'Éc. Pol.*, vol. 24, 1910, p. 532.

[19] "Essai de philosophie économique. La loi du rendement décroissant, sa signification et ses conséquences." *Journ. d. Éc.*, Sér. 6, vol. 43, 1914, pp. 23 and 296.

[20] *Principii di economia della produzione. Il prezzo di produzione*, Turin, 1920.

[21] "La base agronomica della teoria della rendità," articles in the *Giorn. d. Ec.*, vols. 11, 12, and 13, 1895–1896.

[22] *La teoria della "Rendita."* Rome, 1912.

[23] *Cf.* Valenti for an excellent criticism of Loria's theory, which belongs to the last century: "La rendita di monopolio" and "Il diritto alla terra e il salario territoriale," *Giorn. d. Ec.*, vol. 21, 1900, p. 216 and 449.

[24] "I 'benefici' del produttore," *Giorn. d. Ec.*, vols. 62–63, 1922, p. 101.

[25] "Intorno ad alcuni punti della teoria della rendita," *Giorn. d. Ec.*, vol. 64, 1923, p. 397.

[26] *Esquisse d'une théorie générale de la rente suivie d'une critique des principales opinions émises sur le même sujet.* Lausanne, 1912.

[27] *La théorie de la rente et son extension récente dans la science économique.* Montpellier, 1908.

[28] *Disarmonie economiche e disarmonie morali. Saggio di un estensione della teoria ricardiana della rendita.* Florence, 1906.

[29] "Sulla misura del vantaggio che il consumatore ritrae da uno scambio," *Giorn. d. Ec.*, vol. 52, 1916, p. 101.

[30] "Discussione del systema di equazioni che definiscono l'equilibrio del consumatore," *Ann. d. Ec.*, vol. 4, 1928, p. 31.

[31] "La loi de la demande individuelle et la rente de consommateur," *Rev. d'Éc. Pol.*, vol. 40, 1926, p. 5.

[32] "Sur la rente des consommateurs," *Rev. d'Éc. Pol.*, vol. 18, 1904, pp. 477 and 611.

[33] "La rendita del consumatore e le sue applicazioni finanziarie," *Giorn. d. Ec.*, vol. 61, 1921, p. 157.

[34] *Relazioni fra entrata e consumo.* Rome, 1912.

[35] "Sulla teoria del bilancio del consumatore," *Giorn. d. Ec.*, vol. 50, 1914, p. 1.

[36] "Sul concetto di reddito in relazione al consumo," *Giorn. d. Ec.*, vol. 42, 1911, p. 160.

[37] *Le rôle du consommateur dans l'économie moderne.* Paris, 1922.

[38] "Sulla teoria economica della capitalizzazione," *Giorn. d. Ec.*, vol. 49, 1914, p. 225.

[39] *L'épargne, son mécanisme social et psychologique*, in the collection, *Problèmes actuels de l'économique*, Paris, 1921, and "Quelques définitions de l'épargne. Essai critique," *Rev. d'Éc. Pol.*, vol. 35, 1921, p. 729.

[40] "Le capital provient-il uniquement du travail?" *Rev. d'Éc. Pol.*, vol. 20, 1906, p. 105.

[41] "Contributions aux théories du capital et du revenu," *Rev. d'Éc. Pol.*, vol. 36, 1922, pp. 157 and 465.

[42] "Les causes des variations du taux de l'intérê," *Rev. d'Éc. Pol.*, vol. 36, 1922, pp. 157 and 465.

[43] "L'offerta del risparmio," *Giorn. d. Ec.*, vol. 67, 1926, p. 73 and p. 117; "Ancora sull'offerta del risparmio," *ibid.*, vol. 68, 1927, p. 480.

[44] *Il capitale. Saggio di economia teoretica.* Turin, 1910. *Cf.* also the detailed review of the work of Irving Fisher, which we shall discuss later: "Natura del capitale e del reddito," *Giorn. d. Ec.*, vol. 35, 1907, p. 821.

[45] "Observations sur l'intérêt du capital," *Rev. d'Éc. Pol.*, vol. 41, 1927, p. 1088.

[46] "Revisione critica dei recenti concetti nella teoria del capitale e delle loro fondamentali applicazioni," *Giorn. d. Ec.*, vol. 38, 1909, p. 327.

[47] "Lineamenti generali della teoria dell'interesse," *Giorn. d. Ec.*, vol. 51, 1914, pp. 273 and 366.

[48] *Cf.* besides the *Istituzioni*, also *Capitale e interesse.* Naples, 1923.

[49] *Saggio sulla teoria dell'interesse in economia e finanza.* Turin, 1901.

[50] *L'intérêt du capital.* Paris, 1903. *Cf.* also his above mentioned *Manuel.*

[51] *Il capitale salari.* Turin, 1900.

[52] *La teoria del salario nella storia delle dottrine e nei fatti economici.* Palermo, 1900.

[53] *Cf.* his review of Ricca-Salerno's work in the *Giorn. d. Ec.*, vol. 22, 1901, p. 273.

[54] *Il Salario.* Milan, 1916.

[55] *Capitale e colonie.* Milan, 1927, and *Capitale e salari.* Milan, 1928.

[56] "Dell'influenza delle coalizioni operaie sull'aumento nel saggio del salari," *Giorn. d. Ec.*, vol. 40, 1910, pp. 407 and 553.

[57] *Salariat et salaires.* Paris, 1909.

[58] "Causes déterminants du taux des salaires," *Rev. d'Ec. Pol.*, vol. 21, 1907, p. 729.

[59] *Théorie du salaire et du travail salarié*, Paris, 1908.

[60] *Le salaire des ouvriers des mines de charbon en France.* Paris, 1907.

[61] "Une théorie negligée. De l'influence de la direction de la demande, sur la productivité du travail, les salaires et la population," *Rev. d'Éc. Pol.*, vol. 24, 1910, p. 314, 364, 747, and 773.

[62] *L'idée du juste salaire*, Paris, 1903.

[63] *Vers le salaire minimum.* Paris, 1912.

[64] *Le travail humain, son utilisation et sa rémunération*, in the collection *Problèmes actuels de l'économique.* Paris, 1921.

[65] "Die Lohntheorie," in the collection: *Die Wirtschaftstheorie der Gegenwart*, ed. by Hans Mayer, etc., vol. 3, Vienna, 1928, p. 98.

[66] *Il profitto. Appunti di critica economica intorno ad un particolare aspetto dell'odierna questione sociale.* Roma, 1901.

[67] "L'inesistenza di plus-valore nel lavoro e la fonte del profitto," *Giorn. d. Ec.*, vol. 34, 1906, p. 48.

[68] *Traité général de science économique.* Tome 3: *Théorie du capital et du profit*, 2 vols. Paris, 1926.

[69] *Le problème du profit.* Paris, 1926.

[70] "Intorno alla teoria del 'profitto,'" *Giorn. d. Ec.*, vol. 69, 1928, p. 27.

[71] "Untersuchungen zur Theorie des Unternehmergewinns," in the collection: *Die Wirtschaftstheorie der Gegenwart*, ed. by Hans Mayer, etc., 3rd vol. Vienna, 1928, p. 281.

[72] "La classificazione dei rischi," *Rivista di Politica Economica*, 1927, pp. 101, 205, and 317; "La nozione economica del rischio," *Giorn. d. Ec.*, vol. 68, 1927, p. 65 and "Il caso, la congiuntura ed il rischio nell'evoluzione economica," *ibid.*, vol. 69, 1928, p. 131.

[73] *I profitti industriali nella costituzione economica odierna*, Turin, 1907.

PART FOUR

CHAPTER I

[1] *Memorials of Alfred Marshall*, edited by A. C. Pigou. London—New York, 1925, p. 427.

[2] *Papers Relating to Political Economy*, 3 vols. London, 1925.

[3] A *Geometrical Political Economy. Being an Elementary Treatise on the Method of Explaining Some of the Theories of Pure Economic Science by Means of Diagrams.* Oxford, 1904.

[4] *The Mathematical Groundwork of Economics.* New York, 1924.

[5] For example, Jones D. Caradog and G. W. Daniels, *Elements of Mathematics, for Students of Economics and Statistics.* Liverpool, 1926. *Cf.* the above mentioned similar attempt of the Frenchmen Leseine and Suret.

[6] "The Statistical Complement of Pure Economics," *Quart. Journ. of Ec.*, vol. 23, 1908–09, p. 1.

[7] Besides the corresponding passages in his systematic works, which we shall mention later, *cf.* esp.: "A Suggestion for a New Economic Arithmetic," *Ec. Journ.*, vol. 18, 1908, p. 19.

[8] *Graphic Methods for Presenting Facts.* New York, 1914.

[9] "A Study in the Science of Welfare," *Quart. Journ. of Ec.*, vol. 17, p. 199.

[10] "The Fundamental Economic Principle," *Quart. Journ. of Ec.*, vol. 15, 1900, p. 218.

[11] *Natural Economy, an Introduction to Political Economy.* Birmingham, 1900.

[12] "One of the Physical Foundations of Economics," *Quart. Journ. of Ec.*, vol. 33, 1918–19, p. 717.

[13] *Physical Economics: An Essay on Fundamental Principles.* London, 1921.

[14] *Economic Method and Economic Fallacies.* London, 1904.

[15] *Disturbing Elements in the Study and Teaching of Political Economy.* Baltimore, 1911.

[16] "A Functional approach to Social-Economic Data," *Journ. of Pol. Ec.*, vol. 28, 1920, p. 529.

[17] *Free Thought in the Social Sciences.* New York, 1926.

[18] *The Casual Laborer and Other Essays.* New York, 1920, esp. "Motives of Economic Life."

[19] "A Revaluation of Traditional Economic Theory," *Am. Ec. Rev.*, vol. 11, 1921, Suppl. p. 123.

[20] *A Critique of Economics.* New York, 1922.

[21] "The Emancipation of Economics," *Am. Ec. Rev.*, vol. 14, 1924, p. 17.

[22] "Psychology in Economic Theory," *Journ. of Pol. Ec.*, vol. 32, 1924, p. 487.

[23] "The Behavioristic Man," *Quart. Journ. of Ec.*, vol. 33, 1919, p. 195.

[24] Besides his book, *Economic Motives, a Study in the Psychological Foundations of Economical Theory with Some Reference to Other Social Sciences*, Cambridge and New York, 1922, *cf.* esp. the articles: "The Relations of Recent Psychological Developments to Economic Theory," *Quart. Journ. of Ec.*, vol. 33, 1918–19, p. 377, and "Quantitative Methods in Psychological Economics," *Am. Ec. Rev.*, vol. 14, 1924, p. 117.

[25] *Cf.* his article on the latest development of economic research in America in the collection *Die Wirtschaftstheorie der Gegenwart*, edited by Hans Mayer *et al.*, vol. 1, Vienna, 1927, p. 31.

[26] *Economics and Human Behaviour. A Rejoinder to Social Psychologists*, London, 1927; and "Irrtümer einer Wirtschaftstheorie ohne statistische Grundlage," *Arch. f. Sozwiss.*, vol. 59, 1928, p. 526.

[27] "Economics as a Field of Research," *Quart. Journ. of Ec.*, vol. 42, 1927–28, p. 1.

[28] "Some Problems of Logical Method in Political Economy," *Journ. of Pol. Ec.*, vol. 25, 1917, p. 236.

[29] "Some Positive Contributions of the Institutional Concept," *Quart. Journ. of Ec.*, vol. 41, 1926–27, p. 405.

[30] A list of independent treatises gathered together in the volume: *Contemporary Economic Thought*, New York, 1928.

[31] "Social Aspects of Economic Law," Publ. of the *Am. Ec. Assn.*, Ser. 3, vol. 5, 1904, p. 49.

[32] *The Economic Interpretation of History.* New York and London, 1902.

[33] "The Present State of the Theory of Distribution," *Publ. of the Am. Ec. Ass.*, Ser. 3, vol. 7, 1906, p. 24.

[34] "The Making of Economic Literature," *Publ. of the Am. Ec. Ass.*, Ser. 3, vol. 10, 1909, p. 1.

[35] "Distribution by the Law of Rent," *Publ. of the Am. Ec. Ass.*, Ser. 3, vol. 4, 1903, p. 154.

[36] *Am. Ec. Rev.*, vol. 3, 1913, Suppl. p. 89.

[37] *The Reconstruction of Economic Theory.* Philadelphia, 1912.

[38] "Observations in Economics," *Publ. of the Am. Ec. Ass.*, Ser. 3, vol. 11, 1910, p. 29.

[39] "Economic Theorizing and Scientific Progress," *Am. Ec. Rev.*, vol. 6, 1916, Suppl. p. 124.

[40] "Economic Theory in the Calculable Future," *Am. Ec. Rev.*, vol. 15, 1925, Suppl. p. 48.—Notice esp. too, *The Place of Science in Modern Civilization and Other Essays*, New York, 1919, in which there is a collection of Veblen's most important critical works.

[41] "The Use of the Quantitative Method in the Study of Economic Theory," *Am. Ec. Rev.*, vol. 27, 1927, Suppl. p. 18.

[42] "The Present Status and Future Prospects of Quantitative Economics," *Am. Ec. Rev.*, vol. 18, 1928, Suppl. p. 28.

[43] "Quantitative Analysis and the Evolution of Economic Science," *Am. Ec. Rev.*, vol. 16, 1926, pp. 426; and "The Significance and Use of Data in the Social Sciences," *Ec. Journ.*, vol. 38, 1928, p. 63.

[44] *The Trend of Economics.* New York, 1924.

[45] The average age of the authors at the time of the publication was 37 years.

[46] *Some Recent Developments of Economic Theory*, p. 271.

[47] *The Limitations of Scientific Method in Economics*," p. 229.

[48] *Cf.* his more recent treatises: "Ethics and the Economic Interpretation," *Quart. Journ. of Ec.*, vol. 36, 1921–22, p. 454; "The Ethics of Competition," *ibid.*, vol. 37, 1922–23, p. 579; "Facts and Metaphysics in Economic Psychology," *Am. Ec. Rev.*, vol. 15, 1925, p. 247.

[49] *Amer. Ec. Rev.*, vol. 11, 1921, Suppl. p. 143.

[50] "Professor Knight on Psychology," *Quart. Journ. of Ec.*, vol. 40, 1925–26, p. 134.

[51] *Functional Economics*, p. 445.

[52] "Economics and Modern Psychology," *Journ. of Pol. Ec.*, vol. 26, 1918, pp. 1 and 136.

[53] "Soundings in Non-Euclidean Economics," *Am. Ec. Rev.*, vol. 11, 1921, p. 132.

[54] *The Socializing of Theoretical Economics*, p. 73. *Cf.* also his latest essay "Recent Developments in Economics" in the collection *Recent Developments in the Social Sciences*, ed. by E. C. Hayes. Philadelphia and London, 1927.

[55] "The Relation between Statics and Dynamics," in the collection *Economic Essays, Contributed in Honor of John Bates Clark*, pub. by J. H. Hollander, New York, 1927, p. 46.

[56] *Experimental Economics*, p. 371.

[57] *The Organization and Control of Economic Activity*, p. 303.

[58] "Human Nature in Economic Theory," *Journ. of Pol. Ec.*, vol. 30, 1922, p. 317.

[59] *On Measurement in Economics*, p. 37.

[60] *Statistical Methods Applied to Economics and Business.* New York, 1927.

[61] *Regional Comparison and Economic Progress*, p. 425.

[62] *The Prospects of Economics*, p. 3.

[63] "Quantitative Analysis in Economic Theory," *Am. Ec. Rev.*, vol. 15, 1925, p. 1.

[64] "Human Behavior and Economics: A Survey of Recent Literature," *Quart. Journ. of Ec.*, vol. 29, 1914–15, p. 1; "Wieser's Theory of Social Economics," *Pol. Sci. Quart.*, vol. 32, 1917, p. 95; "Bentham's Felicific Calculus, *ibid.*, vol. 33, 1918, p. 161.

[65] *Legal Foundations of Capitalism.* New York, 1924; also, recently, a short treatise "Das Anglo-Amerikanische Recht und die Wirtschaftstheorie," in the collection *Die Wirtschaftstheorie der Gegenwart*, ed. by Hans Mayer *et al.*, vol. 3. Vienna, 1928, p. 293.

[66] *Cf.* the two treatises: "The Present Position of Political Economy," *Ec. Journ.*, vol. 17, 1907, p. 467, and "The Enlargement of Economics," *ibid.*, vol. 18, 1908, p. 181.

[67] "The Social Point of View in Economics," *Quart. Journ. of Ec.*, vol. 28, 1913–14, pp. 115 and 292.

[68] *Economics as the Basis of Living Ethics.* New York, 1913.

[69] *Economics and Ethics: a Treatise on Wealth and Life.* London, 1923.

[70] "Economic Theory and Political Morality," *Pub. of the Am. Ec. Ass.*, Ser. 3, vol. 1, 1900, p. 45.

[71] *Cf. Am. Ec. Rev.*, vol. 12, 1922, Suppl., p. 192.

[72] *The Principles of Business Economics.* London, 1924.

[73] *Problems in Business Economics.* Chicago, 1924.

[74] *The Principles of Scientific Management.* New York, 1911.

[75] *The Political Economy of War.* London, 1915.

[76] *Economics in the Light of War.* London, 1916.

[77] *An Economic Interpretation of the War.* New York, 1915.

[78] *On the Relations of Political Economy to War.* Oxford, 1915.

[79] *The Economic Consequences of the Peace.* London, 1919.

[80] *Political Economy of War.* London, 1921.

[81] "Economics and War," *Am. Ec. Rev.*, vol. 16, 1926, p. 1.

CHAPTER II

[1] *The Theory of Political Economy*, 4th ed. London, 1911.

[2] *The Principles of Economics. A Fragment of a Treatise on the Industrial Mechanics of Society and Other Papers.* London, 1905.

[3] *Essays on Economics.* London, 1905.

[4] *The Principles of Economics*, 5th ed. London, 1907; the last edition revised by Marshall was published in 1920.

[5] *Industry and Trade. A Study of Industrial Technic and Business Organization, and of their Influences on the Conditions of Various Classes and Nations.* London, 1920, 5th ed. 1923; and *Money, Credit and Commerce*, London, 1923.

[6] *Principles of Political Economy*, 3 vols., London, 1893–1901.

[7] "The Use and Abuse of Authority in Economics," *Ec. Journ.*, vol. 13, 1903, p. 554.

[8] "The Vagaries of Recent Political Economy" (a collective review of the works of Sidgwick, Pareto, Colson, Wicksteed, Pigou, and Pierson), *Quart. Rev.*, vol. 219, 1913, p. 406.

[9] *Elements of Political Economy.* London, 1903.

[10] *Economic Principles: An Introductory Study*, London, 1904; 2nd ed. *ibid.*, 1923.

[11] *Principles of Economics*, 2 vols. London, 1902–12.

[12] *The Common Sense of Political Economy, including a Study of the Human Basis of Economic Law.* London, 1910.

[13] "The Scope and Method of Political Economy in the Light of the 'Marginal' Theory of Value and Distribution," *Ec. Journ.*, vol. 24, 1914, p. 1.

[14] *Cf.* in Pigou's edition: *Memorials of Alfred Marshall*, New York, 1925, which contains, besides some rare essays of Marshall and his scientific correspondence, valuable representations of the master's efficacy, especially by Keynes, Edgeworth and the editor.

[15] *Wealth and Welfare.* London, 1912; *The Economics of Welfare.* London, 1920, 2nd ed. *ibid.*, 1924.

[16] *Industrial Fluctuations.* London, 1927.

[17] *Essays in Applied Economics.* London, 1923.

[18] *Ec. Journ.*, vol. 23, 1913, p. 62, and vol. 35, 1925, p. 30.

[19] *Quart. Rev.*, vol. 219, 1913, p. 415.

[20] *Ec. Journ.*, vol. 31, 1921, p. 206.

[21] *Quart. Journ. of Ec.*, vol. 27, 1912–13, p. 672.

[22] *Am. Ec. Rev.*, vol. 16, 1926, p. 51.

[23] *Outlines of Political Economy*, London, 1911, 3rd ed. *ibid.*, 1917; *Political Economy*. London, 1912; *Elementary Economics*. London, 1913.

[24] *The Theory of Marginal Value*. London and New York, 1922.

[25] *The Relation of Wealth to Welfare*. New York, 1925.

[26] *The Essentials of Economic Theory as Applied to Modern Problems of Industry and Public Policy*. New York, 1907.

[27] *Principles of Economics with Special Reference to American Conditions*. London and New York, 1905; 11th ed., New York, 1926. *Cf.* also the recent collection of his economic essays, *Essays in Economics*. New York, 1925.

[28] *The Economics of Installment Selling. A Study in Consumer's Credit with Special Reference to the Automobile*. 2 vols., New York, 1927. This has since been translated into French, German, Spanish and Italian.

[29] "Seligman's Principles of Economics," *Quart. Journ. of Ec.*, vol. 20, 1905–06, p. 622.

[30] *Quart. Journ. of Ec.*, vol. 21, 1906–07, p. 151.

[31] *Principles of Economics*, 2 vols. New York, 1911; 3rd ed., New York, 1921.

[32] "Die Sozialökonomie in den Vereinigten Staaten," in the *Festschrift* for Lujo Brentano on his 80th birthday, Munich and Leipsic, 1925, vol. II, p. 70.

[33] *Introduction to Economics*, New York, 1904; *Principles of Economics, Being a Revision of Introduction to Economics*, New York, 1913; 3rd ed. revised and augmented, New York, 1923.

[34] *Economics (Briefer Course)*. New York, 1909.

[34a] Elementary Principles of Economics. New York, 1912.

[35] *The Economics of Enterprise*. New York, 1913. Most of the essential ideas in this book were contained in Davenport's earlier work: *Value and Distribution. A Critical and Constructive Study*. Chicago, 1908.

[36] "Davenport's Economics and the Present Problems of Theory," *Quart. Journ. of Ec.*, vol. 28, 1913–14, p. 417.

[37] *Introductory Economics*. New York, 1907.

[38] *Introduction to Economics*. New York, 1909.

[39] "The Next Decade of Economic Theory," *Publ. of the Am. Ec. Ass.*, Ser. 3, vol. 2, 1901, p. 236.

[40] *The Principles of Economics, with Applications to Practical Problems*. New York, 1904.

[41] *Cf.* esp. the later edition of his system: *Economics, vol. I. Economic Principles*, New York 1915, *vol. II. Modern Economic Problems, ibid.*, 1916; 2nd ed. *ibid.* 1922–23.

[42] *Cf.* Price Economics versus Welfare Economics," *Am. Ec. Rev.*, vol. 9, 1919, p. 467 and "The Economists and the Public," *ibid.*, vol. 15, 1925, p. 13.

[43] *Principles of Political Economy*. Boston, 1919. The main lines of his system have appeared in his earlier works.

[44] *Cf.* "The Concept of Economic Quantity," *Quart. Journ. of Ec.*, vol. 21, 1906–07, p. 427, and the remarks of George Ray Wickers: "Professor Carver's Concept of an Economic Quantity," *ibid.*, vol. 22, 1907–08, p. 645.

[45] *Essays in Social Justice*. Cambridge, Mass., 1915.

[46] *Elementary Economics.* Boston, 1921.

[47] *The Present Economic Revolution in the United States.* Boston, 1925.

[48] *Cf.* "An Eminent Economist Confused," also "A Rejoinder" of Carver's, and "A Re-rejoinder" of Brown's, *Quart. Journ. of Ec.*, vol. 23, 1918–19, p. 567.

[49] *Economic Science and Common Welfare.* Columbia, 1923.

[50] *Introduction into Economics.* London, 1919.

[51] *Principles of Economics.* New York, 1921.

[52] *Essentials of Economics.* New York, 1923.

[53] *Elementary Economics.* New York, 1926.

[54] *Principles of Economics.* New York, 1924.

[55] *Applied Economics.* New York, 1928.

[56] *Rudiments of Economics.* New York, 1927.

[57] *Principles of Economics.* New York, 1925.

[58] *Principles of the New Economics.* New York, 1922; and recently, *Economics: Principles and Problems.* New York, 1926.

[59] *American Economic Life and the Means of Its Improvement.* New York, 1925.

[60] *Wealth: A Brief Explanation of the Causes of Economic Welfare.* London, 1914.

[61] *The Economic Outlook.* London, 1912, and *An Economist's Protest.* London, 1927.

[62] *Principles of Comparative Economics,* with a Preface by Raphael Georges Lévy. 2 vols., London, 1921–22.

[63] *Borderlands of Economics.* London, 1925, and *Ground Work of Economics.* New York, 1925.

[64] *A National System of Economics: With a Consideration of the Paris Economic Resolutions and of Their Influence on Nationality.* London, 1917.

[65] *Economics: An Introduction for the General Reader.* London, 1916.

[66] *Cf.* the American edition, published by Agger, New York, 1918.

[67] *The Economic Problem.* New York, 1926.

[68] *Political Economy.* 2nd ed., London, 1901.

[69] *Political Economy.* New York, 1913.

[70] *Essays in Economic Theory,* ed. by R. G. Tugwell, with an introd. by H. R. Seager. New York, 1924.

[71] *The Theory of Prosperity.* New York, 1902.

[72] *The Principles of Wealth and Welfare.* New York and London, 1906.

[73] *The Science of Wealth.* New York, 1912.

[74] *Elements of Political Economy.* London, 1903.

[75] *Elementary Principles of Economics.* New York, 1904.

[76] *Outlines of Economics.* New York, 1908; 4th ed., *ibid.*, 1923.

[77] *The Elements of Economics.* New York, 1905; rev. and enlarged ed. Boston, 1923. Bullock's earliest text-book was *Introduction to Economics.* New York, 1887.

[78] *Elementary Economics, with Special Reference to Social and Business Conditions in the United States.* Boston, 1920.

[79] *Introduction to Economic Problems.* New York, 1922.

[80] *Principles of Economic: An Elementary Text.* New York, 1923.

[81] *Economics.* New York, 1908.

[82] *Elements of Economics, with Special Reference to American Conditions.* New York, 1912.

[83] *Economics, Descriptive and Theoretical.* London, 1911.

[84] *The Economics of Everyday Life: A First Book of Economic Study.* 2 vols., Cambridge, Mass., 1913–21.
[85] *Introduction to the Study of Economics.* Boston, 1924.
[86] *The Science of Prices: A Handbook of Economics (Production, Consumption and Value).* New York, 1925; and *The Mechanism of Exchange.* London, 1927.
[87] *Everyone's Economics.* London, 1924.
[88] *Elements of Economics.* St. Albans, 1924.
[89] *A Text-book of Economics.* London, 1921.
[90] *Groundwork of Economics.* Cambridge, 1928.
[91] *Elements of Economics.* New York, 1927.
[92] *Economics, Principles and Interpretation.* Chicago and New York, 1928.
[93] *Principles of Economics.* Boston, 1927.
[94] *Practical Economics.* New York, 1922.
[95] *Wealth and Work*, London, 1921.
[96] *Materials for the Study of Elementary Economics.* Chicago, 1913.
[97] *Our Economic System.* 2 vols., New York, 1928.
[98] *Economics: Practical Exposition of Science of Business.* Chicago, 1909.
[99] *Data of Economics.* London, 1916.
[100] *The Economics of Progress.* London, 1918.
[101] *An Introduction to Social Economics.* New York, 1923.
[102] *Introduction to Economics.* Boston, 1923.
[103] *A Short Course of Economic Science.* London, 1923.
[104] *A Groundwork of Economics.* Dublin, 1925.
[105] *National Economy.* London, 1917.
[106] *Economics for Beginners.* London, 1921.
[107] *The Economic World.* London, 1927.
[108] *Economics.* New York, 1920.
[109] *Elementary Economics.* New York, 1920.
[110] *Social Economics.* London, 1920; *cf.* also his larger work, *The Economics of Private Enterprise.* London, 1926.
[111] *Plain Economics.* London, 1921.

CHAPTER III

[1] "Is 'Utility' the Most Suitable Term for the Concept it is used to denote?" *Am. Ec. Rev.*, vol. 8, 1918, p. 335.
[2] *Mathematical Investigations in the Theory of Value and Prices.* New Haven, 1925.
[3] "Social Elements in the Theory of Value," *Quart. Journ. of Ec.*, vol. 15, 1900–01, p. 321.
[4] *The Theory of Value before Adam Smith*, Publ. of the Am. Ec. Ass., Ser. 3, vol. 2, 1901, p. 633.
[5] *Competitive and Social Value, Economica*, vol. 2, 1922, p. 278.
[6] "Marginal Utility and Marginal Disutility as Ultimate Standards of Value," *Quart. Journ. of Ec.*, vol. 27, 1912–1913, p. 547.
[7] *Cf.* especially recently: "Non-Competing Groups," *Quart. Journ. of Ec.*, vol. 40, 1925–26, p. 52.
[8] "Suggestions on the Theory of Value," *Quart. Journ. of Ec.* vol. 19, 1904–05, p. 571.
[9] "Prestige Value," *ibid.*, vol. 17, 1902–03, p. 465.
[10] "A Statistical Method for Measuring 'Marginal Utility' and Testing the Justice of a Progressive Income Tax," in the collection *Economic Essays Con-*

tributed in Honor of John Bates Clark, pub. by J. A. Hollander. New York, 1927, p. 157.

[11] *The Measurement of Economic Value*. San Francisco, 1925.

[12] "The Measurement of Time Valuation," *Am. Ec. Rev.*, vol. 18, 1928, p. 227.

[13] "Parity in the Exchange of Future Money and Future Commodities," *Quart. Journ. of Ec.*, vol. 42, 1927–28, p. 366.

[14] *The Flow of Value*. New York, 1919.

[15] *Prices and Wages: an Investigation of the Dynamic Forces in Social Economics*. London, 1921.

[16] *History and Criticism of the Labor Theory of Value in English Political Economy*. New York, 1904.

[17] *The Labour Theory of Value in Karl Marx*. London, 1923.

[18] Besides Davenport's two large works mentioned above, *cf.* esp. his essays: "Proposed Modifications in Austrian Theory and Terminology," *Quart. Journ. of Ec.*, vol. 16, 1901–02, p. 355; and "Cost and its Significance," *Am. Ec. Rev.*, vol. 1, 1911, p. 724.

[19] *Quart. Journ. of Ec.*, vol. 23, 1908–09, p. 151.

[20] Besides his famous *Common Sense* and earlier works, *cf.* esp. his more recent speech: "The Scope and Method of Political Economy in the Light of the 'Marginal' Theory of Value and Distribution," *Ec. Journ.*, vol. 24, 1914, p. 1.

[21] *Ec. Journ.*, vol. 24, 1914, p. 421.

[22] "The Pure Theory of Utility Curves," *Ec. Journ.*, vol. 23, 1913, p. 483.

[23] *Ec. Journ.*, vol. 25, 1915, p. 36.

[24] "Cost and Its Relation to Value," *Quart. Journ. of Ec.*, vol. 42, 1927–28, p. 530.

[25] *Social Value*, Boston, 1911.

[26] J. M. Clark, "The Concept of Value," Anderson: "The Concept of Value Further Considered," again Clark: "A Rejoinder," *Quart. Journ. of Ec.*, vol. 29, 1914–15, p. 663.

[27] "Economic Value and Moral Value," *Quart. Journ. of Ec.*, vol. 30, 1915–16, p. 443.

[28] "The Content of the Value Concept," *Quart. Journ. of Ec.*, vol. 31, 1916–17, p. 711.

[29] *The Psychological Theory of Value*. London, 1924.

[30] *The Four Kinds of Economic Value*. Cambridge, 1926.

[31] *Cf.* besides his important early works, esp.: "The Limitations of Marginal Utility," *Journ. of Pol. Ec.*, vol. 17, 1909, p. 620.

[32] "The Futility of Marginal Utility," *Journ. of Pol. Ec.*, vol. 18, p. 253.

[33] "The Place of Value Theory in Economics," *Journ. of Pol. Ec.*, vol. 26, 1918, pp. 217 and 375.

[34] *Cf.* his recent work on the subject: "Economic Psychology and the Value Problem," *Quart. Journ. of Ec.*, vol. 39, 1924–25, p. 372.

[35] "An Extension of Value Theory," *Quart. Journ. of Ec.*, vol. 36, 1921–22, p. 197.

[36] "Value and Larger Economics. I, Rise of the Marginal Doctrine," *Journ. of Pol. Ec.*, vol. 31, 1923, p. 587; and "II, Conditional Validity of Marginality Doctrine," *ibid.*, p. 790.

[37] "The Utility Concept of Value Theory and Its Critics," *Journ. of Pol. Ec.*, vol. 32, 1925, pp. 369 and 638.

[38] "Some Limitations of the Value Concept," *Quart. Journ. of Ec.*, vol. 25, 1910–11, p. 409.

CHAPTER IV

[1] "Marshall and Edgeworth on Value," *Ec. Journ.*, vol. 16, 1906, p. 365.

[2] "The Interdependence of Different Sources of Demand and Supply in a Market," *Ec. Journ.*, vol. 23, 1913, p. 18.

[3] "An Analysis of Supply," *Ec. Journ.*, vol. 38, 1928, p. 238.

[4] "The Representative Firm," *Ec. Journ.*, vol. 38, 1928, p. 387.

[5] "Are Manufactures Unstable Internationally?" *Ec. Journ.*, vol. 15, 1905, p. 186.

[5a] A Method of Determining the Numerical Value of Elasticities of Demand," *Ec. Journ.* vol. 20, 1910, p. 636.

[6] "Fetter's Theory of Value," *Quart. Journ. of Ec.*, vol. 19, 1904–05, p. 210.

[7] "The Definition of Price," *Am. Ec. Rev.*, vol. 2, 1912, p. 783.

[8] *Cf. Am. Ec. Rev.*, vol. 2, 1912, Suppl. p. 89.

[9] "The Economic Law of Market Areas," *Quart. Journ. of Ec.*, vol. 38, 1923–24, p. 520.

[10] *The Economics of Distribution.* New York, 1900.

[11] "The Higgling of the Market," *Quart. Journ. of Ec.*, vol. 17, 1902–03, p. 670.

[12] *Ec. Journ.*, vol. 10, 1900, p. 380.

[13] "A Suggestion for Simplifying the Statement of the General Theory of Price," *Journ. of Pol. Ec.*, vol. 36, 1928, p. 353.

[14] "Elasticity of Demand and Flexibility of Prices," *Journal of the American Statistical Society*, vol. 18, 1922–23, p. 8; "A Moving Equilibrium of Demand and Supply," *Quart. Journ. of Ec.*, vol. 39, 1924–25, p. 357; "Partial Elasticity of Demand," *ibid.*, vol. 40, 1925–26, p. 393; "Pantaleoni's Problem in the Oscillation of Prices," *ibid.*, p. 587; "A Theory of Economic Oscillation," *ibid.*, vol. 41, 1926–27, p. 1.

[15] "The Statistical Law of Demand as Illustrated by the Demand for Sugar," *Journ. of Pol. Ec.*, vol. 33, 1925, pp. 481 and 577; *Statistical Laws of Demand and Supply.* Chicago, 1928.

[16] "A Dynamical Theory of Economics," *Journ. of Pol. Ec.*, vol. 35, 1927, p. 632.

[17] "Graphic Illustration of the Laws of Price," *Am. Ec. Rev.*, vol. 14, 1924, p. 417.

[18] *The Behavior of Prices.* New York, 1927.

[19] "Mills' Behavior of Prices," *Quart. Journ. of Ec.*, vol. 43, 1928–29, p. 337.

[20] *Inter-Relationship of Supply and Prices.* Ithaca, 1928.

[21] *The Stabilization of Wheat during the War and Its Effect upon the Returns to the Producer.* Washington, 1925.

[22] "The Elasticity of Demand for Wheat," *Ec. Journ.*, vol. 24, 1914, p. 212.

[23] "The Statistical Determination of Demand Curves," *Quart. Journ. of Ec.*, vol. 39, 1924–25, p. 503.

[24] "What Do Statistical 'Demand Curves' show?" *Quart. Journ. of Ec.*, vol., 41, 1926–27, p. 212.

[25] "Supply Curves and Maximum Satisfaction," *Quart. Journ. of Ec.*, vol. 42, 1927–28, p. 170.

[26] "Statistical Analyses and the 'Laws of Price,'" *Quart. Journ. of Ec.*, vol. 42, 1927–28, p. 199; and "A Statistical Examination of Factors Related to Lamb Prices," *Journ. of Pol. Ec.*, vol. 35, 1927, p. 233.

[27] *The Theory of International Prices. History, Criticism and Restatement.* Cambridge, Mass., 1926.

[28] "Consumer's Demand," *Quart. Journ. of Ec.*, vol. 39, 1924–25, p. 584.

[29] *Dumping: A Problem of International Trade.* Chicago, 1923; and *Canada's Balance of International Indebtedness 1900–1913; An Inductive Study in the Theory of International Trade.* Cambridge, Mass., 1924.—Some of Viner's pupils have also worked with success in this direction, e. g., Theodore O. Yntema: "The Influence of Dumping on Monopoly Price," *Journ. of Pol. Ec.*, vol. 36, 1928, p. 686.

[30] *International Trade.* New York, 1927.

[31] "Some Aspects of Protection Further Considered," *Quart. Journ. of Ec.*, vol. 37, 1922–23, p. 199; "The Theory of International Values Re-examined," *ibid.*, vol. 38, 1923–24, p. 54.

[32] "Some Fallacies in the Interpretation of Social Cost," *Quart. Journ. of Ec.*, vol. 38, 1923–24, p. 582; also Graham's answer, *ibid.*, vol. 39, 1924–25, p. 324; and Knight's reply, *ibid.*, p. 331.

[33] "A Re-examination of the Doctrine of Comparative Costs," *Journ. of Pol. Ec.*, vol. 35, 1927, p. 464.

[34] "The Doctrine of Comparative Costs," *Quart. Journ. of Ec.*, vol. 41, 1926–27, p. 63.

[35] *Cf.* besides his two large works already mentioned several times, especially: "Cost and Its Significance," *Am. Ec. Rev.*, vol. 1, 1911, p. 724.

[36] *Supply and Demand.* London, 1922.

[37] "Economic Incentive," *Economica*, vol. 1, 1921, p. 231.

[38] "A Contribution to the Theory of Competitive Price," *Quart. Journ. of Ec.*, vol. 28, 1913–14, p. 747.

[39] *Studies in the Economics of Overhead Costs.* Chicago, 1923.

[40] *Cf.* esp. his recent work, *Social Control of Business.* Chicago, 1926.

[41] "Price-Fixing as Seen by a Price-Fixer," *Quart. Journ. of Ec.*, vol. 33, 1918–19, p. 205.

[42] "Is Market Price Determinate?" *Quart. Journ. of Ec.*, vol. 35, 1920–21, p. 395.

[43] "Cost of Production and Price," *Quart. Journ. of Ec.*, vol. 33, 1918–19, p. 560.

[44] "Price-fixing and the Theory of Profit," *Quart. Journ. of Ec.*, vol. 34, 1919–20, p. 139; "A Statistical Analysis of the Relation between Cost and Price," *ibid.*, vol. 35, 1920–21, p. 265, and vol. 37, 1922–23, p. 476.

[45] "The Nature and Fundamental Elements of Costs," *Quart. Journ. of Ec.*, vol. 41, 1926–27, p. 30; *cf.* also Willard C. Beatty: "Sinking Fund and Cost: Criticism of Bye's Analysis," *ibid.*, p. 353.

[46] "Professor Edgeworth's Collected Papers," *Ec. Journ.*, vol. 35, 1925, p. 177.

[47] "Equilibrium under Bilateral Monopoly," *Ec. Journ.*, vol. 18, 1908, p. 205. *Cf.* also among Pigou's earlier works on the subject: "Monopoly and Consumer's Surplus," *Ec. Journ.*, vol. 14, 1904, p. 388.

[48] Besides his "Mathematical Groundwork of Economics," mentioned above, *cf.* esp.: "Bilateral Monopoly," *Ec. Journ.*, vol. 38, 1928, p. 651.

[49] "Monopoly and Business Stability," *Economica*, vol. 6, 1926, p. 135.

[50] "The Relation of Marginal Rents to Price," *Quart. Journ. of Ec.*, vol. 20, 1905–06, p. 596.

[51] *Monopolies and Trusts.* New York, 1900.

[52] "The Relation of Monopoly price to the Rate of Interest," *Quart. Journ. of Ec.*, vol. 22, 1907–08, p. 626.

[53] "Competitive and Monopolistic Price-Making," *Quart. Journ. of Ec.*, vol. 22, 1907–08, p. 626.

[54] *Am. Ec. Rev.*, vol. 15, 1925, p. 480.

[55] "The Concept of Normal Price in Value and Distribution," *Quart. Journ. of Ec.*, vol. 32, 1917–18, p. 66.

[56] "Normal Price as a Market Concept," *Quart. Journ. of Ec.*, vol. 33, 1918–19, p. 632.

[57] *The Laws of Supply and Demand.* London, 1912.

[58] *Business Cycles.* Berkeley, 1913; new revised edition, New York, 1927.

[59] *The Making of Index Numbers. A Study of their Varieties, Tests and Reliability.* Boston and New York, 1922; 3rd ed., Boston, 1927.

CHAPTER V

[1] "The Theory of Distribution," *Quart. Journ. of Ec.*, vol. 18, 1903–04, p. 159.

[2] "The Authoritarian Element in Distribution," *Ec. Journ.*, vol. 37, 1927, p. 1.

[3] *The Distribution of Livelihood*, New York and London, 1908.

[4] *The Theory of Distribution and Consumption.* London, 1911.

[5] *Wealth: Its Production and Distribution.* London, 1920.

[6] "Clark's Distribution of Wealth," *Quart. Journ. of Ec.*, vol. 15, 1900, p. 578.

[7] *The Theory of Distribution.* New York and London, 1904.

[8] "Distribution by a Law of Rent," *Publ. of the Am. Ec. Ass.*, Ser. 3, vol. 4, 1903, p. 154.

[9] "J. B. Clark's Formulae of Wages and Interest," *Journ. of Pol. Ec.*, vol. 9, 1900–01, p. 461; and Clark's defence: "Wages and Interest as Determined by Marginal Productivity," *ibid.*, vol. 10, 1901–02, p. 105.

[10] "Specific Productivity," *Quart. Journ. of Ec.*, vol. 29, 1914–15, p. 149.

[11] "Professor Clark's Economics," *Quart. Journ. of Ec.*, vol. 22, 1907–08, p. 147.

[12] "Elasticity of Supply as a Determinant of Distribution," in the collection, *Economic Essays Contributed in Honor of John Bates Clark*, ed. by J. H. Hollander. New York, 1927, p. 71.

[13] "The Distribution Equilibrium under the Specific Productivity Theory," *Quart. Journ. of Ec.*, vol. 41, 1926–27, p. 349.

[14] *Journ. of Pol. Ec.*, vol. 33, 1925, p. 550.

[15] *Cf.* besides his small text-book mentioned above: "The Distribution of Income," *Quart. Journ. of Ec.*, vol. 19, 1904–05, p. 341.

[16] *A History of the Theories of Production and Distribution in English Political Economy* 1776–1848. London, 1893.

[17] "The Relations between Rent and Interest," and the discussion which followed. Publ. of the *Am. Ec. Ass.*, Ser. 3, vol. 5, 1904, p. 176.

[18] *Welfare as an Economic Quantity.* Boston, 1915.

[19] "A Third Factor in the Variation of Productivity: the Load Factor," *Am. Ec. Rev.*, vol. 18, 1928, p. 65.

[20] *Cf.* Persons: "The Variability in the Distribution of Wealth and Income," *Quart. Journ. of Ec.*, vol. 23, 1908–09, p. 416; Watkins: "The Measurement of Concentration of Wealth," *ibid.*, vol. 24, 1909–10, p. 160; also Persons' last word, *ibid.*, p. 180.

[21] "Income and Wealth," *Am. Ec. Rev.*, vol. 15, 1925, p. 457.

[22] "Economic Terminology: Factors of Production and Distributive Shares," *Am. Ec. Rev.*, vol. 18, 1928, p 65.

[23] "Der Einkommensbegriff im Lichte der Erfahrung," in the collection *Die Wirtschaftstheorie der Gegenwart*, ed. by Hans Mayer, etc., vol. 3, Vienna, 1928, p. 22.

[24] *Cf.* Redvers Opie: "Die Quasirente in Marshall's Lehrgebaüde," *Arch. f. Sozwiss.*, vol. 60, 1928, p. 251.

[25] "Prof. Seligman on the Mathematical Method in Political Economy," *Ec. Journ.*, vol. 9, 1899, p. 286.

[26] "Laws of Increasing and Decreasing Returns in Production and Consumption," *Ec. Journ.*, vol. 18, 1908, p. 52.

[27] *Cf.* Clapham: "On Empty Economic Boxes," *Ec. Journ.*, vol. 32, 1922, p. 305; Pigou: "A Reply," *ibid.*, p. 458; Clapham: "A Rejoinder," *ibid.*, p. 560. Cf. also Pigou's polemic against the discoveries of Piero Sraffa: "The Laws of Diminishing and Increasing Cost," *ibid.*, vol. 37, 1927, p. 188.

[28] "Varying Costs and Marginal Net Products," *Ec. Journ.*, vol. 38, 1928, p. 258.

[29] "The Passing of the Old Rent Concept," *Quart. Journ. of Ec.*, vol. 15, 1901–02, p. 416.

[30] "The Variation of Productive Forces," *Quart. Journ. of Ec.*, vol. 16, 1901–02, p. 473.

[31] *Quart. Journ. of Ec.*, vol. 17, 1902–03, p. 332.

[32] "Diminishing Returns in Manufactures," *Am. Ec. Rev.*, vol. 8, 1918, p. 741.

[33] *Quart. Journ. of Ec.*, vol. 18, 1903–04, p. 280; *cf.* also Bullock: "A Rejoinder," *ibid.*, p. 437.

[34] "The Universal Law of Diminishing Returns," *Quart. Journ. of Ec.*, vol. 22, 1907–08, p. 333.

[35] "Capital, Interest and Diminishing Returns," *Quart. Journ. of Ec.*, vol. 22, 1907–08, p. 333.

[36] "Proportions of Factors—Advantage and Size," *Quart. Journ. of Ec.*, vol. 23, 1908–09, p. 593.

[37] *The Common Sense of Economic Science.* London, 1922.

[38] *The Law of Diminishing Returns.* New York, 1924.

[39] "Increasing Returns and Economic Progress," *Ec. Journ.*, vol. 38, 1928, p. 527.

[40] "A Theory of Production," *Am. Ec. Rev.*, vol. 18, 1928, Suppl. p. 139.

[41] "Inductive Evidence on Marginal Utility," *Am. Ec. Rev.*, vol. 18, 1928, p. 449.

[42] *Introduction to Production Economics.* New York, 1926.

[43] *The Control of Industry.* New York, 1923.

[44] Production: A Study in Economics. London, 1907; 2nd ed., London, 1914.

[45] *La Rif. Soc.*, vol. 34, 1923, p. 234.

[46] "Marshall on Consumer's Surplus in International Trade," *Quart. Journ. of Ec.*, vol. 39, 1924–25, p. 144.

[47] "Total Utility and Consumer's Surplus," *Economica*, vol. 3, 1923, p. 21.

[48] "Consumer's Surplus: A Reply," *ibid.*, p. 131.

[49] "Does Mathematical Analysis Explain? A Note on Consumer's Surplus," *ibid.*, p. 135.

[50] "Utility Curves, Total Utility and Consumer's Surplus," *Quart. Journ. of Ec.*, vol. 41, 1926–27, p. 292.

[51] "Consumer's Surplus," *Am. Ec. Rev.*, vol. 16, 1926, p. 77.

[52] "Psychic Income, Total Utility and Consumer's Surplus," *Am. Ec. Rev.*, vol. 18, 1928, p. 75.

[53] "Total Utility and Consumer's Surplus under Varying Conditions of the Distribution of Income," *Quart. Journ. of Ec.*, vol. 31, 1916–17, p. 307.

[54] *A Theory of Consumption.* London, 1924.

[55] *Economics of Consumption.* New York, 1928.

[56] "Competitive Costs and the Rent of Business Ability," *Quart. Journ. of Ec.*, vol. 39, 1924–25, p. 39.

[57] "Three-Dimensional Diagrams in Illustration of Consumer's Demand and of Interest Rate and Saver's Surpluses," *Am. Ec. Rev.*, vol. 15, 1925, p. 228.

[58] "Further Discussion of Three-Dimensional Price Diagrams," *Am. Ec. Rev.*, vol. 15, 1925, p. 717.

[59] *Rent in Modern Economic Theory, an Essay on Distribution.* New York, 1902.

[60] *The Ricardian Rent Theory in Early American Economics.* New York, 1921.

[61] "Producer's and Consumer's Surplus," *Ec. Journ.*, vol. 20, 1910, p. 358.

[62] "Earnings and Surpluses," *Ec. Journ.*, vol. 18, 1908, p. 532.

[63] "The Differential Rent of Farm Land," *Quart. Journ. of Ec.*, vol. 17, 1902–03, p. 598.

[64] "Rent under the Assumption of Exhaustibility," *Quart. Journ. of Ec.*, vol. 28, 1913–14, p. 467.

[65] "Rent and Price: 'Alternative Use' and 'Scarcity Value,'" *Quart. Journ. of Ec.*, vol. 25, 1910–11, p. 119.

[66] "Price and Rent," *Quart. Journ. of Ec.*, vol. 26, 1911–12, p. 523.

[67] "The Rent Concept, Narrowed and Broadened," *Quart. Journ. of Ec.*, vol. 22, 1906–07, p. 48.

[68] "Land Rent as a Function of Population Growth," *Journ. of Pol. Ec.*, vol. 34, 1926, p. 274.

[69] "Land Income," *Pol. Sci. Quart.*, vol. 43, 1928, p. 408; *cf.* also: "Kosten und Einkommen bei der Bodenverwertung," in the collection *Die Wirtschaftstheorie der Gegenwart*, ed. by Hans Mayer, etc., vol. 3, Vienna, 1928, p. 242.

[70] "Land Rent and the Prices of Commodities," *Am. Ec. Rev.*, vol. 17, 1927, p. 219.

[71] *A Study of English Theories of Rent.* Calcutta, 1924.

[72] *Diminishing Returns in Agriculture.* New York, 1926.

[73] "Uncertainty in its Relations to the Net Rent of Interest," *Ec. Journ.*, vol. 22, 1912, p. 398.

[74] *A Theory of Interest.* New York, 1914.

[75] "Neglected Factors in the Problem of Normal Interest," *Quart. Journ. of Ec.*, vol. 31, 1916–17, p. 279.

[76] *The Nature and Necessity of Interest.* London, 1903.

[77] *Interest as a Cost.* New York, 1924.

[78] "Interest on the Enterpriser's Capital as a Cost in the Light of Economic Theory," *Am. Ec. Rev.*, vol. 16, 1926, p. 266.

[79] "Interest, Cost and Business Cycle," *Am. Ec. Rev.*, vol. 16, 1926, p. 209; "Supplementary Note on Interest Cost," *ibid.*, p. 660; "Interest Rates as Factors in the Business Cycle," *ibid.*, vol. 18, 1928, Suppl., p. 217.

[80] "The Influence of the Interest Rate on the Business Cycle," *Am. Ec. Rev.*, vol. 15, 1925, p. 684; "Interest Rates and the Business Cycle, *ibid.*, vol. 16, 1926, p. 451.

[81] "The Impatience Theory of Interest," *Am. Ec. Rev.*, vol. 2, 1912, p. 834.

[82] "The Marginal Productivity versus the Impatience Theory of Interest," *Quart. Journ. of Ec.*, vol. 27, 1912–13, p. 630.

[83] *Cf.* besides his other works which have been repeatedly mentioned: "Interest Theory and Theories," *Am. Ec. Rev.*, vol. 17, 1927, p. 636.

[84] "The Theory of Profit and Interest," *Quart. Journ. of Ec.*, vol. 36, 1921–22, p. 413.

[85] "Economic Theory and Economic Criticism: Cassel on Rent and on Interest," *Pol. Sci. Quart.*, vol. 41, 1926, p. 240.

[86] Böhm: "Capital and Interest Once More: I. Capital versus Capital Goods," *Quart. Journ. of Ec.*, vol. 21, 1906–07, p. 1; and II. A Relapse to the Productivity Theory," *ibid.*, p. 247; Clark: "Concerning the Nature of Capital: A Reply," *ibid.*, p. 350; Böhm: "The Nature of Capital: A Rejoinder," *ibid.*, vol. 22, 1907–08, p. 28.

[87] "Recent Discussion of the Capital Concept," *Quart. Journ. of Ec.*, vol. 15, 1900–01, p. 1;—also: "Clark's Reformulation of the Capital Concept," in the collection *Economic Essays, Contributed in Honor of John Bates Clark*, ed. by J. H. Hollander, New York, 1927, p. 136.

[88] "The Real Capital Concept," *Quart. Journ. of Ec.*, vol. 18, 1903–04, p. 54; and "The Fundamental Notion of Capital, Once More," *ibid.*, vol. 19, 1904–05, p. 81.

[89] *Cf.* among his writings on the subject published in the present century: "Precedents for Defining Capital," *Quart. Journ. of Ec.*, vol. 18, 1903–04, p. 386; and: "Professor Tuttle's Capital Concept," *ibid.*, vol. 19, 1904–05, p. 309.

[90] "Fisher's Capital and Income," *Pol. Sci. Quart.*, March 1908.

[91] "The Nature of Capital," *Quart. Journ. of Ec.*, vol. 22, 1907–08, p. 517, and vol. 23, 1908–09, p. 104.

[92] "The Controversy about the Capital Concept," *Quart. Journ. of Ec.*, vol. 22, 1907–08, p. 467.

[93] *The Nature of Capital and Income*. New York, 1906.

[94] "Are Savings Income?" *Publ. of the Am. Ec. Ass.*, Ser. 3, vol. 9, 1908, p. 21.

[95] "Irving Fisher on Capital and Interest," *Quart. Journ. of Ec.*, vol. 23, 1908–09, p. 307.

[96] "A Reply to Critics," *Quart. Journ. of Ec.*, vol. 23, 1908–09, p. 536.

[97] "Political Economy and Business Economy: Comment on Fisher's Capital and Income," *Quart. Journ. of Ec.*, vol. 22, 1907–08, p. 120.

[98] *The Rate of Interest, Its Nature, Determination and Relation to Economic Phenomena*. New York, 1907.

[99] "The 'Roundabout Process' in the Interest Theory," *Quart. Journ. of Ec.*, vol. 17, 1902–03, p. 163.

[100] Fetter: "Interest Theories, Old and New," *Am. Ec. Rev.*, vol. 4, 1914, p. 68; Brown: "The Discount versus the Cost-of-Production Theory of Capital Valuation," *ibid.*, p. 340; Fetter: "Capitalization versus Productivity: Rejoinder," *ibid.*, p. 856.

[101] "Interest Theory and Price Movements," *Am. Ec. Rev.*, vol. 17, 1927, Suppl. p. 62.

[102] *Ibid.*, p. 106.

[103] "Value in Its Relation to Interest," *Journ. of Pol. Ec.*, vol. 10, 1901–02, p. 50.

[104] "Factors Determining the Interest Rate," *Quart. Journ. of Ec.*, vol. 34, 1919–20, p. 445.

[105] "Clark's Distribution of Wealth," *Quart. Journ. of Ec.*, vol. 15, 1900–01, p. 578.

[106] "The Relation of Abstinence to Interest," *Quart. Journ. of Ec.*, vol. 18, 1903–04, p. 142.

[107] "Die Theorie des Zinses," in the collection *Die Wirtschaftstheorie der Gegenwart*, ed. by Hans Mayer, etc., vol. 3, Vienna, 1928, p. 151.

[108] The Nature of Interest and the Causes of Its Fluctuations," *Quart. Journ. of Ec.*, vol. 31, 1916–17, p. 547.

[109] "The Theory of Saver's Rent and Some of Its Applications," *Quart. Journ. of Ec.*, vol. 14, 1899–1900, p. 249.

[110] "Interest and Saving." London, 1906, and "Some Considerations about Interest," *Ec. Journ.*, vol. 18, 1908, p. 42.

[111] "Saver's Surplus and the Interest Rate," *Quart. Journ. of Ec.*, vol. 35, 1920–21, p. 1.

[112] "A Mathematical Theory of Saving," *Ec. Journ.*, vol. 38, 1928, p. 543.

[113] "The Income of Capital," *Quart. Journ. of Ec.*, vol. 35, 1920–21, p. 1.

[114] *The Adjustment of Wages. A Study in the Coal and Iron Industries of Great Britain and America.* London, 1903.

[115] *Wages in the United Kingdom in the 19th Century. Notes for the Use of Students of Social and Economic Questions.* Cambridge, 1900; *Prices and Wages in the United Kingdom, 1914–20.* Oxford, 1921.

[116] Work and Wages, 3 vols. (I. *Foreign Competition*, II. *Wages and Employment*, III. *Social Betterment*). London, 1904–1914.

[117] "The Dynamics of the Wages Question," *Publ. of the Am. Ec. Association*, Ser. 3, vol. 4, 1903, p. 130.

[118] *The Social Problem. Life and Work.* London-New York, 1901; *Industrial Systems: An Inquiry into Earned and Unearned Income.* New York, 1909; *Work and Wealth: A Human Valuation.* London, 1914.

[119] "The Rate of Wages and the Use of Machinery," *Am. Ec. Rev.*, vol. 13, 1923, p. 461.

[120] "An Issue in Economic Theory: The Rate of Wages and the Use of Machinery," *Am. Ec. Rev.*, vol. 13, 1923, p. 654.

[121] *Ibid.*, vol. 14, 1924, p. 283.

[122] *Ibid.*, p. 284.

[123] "Note on the Effect of Wage Rates on Machine Use," *Am. Ec. Rev.*, vol. 17, 1927, p. 50.

[124] "Relation of Wage Rates to the Use of Machinery," *ibid.*, vol. 16, 1926, p. 434.

[125] "Wage Rates and the Use of Machinery," *ibid.*, vol. 17, 1927, p. 675.

[126] *Machinery and Labor.* Cambridge, Mass., 1926.

[127] *Wages and Labor Costs.* London, 1927.

[128] *Capital and Labor.* London, 1914.

[129] *Economics of Social Problems.* London, 1925.

[130] *Labor and Economics.* New York, 1925.

[131] "The Principles of Wages," London, 1928; "Zur Frage der Grenzproduktivität," *Schmoller's Jahrb.* N.F. vol. 51, 1927, p. 653. *Cf.* also Joseph Schumpeter's reply, *ibid.*, p. 671.

[132] "Outlines of a Theory of Wages," *Publ. of the Am. Ec. Ass.*, Ser. 3, vol. 11, 1910, p. 136.

[133] "Present Work and Present Wages," *Quart. Journ. of Ec.*, vol. 24, 1909–10, p. 515.

[134] *Ibid.*, p. 535.

[135] "Kleene's Profit and Wages," *Quart. Journ. of Ec.*, vol. 31, 1916–17, p. 705.

[136] "The Supply Price of Labor," *Quart. Journ. of Ec.*, vol. 32, 1917–18, p. 400.

[137] *Am. Ec. Rev.*, vol. 16, Suppl., 1926, p. 240.

[138] "Wages Theory and Theories," *Quart. Journ. of Ec.*, vol. 33, 1918–19, p. 256.

[139] *Wages. An Introductory Analysis of the Wage System under Modern Capitalism.* London (n. d., probably 1926).

[140] *The Economics of Wages and Labor.* London, 1926.

[141] *The Economic Basis of Fair Wages.* New York, 1926.

[142] "Wages and the Collective Wage Bargain," *Am. Ec. Rev.*, vol. 18, 1928, p. 670.

[143] *Laws of Wages. An Essay on Statistical Economics.* New York, 1911.

[144] *Ec. Journ.*, vol. 22, 1912, p. 314.

[145] *Ibid.*, p. 66.

[146] "Paradoxes of Competition," *Quart. Journ. of Ec.*, vol. 20, 1905–06, p. 211.

[147] *A Living Wage. Its Ethical and Economic Aspects.* New York, 1906.

[148] "A Theory of the Rate of Wages," *Quart. Journ. of Ec.*, vol. 36, 1921–22, p. 581. *Cf.* also his book with Stacy May: *The Control of Wages.* New York, 1923.

[149] "General Intelligence and Wages," *Quart. Journ. of Ec.*, vol. 31, 1916–17, p. 690.

[150] "The Minimum Wage and Efficiency," *Am. Ec. Rev.*, vol. 13, 1923, p. 411.

[151] *Wages and the State: A Comparative Study of the Problems of State Wage Regulation.* London, 1926.

[152] *A Study on the Minimum Wage.* New York, 1927.

[153] "Productivity and the Theory of Wages," in the collection *London Essays in Economics: in Honour of Edwin Cannan*, ed. by T. E. Gregory and H. Dalton. London, 1927, p. 183.

[154] "Real Wages and the Control of Industry," *Am. Ec. Rev.*, vol. 16, 1926, Suppl., p. 54.

[155] "Wage Theories and Wage Policies," *Am. Ec. Rev.*, vol. 16, 1926, Suppl., p. 54.

[156] *The Secret of High Wages.* New York, 1926.

[157] *Capital for Labor.* New York, 1927.

[158] *Wages and the Family.* Chicago, 1925.

[159] "The Movement of Real Wages and Its Economic Significance," *Am. Ec. Rev.*, vol. 16, 1926, Suppl., p. 17.

[160] *Profits, Wages and Prices.* New York, 1920.

[161] "Factors Affecting the Trend of Real Wages," *Am. Ec. Rev.*, vol. 15, 1925, p. 27.

[162] "The Best Measure of Real Wages," *Am. Ec. Rev.*, vol. 16, 1926, Suppl., p. 5.

[163] *Wages and Labor's Share in the Value Added by Manufacture.* Washington, 1928.

[164] "The Productivity Factor in Wage Determinations," *Am. Ec. Rev.*, vol. 13, 1923, p. 129.

[165] "The Theory of Distribution," *Quart. Journ. of Ec.*, vol. 18, 1903–04, p. 159.

[166] "The Remuneration of Employers," *Ec. Journ.*, vol. 16, 1906, p. 523.

[167] "Analysis of Profit," *Journ. of Pol. Ec.*, vol. 33, 1925, p. 278.

[168] "Bemerkungen zur Theorie des Unternehmergewinns," in the collection *Die Wirtschaftstheorie der Gegenwart*, ed. by Hans Mayer, etc., vol. 3, Vienna, 1928, p. 271.

[169] "Profits of Efficiency," *Am. Ec. Rev.*, vol. 8, 1918, p. 317; "A Division among Theorists in Their Analysis of Profits," *Quart. Journ. of Ec.*, vol. 34, 1919–20, p. 114; "Computation of Good-Will Profits," *Am. Ec. Rev.*, vol. 15, 1925, p. 652.

[170] "The Place of the Speculator in the Theory of Distribution," *Publ. of the Am. Ec. Ass.*, Ser. 3, vol. 1, 1900, p. 103.

[171] Hawley: "Enterprise and Profit," *Quart. Journ. of Ec.*, vol. 15, 1900–01, p. 75; Carver: "The Risk Theory of Profits," *ibid.*, p. 456; Hawley: "Reply to Final Objections to the Risk Theory of Profit," *ibid.*, p. 603.

[172] "A Positive Theory of Economics," *Quart. Journ. of Ec.*, vol. 16, 1901–02, p. 233.

[173] *Enterprise and the Productive Process; A Theory of Economic Productivity Presented from the Point of View of the Entrepreneur.* New York and London, 1907.

[174] Hawley has recently deplored this: "The Orientation of Economics on Enterprise," *Am. Ec. Rev.*, vol. 17, 1927, p. 409.

[175] *Risk, Uncertainty and Profit.* Boston and New York, 1921.

[176] *Risk and Risk-Bearing.* Chicago, 1923.

[177] "The Residual Claimant Theory of Distribution," *Quart. Journ. of Ec.*, vol. 17, 1902–03, p. 261.

[178] "A Functional Theory of Economic Profit," in the collection *Economic* Essays, Contributed in Honor of John Bates Clark, ed. by J. H. Hollander, New York, 1927, p. 321; "The Function of the Entrepreneur," *Am. Ec. Rev.*, vol. 17, 1927, p. 13; "The Entrepreneur Function in Economic Literature," *Journ. of Pol. Ec.*, vol. 35, 1927, p. 501.

[179] *Capitalist Enterprise and Social Progress.* London, 1925.

[180] *Profits.* Boston and New York, 1925.

SUMMARY AND PROSPECTS

[1] *Quart. Journ. of Ec.*, vol. 16, 1901–02, p. 69.

[2] *Rev. d'Ec. Pol.*, vol. 24, 1910, p. 496.

[3] *Quart. Journ. of Ec.*, vol. 27, 1912–13, p. 520.

[4] *Quart. Journ. of Ec.*, vol. 39, 1924–25, p. 124.

[5] *Ibid.*, vol. 35, 1920–21, p. 461.

[6] *Ibid.*, vol. 36, 1921–22, p. 335.

[7] *Am. Ec. Rev.*, vol. 16, 1926, p. 59.

[8] *Pol. Sci. Quart.*, vol. 41, 1926, p. 240.

[9] *Quart. Journ. of Ec.*, vol. 36, 1921–22, p. 145.

[10] *Ibid.*, vol. 43, 1928–29, p. 303.

[11] *Am. Ec. Rev.*, vol. 19, 1929, p. 78.

[12] *Journ. of Pol. Ec.*, vol. 36, 1928, p. 641.

[13] "The Phenomena of Economic Dynamics," *Publ. of the Am. Ec. Ass.*, Ser. 3, vol. 11, 1910, p. 112.

[14] "Professor Cassel's Treatise," *Ec. Journ.*, vol. 30, 1920, p. 533.—In 1923 Cassel's text-book was translated into English.

[15] For a further discussion of this subject, *cf.* the author's book: *A gazdaságpolitika tudományos alapkérdései* (The fundamental scientific problems of economic policy), Budapest, 1927.

INDEX OF NAMES

The numbers refer to the pages on which the authors are mentioned; those in thick type refer to the pages in which the authors are discussed. Numbers with an asterisk refer to notes on the given page.

Adams, 221, 251
Adriance, 281
Aereboe, 116
Aftalion, 172, 183, **191**
Albrecht, 112
Alessio, **161**
Almada, 366 *
Amantia, **166**
Amonn, **30**, 47, 66, 67, 71, 74, 77, 79, **80**, **81**, 82, 95, 97, 103, 320, 334, 337, 349,* 351,* 354 *
Ambrozovics, 197 *
Amoroso, 130, 143, **144**, 181, 197, 200, 201
Anderson, 19, 260, **261**, 262, **316**, 376 *
Andler, 162
Andreae, 77
Angell, 38, 270, **271**
Ansiaux, **151**, 185, 192, 202
Antonelli, **145**, **146**, 184, 193
Aria, 139
Arias, 193
Ariès, 159
Aristotle, 33, 36
Arndt, 120
Ashley, 225, 229, 298
Atkins, **257**, **258**
Atkinson, 252
Aubry, 193
Auhagen, 116
Auspitz, 221
Austin, 304
Avenati, 194

Bach, 6
Back, 97
Bain, 26, 36
Balás, 112, 113, 120, 318
Balbi, 165
Baldwin, 38
Barnett, 300
Barone, **143**, **144**, 175, 190, 313, 330
Bastiat, 151, 165, 192, 287
Bateson, 38
Baudin, 131 *
Bauer-Mengelberg, 92
Baxa, 77, 107
Beatty, 378 *
Béchaux, 131
Beckerath, 61
Bellet, 10
Bellom, 136, 192
Below, 77
Beneduce, 190
Benini, 134
Bentham, 28, 243, 371 *
Berardi, 130, 133, **175**, 176
Bergson, 41
Bernhardi, 161
Berolzheimer, **57**
Biermann, 46, 62
Bigge, 300
Bilimowitsch, 92
Birck, 118, **238**, **258**
Bismarck, 6
Bizzel, 252
Black, 49, 221, 288
Blanchard, **166**
Blaustein, 62
Blue, 215
Blum, 301
Boaz, 38
Bochard, 137
Boden, 94
Bodeville, 150
Bodin, 133, **153**, **154**, 170, 171, 200, **322**
Bogdanoff, 253
Böhm-Bawerk, 15, 47, 49, **88**, 89, **90**, 91, 92, 106, 108, 109, 110, **117**, **118**, 119, 120, 148, 172, 191, 198, 199, 201, 202, 239, 258, 268, 283, 287, 291, 292, **293**, **294**, 295, 296, 297, 313, 321, 330, 352,* 357,* 358,* 382 *
Bonar, 216, 251
Boninsegni, **145**, **146**, 178, 180
Bonn, 61
Borgatta, 197
Bortkiewicz, 118
Boucke, 40, 217, **247**, 282
Bounatian, **183**, 313

Bousquet, 134, 143, 150, 200, 201, 313
Bouvier, 129
Bovens, 129
Bowley, 215, 275, 288, 298, 343 *
Brants, **160**
Brassey, 298
Brentano (F.), 31
Brentano (L.), 10, 50, 111, 129, 355,* 373 *
Bresciani-Turroni, 181, 190
Briefs, 61, 63, 120, 358 *
Briggs, 252
Brinkmann, 347 *
Brinton, 215
Broda, 89
Broggi, 144
Brouilhet, **154, 155, 318,** 320
Brown, **246,** 262, 276, 290, 292, 295, 297, 374,* 382 *
Bücher, 61, 86, 239, 345 *
Buck, 247, 291
Budge, 71, **72,** 119
Buer, 253
Bulgakoff, 58
Bullock, 251, **287,** 306, 374,* 380 *
Bunke, 31
Bunzel, 46
Burch, 252
Burke, **249**
Burns (A. R.), 253
Burns (E. M.), 253, 304
Butler, 28
Bye, 221, 222, 223, **247, 274,** 292, 303, 378 *

Cabiati, 175, 194
Cæsari, 144
Cahen, 192
Calderoni, **196**
Cannan, 236, 237, **248,** 249, **282,** 288
Cannon, 38
Cantillon, 206
Caradog, 369 *
Carey, 35, 195, 213, 287, 314
Carli, **175**
Carlile, 216
Carlton, 253, 276, 290
Carlyle, 249
Carver, 215,* 217, **245, 246,** 260, 266, 280, 281, 284, 287, 297, **300,** 301, 306, 307, 309, 329, 374 *
Cassel, 12, 16, **21,** 22, 29, 48, 67, **70,** 71, 72, 73, 75, 96, 97, **102, 103, 109,** 114, 120, 121, 168, 200, 292, 293, 300, 301, 314, **319, 320,** 330, 335, 338, 348,* 354,* 355,* 356,* 382,* 385*
Cassirer, 21, 49
Castberg, 288
Catchings, 309
Cauwés, 11, 166
Chapman, **237,** 238, 266, 286, 298, 306
Chessa, 204, 208, 307
Chiro, 49
Clapham, 286, 380 *
Clark (J. B.), 15, 19, 34, 35, 41, 107, 118, 206, 213, 219, 220, **238, 239,** 240, 241, 242, 243, 245, 252, 254, 255, 256, 257, 260, 261, 262, 263, **268,** 276, **279, 280,** 281, 284, 286, 287, 289, 292, **293, 294,** 297, **299,** 301, 302, **308,** 309, 313, 314, 316, 319, **328, 329, 335, 336,** 338, 376,* 379,* 382,* 385 *
Clark (J. M.), 40, 221, 222, **223,** 261, **272, 273, 274,** 281, 288, 289, **300, 328, 329,** 376 *
Clay, **249,** 279
Clerget, 139
Cobb (Ch. W.), 287
Cobb (J. C.), 221
Cohen, 21
Cohn (A. W.), 342 *
Cohn (G.), 50, 53, 64, 213
Colson, **147,** 148, 149, 166, **184,** 185, **322,** 372 *
Commons, 40, **225,** 227, 276, 286, 295, 304, 307, 314, 318
Comte, 22, 23, 26, 135, 157
Conrad (O.), 70, 71, 86, 94, 100, 114, 117, 119, 122, 213, 321, 345,* 355 *
Cooley, 19, 38, 261, 316
Copeland, 223
Cornélissen, **173, 174, 184,** 204, **205, 208,** 313, 321
Cossa (E.), 134, 207, 322
Cournot, 129, 165, 181, 186, 221, 275, 313, 336
Cox, 303
Croce, 20, **137,** 143, 178, 317
Čuhel, 92
Cunnison, 253
Cunynghame, 215, 266
Curtis, 252

Dane, 287, 300
Daniels, 295, 369 *
Darwin, 26
Davenport, 40, 171, **242,** 256, **258, 259,** 260, 262, **272, 282,** 287, 290, 293, 303, 318, 322, 373,* 376 *
Davidson, 216
Davies, 297
Defourny, 134

Delevsky, 182
Denoel, 160
Descartes, 36
Devas, **249**
Dewey, 220
Dibblee, 19, 261, 277
Dickinson, 41, **217**, 262
Diehl, 15, 30, 61, 67, 69, 71, 75, 78, **79**, **80**, 81, 94, 97, 104, 107, 116, 117, 155, 314, **318**, 320, 329, 331, 337, 357 *
Dietrich, 60
Dietzel, 61, 96, 320
Dilthey, 31
Diogenes, 36
Divisia, 146
Dobb, **309**
Dobretsberger, 49
Dostojewsky, 41
Douglas, 281, 288, 305
Downey, 262
Driesch, **31**, **32**, 33, 49
Dühring, 112
Dunkmann, 349 *
Dunlap, 38
Dupont, 157
Dupuit, 186 *
Durkheim, **19**, **20**, 22, 136, 137, 172, 205, 317

Eberstadt, 45, 116
Eckehart, 33
Edgeworth, 142, 144, 182, **214**, **215**, 228, **232**, 237, 254, 260, 266, **275**, 278, 286, 288, 291, 304, **305**, 313, 319, 330, 372,* 377 *
Edie, 40, 218, **247**, **248**, 282
Edwards, 34, 40
Effertz, **162**, 186, 206
Ehrenberg, 53, **55**, **56**, **59**, 60, 61, 136, **317**, 330
Ehrenfels, 31
Einaudi, 151
Eleutheropulos, 59
Elster, 336
Ely, **251**, 276, 284, 291, 293, 297, 306
Emery, 307
Empoli, 182, 336
Engländer, 54, 85, **103**, 104, 119, 120, 123, 355 *
Engliš, 75, **79**, 104
Esslen, 74, 116, 349 *
Eucken, 30
Eulenburg, 49, 63, 70, 71
Ezekiel, 271

Fairchild, **246**, **247**, 257, 291, 294
Falckenberg, 30
Fanno, 181
Faubel, 251
Fay, 252
Fechner, 37, 287
Fenoglio, 162
Ferrara, 175, 176, 201
Fetter, 40, 99, 217, **220**, **243**, **244**, 245, 251, 258, **260**, **261**, 262, **263**, **267**, 272, **283**, **284**, 286, 287, 290, **294**, **295**, **296**, 300, 301, 306, 314, **315**, **318**, 320, **327**, 341,* 353,* 357,* 382 *
Fichte, 30, 31
Field, 252
Filene, 304
Fisher (C. O.), 300
Fisher (G.), 146, 215, 217, 220, **241**, **242**, 246, 251, 255, 256, 257, 277, 285, 291, 292, **294**, **295**, 296, 368 *
Fleischl, 106
Florence, 217
Flux, **233**, 234, 235, **269**, **270**, 287, 295
Follin, 165
Foreman, 306
Foster, 309
Frank, 217
Franklin (B.), 34, 35, 40
Franklin (F.), 71, 293, 314
Freyer, 59
Frézouls, **196**
Friday, 40, 262, 305, 320
Fulda, 61
Furlan, 171, 190
Furniss, 247, 291

Garrett, 303
Gearhart, 300
Gebauer, 120
Gehrig, 347 *
Gelesnoff, **83**, 95
George, 213
Gerbino, 198
Gerlach, 61
Gestrich, 72
Ghio, 166
Gibson, 216
Giddings, 19, 316
Gide, 10, 11, 129, 151, **157**, **158**, 166, **174**, 183, 207, 313, 322
Gini, 171, 181, 190
Giovannini, **167**
Gluck, 6
Gobbi, **153**, **178**, 197, 288, 320
Goldscheid, 85
Gömöry, 185
Gonnard, 159
Gonner, 297
Gosh, 291
Gossen, 73, 91, 92, 336, 349 *
Gottl, 48, 97, 320, 343 *
Gottl-Ottlilienfeld, 96, 320
Gough, 252
Grabski, 45
Graham, 272, **300**, 378 *
Gray, 290
Graziadei, **172**, 176, 177, 204, 313, 320

Graziani, 130, 132, **148**, 149, 172, **174**, **175**, **181**, 185, 194, 197, **201**, 203
Greef, 135
Gruntzel, 86, **87**, 95, 104
Guyot, 10, 131, **150**, 165, 177, 185, 341 *

Haas, 49
Hadley, 226, 227, 307
Haenel, 86, 94
Hainisch, 118
Halm, 119
Hamilton, 40, 262, **304**
Händel, 6
Haney, 225, 290
Hansen, 305
Hanstein, 31
Hardy, 307
Haret, 130
Harms, 56, 60, **61**, 62
Hartley, 36, 37
Hasbach, 45, 46, 53
Hauser, 135
Hawley, 294, **307**, 385 *
Hawtrey, 226, **249**
Hayek, 91, 99, 118
Hayes, 227, 252, 291, **300**, 371 *
Hegel, 31, 49
Heimann, 95
Heinrich, 77
Heinze, 119
Held, 213
Heller, 63, **67**, 77, 109
Helmholtz, 37
Henderson, 256, 272, 282, 313
Herkner, 54
Hermann, 161, 195
Herzfelder, 85, 86, 104
Hesse, 54, 77, 345 *
Hewett, 247
Higgs, 230, 253
Hildebrand, 40, 64, 65, 135
Hirst, 228 *

Hoag, **291**
Hobbes, 36
Hobhouse, 256
Hobson, 216, 250, **269**, **281**, **282**, 284, 290, **292**, 297, **299**, 300, 301, 302, 304, **309**, **316**
Hohoff, 119
Hollander, **219**, 220, 221, 284, 302, 304, 308, 371,* 376,* 379,* 382,* 385 *
Homan, 219
Honegger, 47, 77, 81
Houques-Fourcade, 161, 188
Hoxsie, 267
Hume, 28, 36
Husserl, 49

Inama-Sternegg, 65

Jaeger, 52
Jaffé, 75
Jahn, 86, **87**, 349 *
James, 38
Jannacone, 177, 194, **323**, **324**
Jellinek, 32
Jevons (H. S.), 229, 230
Jevons (W. S.), 165, 213, 229, 237, 238, 252, 254, 259, 263, 298, 315, 335, 349 *
Johnson (A. S.), **242**, 260, **276**, 281, 289, 304, 308
Johnson (S.), 40
Johnson (W. E.), 260
Johnston, 253
Jollivet-Castelot, 160
Jones (J. H.), 253
Jones (R.), 252
Joseph, 258
Josephy, **79**, 112
Journé, **166**
Juvalta, 130

Kant, 21, 28, 31, 36, 51, 110
Katser, 91
Kaulla, 47, 97, 342 *
Kautz, 64
Keasbey, 257, 261
Keilhau, 85
Kellenberger, 75, 99, 123
Kemmerer, 269
Kerschagl, 77, 92
Ketelhodt, 96
Keynes, 215, 228, 372 *
King (G.), 182, 183
King (W. T.), 227, 285
Kinley, 219
Kirk, **289**
Kirkaldy, 279
Kleene, 227, 298, **302**, **303**, 306, 314
Kleinwächter (F. jun.), 117
Kleinwächter (F. sen.), 65, 95
Klien, 121
Knapp, 213, 330
Knies, 64, 161, 213, 294
Knight, 221, **222**, 227, 236, 237, 262, 264, **270**, 272, **276**, 281, 291, 296, **307**, 314, 323, 371,* 378 *
Kobatsch, 61
Koehne, 349 *
Köhler, 49, 54
Kostanecki, 96
Kotany, 257, 293
Krafft, 61, 83
Kramphardt, 71
Kraus, 90
Krzymorski, 59
Kuczynski, 305
Kühne, 49
Külpe, 21, 31
Kupper, 75

Labriola, **135**, **136**, **164**, **165**, 176, 186, 193

Lampe, 123
Lamprecht, 48
Landauer, 47, 91, 108, 356 *
Landry, **162**, **163**, **186**, 193, 196, **201**, **202**, 206, 207, 364 *
Lang, 287
Langfeldt, 348 *
Lasson, 31
Laurent, **145**
Lavergne, **146**, **147**, 183, 192, 196, **202**, 206, **209**
Lavington, 275, 291
Layton, 301
Lazard, 206
Lederer, 62, **67**, 75, 78, 348 *
Leduc, 182
Lee, 253
Lefort, 9
Lehfeldt, 228, 271, 306
Lehmann, 54
Lenoir, 182
Lenz, 77
Leone, **163**, **164**
Leonhard, 96
Le Rossignol, 253
Leroux, 129
Leroy-Beaulieu, 147, **150**
Lescure, 185
Leseine, 133, 369 *
Letrosue, 337
Leudet, 9
Levasseur, **204**
Levy (H.), 61
Lévy (R. G.), 341,* 374 *
Lewin, 122
Lexis, 69, **72**, 76, **111**, 112
Lieben, 221
Liefmann, 15, **22**, 29, 48, **73**, **74**, **75**, 77, 79, 81, 91, 94, 96, **99**, **100**, 101, **108**, 114, 120, 192, 243, 260, 314, **317**, **318**, 320, 321, 330, **331**, 349,* 355,* 356 *
Lifschitz, 46
List, 77, 78, 248
Lloyd (T.), 279
Lloyd (W. F.), 304
Locke, 36
Lorenz, 251
Loria, **134**, **135**, **161**, 162, 176, **192**, **193**, 195, 203, 207, 266, 288, 313, **316**, 367 *
Lorini, **207**
Lotze, 31
Lowie, 38
Lukas, 71, 356 *
Lyon, 216

MacCrea, 314
MacDougall, 38
MacFarlane, 220, 281, 284
MacGoun, 297
MacGregor, 288, 290, 306
MacKillop, 252
MacPherson, **258**
MacVane, 259, 297
Magee, 251
Mahaim, 157
Majorana, 176 *
Malebranche, 36
Mangoldt, 195, 209
Mannstaedt, 71
March, 134
Marriot, 226
Marschak, 48
Marshall (A.), 15, 26, 147, 148, 158, 166, 170, 174, 179, 180, 182, 184, 190, **214**, 221, 224, 226, **230**, **231**, 232, 233, 234, 235, 236, 237, 238, 239, 240, 246, 249, 252, 253, 254, 258, 260, 263, **265**, **266**, 268, 270, 271, 276, 277, **278**, 280, 281, **285**, **286**, 287, **288**, 289, 291, 298, 303, 305, 309, 321, 322, 323, 324, 327, 330, 335, 369,* 372,* 377 *
Marshall (L. C.), 252
Martello, 176
Marx, 3, 6, 20, 48, 79, 82, 83, 143, 164, 176, 204, 234, 249, 376 *
Mason, 272
Masslow, **83**, 95
Maunier, 136
Mayer (H.), 69, 89, 99, 106, 341,* 353,* 357,* 358,* 369,* 370,* 371,* 380,* 381,* 383,* 385 *
Mayer (J.), 289
Mayer (O.), 75
Mayer (Th.), 77
Mayo-Smith, 226
Mayr, 60, 63
Meade, 252
Medicus, 31
Meerwarth, 86
Meinong, 31
Melrose, 253
Menger, 52, 68, 71, 92, 148, 259, 283, 314, 315, 330, 335, 336, 349 *
Meriam, 271, 303, 314
Michels, 132, 313
Mill (J.), 36, 229, 244
Mill (J. S.), 28, 36, 229, 232, 233, 240
Miller, 288
Mills, 40, 221, **223**, 270, 271
Milnes, 303
Mises, 92
Mitchell (W. C.), 40, 221, **224**, 277, 292, 296, 314
Mitchell (W. F.), 296
Mitscherlich, 45, 77
Mixter, 287, 297
Moeller, 71, 97
Mohrmann, 95
Molinari, 29, 150
Moll, 123
Montemartini, 178

Moore, 215, 260, 270, 271, **303**, **304**
Moret, 129, 182
Morgan, 38
Morrison, 300
Morss, 281
Mortara, 190
Mourre, 200
Muhs, 48, 97, 119
Mukerjee, **248**
Müller (A.), 75, 77
Müller (H.), 104
Müller (J.), 37
Munro, 248
Münsterberg, **18**, 22, 30
Murdock, 226
Murray, 134, **144**, 171

Napolitano, **159**
Natoli, **175**, 193
Natorp, 21
Navratil, 47, 69
Nearing, 252
Neisser, 71, 116
Neumann, 161
Neurath (O.), 62, 63, 86, 97
Neurath (W.), 86
Newcomb, 294
Nicholson, 226, **232**, 233, 234, 235, 237, 306, 330
Nickel, 54, 58, 349 *
Nicklisch, 60
Nietzsche, 6, 41
Noël, 151
Nogaro, **154**
Nordenholz, 107
Nourse, **277**

Offner, 85
Ogburn, 38
Oppenheimer (F.), 74, 81, **82**, **83**, 94, 95, 100, 101, **109**, **110**, 114, 119, 122, 195, **316**, 317, 354,* 355,* 356 *
Oppenheimer (H.), 67, 122
Osorio, 170, 182
Oswalt, 71
Ottolenghi, **208**, **209**

Padan, 281, 297
Pantaleoni, 127, 129, 133, 140, 149, 179, 181, 314, 330, 359 *
Paoletti, 165
Papi, 182
Pareto, 15, **25**, **26**, 27, **128**, 129, 130, 134, 136, 137, **140**, **141**, **142**, 143, 144, 145, 146, 148, 150, 165, **168**, **169**, **170**, **179**, **180**, 182, 185, 189, 190, **195**, 199, 203, 256, 257, 330, 362,* 372 *
Parker, 217
Parmenides, 36
Parry, 217, 222
Parson, 314
Patten, 35, **220**, 241, **249**, **250**,* 252, **256**, **257**, **266**, 267, 276, 280, 287, **296**, 299, 308, 314
Patton, 291
Pearson, 271
Peddie, **248**
Penson, 252
Perlman, 314
Perreau, **154**
Perroux, 208
Perry, 19, 261
Persons, 10, 256, 285, 379 *
Pesch, **84**, **85**
Petit, 9
Pfleiderer, 31
Philippovich, 54, 68, 117, 330
Pierson, **233**, **234**, 278, 306, 372 *
Pietri-Tonelli, 165
Pigou, 27, 28, 215, 228, **235**, **236**, **237**, 238, 245, 253, 263, 264, 266, 275, 279, 286, 288, 290, 291, 298, 327, 335, 369,* 372,* 378,* 380 *
Pirou, 173, 359 *
Plato, 36
Platter, **82**
Plenge, 62, 86
Plotinus, 33
Pohle, 53, 69, 70, 124, 345,* 348 *
Polier, 206 *
Prion, 61

Quesnay, 136

Ramsey, 298
Raper, **250**
Ratzenhofer, 49
Rau, 60, 161
Raynaud, 206
Rebaud, **166**, 184
Reinke, 31
Reisch, 341,* 353,* 357 *
Renner, 95
Ricardo, 71, 75, 114, 147, 192, 195, 196, 208, 229, 244, 253, 254, 284, 290, 291, 298, 302, 338, 356 *
Ricca-Salerno, 201, **203**, 204, 368 *
Ricci, 150, **170**, 176, 180, 190, 197, 200
Richards, 252, 341 *
Richardson, 304
Rickert, 16, 17, 30, 31, 45, 51
Riedenauer, 104
Riehl, 21
Rist, 41, 129, 191, 192, **199**, **200**, 314, 360 *
Robbins, 266, 303
Robeck, 356 *
Robertson (D. H.), 272, 288

Robertson (J. M.), 253
Robinson, 295
Robson, 238
Roche-Agussol, 157, 172
Rodbertus, 79, 143
Roscher, 50, 64, 65, 135, 157, 213
Rosewater, 219
Ross, 271
Rost, 95
Rouxel, 131, 192
Rueff, 134
Rufener, 252
Ruggiero, 133
Ruhland, 65
Ruskin, 249
Ryan, 304

Sachot, 186
Salin, 71
Salz, 92, 120
Samsonoff, **195**
Sander, 77, 83, 351 *
Saspach, 121
Sax, 92, 118
Schack, 48, 54, 100
Schäffle, 16, 161, 195, 209
Schams, 71
Schaposchnikoff, 118 *
Schär, 60
Scharling, 92
Schatz, 131
Schelle, 131
Schelting, 37, 344 *
Schiele, **107**
Schlesinger, 49, 70
Schmalenbach, 60
Schmidt (F.), 62, 63
Schmidt (M.), 85
Schmoller, 10, 15, 45, 46, 50, 53, 54, 64, 65, 86, 111, 121, 128, 134, 213, 248, 314, 330, 337, 342,* 347 *
Schönfeld, 70, 91
Schönitz, 60, 346 *
Schoolmeester, 185
Schor, 94
Schröder, 112
Schubert, 85
Schüller, 106, **115**, **121**, 122, 194, **323**, **324**
Schullern, 68
Schultz, 221, 270, **271**
Schumpeter, 47, 48, 67, **68**, **69**, 70, 71, 72, 75, 76, 78, 82, 90, 98, 99, 106, 110, 115, 116, **118**, **119**, 120, 123, 308, 313 314, **319**, 338, 348,* 356,* 358,* 383 *
Schuster, 110
Schwarz, 31
Schwiedland, 86, **87**, 314
Schwoner, 96
Scorza, 180
Scovell, 292
Seager, 219, **240**, **241**, 251, 255, 256, **269**, 280, 292, 300, 308, 329, 374 *
Secrist, 221
Seidler-Schmid, 77
Seignobos, 135
Seligman, 19, 35, **219**, 226, 228, **239**, 240, 251, 255, 256, 261, **268**, **269**, 280, 286, 292, 301, 308, 313, 314, 316, 329, 373 *
Sella, 133, 186, 317
Senior, 119, 176, 297
Sensini, 195, 208
Sewall, 256
Shearman, 252
Shove, 286
Sidgwick, 27, **28**, 235, 236, 372 *
Sieveking, 65, 120
Sigwart, 49
Silberling, 271, 289
Silverman, 301
Simiand, 20, 22, **132**, **133**, 136, 204, **205**, **206**, 317
Simmel, 51, 59, 185
Simpson, 221, 272, 274
Sivers, 118
Slichter, 223, 303
Slutsky, 198
Smith (A.), 3, 18, 75, 81, 147, 150, 229, 244, 375 *
Smith (J. G.), 258
Snow, 217
Snyder, 221, 292, 296
Sombart, 46, 50, 52, 75, 86, 95, 101, 102, 107, 109, 123, 137, 224, 314, 342 *
Sommer, 45
Soule, 305
Southern, 216
Spann, 16, 30, 31, **32**, **33**, 34, 48, 49, 67, 69, **75**, **76**, 77, 79, 89, **92**, **93**, 103, **104**, **105**, 107, **113**, 115, 156, 243, **315**, **316**, 320, 323, **331**, **332**, 334, 337, 349,* 350 *
Spencer, 22, **23**, **24**, **25**, **26**, **27**, 28, 29, 34, **36**, **37**, 38, 39
Spengler, 41, 334
Spiethoff, 120
Spillmann, 287
Spirito, 143
Splawn, 252
Spranger, 54
Sraffa, 380 *
Staberow, 123
Stammler (H.), 81
Stammler (R.), **29**, 30, 54, 57, 58, 78, 79, 81, 112, 155, 329, 337
Stanton, 279
Steinberg, 74
Stephenson, 228
Stephinger, 45, 77, 86, 94
Stieda, 347 *
Stier-Somló, 89
Stolzmann, 30, **58**, 74, 76,

78, 79, 81, 93, 112, 119, 329, 337
Strat, 198
Streller, 49, 79, 123
Strigl, 48, 120, 122
Struve, 132, 185
Stryker, 248
Stuart, **67**, **121**, 122, 123
Stucken, 116, 123
Supino, 132, **149**, 150, **203**
Suret, 133, 369 *
Surface, 271

Tangorra, 132, 175, 201
Tarde (A.), **187**
Tarde (G.), **33**, **34**, 137, **155**, **156**, **157**, 172, **177**, 178, **186**, **187**, 193, **316**, 323
Taussig, 221, 239, **240**, 251, 252, 255, 256, 271, 272, **274**, 280, 287, 296, **301**, **302**, 303, 306
Taylor (F. M.), **246**, **270**, 306, 336
Taylor (F. W.), **228**
Taylor (H. C.), 290
Taylor (L.), 284
Terbourgh, 289
Théodotou, 178
Thomas Aquinas, 33, 160
Thomas (S. E.), 252
Thompson (C. M.), 251
Thompson (J. G.), **302**
Thorndike, 38
Thünen, 120, 280
Tiburtius, 92
Titchener, 38
Todd, 252
Tolstoi, 41
Toniolo, **160**, **161**
Tönnies, 58
Tosi, 139
Trivero, 171
Truchy, **151**, 192
Tschajanow, 84
Tugan-Baranowsky, **111**, **112**, 113, 114, 122
Tugwell, 40, **222**, **223**, **224**, 248, 374 *
Turgeon (Ch.), **173**, 188, 365 *
Turgeon (Ch. H.), **173**, 365 *
Turgot, 161, 185
Turner, **246**, 251, 262, 282, 290, 308
Tuttle, 216, 294, 308, 309, 336

Uexküll, 32
Usher, 19, 261

Vaihinger, **17**, **18**, 85
Valenti, 132,* **149**,* **150**, **194**, 209, 367 *
Valk, **301**
Valois, **158**, **159**, 177, 188, **315**, **316**, 323
Vanderblue, 228
Veblen, 15, 38, 40, **220**, 223, 224, 262, 281, 289, 294, 314, 371 *
Vecchio, **145**, 181, 182, 198, **200**, 201, 208
Verweyen, 31
Victor, 10
Villey, 131
Vinci, 199
Viner, 218, 221, 227, 263, 271, 272, 378 *
Virgilii, 194
Vleugels, 95
Voelcker, 62
Vogel, 49, 77, 119, 124
Vogelstein, 116
Voigt, 46, 53, 97, 117
Volta, 172
Volterra, 130, 143

Waffenschmidt, 48
Wagenführ, 77, 343 *
Wagner (R.), 62, 213, 330
Waite, 289
Walker, 213, 274
Wallas, 38
Wallis (A.), 258
Wallis (P.), 258
Walras, 15, 25, 109, 129, 140, 142, 144, 145, 146, 165, 168, 170, 179, 182, 189, 198, 199, 221, 237, 280, 301, 315, 325, 335, 336, 349 *
Walsh, 261
Waltershausen, 61, 62
Warburton, 285
Ward, 19, 316
Warren, 271
Wasserrab, 47
Watkins, 258, **284**, **285**, 379 *
Watson (F.), 251
Watson (J. B.), 38
Webb, 224
Weber (Ad.), 53, 63, **73**, 109, 117, 120, 336, 347 *
Weber (Alfr.), 194, 323
Weber (E. H.), 37
Weber (M.), 19, 20, 22, **51**, **52**, 53, 54, 55, 133, 227, 313, 317, 330, 344,* 345 *
Weddigen, 54, 77, **115**, 356 *
Wehberg, 341 *
Weinberger, 92
Weiss, 116, 118, 358 *
Weld, 224
Wenckstern, 86, **87**
Weyermann, 60, 75, 346 *
Whitaker, 258
Wicker, 251, 373 *
Wicksel, 49, **66**, 97, 116, 118, 120, 358 *
Wicksteed, **234**, **235**, 259,

267, 272, 278, 322, 330, 372 *
Wiedenfeld, 124
Wieser, 47, 65, 66, 69, 88, 89, 90, 91, 92, 98, 99, 106, 117, 122, 191, 260, 283, 284, 313, 329, 330, 336, 337, 347,* 352,* 371 *
Wilbrandt, 55, 58, 82
Williamson, 253
Windelband, 16, 22, 30, 31, 51
Wirz, 112
Wissler, 300
Wolf, 53, 86, 87
Wolfe, 40, 223, 227, 289, 297, 303, 314
Wolzel, 233
Woodbury, 304
Woodworth, 38
Working (E. J.), 271
Working (H.), 271
Worms (E.), 137
Worms (R.), 137
Wright (C. W.), 252
Wright (P. G.), 274, 289
Wunderlich, 107 *
Wundt, 37, 53
Wygodzinski, 86, 87
Wyler, 93

Yerkes, 38
Yntema, 378 *
Young, 218, 228, 237, 251, 264, 287, 288, 289

Zaleskij, 59
Zankoff, 118
Zawadawski, 129
Zorli, 152, 153, 317, 318, 320
Zuccarini, 131
Zuckerkandl, 89, 99, 106
Zwiedineck-Südenhorst, 47, 74, 103, 116, 120

For Product Safety Concerns and Information please contact our EU
representative GPSR@taylorandfrancis.com
Taylor & Francis Verlag GmbH, Kaufingerstraße 24, 80331 München, Germany

www.ingramcontent.com/pod-product-compliance
Lightning Source LLC
LaVergne TN
LVHW011106300926
849160LV00008B/293

* 9 7 8 0 4 1 5 6 0 7 3 0 8 *